MHW00989481

MOURNING HEADBAND FOR HUE

Mourning Headband for Hue is a personal account of what happened in Hue during the month-long occupation of parts of the city by communist troops during the 1968 Tết Offensive, a very bloody episode of the Vietnam War that inflicted extremely heavy losses on the civilian population in both human and material terms. Stranded in Hue where she had come to visit her family, the author found herself face-to-face with the war. . . . Horrified, she recounts her experiences day by day as if weeping and wailing in the remembrance of the atrocities she has seen and heard. It is indeed a book laden with blood, sweat, and tears but records events without distorting them. With explanatory information on many persons and events provided by the translator, the book is a valuable document for the history of the Vietnam War.

NGUYEN THE ANH, Rector of Hue University at the time of the events described in this book; professor emeritus, Ecole Pratique des Hautes Etudes, Paris-Sorbonne; and author most recently of *Vietnam: A Journey into History* (in French)

MOURNING HEADBAND FOR HUE

An Account of the Battle for Hue, Vietnam 1968

Nhã Ca

Translated and with an Introduction by Olga Dror

INDIANA UNIVERSITY PRESS *Bloomington & Indianapolis*

Frontis: Nhã Ca with a mourning headband, at her father's funeral on the eve of the Tết Offensive in Hue.

This book is a co-publication of

INDIANA UNIVERSITY PRESS
Office of Scholarly Publishing
Herman B Wells Library 350
1320 East 10th Street
Bloomington, Indiana 47405 USA

iupress.indiana.edu

First paperback edition 2016

The paper used in this publication meets the minimum requirements of the American National Standard for Information Sciences–Permanence of Paper for Printed Library Materials, ANSI Z39.48–1992.

Manufactured in the United States of America

Library of Congress Cataloging-in-Publication Data

Nhã Ca, [date] author.
[Giải khăn sô cho Huế. English]
Mourning headband for Hue : an account of the battle for Hue, Vietnam 1968 / Nhã Ca ; translated and with an introduction by Olga Dror.
pages cm
Includes bibliographical references.
ISBN 978-0-253-01417-7 (cloth : alk. paper) – ISBN 978-0-253-01432-0 (ebook) 1. Nhã Ca, [date] 2. Vietnam War, 1961–1975 – Personal narratives, Vietnamese. 3. Vietnam War, 1961–1975 – Campaigns – Vietnam – Huế. 4. Tet Offensive, 1968. I. Dror, Olga, translator, writer of introduction. II. Nhã Ca, [date] Giải khăn sô cho Huế. Translation of: III. Title.
DS559.5.N59613 2014
959.704'3092 – dc23

2014005693

ISBN 978-0-253-02164-9 (pbk.)

1 2 3 4 5 21 20 19 18 17 16

In Vietnam, when a person dies, the family members tie a white crepe mourning band around their heads.

CONTENTS

ACKNOWLEDGMENTS

THE WORK YOU ARE ABOUT TO READ, *GIẢI KHĂN SÔ CHO HUẾ* (Mourning Headband for Hue), was written by a prominent South Vietnamese female writer, Nhã Ca, and is an account of events as seen through her own eyes and the eyes of other civilians caught in the midst of the Tết Offensive in the city of Hue between January 30 and February 28, 1968.

In the course of my work on *Mourning Headband for Hue,* I consulted with many Vietnamese who were on both sides of the war and who in its aftermath have held different views about the book, and this has afforded to me a more inclusive, if not comprehensive, perspective on Nhã Ca's work and the events in Hue during the Tết Offensive. Some of the people I consulted are mentioned by name in my introduction, and I would like to express here my sincere appreciation for their willingness to share their views. The names of the others I do not provide, not out of disrespect but in honoring their wishes, as the events in Hue during 1968 are still a highly sensitive topic both in Vietnam and in the Vietnamese diaspora. While for the readers they remain anonymous, I warmly remember all of them as a great source of encouragement for my work and of knowledge about the country and the language. I also felt their love for their country and for their countrymen, whether in Vietnam or overseas.

I benefited from anonymous reviewers who supported the publication and who drew my attention to the places that could be improved.

Shawn McHale of George Washington University; Patricia Pelley of Texas Tech University; Dale Baum, Terry Anderson, and Brian Rouleau, my colleagues at Texas A&M; and Đinh Từ Bích Thúy of Da Màu literary magazine read and commented on my work at various stages, lending their kind hearts and sharp eyes and significantly improving the manuscript. Peter Zinoman of the University of California, Berkeley, has been a strong supporter of the project, its careful reader, and a treasury of excellent advice.

I found a most patient and engaged ally in Robert Sloan, the editor-in-chief of Indiana University Press. He guided me gently but firmly through the entire process. Michelle Sybert very effectively managed the production of the book. In Julie Bush I found an extremely thorough and astute editor who not only improved my English rendition of Nhã Ca's work but also identified my typos in Vietnamese without knowing the language – not a small feat. Her ability to do this will always remain a mystery to me and is proof of her excellent editorial work.

My parents, Ella Levitskaya and Alexander Massarsky, and my grandmother, Olga Zhivotovskaya, all lived and suffered through World War II in St. Petersburg, Russia. They have always been a source of strength and inspiration for me. Their lives, as well as the lives of my other close relatives who lived through the war ignited my desire to better understand the experience of civilians in wartime. In many ways my work on this book is a legacy of their influence on me. My son, Michael Dror, read portions of the translation and helped me to clarify my introduction, posing pertinent and well-focused questions. My husband, Keith Taylor of Cornell University and a veteran of the war in Vietnam, was and is always there for me and for the translation, and perhaps he knows it already by heart; he also made the map.

Finally, my deepest gratitude goes to Nhã Ca, the author of *Mourning Headband for Hue,* and her husband, poet Trần Dạ Từ, for their generous cooperation and willingness to share with me their painful memories of the war.

All the mistakes are mine.

NOTE ON TRANSLATION

WHATEVER PEOPLE THINK ABOUT THE WAR IN VIETNAM, MOST agree that in many ways Americans appropriated that war and very often did not try to understand their Vietnamese allies and opponents. Thus, my main goal in translating *Mourning Headband for Hue* was not to misappropriate Nhã Ca's work by turning it into an American wartime horror story with Vietnamese names but rather to give readers a chance to hear otherwise silenced Vietnamese voices. To achieve this, I tried to stay as close as possible to Nhã Ca's original work while at the same time not forgetting that it should be easily accessible for English-speaking readers. This proved to be a difficult task. I often consulted with Nhã Ca to be sure that I did not violate her intent. She helped me with amazing grace and patience.

The work was written in 1969, in the midst of war, with the author still in a state of shock. Thus, there were some points in her writing that needed clarification. I intentionally chose to translate the original 1969 edition so that I could work with the unadulterated voice from the time of the war, the version written shortly after the events of the 1968 Tết Offensive and the tragedy of Hue took place, not the later, perhaps slightly edited, version that was published in the United States in 2008 on the fortieth anniversary of the events described in *Mourning Headband for Hue*. As requested by the author, I made some minor corrections in the text, and they should not be perceived as mistranslation. I also made necessary clarifications because of the Vietnamese grammar or because of some confusion that became apparent during translation. In addition, with the permission of the author, I reordered chapters 3 and 4 for the sake of the flow of the narrative.

I attempted to stay faithful to the Vietnamese spirit and idiom of the work. I found it to be important to keep, at least partially, the Vietnamese system of personal pronouns when people address each other because the Vietnamese language does not have a simple "you." Unlike in English, Vietnamese pronouns reflect the structure of society and a constant awareness of one's position vis-à-vis other people, be it at work, with neighbors, or within a family. That's why the "you" on the following pages will be in such forms as "elder brother," "elder sister," "aunt," and "uncle" but also in compounds like "I and my sister," in which the word order will immediately indicate that the person calling himself or herself "I" in any situation is older or holds a more important status in age or position than the other person being mentioned. There is nothing denigrating or even impolite in these pecking orders. On the contrary, all these elements highlight the intensity of human relations on which the account is based and which give some semblance of order amid the chaos of war.

While I have adjusted certain features of the original to increase its accessibility to readers of English, I have retained other aspects that may seem odd or stilted in certain respects but that nevertheless help to convey the strangeness of encountering not only another culture but also a society directly experiencing the terrible fear and violence of war. For example, the original contains very few exclamation points. Some readers may imagine that this book should be studded with exclamation points, but adding them not only would disfigure the translation with emphases not in the original but also would remove the understated quality of the author's voice as she narrates horrific events that had become everyday occurrences. The entire text is an exclamation point, and to use exclamation points would simply imply that there is something in the text not needing such punctuation.

These and some other elements hopefully help to preserve *Mourning Headband for Hue* as a faithful document of wartime Vietnamese culture and history and to establish it as a necessary text for a better understanding of the Tết Offensive and of the war in Vietnam from a voice of that time. Many dozens of people come to life (and die) on the pages of the book; some of them remain anonymous while others are identified. I provide a list of the recurring names before the beginning of the translation to assure an easier comprehension of the work.

Quite often Nhã Ca uses the pronoun "they" or an equivalent. In most cases it refers to the Communist forces. As she wrote in the book: "We usually use the word 'they' to refer to the Việt Cộng and to avoid the word 'liberators.' In fact, would it not be ironic and cruel to use the word 'liberation' at the sight of such pain and utter destruction in the city?" While it was apparently clear at the time to the Vietnamese to whom she referred in such cases, it is not always as clear in translation. Thus, to avoid possible confusion in ambiguous contexts, I clarified in brackets to whom reference is being made. I used "the Communist forces" to identify the Việt Cộng and the North Vietnamese Army and "the Nationalists" for the Army of the Republic of Vietnam and its supporting units, for whom Nhã Ca uses the term *lính Quốc gia.* This term is distinct from the term translated into English as the Armed Forces of South Vietnam (ARVN). *Quốc gia* has different meanings: "country," "state," "national," or "nationalist" as, for example, in the expression *chủ nghĩa quốc gia*—"nationalism." I could not use the term "state" because Nhã Ca uses it as an adjective in expressions such as *xác* [corpses] *Quốc gia,* referring to the corpses of the people from the South Vietnamese anti-communist forces. Moreover, North Vietnamese forces were also state forces. I also wanted to avoid the confusion between the Communist forces in the South known in English as the National Liberation Front and members of the anti-communist forces of the Republic of Vietnam, who considered themselves to be nationalists. Thus, referring to South Vietnamese forces I use the term "nationalist."

After much deliberation and consultation, I decided to keep Vietnamese script with diacritical marks in the text for a number of reasons. First, I hope that it will help to preserve some of the Vietnamese spirit. Second, for those who know Vietnamese, it will be easier to identify people and places as they know them. Third, the diacritics will not prevent those who do not know Vietnamese from engaging with the text. They can be disregarded in most cases; however, sometimes they are important as most Vietnamese are mentioned here only by their personal names, and some of these personal names, while pronounced differently (for example, Lễ and Lê), look identical in print without diacritics, thus causing confusion. Including diacritics also precludes instances of similarity, in the absence of diacritics, between English and Vietnamese monosyllabic words. For example, the often-mentioned Vietnamese name "Bé," when occurring without its diacritic as the first word in a translated sentence, might cause confusion about whether it is a Vietnamese name or an English verb. As an exception, I dispensed with diacritics for the names of two cities – Hue and Saigon – as they are already firmly rooted in the English language in this form.

Working on this project, I envisioned myself as merely a conduit for Nhã Ca's voice and, through her, for the voices of the people of Hue at the time of the Tết Offensive. It was a hard and exhilarating task as the amount of information that can be and should be brought to light and that I read, heard, and collected is overwhelming. In order to keep my focus on her work, I have tried to stay as concise as possible in my introduction to the work so that it will provide only necessary information and not turn into a thorough study of the Tết Offensive, the Hue massacre, or the general situation in the South.

Each of these subjects deserves separate study, and while some aspects of them are covered extensively elsewhere, others still wait their turn. This project is not about these topics. My aim is to bring into English, for the first time, the voice of one of the best South Vietnamese writers who, along with her countrymen, lived through the nightmare of war: the nightmare of Hue during the Tết Offensive.

In the notes to my introduction, I have attempted to give a significant number of references to English-language sources for those readers who do not know Vietnamese but would like to read further on the subjects touched on in the book.

TRANSLATOR'S INTRODUCTION

THE AUTHOR AND HER WORK

> He: How beautiful you are, my darling!
> Oh, how beautiful!
> Your eyes behind your veil are doves.
> Your hair is like a flock of goats
> descending from the hills of Gilead. . . .
> She: Daughters of Jerusalem, I charge you –
> if you find my beloved,
> what will you tell him?
> Tell him I am faint with love.
>
> *Song of Solomon 4:1, 5:8 (NIV)*

What do these poetic verses from the Song of Solomon have to do with the book you are about to read? Is there any connection between the hills of Gilead, a mountainous area near the Jordan River and Jerusalem, and the hills surrounding the Perfume River and the city of Hue? As you will see below, the connection is with the author of *Giải khăn sô cho Huế* (Mourning Headband for Hue), Nhã Ca. Nhã Ca, meaning "courteous, elegant song" in Vietnamese, is the pen name of one of the most famous Vietnamese writers of the second half of the twentieth century.[1] Her real name is Trần Thị Thu Vân. She was born on October 20, 1939, in Hue and spent her youth there. Her father, Trần Vĩnh Phú, worked for the Office of Public Works in Hue and was a leading figure in one of the Buddhist communities of Hue. A middle child of a devout Buddhist family, she grew up in and among different Buddhist pagodas, closely acquainted with many dignitaries of Vietnamese Buddhism.[2] She attended Đồng

Khánh School, which she mentions in the account, and while there she started to publish poetry and short stories under her real name in some literary magazines in Saigon, most notably in the newspaper *Văn Nghệ Học Sinh* (Student Literature and Arts). This newspaper was established by a group of students from the North who had relocated to the South after the partition of the country in 1954. Among those who published in it were future famous writers and poets Dương Nghiễm Mậu, Lê Tất Điều, Lê Đình Điểu, Nguyễn Thụy Long, Đỗ Quí Toàn, Viên Linh,[3] Nhã Ca's future husband Trần Dạ Từ (b. 1940), and a number of others. In 1956 Nhã Ca saw this newspaper in a bookstore in Hue and established a connection with it.

In 1959 Trần Thị Thu Vân left Hue for Saigon and started her writing career. There she published in a variety of different magazines. In 1960, while reading the Old Testament translated into Vietnamese, this young woman, although raised as a Buddhist, was immensely impressed by the Song of Songs or Song of Solomon, also known in its Catholic version as the Canticle of Canticles – one of the most poetic books in the Bible – pulsating with passion between its protagonists, a man and a woman. The word "canticle" was translated into Vietnamese as *nhã ca*. The love, passion, longing, and poetic power that permeated each word mesmerized and overwhelmed Trần Thị Thu Vân, so much so that she decided to take the word "canticle" as her pen name. Thus, the author Nhã Ca was born. From 1960 Nhã Ca's poems and short stories were published in South Vietnam's leading literary magazines. In 1963 she founded a short-lived weekly newspaper, *Ngàn Khơi* (Forests and Seas). She also worked at a number of the most popular newspapers in the South, such as *Hiện Đại* (Modernity), *Văn* (Literature), *Dân Việt* (Vietnamese People), *Sống* (Life), *Hòa Bình* (Peace), and *Độc Lập* (Independence). She also associated with members of a group that published a literary journal called *Sáng Tạo* (Creativity).

Indeed, until the mid-1960s Nhã Ca stayed away from political topics and focused her writings on love, passion, and longing. Many other authors wrote along similar lines. The literary scene in the South, especially after the overthrow of President Ngô Đình Diệm in 1963, presented a wide palette of publications. More than a hundred privately owned newspapers, magazines, and journals were published at that time; some of them survived only a few months while others found a significant readership that followed them for years. According to Neil Jamieson, "There were nearly 700,000 copies of Vietnamese-language newspapers printed daily in Saigon."[4] Though the contemporary Vietnamese publishers I consulted think that this number is exaggerated, this vibrancy, the lack of which was evident in the North at the time with but a few newspapers and extremely tight censorship, demonstrated the relative freedom in the South. The predominant feature of many literary works of the time revealed that the war did not "seem to have [found] its way into literature and the arts.... The favorite theme of the great majority of poetic and prose works is love."[5]

Nhã Ca's first book, published in 1965, is a collection of poems called *Nhã ca mới* (New Canticles). An instant and huge success, it describes the joys and sorrows of a woman's life through Nhã Ca's exploration of her own feelings and experiences; this book recieved a National Literature Award for poetry in 1966.[6] The same year, she started working for the Voice of Freedom radio that transmitted programs into North Vietnam. Nhã Ca was a staff writer and also in charge of some music programs and programs focusing on women. She included no politics in her writings there, either. Nevertheless, her focus started to steadily shift. While women and their feelings still played an important role in her writings, family became more prominent in her work, which she began to situate within the intensifying war. Moreover, Nhã Ca began to explore new genres, including longer works of prose.

In 1966 her first novella, *Đêm nghe tiếng đại bác* (At Night I Hear Cannons), appeared and became a best seller. Reprinted six times and selling over 100,000 copies, it describes the plight of a family waiting in vain for their young male members – a son and a son-in-law – to come back from the front to celebrate the most important Vietnamese holiday, the Lunar New Year called Tết. The son of the family was killed and the son-in-law went missing.[7]

In *At Night I Hear Cannons,* Nhã Ca sided with neither political faction in the ongoing conflict. She stood for the family. Even as prose, this work was her canticle for perseverance, for human love, for family. But it also lamented the situation that put the family into these unbearable circumstances of hope and despair caused by the civil and international war ravaging her country. Nhã Ca's voice became more powerful in her next work, *Mourning Headband for Hue.*

By 1968 Nhã Ca and her husband, fellow poet Trần Dạ Từ, had been married for seven years. They had two young children and lived in Saigon. Their success as authors afforded them financial freedom with a very comfortable life in an affluent neighborhood. On January 25, 1968, Nhã Ca's father died in her native city of Hue and she left for his funeral, which took place on January 29. The next day the Communists attacked, beginning the Tết Offensive.[8] Nhã Ca was stranded in Hue during battles that lasted for almost the entire month of February. Her experiences and the experiences of those around her in Hue shocked her. Longing for peace, she decried the war in the book she completed in November 1968 with the title that speaks for itself, *Một mai khi hòa bình* (One Day When There Is Peace). In 1969 she wrote almost simultaneously three works about Hue: a collection of stories, *Tình ca cho Huế đổ nát* (A Love Song for Destroyed Hue), and a sequel to it titled *Tình ca trong lửa đỏ* (A Love Song in the Fire).[9] The latter is a story of love between a South Vietnamese girl and a North Vietnamese soldier. Bringing these two people together, Nhã Ca again demonstrated her faith in a shared humanity that could transcend political difference and put an end to the atrocious war. It was also in 1969 that she wrote *Mourning Headband for Hue.*

All people and events in this work are real. Nhã Ca either witnessed the events she described or heard about them from people she encountered during the ordeal. It is an account or a collection of accounts written in the wake of the tragic events.

Mourning Headband for Hue is infused with a plaintive love for the city of Hue, for its people, for the country of Vietnam, and for life itself. In its language, however, it is very different from the poetry of a song; its staccato tempo fires at the reader like the machine guns used in Hue in February 1968. The frequent repetition of the same words, compounds, and phrases create a rhythm of both monotony and anxiety, dramatically and palpably reflecting life in raw and desperate eloquence in the middle of the battlefield that was Hue. Each day, day after day, people struggled to survive; they fled from one place to another; they searched for food and shelter; they buried the dead; always the same and always anew and always in fear. The rhythm of the language demonstrates a sense of immediacy and at the same time reflection. Nhã Ca's goal was to bring these events out for display, to remember the atrocities that were committed upon the city of Hue and its people, and to take responsibility for them. Her account of events is not perfectly polished – a quality that usually betrays (and requires) a much greater distance from a traumatic event – and in this lies one of its greatest values. The language burns and smokes with the horrific violence and mayhem that war visits upon civilians.

Mourning Headband for Hue is also an accusation. Nhã Ca is very explicit in her antiwar message. One can hear her shouting against the geopolitical calculations of big powers engaged in the Cold War that took advantage of divisions among the Vietnamese. She conveys this idea through a comparison of Vietnam to a "small dog floundering in the water," not being able to reach the shore because of the constant shots that bored soldiers fire at it for their own entertainment. One can also hear Nhã Ca's clear and loud voice against brutality, having seen Vietnamese killing each other in what was also a civil war.

Her voice becomes especially bitter when she describes atrocities committed by the Communists and those who joined forces with them. Indeed, the Communist and their allies' brutality during the Tết Offensive of 1968 pushed Nhã Ca for the first time to move from blaming the war itself for the tragedy of the Vietnamese people, as she does in *At Night I Hear Cannons,* toward a more pronounced anti-Communist position. It also pushed her even further away from the original Canticle of Canticles and the subjects it raised, which were so close to her heart before the mid-1960s.[10] However, she did not make sweeping generalizations regarding Communists, Nationalists, or Americans by depicting them in black and white. Even amid the nightmare of Hue, and later while writing about it, she described positive examples of humanity in each group of combatants. In her "Small Preface" to *Mourning Headband for Hue,* she assumes the responsibility of her generation for the plight of Vietnam and of Hue, having let the country fall into a ruinous civil war that left a broken legacy for future generations. As I discuss below, it was and is not a view accepted by everyone, then or now.

Nhã Ca's account was first published in 1969, serialized in the daily South Vietnamese newspaper *Hòa Bình* (Peace) from March 30 to August 18. She remembers being threatened by the Communists, who sent letters demanding that the publication be stopped, but she continued anyway. Later in 1969 her serialized account was issued as a book by the publishing house Thương Yêu (Love), founded by Nhã Ca herself.[11] That same year it also published the abovementioned *One Day When There Is Peace* and *A Love Song for Destroyed Hue,* and then in 1970 it published the sequel to the latter, *A Love Song in the Fire.*

But *Mourning Headband for Hue* was (and still is) Nhã Ca's most famous work. The author donated all the proceeds from the first and later Vietnamese editions of *Mourning Headband for Hue* to her beloved city of Hue to contribute to its restoration after the destruction of the offensive. In 1970 Nhã Ca received a governmental honor for *Mourning Headband for Hue* – third prize in the Presidential National Literary Award in the category "Long Stories."[12]

The literary scene in the South at that time was incredibly diverse. As was already mentioned above, hundreds of newspapers, magazines, and journals were published, and numerous publishing houses printed new and old works. A prominent Vietnamese writer, Võ Phiến, described this burgeoning diversity: while such writers as Vũ Khắc Khoan, Nghiêm Xuân Hồng, Vũ Hoàng Chương, and Võ Phiến himself "had gone from political concerns and subjects to thoughts of a world far removed from current events. . . . Phan Nhật Nam, Nhã Ca, and Dương Nghiễm Mậu denounced communist atrocities all they wanted while Thế Nguyên, Nguyễn Ngọc Lan, Nhất Hạnh, Nguyễn Trọng Văn, Lữ Phương, etc. continued to accuse the government (of the South) of being dictatorial and corrupt and the society (of the South) of being unjust and decadent."[13]

While some, like Võ Phiến, saw *Mourning Headband for Hue* as a denunciation of Communist atrocities, it is also an undeniably antiwar, and in many ways an anti-American, work. The relationship between Nhã Ca and the Saigon government was not an easy one. The government repeatedly censored some of her publications, as it did those of many other authors. But the fact that *Mourning Headband for Hue* could not only be published but also win a national governmental prize demonstrates that writers in the South enjoyed a much greater degree of intellectual freedom than did their counterparts in the North.

In 1971 director Hà Thúc Cần started to shoot a movie titled *Đất khổ* (Land of Sorrows) partially based on *Mourning Headband for Hue* and *At Night I Hear Cannons.*[14] Nhã Ca wrote the script for the movie and joined the production team. A well-known songwriter, Trịnh Công Sơn, who, like Nhã Ca, also lived through the nightmare of Tết Mậu Thân in Hue and who, like Nhã Ca, hated the war, starred in the film. It was completed in 1972 when the South was in a dire situation amid another Communist offensive and negotiations between the United States and North Vietnam that led to American withdrawal from the war with disregard for the South Vietnamese.[15] The South Vietnamese government banned the film because of its strong antiwar message.

In 1972 director Lê Dân made a movie titled *Hoa mới nở* (Flower That Just Bloomed) based on Nhã Ca's novel *Cô hippy lạc loài* (A Stray Hippie Girl). This book vividly pictures the degradation of groups of Vietnamese youth caused by the war, the presence of Americans, and the Americanization of Vietnamese culture.

Nhã Ca remained in Saigon until the end of the war, publishing more than thirty volumes of poems, stories, and novels. Moreover, she and her husband were chief editors of the newspaper *Báo Đen* (Black Journal), which existed from 1971 to 1973. They also organized a magazine with the title *Nhà Văn* (Writer), but only several issues were published before the fall of South Vietnam in April 1975.

After the fall of Saigon on April 30, 1975, and the subsequent unification of Vietnam under Communist rule, *Mourning Headband for Hue* was publicly burned alongside many other South Vietnamese works officially deemed subversive. Authorities nevertheless put a copy on display in the Museum of War Crimes Committed by Americans and Their Puppets, established in September 1975 in Saigon, re-named Hồ Chí Minh City. The movie *Land of Sorrows* was also banned.[16]

The author, like her book *Mourning Headband for Hue,* was deemed subversive. By March 1976 the Communist government launched an official campaign against South Vietnamese intellectuals. Neil Jamieson, a scholar of Vietnamese literature, describes the situation in South Vietnam after 1975 that affected the writers, poets, and journalists of the Republic of Vietnam: "In April 1976 those literary artists who had not already fled the country or been arrested were rounded up in a series of swift raids, as if they were dangerous criminals, and trucked off to forced labor camps like a consignment of pigs to the market."[17]

In his thought-provoking book *Bên thắng cuộc* (The Winning Side) the Vietnamese correspondent Húy Đức, who interviewed many participants of the events of that time, discussed this painful period in the life of South Vietnam. He recounts that on April 3, 1976, Nhã Ca and her husband, Trần Dạ Từ, were arrested as a result of this campaign and, like hundreds of other intellectuals who were perceived as a danger to the new regime, sent to reeducation camps.[18] By that time they had six children, aged from one to thirteen years old, who, as a result of their parents' arrest and the confiscation of their property, were left without a means for survival. The eldest daughter, still herself a child at the age of thirteen, had to take care of her siblings. Eventually the children moved in with their relatives. After fourteen months, Nhã Ca was released,[19] but Trần Dạ Từ was kept in the camps for twelve years. To survive during that time, the family started to peddle food. While Nhã Ca did not attempt to leave Vietnam without her husband, she did repeatedly try to send some of her children with the groups of boat people who started to leave Vietnam by the thousands. However, each of these attempts ended in failure with her children apprehended and sometimes put into labor camps.[20]

In 1977 a prominent literary figure named Mai Thảo, another northerner who had moved to the South in 1954 and was the founder and editor-in-chief of literary magazines and journals such as *Sáng Tạo* (Creativity), *Văn* (Literature), and *Nghệ Thuật* (Art), managed to escape by boat from Vietnam. He did it with Nhã Ca's assistance. When he settled down in the United States, he revealed the dire situation of South Vietnamese writers and other intellectuals to PEN (Poets, Essayists and Novelists) International, a worldwide association of writers. The vice president of PEN International at the time was Thomas von Vegesack, who was also the president of PEN in Sweden. Through him, the Swedish media learned about the plight of South Vietnamese writers, and Tom Hansson of the *Svenska Dagbladet,* a Swedish daily newspaper, went to Vietnam to learn more. In 1982 he met Nhã Ca and a number of other intellectuals. He also collected information on the pitiful situation of the intellectuals: not only were many of them still imprisoned in the reeducation camps but some had died there, such as the talented writer Nguyễn Mạnh Côn.

Hansson reported his findings in the media and communicated them to the Swedish PEN.

In November 1985 Nhã Ca's and Trần Dạ Từ's eldest son, aged twenty at the time, managed to escape from Vietnam and by September 1986 had reached Sweden, where he was assisted by the Swedish PEN.[21] Due to the efforts of these people, as well as Amnesty International and prime ministers of Sweden Olof Palme and Gösta Ingvar Carlsson, Nhã Ca's husband, Trần Dạ Từ, was released in 1988, and the family was allowed to move to Sweden.

There Nhã Ca resumed her writing. In Sweden she wrote three books, one of which, *A Diary of a Person Who Lost Her Days and Months* (*Hồi ký một người mất ngày tháng*), describes the family experience from the arrest of the parents on April 3, 1976, until their departure from Vietnam on September 8, 1988.[22] In 1992 Nhã Ca and Trần Dạ Từ relocated to California and founded a Vietnamese-language newspaper, *Việt Báo Daily News,* which now has branches in Houston, Texas, and Tacoma, Washington. There are now seven children in their family, five of whom reside in the United States and two in Sweden.

HUE AND ITS PLACE IN THE TẾT OFFENSIVE

> I grew up on this side of the Perfume River
> The river splits my life into patches I long for –
> Fruit trees of Kim Long, iron and steel of Bạch Hổ Bridge,
> The gateway of mercy greets me with great warmth as I step into the river,
> Into the turquoise transparent water of my innocent childhood,
> Ancient stupas, bells from times past, gentle river, small waves.
>
> NHÃ CA, *"Tiếng Chuông Thiên Mụ" (Bell of Thiên Mụ Pagoda)*

The beautiful city of Hue lies in central Vietnam, about four hundred miles from Hanoi in northern Vietnam and about seven hundred miles from Saigon (now Hồ Chí Minh City) in southern Vietnam. The Perfume River runs through the city. For several centuries Vietnam was divided between two ruling families: the northern lords ruled from Hanoi, and in the seventeenth century the southern lords, the Nguyễn, established their capital at Hue. In 1802 one of the Nguyễn lords was able to unify all the Vietnamese lands under his authority, and he placed the national capital at Hue. The city became an imperial enclave with palaces, mansions, and royal tombs. These were concentrated on the northern bank of the Perfume River in the part of the city called the Citadel, which was surrounded by fortified walls. By 1968 between 120,000 and 140,000 people lived in Hue, and most of them resided in the Citadel. There were also newer but significantly smaller residential areas south of the Perfume River. The Demilitarized Zone (DMZ) that in 1954 partitioned Vietnam into two parts lay forty-five miles north of Hue.

Because of its imperial legacy, Hue became a symbol of education, culture, and tradition. One of the most famous schools of colonial Vietnam, a Franco-Vietnamese lycée named Quốc Học (National Academy), was established there in 1896. Among its founders was Ngô Đình Khả, father of the first president of the Republic of Vietnam (South Vietnam), Ngô Đình Diệm, in office from 1955 to 1963, and of Pierre Martin Ngô Đình Thục, the Roman Catholic archbishop of Hue from 1960 to 1963.[23] Ngô Đình Diệm studied at that school as did many other prominent Vietnamese figures, including Ngô Đình Diệm's opponents Hồ Chí Minh, known during his time at school as Nguyễn Tất Thành, and General Võ Nguyễn Giáp, both later leaders of North Vietnam. Many famous poets, writers, and scientists who later joined different sides of the conflict in Vietnam received their education at the National Academy.

Hue was also the Buddhist stronghold of the country. Historically, Buddhists were often on the defensive. Before the French colonization of Vietnam in the second half of the nineteenth century, Buddhists contended with the prevailing Confucianism, which had become the official socio-philosophical basis of Vietnamese society. After the French conquest, they struggled with Christianity and French colonialism itself. This tendency toward resisting authority continued after the French left Vietnam. Hue Buddhists became a consistent source of opposition to the ruling regimes in Saigon. Hue-based Buddhist uprisings in South Vietnam included the campaign of 1963 against the president of South Vietnam, Ngô Đình Diệm. Pictures of the self-immolation of one of the Buddhist monks, a Hue native, shocked the world and brought relations between the United States and Ngô Đình Diệm to a breaking point.

The Buddhist movement did not end after the assassination of Ngô Đình Diệm during a military coup on November 1, 1963. The Buddhists, joined by students, continued to demonstrate against the various governments established in 1964 and 1965, and particularly against the government established in June 1965 by a group of military officers, which finally brought some stability to the political situation in Saigon. For nearly a year, southern Vietnamese politics was dominated by the triumvirate comprising air force marshal Nguyễn Cao Kỳ and army general Nguyễn Văn Thiệu, a Catholic, both of whom were based in Saigon, and army general Nguyễn Chánh Thi, commander of the I Corps in charge of the region that included the cities of Hue and Đà Nẵng, the second and third largest cities in South Vietnam. In 1965 Buddhist monks together with students established the Military-Civilian Struggle Committee, also known as the Struggle Movement, in Hue. The tension escalated further and climaxed in 1966 when Nguyễn Cao Kỳ dismissed his rival Nguyễn Chánh Thi, who was popular among troops in the northern part of South Vietnam. The Struggle Movement led an uprising in the spring of 1966. The uprising was suppressed by the government with the assistance of the United States. A substantial number of supporters of the uprising and members of the movement fled to the mountains and joined the Communist forces there. During the Tết Offensive in the spring of 1968, these people returned and played a significant role in events during the Battle of Hue.

The Tết Offensive was launched on January 30, 1968, during the most important of Vietnamese holidays – the Lunar New Year, commonly called Tết in Vietnamese. Among Vietnamese, this offensive became known as Tết Mậu Thân, indicating the 1968 New Year specifically. It was a part of the Communist winter–spring campaign of 1967–68. Forgoing the usual guerrilla methods employed by the Communists previously, this campaign employed conventional warfare, fought chiefly in mountainous areas near the northern and western borders of South Vietnam. The primary striking forces in this campaign were North Vietnamese regular army units.[24]

The Tết Offensive was the second phase of the winter–spring campaign. This time, the Communist forces, jointly known as the Liberation Army, consisted of members from South Vietnam belonging to the National Liberation Front (NLF) and its military wing, the People's Liberation Armed Forces (PLAF), known in the South as the Việt Cộng or Vietnamese Communists, as well as units of the regular North Vietnamese

Army (People's Army of Viet Nam, PAVN). During the Tết Offensive, the Communists employed a strategy completely different from that used in the winter campaign. They made extensive use of guerrilla tactics and simultaneously attacked cities, towns, and hamlets all over South Vietnam, including Saigon and major provincial administrative centers. With this large-scale operation, they aimed to achieve a military victory. They hoped that the people of South Vietnam would support them and rise up against the Saigon government. It did not happen.

The Communists suffered a crushing military defeat. However, the political effect of the Tết Offensive in the United States marked the turning point of public opinion against the war, with Americans increasingly opposed to any further involvement. On March 31, 1968, President Lyndon B. Johnson announced his decision not to seek reelection in the upcoming presidential elections in November. Within a few months, the offensive led to the beginning of negotiations between the Americans and the North Vietnamese and to the end of American bombing of North Vietnam. Richard Nixon replaced Johnson in the Oval Office and began to disengage from the conflict.

The battle for Hue started with the Communist assault in the wee hours of January 30, 1968. The defenders of Hue – the side opposing the Communists – consisted of the Nationalist Army (ARVN or Army of the Republic of Vietnam) supported by local militia units (Regional Forces and Self-Defense Forces) and by the U.S. Marines and the U.S. Air Force.

The initial Communist assault was strong, organized, and successful. By the dawn of February 1, the Communists had established control over the entire city with the exception of the headquarters of an ARVN division and the compound housing American military advisors. The ARVN and the Americans started to reinforce their positions in the face of Communist attacks.

The Communists established their main stronghold in the Citadel, the heart of the imperial capital. The Communists also occupied the western side of the city, while the ARVN and the Americans controlled the other three sides. Initial efforts to retake the Citadel from the Communists by relying primarily upon firepower failed, so in the third week of February, Nationalist and American soldiers entered the Citadel and engaged in a difficult battle with close-order combat, block by block, yard by yard, house by house.

On February 24 ARVN soldiers replaced the Communist flag that had flown over the Citadel of Hue for almost four weeks and raised their own flag of the Republic of Vietnam. On February 26, 1968, the Communist forces were pushed out of Hue by the Nationalist and American forces.

The battle for Hue was the heaviest in the history of urban warfare in Vietnam. The Communists lost an estimated 5,000 people in the city itself; the ARVN losses stood at around 400, and the Americans had 216 killed in action. Some 80 percent of the city of Hue was destroyed, mainly by American and ARVN firepower and bombing.[25]

Regular North Vietnamese forces – North Vietnamese Army, NVA – shouldered the brunt of fighting at Hue. The South Vietnamese NLF was in charge of organizing liberated zones, conducting indoctrination sessions, rationing food, conscripting youth for labor and fighting, and dealing with those in the local population whom the NLF identified as its enemies. Along with the Communist forces, many former members of the defunct Struggle Movement who had left Hue after the defeat of the Buddhist Uprising in 1966 returned to the city. Intimately familiar with the city and its inhabitants, they, as *Mourning Headband for Hue* shows, were a major force behind the executions in Hue. Not only were government and military officials massacred but innocent civilians, including women and children, were tortured, killed, or buried alive.

Douglas Pike, one of the scholars of Vietnamese Communist strategies whose writings will be discussed below, has divided the period of Communist control of Hue into three phases. During the first stage, immediately upon taking control of the city, "the civilian cadres, accompanied by execution squads, were to round up and execute key individuals whose elimination would greatly weaken the government's administrative apparatus following Communist withdrawal." Those arrested were brought into kangaroo courts. Their trials were public, lasting about ten minutes each, and "there are no known not-guilty verdicts. Punishment, invariably execution, was meted out immediately."[26]

Alje Vennema was a Dutchman who had been in Vietnam from 1962 as a medical volunteer running a provincial hospital and later was the director of Canadian Medical Assistance to Vietnam. His account corroborates Pike's findings. According to Vennema, who was a medical volunteer in Hue at the time, tribunals were conducted at a "small seminary in the Catholic area of the town," in the Citadel, and in a neighborhood just east of the Citadel wall called Gia Hội, a location mentioned numerous times in *Mourning Headband for Hue.* Vennema also reports about the people who appear in Nhã Ca's book:

> At the seminary, a drumhead court had been presided over by Hoang Phu Ngoc Tuong [Hoàng Phủ Ngọc Tường], a Hue University graduate, and in 1966 a prominent student leader of the Buddhist Government Struggle Committee. At Gia Hoi [Gia Hội], a man, Nguyen Dac Xuan [Nguyễn Đắc Xuân], previously a Viet Cong [Việt Cộng] informer who had suddenly reappeared, presided, and in the Citadel two students, Nguyen Doc [unidentified] and Nguyen Thi Doan [Nguyễn Thị Đoan Trinh], a girl, had been in charge. At the session of these tribunals menacing words often mixed with propaganda slogans, accusations, threats, and warnings were commonplace. Most of those who were dragged before the tribunals were convicted for unknown reasons. All were sentenced; some were sentenced to die immediately.[27]

Phase 2 began after several days of the Communist presence in Hue. Some 68,000 refugees from the city escaped and settled in refugee camps, and reports about massacres started to appear in the Saigon press.[28] Pike defines Phase 2 as a period of "social reconstruction, communist style," that is, rounding up those who presented a potential danger to the Communist order. However, only a small number of executions were done publicly to set an example, while "most of the killings were done secretly with extraordinary effort made to hide the bodies."[29] Among those executed were not only government officials, police, and military personnel but also Buddhist bonzes, Catholic priests, intellectuals, and leaders of social movements. Sometimes their families were rounded up and executed with them. Don Oberdorfer, a journalist for the *Washington Post* who was in Vietnam at the time, added that not only Vietnamese but also Americans, Germans, Filipinos, Koreans, and other foreigners were executed by the Communists.[30] One of the examples he presents is Dr. Horst Gunther Krainick and his wife. Dr. Krainick was a German pediatrician and professor of internal medicine who arrived in Vietnam in 1960 to help establish a medical school at Hue University. On the fifth day of the occupation, the South Vietnamese Communist soldiers came to their house: "Elizabeth Krainick screamed and when she and her husband were led away she was heard to shout in English, 'Keep your hands off my husband.' The couple and the two other German doctors in residence, Dr. Raimund Discher and Dr. Alois Altekoester, were taken away in a Volkswagen bus. The four bodies were found later in a shallow grave in a potato field a half mile away, all victims of executioner's bullets."[31]

Phase 3 started when the Communists began to lose control of Hue and strove to eliminate witnesses. "Probably the largest number of killings came during this period and for this reason. Those taken for political indoctrination probably were slated to be returned. But they were local people as were their captors; names and faces were familiar. So, as the end approached they became not just a burden but a positive danger."[32] Even the Soviet authorities grew tired of the violence engulfing South Vietnam during Tet. As the Hungarian embassy in Moscow reported,

> Our [Soviet] comrades say that on the basis of the information available, in those rural areas which temporarily came under NLF control during the offensive, our friends, while taking repressive measures against the members of local authorities, overstepped the necessary and desirable limits. . . . if the terror is extended, for instance, to the family members [of policemen or local administrative leaders], intimidation will no longer yield positive results.[33]

Determining whether those killings were done due to rage, frustration, and panic or were a result of calculated decisions will require additional research, if and when documents in Vietnam about the events of Hue are made available to scholars.

The events in the city not only took a deadly physical toll on its people but also produced a heavy breakdown in morale. As one old man related to a correspondent of the newspaper *Sống* (Life) after the battle, people of Hue were like scared birds because of what they had gone through; they had seen how some Communist soldiers killed their own friends and relatives. He asked rhetorically: "Now who is it possible to trust?"[34]

Dương Nghiễm Mậu, a famous Vietnamese writer, like many other writers a northerner who moved in 1954 to South Vietnam, lived in Hue initially. In 1967 he joined the ARVN and became a war correspondent. He was in Hue on the eve of the Tết Offensive and during its first several days, and then twice he visited the city in the post-offensive period in 1968. At the beginning of 1969 he published a diary, *Hell Is Real,* in which he reflected on the unbearable confusion among people after they witnessed how their neighbors and friends turned into completely different people during the days that followed Tết Mậu Thân in Hue: "Now when people see something, they doubt it, they don't dare to believe anything, don't dare to reveal their attitude to anyone, don't dare to talk with anyone because possibly this other person has a different truth."[35] He compared a picture of Hue before and after the Tết Offensive. Before Tết Mậu Thân, "amidst rounds of whisky and packets of American cigarettes and American candies, everybody was talking about war and peace, against the war. I lived in this atmosphere during my first visit to Hue. The vivacious ancient capital with afternoons of drinking and laughter – the people of Hue go to work and then come back with fresh and smiling faces."[36] But in his later visits his impression of the city changed dramatically:

> Hue was alive but panic-stricken as it emerged from the terrible nightmare – doubtful looks, surreptitious whispering to each other of secrets and of things that people don't want to talk about, don't want to recollect. Not only traces of bullet holes and bomb craters . . . wounds can be bandaged, destruction can be repaired, but there are traces that will not disappear, will not fade, not only for those who live now but also for those who will live later. . . . These are devastations of confidence, imprints of powerlessness in the consciousness – they have become facts of life and bitter-sweet illusions.[37]

This situation was further aggravated by the fact that thousands of people were missing. People did not know where their loved ones were. They were roaming the streets, searching buildings, digging, and finding bodies. People dug up corpses even in the heart of the imperial city, in the Citadel, and around the emperors' mausoleums outside of the city. A correspondent, Huyền Anh, wrote at the beginning of April 1968: "Exhumed corpses of victims were rotten and slimy. After about ten minutes in the air the newly dug up corpses, grey-black and swollen, would gradually start leaking stinky water."[38]

On May 1, 1968, the *Chicago Tribune* cited an official report released in Saigon about the number of civilian victims in Hue rising to 1,000: "Evidence indicated that many victims had been beaten to death, shot, beheaded, or buried alive. . . . A number of bodies showed signs of mutilation. Most were found with hands tied behind their backs. It was estimated that nearly half the civilian victims were found in conditions that indicated they were buried alive. Some were tied up on [*sic*] groups of a dozen or so, with eyes open, with dirt or cloth forced into their mouths."[39]

The number of bodies continued to rise; in April 1969 the newspaper *Trắng Đen* (White and Black) reported that with 580 recently recovered bodies, the count was up to 2,000. The article said that people were able to recognize their friends and relatives only by the clothing found on them.[40] The people of Hue kept digging and finding corpses through the fall of 1969. The condition of the bodies further deteriorated to the extent that only bones and skulls could be extracted from the mass graves.[41] By late 1969 the total number of bodies unearthed around Hue had risen to around 2,800.[42]

Aside from the terrible death and destruction caused by battle, the massacre of unarmed civilians on such a scale in Hue by the Communist forces left a deep scar in the memories of survivors because it meant that the war had reached such a point of mistrust and hatred that a shared sense of being Vietnamese could no longer be taken for granted.

As in other matters concerning the events in Hue, there are different opinions about who were the perpetrators of the mass murders. Stephen Hosmer, a researcher for RAND Corporation, contended in 1970 that "the savagery and indiscriminate nature of much of the repression in Hue seemed uncharacteristic of the Viet Cong's Security Service. It is possible that some of the more brutal killings were not carried out by security cadres at all but were performed by the North Vietnamese or other military forces."[43] On the other hand, that same year Douglas Pike suggested that

> as far as can be determined, virtually all killings were done by local communist cadres and not by the PAVN troops or Northerners or other outside communists. Some 12,000 PAVN troops fought the battle of Hue and killed civilians in the process but this was incidental to their military effort. Most of the 150 communist civilian cadres operating within the city were local, that is from the Thua Thien [Thựa Thiên] Province area. They were the ones who issued the death orders. Whether they acted on instructions from higher headquarters (and the communist organizational system is such that one must assume they did), and, if so, what exactly those orders were, no one knows for sure.[44]

No one knows still.

TẾT MẬU THÂN IN HUE AND *MOURNING HEADBAND FOR HUE* IN AMERICAN AND SOVIET/RUSSIAN CONTEXTS

> For most Americans, the war always has involved selective consciousness, and now even these memories are fading.
>
> JOHN W. DOWER, *Japan in War and Peace*

In this statement, John W. Dower, a renowned scholar of Japan, referred to another war, the Pacific War, and how it was seen and is remembered by Americans.[45] But I would be hard-pressed to find a more apt description to apply to the war in Vietnam.

There is no lack of literature on the Tết Offensive – memoirs along with works of literature, journalism, and scholarship produced by Americans have appeared in abundance, presenting different vantages on the American involvement and describing a plethora of American experiences while analyzing events and seeking to establish or to refute various versions of the facts. Not so, however, with Vietnamese perceptions of the conflict. There exist relatively few English translations of Vietnamese works from any time period. Even fewer have come out from the war period between 1965 and 1975. Most of those that have been translated during and after the war have come from the North. The voices from the South have been intentionally or accidentally left in silence.[46]

Although a number of South Vietnamese short stories have been translated and published in the United States, they have failed to achieve any significant exposure to the reading public. South Vietnam boasted many excellent writers of different political and intellectual persuasions, but for decades after the war no major works found their way into the hands of American readers. *Mourning Headband for Hue* was the first major account of wartime experience by a major author that appeared in South Vietnam during the war. The existence of the work has been mentioned by journalists and scholars alike in English-language publications with significant differences. While journalists such as James Markham and Barbara Crossette and such scholars as Neil Jamieson highlight the work's antiwar spirit, prominent Vietnamese literary figures such as Võ Phiến stress its anti-Communist character.[47]

The lack of previous attention to South Vietnamese literature perhaps reflects an overall skewed perception and representation of the war as one solely between the United States and the Vietnamese Communists. South Vietnam's government and its people – those not allied with the Communists – were either labeled as "American puppets" by the Communists or were given very little regard by Americans because they did not fit into the framework of the dominant representation of the conflict. Yet the war was very much about South Vietnam and its people. Without their voices, an understanding of both sides of the long, tragic conflict is unattainable.

Mourning Headband for Hue fills a serious lacuna in our knowledge of the events that transpired in Hue in 1968 and in our knowledge of South Vietnamese writings. This book uncovers an event not widely known to the American public during and after the war: the actions of the Communists that resulted in thousands of civilians being shot, bludgeoned, and buried alive in mass graves, horrible events that survivors have since considered a massacre.

Tết Mậu Thân in American Media during the War

In 1968 the American media of course covered the Tết Offensive. The fighting was "brought home" when it appeared nightly on U.S. television. To claim that no information whatsoever appeared about the Hue massacre in the American media would be incorrect. In some major publications like the *New York Times*, the *Washington Post*, the *Los Angeles Times*, and the *Chicago Tribune*, scores of articles described or mentioned Communist atrocities committed in the city.[48] However, they were overshadowed by the explosive news about the presumed Communist successes during the offensive and discussions about the hopelessness of the American cause in Vietnam. Moreover, at that time even the people of Hue did not know how many people had been killed; they only realized that thousands had disappeared. Gradually the local citizens started to discover and unearth, one by one, mass graves. Hundreds of names were moved from the category of "unaccounted for" to "dead," but thousands were still unaccounted for.[49]

While the discovery of the atrocities unfolded in Hue, the attention of the American public was diverted to the shocking domestic events of 1968: on March 31, 1968, President Johnson announced that he would not run for reelection; on April 4, 1968, the leader of the African American civil rights movement, Dr. Martin Luther King Jr., was assassinated, an event that provoked days of rioting in American cities; on June 6, 1968, Democratic presidential candidate Robert F. Kennedy was assassinated; in August 1968 violent clashes between police and protesters accompanied the national convention of the Democratic Party in Chicago; and, finally, the tumultuous presidential campaign resulted in the election of Republican Richard M. Nixon. The fate of the Hue victims did not break through these headlines.

Then, even though in Hue local people continued to unearth corpses of missing people through September 1969 and the numbers of uncovered dead were rising into several thousands, the news of another tragedy overshadowed Hue again. On March 16, 1968, less than a month after the events in Hue, a U.S. Army platoon entered the Vietnamese hamlet of Mỹ Lai and within several hours killed between three hundred and four hundred of its inhabitants, including children, old men, and women. Many women, even old ones, were raped. The military tried to sweep news about Mỹ Lai under the rug, but in March 1969 information about the event began to surface. On November 12, 1969, journalist Seymour Hersh broke the Mỹ Lai story on the Associated Press wire service, and shortly thereafter it appeared in several major publications, including *Time* and *Newsweek*. Information about the terrible events in Mỹ Lai, accompanied by graphic pictures of the atrocity, captured the attention of the American public. Americans were rightly appalled by the actions of their countrymen in Vietnam, and the Mỹ Lai victims of Americans pushed the Hue victims of the Communists from the American media and, by extension, from the attention of the American public and of the world.[50] Stanley Karnow, a journalist and historian, author of the much-cited and much-acclaimed *Vietnam: A History,* and later chief correspondent for the thirteen-hour PBS television series on the war in Vietnam, described the reaction of U.S. citizens to the tragedy of Hue during the war: "Paradoxically, the American public barely noticed these atrocities, preoccupied as it was by the incident at Mylai [*sic*]."[51]

Tết Mậu Thân, Douglas Pike, Gareth Porter, and American Politics during the War

Rather than becoming common knowledge, as happened with Mỹ Lai, and rather than becoming a point of serious reckoning about the nature of the war, the events of Hue turned into a political football. Both sides of the American political aisle used it in their constant scrimmages. While Don Oberdorfer's book on the Tết Offensive, published in 1971, provided more than casual information about events in Hue, two other people proved to be especially influential in providing arguments for the contesting camps. One was Douglas Pike, who was instrumental in bringing to light the events that took place in Hue. A professional journalist, Pike joined the U.S. Information Agency in Vietnam in 1960 and stayed there for many years. By 1968 he was also working for the State Department and by the time of the Tết Offensive had already gathered a number of materials on and written a significant amount about Vietnam, Communist strategies, and the National Liberation Front.[52] After Tết he conducted research, using documents seized from Vietnamese Communists, and made his findings known both in interviews and in books written specifically about Tết and, after the war, on Vietnamese Communism more generally.[53] He argued that Communists had committed a massacre in Hue, killing thousands of people when they controlled the city.

Politicians used Pike's findings, as well as some of the reports published at the time, to argue that an inevitable bloodbath would ensue in Vietnam if the Communists took over the country.[54] In his famous "peace with honor" speech delivered on November 3, 1969, Richard Nixon used Hue as justification for avoiding a sudden withdrawal from Vietnam: "We saw a prelude of what would happen in South Vietnam when the Communists entered the city of Hue last year. During their brief rule there, there was a bloody reign of terror in which 3,000 civilians were clubbed, shot to death, and buried in mass graves."[55] A month later, Senator George Murphy from California advanced the same idea on the floor of Congress,[56] citing an article in the *Los Angeles Times*, for which Douglas Pike was the primary source.[57]

Pike's antagonist was Gareth Porter, an antiwar activist, political scientist, and journalist. He was in Vietnam as Saigon bureau chief for

Dispatch News Service in 1970 and 1971. Even before he left for Vietnam, he was opposed to viewing the events in Hue as a massacre. In 1969, as a graduate student at Cornell University, he coauthored an article in *Christian Century* that argued that the killings in Hue were committed on a smaller scale than had been reported and were "the revenge of an army in retreat and were not the deliberate policy of Hanoi."[58] As with Pike's findings, Porter's views were appropriated by politicians. On May 19, 1970, in a response to Nixon's argument about a potential bloodbath in case of a Communist victory, reiterated by the president during a news conference on May 8, 1970, Senator Mark Hatfield of Oregon evoked Porter's point of view by citing *New York Times* correspondent Tom Wicker's article on the events in Hue, which was based solely on Porter's 1969 piece in *Christian Century.*[59]

After returning from Vietnam in 1972, Porter, a research associate at Cornell University, published a work rebutting the claims that the Land Reform in Vietnam in 1953–55 had resulted in a bloodbath that took the lives of thousands of people.[60] In his later works he continued to press his view of the events in Hue and tried to refute Pike's findings. In 1973 Porter wrote: "For professional apologists of American imperialism, Hue has already served as a catchword which helps them to justify years of American war crimes. But it was the work of the U.S. Information Agency and the ARVN Political Warfare Directorate, who used both overt and official propaganda and more devious semi-covert methods, such as misrepresentation of captured documents to the press and fabricating the testimonies of defectors to back up the official account."[61] In 1974 he wrote: "A careful study of the official story of the Hue 'massacre' on the one hand, and of the evidence from independent or anti-communist sources on the other, provides a revealing glimpse into efforts by the U.S. press to keep alive fears of a massive 'bloodbath.'"[62] Antiwar politicians used this 1974 work in their arguments to disengage from Vietnam. For example, Senator George McGovern of South Dakota accused the Nixon administration of using the events in Hue as a pretext to continue American involvement there; he went as far as referring to the killings in Hue as the "so-called Hue massacre."[63]

To support his argument, Porter cited an unpublished manuscript by Alje Vennema, mentioned above.[64] Indeed, until the events of Tết Mậu Thân in Hue, Vennema was a strong Communist sympathizer. According to Vennema, he was appalled by the war and by American involvement. He felt that "the National Liberation Front offered the only solution to the corruption and incessant warfare." But Vennema was in Hue when the tragedy unfolded, and it significantly changed his perspective. He remembered later: "My stay in Hue, however, showed me another aspect of war, which was that the enemy had even greater disregard for human life – by capturing innocent bystanders, eliminating them in cold blood, or letting them rot away in jungle camps until death rescued them." Vennema left Vietnam in April 1968 when the scope of the tragedy had not yet emerged. He was approached to refute the South Vietnamese government claims about the losses in Hue, and it made him reflect on what really happened in Hue, especially because more and more mass graves were being discovered. Obsessed with the urge to find out what really happened there, he "returned to Hue several times, again and again looking, searching, tracing contacts, visiting villages and families of the bereaved."[65] In 1976 Vennema's book was published, detailing the killings in Hue. A source of invaluable information, it did not make a splash back then, perhaps because after 1975 Americans wanted to forget about that war altogether and because both politicians and the public tried to move on, leaving the tragedy of Vietnam behind. His book almost slipped into oblivion, becoming a rarity to find for nonspecialists.

The lack of attention to the events in Hue continued after the war. Unlike the Mỹ Lai massacre, which is mentioned in the majority of general books on the war and analyzed in dozens of specialized books published from the 1970s to the present time,[66] the events in Hue have not received any serious study and have largely, if not completely, faded from the radar of American memory and scholarship. Some continued Porter's line on the fabricated nature of the Hue tragedy.[67] Other postwar writings on the war in Vietnam either dispense entirely with any discussion of it or mention it only briefly.[68] James Robbins, a senior editorial writer for foreign affairs at the *Washington Times,* is one who, besides

Pike, Vennema, and Oberdorfer, has discussed at significant length the massacre in Hue and press coverage of it.[69]

Tết Mậu Thân in the Soviet Union and Russia

While the victims of the Hue tragedy have received little attention in the United States, they have received even less attention in the country with which the Vietnamese Communists were allied, the Soviet Union. No mention of the massacre occurred in the Soviet press or in any other forum in 1968 or in later years; it was as though it never happened. Those who knew and had the courage to speak out had no way to raise the topic in Soviet discourse. In 1973, while still in the Soviet Union, Aleksandr Solzhenitsyn, one of the most famous Soviet dissidents, managed to publish an open letter in the Norwegian newspaper *Aftenpost* denouncing what he called the Hue massacre and the lack of attention to it in the West. He blamed the liberals for their willingness to look the other way when "the bestial mass killings in Hue, though reliably proven, were only lightly noticed and almost immediately forgiven because the sympathy of society was on the other side, and the inertia could not be disturbed. . . . It was just too bad that information did seep into the free press and for a time (very briefly) did cause embarrassment (just a tiny bit) to the passionate defenders of that other social system."[70] Shortly thereafter Solzhenitsyn was expelled from his motherland. As far as I know, his letter was the only public acknowledgment of the events in Hue to emerge from the Soviet Union, but predictably not from within the Soviet Union.

On a personal note, during the 1980s when I studied at Leningrad State University for my bachelor's and master's degrees in Asian studies with a specialized focus on Vietnam, my classmates and I were not taught about the Hue massacre, just as very few students in the United States are exposed to knowledge of this issue even now. The people of Hue failed to attract the attention of either of the two superpowers that were waging a Cold War in pursuit of their own goals in the hot war then tearing Vietnam apart. Not much has changed since then. In 2012 I gave a presentation about *Mourning Headband for Hue* at a conference in Moscow titled "Current Issues in Russian Vietnamese Studies." The attendees of the panel repeatedly interrupted me, saying that what we must talk about is American atrocities in Vietnam. My attempt to call their attention to the fact that American atrocities and those committed by the South Vietnamese government have been exposed time and again and that we have to take a look at all sides of the conflict in order to better understand the past fell on deaf or openly hostile ears. Even as some Americans did not or do not want to consider the tragedy in Hue, preferring to focus on American guilt, the Soviet approach and that of the contemporary scholars of Vietnam in Russia, at least of those who were present at this conference, remains landlocked in Communist self-righteousness. Nhã Ca's name or work did not ring a bell to the audience of the Russian scholars of Vietnam; some of them characterized her as an unknown woman whose stories could not serve as a basis for scholarly consideration and instead would distract us from the consideration of American and South Vietnamese atrocities. Not only did I feel as if I were back in the country that I had left almost twenty-five years before, but more than ever I felt the necessity to make the voices of the people of Hue heard, to bring up the issue of Hue, not to replace the issue of the atrocities committed by Americans and the South Vietnamese army but to join it.

The proceedings of the conference reiterated the hostile scholars' position. The text reads that the attendees "reminded the presenter" that it was the Saigon (not the Communist) troops that distinguished themselves with the cruel treatment of the population, especially of those known as Communist sympathizers.[71]

TẾT MẬU THÂN IN HUE AND *MOURNING HEADBAND FOR HUE* IN VIETNAMESE CONTEXT

> Believe me, it is not easy to rationalize the stamping out of vineyards where the grapes of wrath are stored.
>
> KURT VONNEGUT, *Armageddon in Retrospect*

There are different ways to deal with a tragedy: it is possible to discuss it and through this discussion to potentially initiate a process of healing, or it is possible to pretend that it never happened and forget it, to pretend that if it is not discussed it will go away. There are numerous examples of both approaches in human history in dealing with tragedies of different scales. There has been significant willingness and openness in Germany to discuss and analyze German policies and realities prior to and during World War II that led to the unimaginable sufferings and deaths of millions and millions of people. There has been much more resistance and reluctance to do the same in Japan, and this has resulted in numerous difficulties and tensions in the relationship between Japan and other Asian countries, specifically China and Korea. The U.S. military authorities tried to sweep the tragedy of Mỹ Lai under the rug in 1968, and if they had been successful it would never have become a point of reckoning for Americans.

It took fifty years for the Soviet government to acknowledge what happened in 1940 at Katyn Forest, a wooded area near Gneizdovo village outside the city of Smolensk, where on Stalin's orders the NKVD (People's Commissariat for Internal Affairs) shot and buried thousands of Polish service personnel and civilians who had been taken prisoner when the Soviet Union invaded Poland in September 1939 in alliance with Nazi Germany. The Soviets blamed the Germans for the atrocity until 1990, when then-president Mikhail Gorbachev admitted Soviet guilt and, subsequently, archival documents were opened to give a fuller picture of what happened there. Gorbachev said that the truth of what happened in the forests of Katyn is one of the "historical knots" that has complicated Soviet-Polish relations.[72]

The situation in Vietnam is in many ways more complex because the Hue events unfolded not only against the background of the war between the Vietnamese Communist forces and the United States but also in the context of the civil war with contesting powers in North and South Vietnam. Since then, one of the Vietnamese sides (the Communists) won; the other side (the South Vietnamese anti-Communists) lost. The price that both sides paid is enormous. The Communists suffered the destruction of the northern economy and infrastructure from bombing and thereafter were enmeshed in another long and devastating war as a pawn in the Sino-Soviet competition to dominate Indochina after the American withdrawal. For the anti-Communists, the losses continued long after the war through reeducation camps, discriminatory policies in education and employment, or exodus by boat from unified Vietnam with a loss of their homeland, if their escape succeeded, or with a loss of their lives to sea, pirates, or harsh conditions, if their escape failed.

Now the situation seems to have stabilized with one Vietnam and millions of overseas Vietnamese. A possibility of reconciliation or at least partial healing might be there for many Vietnamese, not in the absence of discourse about the war in general and of Tết Mậu Thân in Hue in particular but through it. It may become a reality not through silence but through an open, if extremely painful, discussion of the history and the course of the conflict. In such a discussion, *Mourning Headband for Hue* and the views expressed in it would become but one of the voices.

Government

When the events in Hue were unfolding, the Vietnamese government in the North and the Communist forces in the South did not address the tragedy. On February 2, 1968, just days after the beginning of the Tết Offensive, the command of the People's Liberation Armed Forces of South Vietnam heralded the success of the Communist forces: "The People's Revolutionary Committee of Thừa-thiên province and Hue came into being to accept the glorious responsibility of the people's government in the province and in the city."[73] On March 3, 1968, after the Communists had already lost the battle in Hue, the Central Committee of the National Liberation Front of South Vietnam still proclaimed a victory over the enemy, stating that in addition to inflicting serious damage to the American and South Vietnamese government forces and installations, the Communist forces also "killed enemy thugs, wiped out evil-doers, essentially liberated the entire countryside, established the revolutionary administration, and expanded the national unity against Americans to save the country." The document continued: "The city of Hue has demonstrated a brilliant example of spirit and ability to launch an offensive against the enemy, with stamina and sense of purpose, defeating all enemy counterattacks, creatively applying tactics of people's war in the city against the enemy, beautifully combining together military attack with political attack."[74] On March 19, 1968, the command of the People's Liberation Armed Forces of South Vietnam further reinforced these ideas, citing not only the Communist forces' heroism and success in strategy but also "richness in creativity and wit" in applying those strategies.[75] The main publishing house of the government in Hanoi produced these documents in April 1968, thus giving them its stamp of approval.

On April 27, 1969, following a series of discoveries of mass graves in Hue and its suburbs, Hanoi Radio reacted: "In order to cover up their cruel acts, the puppet administration in Hue recently played the farce of setting up a so-called committee for the search and burial of the hooligan lackeys who owed blood debts to the Tri-Thien-Hue compatriots and who were annihilated by the southern armed forces and people in early Mau Than spring."[76] This statement, as well as the one from the southern Communist forces cited above, openly admits the killings of at least some people but does not reflect any willingness of the Communist side to shoulder responsibility for them; on the contrary, the Communists portrayed the killings as a necessary act against "enemy thugs," "evildoers," and "hooligan lackeys."

Since the end of the war, the government of Vietnam has not yet acknowledged, or at least openly discussed, the events of Tết Mậu Thân in Hue. At the beginning of the 1980s Stanley Karnow interviewed General Trần Đỗ, one of the senior Communist architects of the Tết Offensive, who flatly denied that Hue atrocities had ever occurred, contending that films and photographs of the corpses had been "fabricated."[77]

Personal Perspectives: The Communist Side

TRƯƠNG NHƯ TẢNG AND BÙI TÍN. Two high-ranking officials from North and South Vietnam, while not directly involved in the events in Hue, have offered their insights about them. The first is Trương Như Tảng, a founding member of the Communist movement in the South and former minister of justice of the Provisional Revolutionary Government, an underground government in South Vietnam formed in 1969 in opposition to the Saigon government and consisting primarily of the members of the National Liberation Front, the Việt Cộng. Disillusioned with Communist policies after the fall of Saigon and reunification of the country, Trương Như Tảng fled the country by boat in 1978 and currently resides in France. In his memoirs written in exile, Trương Như Tảng describes his conversation with the chair of the Provisional Revolutionary Government, Huỳnh Tấn Phát. According to Trương Như Tảng, Huỳnh Tấn Phát expressed his sorrow and disappointment about what had happened and explained that discipline in Hue had been seriously inadequate, which resulted in fanatic young soldiers indiscriminately shooting people and angry local citizens who supported the revolution on various occasions taking justice into their own hands. Huỳnh Tấn Phát stated that there was no policy or directives from the NLF to carry out any massacre: "It had simply been one of those terrible spontaneous tragedies that inevitably accompany war." When Trương Như Tảng heard this explanation, he did not find it "particularly satisfying," but neither did he "pursue the issue."[78]

Unlike Trương Như Tảng who was in the South, Colonel Bùi Tín served with the general staff of the North Vietnamese Army, who during the fall of Saigon in 1975 accepted the surrender from the last South Vietnamese president, Dương Văn Minh. After the war, Bùi Tín worked as vice chief editor of the official daily newspaper of the Communist Party, *Nhân Dân* (People). Similarly disillusioned with Communist authority, he asked for and received political asylum in France when attending a conference organized by the French paper *L'Humanité* in 1990.

From Bùi Tín's memoir published in 1993, a reader can deduce what, in Bùi Tín's opinion, constituted three main contributing factors of the Hue tragedy. The first factor stemmed from the frustration of the Vietnamese Communist forces. According to him, "During that time in the tense atmosphere that permeated the city [of Hue], seeing that people did not rise [against the South Vietnamese government], but on the contrary fled, with very few people coming to greet [Communist forces], to help the [Communist] army, was a reason that when the army took over the city, it was already prejudiced against the people of Hue."[79]

The second factor concerned the Communist loss in Hue. As Bùi Tín explains, when in retreat, an army wants to eliminate witnesses because they might be in a position to disclose information that an army desires to keep secret.

Bùi Tín saw the third cause in the Communist education system existing at the time, which was, in his opinion, rooted in hatred. "Education in hatred, necessary at the time of war, was elevated to the extreme, [and] directions were spread that 'mercenaries-killers,' [and the other] most dangerous enemies, must not be allowed to escape." As Bùi Tín put it, such an education system created a basis for the disastrous massacre.[80]

Like Huỳnh Tấn Phát to whom Trương Như Tảng referred, Bùi Tín suggests that there were no execution orders issued in advance. Even though both Huỳnh Tấn Phát, as expressed by Trương Như Tảng, and Bùi Tín deny the existence of orders from the top authority in advance of the offensive, they differ in their explanations of the killings – the former suggests spontaneity from the rank-and-file, while the latter suggests a possibility of such orders from an unspecified body at the time of the Communist forces' retreat. Neither addresses the issue of killings taking place long before the retreat started.

Bùi Tín relates that the decision-making process of the government and the Communist Party has never been disclosed, but he contends that the party and the government did not put significant effort into a thorough investigation or subsequent punishment: "Leaders of the Communist Party have a tendency to see 'leftist deviations' as light-weighted as, for example, [it happened] during the Land Reform and anti-religion campaigns" when people and issues were "all dealt with summarily."[81]

Bùi Tín names three people who were "criticized" for the Hue tragedy. General Trần Văn Quang, commander and political commissar of the area where Hue was located, was criticized but continued his military career and in 1981 was appointed deputy minister of the Ministry of Defense and promoted to the rank of colonel general in 1984. Major General Lê Chưởng, political commissar of the South Vietnamese Communist forces of the NLF, upon criticism was transferred to become deputy minister of Education. He died in 1973 in a car accident. The third criticized person, according to Bùi Tín, was Colonel Lê Minh, a commander of military operations on the left bank of the Perfume River. According to Bùi Tín, Colonel Lê Minh died of illness after that.[82] Bùi Tín does not indicate Lê Minh's time of death, but Lê Minh certainly lived long after Tết Mậu Thân. Moreover, in 1987 he wrote an essay for a commemorative volume, *Huế, Xuân 68* (Hue, Spring 68), published for the twentieth anniversary of Tết Mậu Thân in Hue in 1988, five years before Bùi Tín's book was published.

LÊ MINH. Lê Minh's essay in *Hue, Spring 68* stands out from the other essays written by politicians and participants in the events. In some ways it represents a significant departure from the official treatment of the tragedy. Lê Minh notes that atrocities are an inevitable part of war. He highly and predictably praises the performance of the Communist forces in Hue during Tết Mậu Thân: "It should be said that after we retreated up into the jungles, if there was something still firmly rooted in the hearts and minds of the people of Hue, first of all, it was the uplifting image of 'Venerable [Uncle] Hồ's [Hồ Chí Minh's] soldiers.'" But then he digresses into the topic of the killings in Hue: "When we were retreating, the enemy counterattacked us with great vigor." He admits that there were some instances of people belonging to the puppet army and administration who were apprehended and who resisted the Communist forces. "In these conditions, some brothers and sisters of our military masses (army, guerilla, self-defense, etc.) were unable to abstain from some *shallow* [italics mine] actions in this situation. We were in such an extremely difficult position that we were not able to control the actions of every fighter and every guerilla . . . including even a number of regional cadres, in their reactions to events."

Indeed, his focus remains rather narrow – he does not mention the number of victims, but from his description they seem to be insignificant and limited to the South Vietnamese military and government officials. Nevertheless, he suggests a measure of culpability to be attributed to the Communist forces, not distinguishing whether it was northerners or southerners. Additionally, he actually assumes his own responsibility for the actions of the Communist forces as the commander of those forces. He concludes on an even more striking note: "The current task of the revolution now is to bring to light the injustice suffered [*minh oan*] for the families and the children of the people who died in that situation when the revolutionary law never had an intention to put them to death."[83]

His essay is especially significant because, unlike Trương Như Tảng and Bùi Tín, who lived outside Vietnam and whose books were published in the United States *after* Lê Minh's essay, it was published in Vietnam. It is hard to imagine that it was a "rogue" work and that it did not go through a regular censorship process. It is possible that because the book was published in Hue, located at some distance from the central authority in Hanoi, the regulations were not as rigid. For comparison, a similarly titled volume, *Mậu Thân 68,* published in Hanoi by the Central

Department of Propaganda and Ideological Education at the same time and on the same occasion, highly praises the Communist achievement at the time and does not even discuss Hue.[84] However, it is more likely that with the advent in 1986 of the *đổi mới* (renovation), the analogue to the Soviet *perestroika,* the country experienced a series of drastic economic and less drastic but still significant political changes. The latter allowed or were expected to allow at the time a larger degree of freedom of expression than previously existed. I would like to think that if Lê Minh's essay was sanctioned by the authorities, perhaps it was a step to open up a possibility of a further discussion. My assumption is supported by the fact that Lê Minh's essay was mentioned by Nguyễn Văn Diệu, a Communist Party foreign liaison officer, to Keith Richburg, a correspondent for the *Washington Post,* who included it in his article "Vietnamese Admit 'Mistakes' in Hue," published in 1988.[85]

While I am not aware of anything that the Vietnamese government has done about what Lê Minh referred to as "bringing to light the injustice suffered" after the publication of the essay, the appearance of his voice not only confirms the fact of the killings but also demonstrates that among those who fought on the Communist side, there are people who feel and/or express guilt for the tragedy of Hue.

HOÀNG PHỦ NGỌC TƯỜNG. Ten years after Lê Minh's essay, in 1997, another person moved even further than Lê Minh in his assessment of the killings in Hue: Hoàng Phủ Ngọc Tường, a native of Hue who during Tết was one of the leaders of the Communist forces in the South. He is directly implicated in the killings in Vennema's account and indirectly implicated in *Mourning Headband for Hue.*

Through his writings we can see a drastic change in his consideration of the Hue tragedy. In 1971 Hoàng Phủ Ngọc Tường wrote a book titled *A Star on the Top of Phu Văn Lâu: A Chronicle (Ngôi sao trên đỉnh Phu Văn Lâu).* Phu Văn Lâu is a tall pavilion in the Citadel of Hue. The title of the book reveals the time and the contents of the events described in it – the period of Communist control in the Citadel when the Communist flag, with a star, fluttered from the top of Phu Văn Lâu pavilion. The date at the end of the book indicates that it was written in 1969; however, it appeared in 1971 from Giải Phóng (Liberation) Publishing House. While the North Vietnamese government and later the government of unified Vietnam claimed that this publishing house was located in the South, in fact it was located in Hanoi.[86] With the publications in the North controlled by the government, it is safe to conclude that the northern authorities were aware of the book.

Unlike in *Mourning Headband for Hue,* there is nothing in the book that goes against the grain of the party line about the events in Hue. Hoàng Phủ Ngọc Tường's chronicle concentrates on battling Americans (Korean forces are also mentioned several times), on the enthusiasm of the population of Hue in greeting the Communist forces after having had to live under the authority of Americans and their Vietnamese puppets, and on the good relations between the population and the Communist forces. Hoàng Phủ Ngọc Tường also describes some of the people who left the city in 1966 and returned with the Communist forces. The book ends on an enthusiastic note, describing how before the Communist defeat, one of the Communist fighters told his mother, "It's peace already, Uncle Hồ will come to visit South Vietnam. He will come to visit you and me."[87] The book does not talk about the indoctrination campaigns, kangaroo courts, mass killings, or mass graves. When I read this book, I could not get rid of the feeling that it was a de facto response to *Mourning Headband for Hue:* Hoàng Phủ Ngọc Tường's chronicle versus Nhã Ca's account.

At the beginning of the 1980s Hoàng Phủ Ngọc Tường was very explicit in his opinion on the killings in Hue. Interviewed by Stanley Karnow for the broadcast series *Vietnam: A Television History,* Hoàng Phủ Ngọc Tường said: "The people so hated those who had tortured them in the past that when the revolution came to Hue they rooted out those despots to get rid of them just as they would poisonous snakes who, if allowed to live, would commit further crimes."[88]

On July 12, 1997, literary critic and journalist Thụy Khuê, hosting programs on literature and arts for Radio France Internationale (RFI)[89] in Vietnamese, interviewed a sixty-year-old Hoàng Phủ Ngọc Tường. By that time Hoàng Phủ Ngọc Tường had become a prominent historian of Hue and an author of literary works. In the course of the interview he reflects on his earlier interview with Karnow, the events in Hue, and *Mourning Headband for Hue.*

Hoàng Phủ Ngọc Tường identifies the person who contacted him for the interview in the series *Vietnam: A Television History* as Burchett. He apparently was referring to Wilfred Burchett, an Australian journalist and strong supporter of the Communist cause who during the war accompanied the Communist forces in the South when they were battling the Americans and South Vietnamese troops.[90] Hoàng Phủ Ngọc Tường reminisces: "It was a long time ago, I simply improvised [when I was giving the interview]; I don't remember exactly everything I said."[91] Since Hoàng Phủ Ngọc Tường had not had a chance to see the film, he did not know "whether his thoughts were reproduced correctly." He only remembered that at the interview for the series, he distinguished three categories of victims. The first was made up of those who died because of the punitive actions by the Liberation Army, intended for those who were guilty. The second category included victims of injustice. The third category consisted of victims who died because of American bombing or who were shot and killed by the South Vietnamese government's forces in their retaliation against people during the counterattack. This categorization, as Hoàng Phủ Ngọc Tường reintroduced it in the interview with Thụy Khuê in 1997, significantly differs from how he expressed his views to Karnow in the early 1980s.

The difference between the two interviews is apparent both in content and in tone. His tone shifts from derogatory to pensive. The difference further deepens when Hoàng Phủ Ngọc Tường addresses the suffering of the people of Hue. According to the RFI interview, it greatly pains him, as a son of Hue, when he thinks "about heart-rending deaths and grief that many families in Hue had to endure being victims of injustice by the uprising [Communist] army at the Hue front in 1968. This is a mistake that cannot be supported with any reasoning, looking at it from the point of view of national conscience and the concept of revolutionary war."

He also dwells, if reluctantly, on the issue of responsibility. Basically, he follows the lead of Lê Minh. Hoàng Phủ Ngọc Tường contends that the people responsible for the tragedy were local commanders, that the revolutionary policy was not to blame for this since similar tragedies did not happen in other places. He also, echoing Lê Minh, suggests that "what should be done now is that the leaders of Hue must clear the injustices for the families of the victims of Hue, to give clear and fair treatment to do them justice and to acknowledge the legitimate rights of citizens toward their relatives." Hoàng Phủ Ngọc Tường evidently heavily draws from Lê Minh's essay. He contends that he himself is "not sufficiently competent [in the knowledge of the events] to evaluate any individual." Hoàng Phủ Ngọc Tường obviously wants to distance himself from the tragedy of Hue.

Whether or not Hoàng Phủ Ngọc Tường was actually present in Hue during Tết Mậu Thân is a controversial issue itself. Vennema, as cited above, and the majority of Vietnamese who lived in Hue and with whom I discussed the issue indicated that, in their opinion, he was there. However, Hoàng Phủ Ngọc Tường himself does not agree on this point. According to him, he "was absent from Hue during Tết Mậu Thân, participating in the Resistance War in the jungles, from summer 1966, and came back to Hue only after March 26, 1975," when Hue was taken by the Communist forces. He says that until then he was the secretary general of the Alliance of Nationalist, Democratic, and Peace Forces of Hue headquartered in Hương Trà District of Thừa Thiên Province, which he locates fifty kilometers (thirty-one miles) from Hue.

The question about Hoàng Phủ Ngọc Tường's book *A Star on the Top of Phu Văn Lâu: A Chronicle,* written in 1969 and published in 1971, never emerged in this or other interviews, as far as I know. But the existence of this book seems to be potentially important as it raises a number of questions: on what basis did he write his 1969 chronicle about the events in Hue if he indeed was absent from Hue from 1966 to 1975? Without knowing the provenance of the sources, can this book really be considered a chronicle? Was Hoàng Phủ Ngọc Tường in Hue but does not want to acknowledge this? Or did he, being far away from Hue, write a work, a kind of response to the account of Nhã Ca (who actually was in Hue during Tết and explains her sources), distinguishing between his account and what she witnessed herself and what she heard? My attempt to approach Hoàng Phủ Ngọc Tường to ask him to help me clarify some of the aforementioned points was unsuccessful. Hoàng Phủ Ngọc Tường's health is declining.

In a rather strange twist in the interview with Thụy Khuê, he states that in *Mourning Headband for Hue,* Nhã Ca exonerated him, "saying that he did not return to Hue during Tết Mậu Thân, but if he did, [he] surely did not kill." He expresses his gratitude to Nhã Ca for allotting him this very important objective point of consideration. In fact, in chapter 7 of *Mourning Headband for Hue,* Nhã Ca relates the words of a young girl named Hường who believes that Hoàng Phủ Ngọc Tường did not come back to Hue, but later Hoàng Phủ Ngọc Tường's comrade-in-arms, Nguyễn Đắc Xuân, confirms the opposite, that Hoàng Phủ Ngọc Tường was in Hue and was at Gia Hội School. Gia Hội School was the location of one of the most infamous tribunals that conducted kangaroo courts and sentenced people to immediate execution. While one can wonder if the information that Nhã Ca indirectly conveys is correct or not, the book does not support his claim that he was absent from Hue. It remains unclear to me what prompted Hoàng Phủ Ngọc Tường to offer this assessment of Nhã Ca's portrayal of him. It is possible that his memory was failing him. I am reluctant to think that Hoàng Phủ Ngọc Tường did not carefully read the book or that he thought her credibility as a witness was strong while at the same time he supposed that what Nhã Ca had actually written was unlikely to be known by or checked by the listeners of his interview.

Nevertheless, Hoàng Phủ Ngọc Tường very positively evaluates *Mourning Headband for Hue:* "Despite such intentional or unintentional factual mistakes of the author, in my opinion, *Mourning Headband for Hue* [contains] interesting notes written about Hue during Tết Mậu Thân; I read them several dozen years ago and then re-read them, I still feel a heartache."

NGUYỄN ĐẮC XUÂN. Another person who appears in the pages of *Mourning Headband for Hue,* Nguyễn Đắc Xuân, has a very different attitude toward Nhã Ca's work. While still a student, as described by Hoàng Phủ Ngọc Tường, he was one of the leading figures of the 1966 Struggle Movement and a commander of the "Suicide Squad" fighting against the South Vietnamese government. This squad consisted mainly of Buddhist students.[92] He and his squad took a very active part in the confrontation between General Nguyễn Chánh Thi and the Saigon government in 1966, known as the Buddhist Uprising. When the uprising was suppressed, he fled and joined the Việt Cộng. Currently, Nguyễn Đắc Xuân, like Hoàng Phủ Ngọc Tường, is a researcher of Hue history and of the history of the Nguyễn dynasty, having published dozens of books. Both men are also members of the Writers' Union.

From his articles and memoirs, it is evident that Nguyễn Đắc Xuân does not share Hoàng Phủ Ngọc Tường's positive sentiment about *Mourning Headband for Hue.* In 1999 and in a number of later publications, including the most recent in 2012, Nguyễn Đắc Xuân reminisces on his first impression of reading Nhã Ca's work.[93] He claims not to have felt angry at the author for her portrayal of him because he understood that it was "a story to serve [the purpose of] cheap psychological war."[94]

Nguyễn Đắc Xuân flatly denies Nhã Ca's portrayal of him in which, according to him, he is described as "killing in a tragic manner" his own friend and classmate Trần Mậu Tý.[95] If Hoàng Phủ Ngọc Tường errs on the positive side in his (mis)interpretation or (mis)representation of Nhã Ca's portrayal of him, Nguyễn Đắc Xuân goes in somewhat the opposite direction. In fact, Nhã Ca does not say in *Mourning Headband for Hue* that Nguyễn Đắc Xuân actually killed Trần Mậu Tý. When she refers to him in her "Small Preface" and later in chapter 7, she describes a scene where Nguyễn Đắc Xuân cruelly tortured Trần Mậu Tý by holding him on the verge of death. She does not say that he killed Trần Mậu Tý. However, it is significant that Nguyễn Đắc Xuân interpreted it as an accusation of murder, which, as he states, affected his relationship with many people in the course of his life.[96]

He suggests that it is not he but another person whom Nhã Ca brings to the pages of *Mourning Headband for Hue* because in the book Nhã Ca refers to him as Đắc, not Xuân, which he says is his personal name.[97] Nguyễn Đắc Xuân's reaction to the new edition of *Mourning Headband for Hue* is bitter and sharp and deserves to be briefly considered here. In 2008, he wrote in his journal *Sông Hương* (Perfume River), published in Hue:

> The content of the new edition of *Mourning Headband for Hue* is still the same as the one published in 1969, I saw only ONE WORD [emphasis in the original], only one word changed, that's it. This is the word XUÂN (my name) on p. 376 in the first edition, which has become Đắc on p. 234 in the new edition (to bring it into accordance with the name of the character Đắc in *Mourning Headband for Hue*). About forty years have passed, and she changed the name from Xuân to Đắc like this, it shows that she realized the difference between the real person Nguyễn Đắc Xuân and the character named Đắc in her *Mourning Headband for Hue*. Such a change has been done because of legal reasons, so that she can defend herself by saying: "I wrote a story about Mr. Đắc, not about Mr. Xuân."[98]

Reading this passage, one can see an understandably desperate person trying to find an exit from a bad situation. First of all, during my work on the translation, I constantly compared the first edition on which

I based the present translation with the one published in 2008. I can assure the readers that Nguyễn Đắc Xuân's assessment is imprecise: more than one word had been changed in the new edition; in fact, on average, more than one word has been changed on each page.

As for the name itself, while Nguyễn Đắc Xuân's last name is Nguyễn, customarily the name Xuân would be considered his personal name. But Nhã Ca in the first edition consistently calls him Đắc, not Xuân, and when once – indeed, on p. 376 of the Vietnamese edition – she calls him Xuân, under circumstances that do not allow any doubt that it is the same person to whom she previously referred as Đắc, this should be considered a pure mistake in writing rather than an attempt to implicate a wrong person. But indeed, for the sake of consistency, he should have been called Đắc. And Nhã Ca fixed this mistake in the new edition of the book. I do not think that she did it in order to avoid potential legal complications – she still meant the same person, Nguyễn Đắc Xuân. It seems that, despite Nguyễn Đắc Xuân's claim to the contrary, at least during the time of Tết Mậu Thân, Nguyễn Đắc Xuân was called Đắc, not Xuân, by more than one person, as I found an identical and unequivocal reference to him also as Đắc, and not Xuân, in Hoàng Phủ Ngọc Tường's book *A Star on the Top of Phu Văn Lâu.*[99]

I have no intention or ability to evaluate here the role of Hoàng Phủ Ngọc Tường, Nguyễn Đắc Xuân, or anyone else in Tết Mậu Thân, both because of the difficulty, if not the impossibility, of gaining access to relevant archival materials and because this lies beyond the goal of my introduction to *Mourning Headband for Hue.* I have solely focused on their memories and memoirs where they reflect on Nhã Ca's work.

Personal Perspectives: The Anti-Communist Side

Unknown to anyone in the West but to specialists in Vietnamese studies, *Mourning Headband for Hue* means something different for different Vietnamese people and different camps. For Communists it was, and perhaps is, anathema. For some South Vietnamese, who lived through the war and its aftermath, either in Vietnam or abroad, based on the materials I have read and on the conversations I have had, it is a painful and treasured representation of what happened in Hue and an anti-Communist accusation.

But there exists one more point of view to be considered. It sees *Mourning Headband for Hue* as too lenient toward Communists. One of the voices supporting this position is that of Nguyễn Tà Cúc, who was a member of the Vietnamese Writers Abroad PEN Center and in 1995 was briefly chair of its Writers in Prison Committee. She also has been an assistant editor for the *Khởi Hành* (Departure) literary magazine in California since 1996. Nguyễn Tà Cúc disagrees with Nhã Ca's call for collective responsibility as expressed in her "Small Preface: Writing to Take Responsibility," where Nhã Ca assumes responsibility for the situation in Hue in particular and in Vietnam more generally, not only on her own behalf but on behalf of her entire generation of Vietnamese, saying: "Our generation, the generation that likes to use the most beautiful and showy words: not only must we tie a mourning headband for Hue and for our homeland, which are being destroyed, but we must also take responsibility for Hue and for our homeland."

Nguyễn Tà Cúc questions who these "we" are. In her opinion, Nhã Ca refers to her generation of South Vietnamese, and Nguyễn Tà Cúc raises a question: who authorized Nhã Ca to speak on behalf of other South Vietnamese? She rejects Nhã Ca's idea of taking collective responsibility. She asks why "we," if it includes other South Vietnamese, should take responsibility for the Communist actions. Why should "we" take responsibility for the destruction of Hue, if it was the result of the Communist actions? Why should "we" feel responsible for the massacre of more than three thousand people? Nguyễn Tà Cúc also questions why Nhã Ca did not address the fundamental problem that if North Vietnam had not attacked South Vietnam, Americans would not have been there in the first place. Nguyễn Tà Cúc sees Nhã Ca's antiwar stance and her willingness to share responsibility "for the destruction of such a historic city as Hue" as a weakness, if not an outright betrayal of the anti-Communist cause of South Vietnam.[100] In the aforementioned article penned by James Markham in the *New York Times* in 1973 after the American withdrawal, based on his interview with Nhã Ca, she finds "everyone guilty" in the conflict, and some South Vietnamese see this admission of guilt as a validation of American abandonment of South Vietnam and as at least partial exoneration of the North.[101]

As an alternative assessment of the nature of the war, Nguyễn Tà Cúc suggests the view of another prominent Vietnamese writer, Lê Tất Điều, as expressed in a passage from his work *Ngừng bắn ngày thứ* (Ceasefire – Day 492), which he finished writing in Saigon on April 17, 1975, less than two weeks before the fall of Saigon. "In the course of several dozen years of war, the free world held and pulled, threatened South Vietnam, demanded that the South must conduct war in a moral way, must search ways to achieve peace. In the end, victory fell into the hands of those whose hands don't shake when they pull a trigger even though they know that at the end of their bullets' trajectory are women and children."[102] This passage indeed differs from Nhã Ca's position as expressed in *Mourning Headband for Hue* about sharing responsibility for the tragedy of Hue and of Vietnam. Comparing these two points of view about responsibility, not only in terms of message but also in consideration of the times and circumstances of their expression, might be a separate, engaging, and important project, which I am not going to undertake here.

Nguyễn Tà Cúc is not alone in her views. One person with a similar perspective is Nhật Tiến, the vice president of Vietnamese PEN before 1975. One of the most active literary figures in South Vietnam during the war, whom Neil Jamieson described as one of Saigon's finest and most respectable writers,[103] he fled Vietnam on a boat in 1979. Comparable considerations have been expressed by some other members of the Vietnamese American literary community, who prefer to remain anonymous.

It is evident that if for some, especially those on the Communist side, Nhã Ca's portrayal of the Communist role in Hue was too much, for others it was too little. I realize that in addition to the array of views presented here, there might exist other views that I have not considered. If so, it is because I am not aware of them, not because I am trying to silence them. While working on this introduction, I decided that it is important to present, as much as I could, the fullest accessible range of representative Vietnamese reactions to *Mourning Headband for Hue* – for the sake of the people who hold them, for the sake of the work, and for the sake of our understanding of this work and the tragedy of Hue in the contemporary context.

Among the views that I have noted here, *Mourning Headband for Hue* occupies a middle ground representing disillusioned people who took a neutralist position in the conflict, condemning the war. Despite possible ideological controversies, Nhã Ca's work is distinguished by its strong voice elucidating the experiences of civilians trapped for weeks in a horrible battle.

WHY WE SHOULD MOURN FOR HUE

> Until now, Hue has not been officially allowed to have a common commemoration day when all people would turn their hearts to those who died a painful death during the Tết Mậu Thân.
>
> NHÃ CA, *Giải khăn sô cho Huế* (Morning Headband for Hue)

There may not have been a bloodbath after the fall of Saigon and the unification of Vietnam, but there were consequences. Many thousands of people were put into reeducation camps, including Nhã Ca and her husband, Trần Dạ Từ; hundreds upon hundreds of thousands fled or tried to flee by boat, with many thousands dying at sea or in transit or apprehended even before they left the shores of Vietnam. A senior-ranking ARVN officer, Nguyễn Công Luận, reflected on the Hue events in his excellent memoir:

> Years later, in 1972, the horrible images of 1968 mass graves drove many tens of thousands of people from all walks of life in Huế and Quảng Trị to take the route of war refugees. The press corps named it "voting with their feet." Panic evacuations from South Việt Nam's northern cities happened once again more tragically in March 1975 before South Việt Nam fell. It was later apparent that people from Huế and the adjacent provinces made up a significant proportion of the Vietnamese boatmen fleeing Việt Nam after the RVN collapsed on April 30, 1975. After April 1975, communist authorities evicted a large number of close relatives of the 1968 carnage victims in the Huế area and resettled them in remote "New Economic Areas." The living conditions in the "New Economic Areas" were much harsher.[104]

Nearly half a century has passed since 1968. The Vietnamese government still trumpets Tết 1968 in general and the battle of Hue in particular as a huge victory. On January 1, 2008, for example, the Ministry of Defense and the Provincial Committee organized a conference, "Offensive and Uprising of the Spring Mậu Thân 1968," to celebrate the fortieth anniversary of the event. Lê Khả Phiêu, the former secretary general of the Communist Party (1997–2001); Colonel General Phan Trung Kiên, a member of the Party Central Committee and deputy minister of the Ministry of Defense; and other officials and scholars attended. The issue of the massacre and who was responsible for it was not officially addressed.

Lê Minh's and Hoàng Phủ Ngọc Tường's reflections on the Hue tragedy, discussed above, show a crack that potentially can lead to more openness, and perhaps even in the direction of having "a common commemoration day when all people would turn their hearts to those who died a painful death during the Tết Mậu Thân."[105] Despite many years having passed after those reflections appeared, nothing has happened yet.

Those who lived through the nightmare of Hue and those who want to see those events recognized have constructed literally dozens upon dozens of websites with pictures and testimonies from that time. But without the official acknowledgment of Hanoi, a dialogue is not possible. Nhã Ca's works have not been published in Vietnam after the war; though many of them, including *Mourning Headband for Hue,* are accessible on the internet, this does not lead to a dialogue with the academic and political establishment or to public consideration in Vietnam today.

It is important not only for Vietnamese but for Americans, too. Whether Nhã Ca's voice and other South Vietnamese and North Vietnamese voices that may potentially be brought to public attention can change our perspective on the war and on what happened in Hue, or at least open a discussion, I do not know. In any case, this is not my most important goal, even though I would be happy if it happens and if one day the people of Vietnam would be able to together commemorate those who died at the time of Tết Mậu Thân in Hue, as Nhã Ca also desires. My goal with this publication is to make our consideration of the war more inclusive and to encourage anyone who wants to think about this issue to have a broader basis for reaching his or her own conclusion.

Mourning Headband for Hue was written in the months after the events in Hue. It presents an opportunity to become acquainted, albeit belatedly, with a South Vietnamese view on what happened in that city. It is a look at the war not through the eyes of a soldier or a politician but through the eyes of civilians. Those civilians did not have a choice in the conflict but were pushed into the middle of a terrible battle by the same military people and politicians who articulated the war policies, conducted the war, and later wrote books about it. This book depicts the experiences of ordinary people whose lives were drastically changed or cut short by wartime violence; it is about the "others," those caught in the crossfire, those who survived, and those who did not. It is not a novel, not a work of fiction, but an unvarnished account of the events as seen through the eyes of the author and of those who surrounded her at that time. It gives us "snapshots" of the ruined and scarred lives at the time of the Tết Offensive. But it also demonstrates a variety of views on the Communist, Nationalist, and American sides of the conflict from the vantages of different people. Some passages in the work relate the same events or describe the same figures as they were perceived by different people, and this adds to our understanding of the complex situation in South Vietnam at that time and creates a style slightly reminiscent of *Rashomon,* the famous movie of the Japanese director Akira Kurosawa based on Akutagawa Ryunosuke's story "In a Grove."

Regardless of one's political persuasion, *Mourning Headband for Hue* prompts us to mourn for the people of Hue, for the Vietnamese, for the self-absorption of great power policies in Vietnam, and for our unwillingness to learn more about "others," which even today continues to haunt our policies toward other countries.

Olga Dror
January 2014

NOTES

1. The information about Nhã Ca and her work comes primarily from my correspondence with her as well as from the works cited here.

2. Neil Jamieson mistakenly identifies Nhã Ca as a Catholic writer. Neil Jamieson, *Understanding Vietnam* (Berkeley: University of California Press, 1995), 321.

3. Dương Nghiễm Mậu currently lives in Hồ Chí Minh City. Nguyễn Thụy Long died in Hồ Chí Minh City in 2009. Lê Tất Điều currently resides in California. Lê Đình Điểu and Đỗ Quí Toàn established the first *Vietnamese Daily* newspaper in California in 1978. Viên Linh is a publisher and editor-in-chief of *Khởi Hành* (Depar-

ture) magazine, a monthly Vietnamese literary magazine in California.

4. Jamieson, *Understanding Vietnam*, 291.

5. According to the PhD dissertation of Hoang Ngoc Thanh, completed at the University of Hawai'i in 1968. He also suggested that there were notable exceptions like Doãn Quốc Sỹ, Đỗ Thúc Vịnh, Diệp Lan Anh, and Ngô Thế Vinh. Cited from the later publication of portions of the dissertation: Hoang Ngoc Thanh, *Vietnam's Social and Political Development as Seen through the Modern Novel* (New York: Peter Lang, 1991), 310.

6. Công Huyền Tô Nhữ Nha Trang, "Women Writers of South Vietnam (1954–1975)," *Vietnam Forum* 9 (Winter–Spring 1987), 174.

7. *Đêm nghe tiếng đại bác* (Saigon: Nam Cường, 1966). This work was translated into English by James Banerian in 1993 but remains only in copies published by the translator himself. In 1997 it was translated into French by Lieu Truong and published by P. Picquier in Arles under the title *Les canons tonnent la nuit*.

8. Called Tết Mậu Thân by Vietnamese to indicate New Year's Day of 1968.

9. Respectively: *Một mai khi hòa bình* (Saigon: Nhà xuất bản Thương Yêu, 1969); *Tình ca cho Huế đổ nát* (Saigon: Nhà xuất bản Thương Yêu, 1969); and *Tình ca trong lửa đỏ*. The last work was serialized in *Hòa Bình* starting August 19, 1969, the day after the last installment of *Mourning Headband for Hue* was published in the same newspaper and later published as a separate book in 1970 by the Thương Yêu publishing house.

10. Well-known Vietnamese writers and literary critics Võ Phiến and Thế Uyên delineated the politicization of Nhã Ca and other authors in the literary journal *Bách Khoa* (Encyclopedia). "Tác phẩm và cuộc đời nói chuyện với Võ Phiến" [Conversations with Võ Phiến about Literary Work and Life], *Bách Khoa* no. 302 (August 1, 1969): 59–72; "Vài vấn đề với Thế Uyên" [Several Issues with Thế Uyên], *Bách Khoa* no. 303 (August 15, 1969): 72–74.

11. It was reissued in 1970 and 1973 in Saigon by the same publishing house, and a revised edition was published in California by Việt Báo publishing house in 2008.

12. The first and second prizes went to two other female writers: the first to Túy Hồng for the work *Những sợi sắc không* (Illusions); the second to Nguyễn Thị Thụy Vũ for the work *Khung rêu* (Frame of Moss).

13. Vo Phien, *Literature in South Vietnam, 1954–1975* (Victoria, Australia: Vietnamese Language and Culture Publications, 1992), 137.

14. The movie is available on YouTube and Amazon. On the history of the creation and the distribution of the movie, see Nguyễn Xuân Nghĩa, "Ngậm ngùi với Đất khổ" [Grieving with the Land of Sorrows], *Việt Báo*, Spring 2008, 56–57.

15. See Larry Berman, *No Peace, No Honor: Nixon, Kissinger, and Betrayal in Vietnam* (New York: Free Press, 2001).

16. See for example Trần Trọng Đăng Đàn, *Văn hóa, văn nghệ phục vụ chủ nghĩa thực dân mới Mỹ tại Nam Việt Nam 1954–1975* [Culture, Literature, and Art Serving American Neo-Colonialism in Vietnam in 1954–1975] (Long An: Thông Tin, 1990), 618–72.

17. Jamieson, *Understanding Vietnam*, 364.

18. Huy Đức, *Bên thắng cuộc* [The Winning Side], vol. 1, *Giải phóng* [Liberation] (Saigon, New York: OsinBook, 2012), 51.

19. Neil Jamieson's statement that Nhã Ca was imprisoned for several years is in-

correct. Jamieson, *Understanding Vietnam*, 364.

20. Tom Hansson, "Han flydde från Vietnam – men familjens hålls kvar" [He Fled from Vietnam – But the Family Still Held There], *Svenska Dagbladet*, April 19, 1987, reproduced in Nhã Ca, *Hồi ký một người mất ngày tháng* [A Diary of a Person Who Lost Her Days and Months] (Westminster, CA: Thương Yêu, 1991), 524–33.

21. Hansson, "Han flydde från Vietnam – men familjens hålls kvar," 524–33.

22. The other two books are a novel, *Hoa phượng, Đừng đỏ nữa!* [Flamboyant Flowers: Please Don't Bloom Again] (Westminster, CA: Thương Yêu, 1989), and a collection of short stories, *Sài gòn cười một mình* [Saigon Smiles Alone] (Westminster, CA: Thương Yêu, 1990).

23. Nguyễn Văn Minh, *Dòng họ Ngô Đình: Ước mơ chưa đạt* [Ngô Đình Clan: Dreams Unrealized] (Garden Grove, CA: Hoàng Nguyên Xuất Bản, 2003), 12–13.

24. For an informative contemporary analysis of the Vietnamese side prior to and during the offensive, see Victoria Pohle, *The Viet Cong in Saigon: Tactics and Objectives during the Tet Offensive* (Santa Monica, CA: RAND, Office of the Assistant Secretary of Defense/International Security Affairs and the Advanced Research Projects Agency, 1969). There is a somewhat less researched and more politicized work on the offensive giving coverage of each area in South Vietnam: Pham Van Son and Le Van Duong, eds., *The Viet Cong Tet Offensive, 1968* (Saigon[?]: Print and Publications Center, A.G./Joint General Staff, RVNAF [1969?]), which discusses the Battle of Hue, including the massacre, pp. 248–96. See also Lien-Hang T. Nguyen, *Hanoi's War* (Chapel Hill: University of North Carolina Press, 2012), 87–109, for an analysis of the political struggle in Hanoi prior to the Tết Offensive.

25. Don Oberdorfer, *Tet! The Story of a Battle and Its Historic Aftermath* (New York: Doubleday, 1971), 232.

26. Douglas Pike, *The Viet-Cong Strategy of Terror* (Saigon: For the United States Mission, Vietnam, February 1970), 54–55. There is also a brochure based on this work: *Massacre at Hue* (Bangkok, Thailand: SEATO, 1970).

27. Alje Vennema, *The Viet Cong Massacre at Hue* (New York: Vantage Press, 1976), 90, 94.

28. "Huế vẫn tiếp tục chiến đấu dù bị Việt Cộng tàn phá" [Hue Continues to Struggle Although Devastated by the Việt Cộng], *Sống* [Life], February 19, 1968. The newspaper continued to report on atrocities in Hue throughout the month of February.

29. Pike, *Viet-Cong Strategy of Terror*, 53.

30. Oberdorfer, *Tet!*, 232.

31. Ibid., 214.

32. Pike, *Viet-Cong Strategy of Terror*, 58.

33. "Report from the Hungarian Embassy in the USSR to the Hungarian Foreign Ministry, 21 March 1968, in Hungarian National Archives, VTS, 1968, 88. doboz, 43, 00631/13/1968" in Balázs Szalontai, "In the Shadow of Vietnam A New Look at North Korea's Militant Strategy, 1962-1970," *Journal of Cold War Studies* 14 (4), Fall 2012, pp. 122–166.

34. Huyền Anh, "Một ngày đi moi những hầm xác ở Huế" [A Day When I Went to Extract Bodies from Graves in Huế], *Sống*, April 3, 1968. This newspaper published a series of articles on the findings in Hue.

35. Dương Nghiễm Mậu, *Địa ngục có thật* [Hell Is Real] (Saigon: Văn-Xã Xuất Bản, 1969), 16.

36. Ibid., 86.

37. Ibid., 87.

38. Huyền Anh, "Một ngày đi moi những hầm xác ở Huế," *Sống,* April 1, 1968.

39. "Find: Reds Murdered 1,000 Hue Civilians," *Chicago Tribune,* May 1, 1968, C10.

40. *Trắng Đen,* April 17, 1969, 1.

41. For a concise timetable of the discoveries of bodies in Hue, see *Massacre at Hue,* 10–14.

42. Stephen Hosmer, *Viet Cong Repression and Its Implications for the Future* (Lexington, MA: Heath Lexington Books, RAND Corporation, 1970), 50. RAND Corporation (RAND standing for Research and Development) is a nonprofit global policy think-tank first formed to offer research and analysis to the U.S. Armed Forces. Mai Elliot gives the estimate of between two thousand and three thousand government employees, police officials, and common residents executed by the Communist forces during the offensive. Mai Elliot, *RAND in Southeast Asia: A History of the Vietnam War Era* (Santa Monica, CA: RAND Corporation, 2010), 294. David Anderson puts the number higher (up to six thousand). David L. Anderson, *The Columbia Guide to the Vietnam War* (New York: Columbia University Press, 2004), 98–99.

43. Hosmer, *Viet Cong Repression,* 50.

44. Pike, *Viet-Cong Strategy of Terror,* 52–53.

45. John W. Dower, "Race, Language, and War in Two Cultures," in *Japan in War & Peace: Selected Essays,* by Dower (New York: New Press, 1993), 257.

46. James Banerian, who studied Vietnamese at Southern Illinois University at Carbondale and currently resides in San Diego, translated in 1979 a collection of short stories presumably written for children by a famous writer, Lê Tất Điều, a northerner who moved to South Vietnam in 1954 and rose to fame there. While perhaps written for children, the author of the foreword to the collection, C. A. Boren, characterized the stories as "like Mark Twain's so-called children's stories. [They] could be read on many levels." The collection was published by the Vietnamese Artist Association. Then, in 1986, Banerian translated another collection of South Vietnamese short stories, which were published by Sphinx under the title *Vietnamese Short Stories: An Introduction.* In 1993 he very skillfully translated Nhã Ca's first piece of prose, a novelette titled *At Night I Hear Cannons,* but unfortunately it seems not to have yet found a professional academic or commercial publisher. Like his first two translations, this work is also very difficult to find. Another book is a collection edited by Nguyễn Ngọc Bích and titled *War and Exile* (East Coast, USA: Vietnamese PEN Abroad, 1989). It includes some wartime writings. Poetry is slightly better represented: Nguyen Chi Thien, *Flowers from Hell,* trans. Huynh Sanh Thong (New Haven, CT: Council on Southeast Asian Studies, Yale University, 1984); Trần Dạ Từ, *Writers and Artists in the Vietnamese Gulag* (Elkhart, IN: Century Publishing House, 1990). Some other publications include poems from the South: Huỳnh Sanh Thông, ed., *An Anthology of Vietnamese Poems* (New Haven, CT: Yale University Press, 1996); Philip Mahony, ed., *From Both Sides Now: The Poetry of the Vietnam War and Its Aftermath* (New York: Scribner, 1998). In 2013 a Vietnamese American author and translator, Linh Dinh, published a collection of translated Vietnamese poetry with Chax Press called *The Deluge: New Vietnamese Poetry.* It includes many poems from the South. Scholarly works are equally limited in numbers, though they are engaging and

informative: Công Huyền Tôn Nữ Nha Trang, "Women Writers of South Vietnam," 149–221; Hoang Ngoc Thanh, *Vietnam's Social and Political Development as Seen through the Modern Novel* (New York: Peter Lang, 1991); Vo Phien, *Literature in South Vietnam;* Jamieson, *Understanding Vietnam;* John C. Schaffer, "Phan Nhật Nam and the Battle of An Lộc" *Crossroads* 13 (1999): 53–102. In this publication Schaffer introduces an account from one of the best South Vietnamese war correspondents, Phan Nhật Nam, about one of the most important battles of the war in Vietnam, which took place in 1972 and in the course of which North Vietnamese forces were stalled on their way to Saigon. Schaffer also published a very interesting and poignant book that introduces the South Vietnamese literary scene: *Vo Phien and the Sadness of Exile,* trans. Võ Đình Mai (DeKalb: Southeast Asia Publications, Northern Illinois University, 2006). Also see his "The Trịnh Công Sơn Phenomenon," *Journal of Asian Studies, 66,* no. 3 (2007): 597–643. Schaffer's analysis of this famous songwriter is very useful for understanding the literary scene in the South during the war.

47. James M. Markham, "Saigon Writer Finds Everyone Guilty," *New York Times,* November 8, 1973, 60; Barbara Crossette, "On Eve of Tet, Vietnam Tries to Ease Friction," *New York Times,* February 12, 1988, A9; John Gittelsohn, "Family Bound by Music: A Song for Christmas," *Accent,* December 23, 2001, 1, 4. In academic works, *Mourning Headband for Hue* is mentioned or discussed in Công Huyền Tôn Nữ Nha Trang, "Women Writers of South Vietnam," 149–221; and Jamieson, *Understanding Vietnam,* 321, 349. Vo Phien highlights a different perspective: Vo Phien, *Literature in South Vietnam,* 135, 147, 148, 175.

48. The events in Hue were also covered in the British and Italian press. For example, Richard Oliver, "More Than 1,000 Civilians Slain in Battle for Hue: Murder of an Ancient Imperial City," *Guardian,* February 23, 1968; "400 in Mass Killings," *Observer,* March 10, 1968, 4; Tony Mockler, "The Mourning and Desolation of an Imperial City: Struggle for Hue Cost the Lives of 2,500 Civilians," *Guardian,* March 15, 1968; "Vatican Says Reds Killed Many Catholics in Hue," an article from *L'Osservatore Romano* [Roman Observer], a daily newspaper published in the Vatican, reproduced in the *Washington Post,* March 14, 1968, A21.

49. For analysis of press coverage of the Tết Offensive in general and the Hue killings in particular, see Peter Braestrup, *Big Story: How the American Press and Television Reported and Interpreted the Crisis of Tet 1968 in Vietnam and Washington,* initially published in 1977 by Westview Press and then republished by other presses in 1977, 1978, 1983, and 1994.

50. There were a few exceptions. For example, London's *Time* published an investigative report conducted by Stewart Harris, a correspondent of the *London Times,* under the title "An Efficient Slaughter," confirming executions in Hue (see April 5, 1968, 36).

51. Stanley Karnow, *Vietnam: A History* (New York: Viking Press, 1983), 530; the book was reprinted in 1987 and in 1997.

52. For example, Douglas Pike wrote the following works: *Documents on the National Liberation Front of South Vietnam (1959–1966)* (Chicago: Center for Research Libraries, 1967); *National Development in Vietnam: 1967* (Saigon: U.S. Information Service, 1967); *Viet Cong: The Organization and Technique of the National Liberation Front of South Vietnam* (Delhi: Altma Ram

and Sons, 1966); *Politics of the Viet Cong* (Saigon, 1968).

53. Pike also wrote *Catalog of Viet Cong Documents* (Saigon, 1969) and *Hanoi's Strategy of Terror* (Bangkok: South-East Asia Treaty Organization, 1970). More of his general works: *War and Peace and the Viet Cong* (Cambridge, MA: MIT Press, 1969); *History of Vietnamese Communism, 1925–1976* (Stanford, CA: Hoover Institution Press, 1978); PAVN*: People's Army of Vietnam* (Novato, CA: Presidio Press, 1986).

54. The Hue atrocities were also addressed in Oberdorfer, *Tet!* A chapter in this book titled "Death in Hue" (197–235) deals, in part, with civilian experiences during the battle. Don Oberdorfer was then a correspondent for the *Washington Post.* His third extensive assignment in Indochina coincided with the Tết Offensive. Hosmer, *Viet Cong Repression,* also supplies a significant amount of information and analysis.

55. "Televised Address to the Nation," November 3, 1969, republished in many newspapers. The citation here is from the *New York Times,* November 4, 1969, "Text of President Nixon's Address to the Nation on U.S. Policy in the War in Vietnam."

56. *Congressional Record,* December 10, 1969, p. 38223.

57. Robert S. Elegant, "Hue Massacre Effort to Destroy Entire Society – Authority Says Murders Were According to Plan and Perhaps 6,000 Died," *Los Angeles Times,* December 6, 1969.

58. D. G. Porter and L. E. Ackland, "Vietnam: The Bloodbath Argument," *Christian Century,* November 5, 1969.

59. *Congressional Record,* May 19, 1970, p. 16061; Tom Wicker, "In the Nation: Mr. Nixon's Scary Dreams," *New York Times,* May 12, 1970, 38.

60. Gareth Porter, *The Myth of the Bloodbath: North Vietnam's Land Reform Reconsidered* (Ithaca, NY: Cornell University, International Relations of East Asia Project, 1972).

61. "National Liberation Front Political Operations (DV). Hue 'Massacre,'" Porter MSS on the Hue Massacre – April 1973, p. 6, folder 13, box 13, Douglas Pike Collection: Unit 05 – National Liberation Front, The Vietnam Center and Archive, Texas Tech University, http://www.vietnam.ttu.edu/virtualarchive/items.php?item=2311313038 (accessed September 2, 2013).

62. D. Gareth Porter, "The 1968 'Hue Massacre,'" *Indochina Chronicle* 33 (June 24, 1974). Also see D. Gareth Porter and Edward S. Herman, "The Myth of the Hue Massacre," *Ramparts* 13, no. 8 (May–June 1975), 1–4.

63. *Congressional Record,* February 19, 1975, p. 3515.

64. Porter, "The 1968 'Hue Massacre,'" 1.

65. Vennema, preface to *The Viet Cong Massacre at Hue,* pages unnumbered.

66. Here are some examples of the books published in the last seven years: Nick Turse, *Kill Anything That Moves: The Real American War in Vietnam* (New York: Metropolitan Books, 2013); Michal R. Belknap, *Vietnam War on Trial* (Lawrence: University Press of Kansas, 2013); William Thomas Allison, *My Lai: An American Atrocity in the Vietnam War* (Baltimore, MD: Johns Hopkins University Press, 2012); Gary W. Bray, *After My Lai: My Year Commanding First Platoon, Charlie Company* (Norman: University of Oklahoma Press, 2010); Kendrick Oliver, *The My Lai Massacre in American History and Memory* (Manchester, UK: Manchester University Press, 2007); Heonik Kwon and Drew Faust, *After the Massacre: Commemoration and Consolation in Ha My and My Lai*

(Berkeley: University of California Press, 2006).

67. See, for example, Noam Chomsky and Edward Herman, *The Washington Connection and Third World Fascism: The Political Economy of Human Rights* (Boston: South End Press, 1979), 348, 353; and Marilyn B. Young, *The Vietnam Wars, 1945–1990* (New York: HarperCollins, 1991), 217–19.

68. Stanley Karnow, in his much-cited and much-acclaimed *Vietnam: A History,* briefly addresses the tragedy that unfolded in Hue and refers to it as a "holocaust" (531). James Willbanks also talks in short about the events in his history of the Tết Offensive (*Tet Offensive: A Concise History* [New York: Columbia University Press, 2006], chapter titled "The Battle of Hue"). Two books that I have found to be particularly useful and good for my classes on the war in Vietnam at Texas A&M University are George Herring's *America's Longest War* (New York: Wiley, 1979; 4th ed., Boston: McGraw-Hill, 2002) and George Donelson Moss's *Vietnam: An American Ordeal* (Englewood Cliffs, NJ: Prentice Hall, 1990; 6th ed., 2010), but they are also very brief on the tragedy in Hue. George Herring's reference to the Hue killings is powerful, if brief: "The bodies of 2,800 South Vietnamese were found in mass graves in and around Hue, the product of NLF and North Vietnamese executions, and another 2,000 citizens were unaccounted for and presumed murdered" (4th ed., 231–32). Moss's treatment of the Hue tragedy is similar to that of Herring's, succinctly occupying several lines in the chapter on the Tết Offensive. Citing Oberdorfer's work, Moss adduces similar numbers and states that Communists "summarily executed about 3,000 people, often in brutal fashion, or they buried them alive" (6th ed., 228). On the other hand, Moss singles out the events in Mỹ Lai into a separate sub-chapter titled "Massacre at My Lai" (259–61) and also places this title into his index (430). Killings in Hue are not mentioned in his index.

69. James S. Robbins, *This Time We Win: Revisiting the Tet Offensive* (New York, London: Encounter Books, 2010).

70. Reprinted as "Peace and Violence," *New York Times,* September 15, 1973, 31. Also cited in Robbins, *This Time We Win,* 206.

71. "Введение: Актуальные проблемы российского вьетнамоведения" [Introduction: Current Problems in Russian Vietnamese Studies], Вьетнамские исследования [Research on Vietnam], no. 3 (Moscow: Far East Institute of the Russian Academy of Science, 2013), 14–15.

72. Esther B. Fein, "Upheaval in the East; Gorbachev Hands Over Katyn Papers," *New York Times,* April 14, 1990, 1.

73. Bộ Chỉ Huy các Lực lượng Vũ trang Nhân dân Giải phóng Miền Nam Việt-Nam [The Command of the People's Liberation Armed Forces of South Vietnam], "Thông cáo đặc biệt số 3 của Bộ Chỉ Huy các Lực lượng Vũ trang Nhân dân Giải phóng Miền Nam Việt-Nam" [Special Communiqué No. 3 of the Command of the People's Liberation Armed Forces of South Vietnam], February 2, 1968, *Tiến công đồng loạt, nổi dậy đều khắp, quyết chiến quyết thắng giặc Mỹ xâm lược!* [All Together Launch an Offense, Rise Everywhere, Be Determined to Fight until Victory, Be Resolute to Achieve Victory over the American Aggression!] (Hanoi: Nhà xuất bản Sự thật, 1968), 48.

74. Ủy ban trung ương Mặt trận Dân tộc Giải phóng Miền Nam Việt Nam [The Central Committee of the National Liberation Front, South Vietnam], "Quyết định của Ủy ban Trung ương Mặt trận Dân tộc

Giải phóng Miền Nam Việt Nam tuyên dương công trạng quân và dân toàn Miền Nam trong những ngày tiến công toàn diện đầu xuân 1968" [Resolution of the Central Committee of the National Liberation Front, South Vietnam, Commending Distinguished Services of the Army and of the People of the South during the Days of the All-Out Offensive at the Beginning of Spring 1968], March 3, 1968, in ibid., 60.

75. Bộ Chỉ Huy các Lực lượng Vũ trang Nhân dân Giải phóng Miền Nam Việt-Nam [The Command of the People's Liberation Armed Forces of South Vietnam], "Thống cáo đặc biệt số 4 của Bộ Chỉ Huy các Lực lượng Vũ trang Nhân dân Giải phóng Miền Nam Việt-Nam"

[Special Communiqué No. 4 of the Command of the People's Liberation Armed Forces of South Vietnam], March 19, 1968, in ibid., 79.

76. *Congressional Record,* May 19, 1970, p. 16079.

77. Karnow, *Vietnam,* 530.

78. Trương Như Tảng, *A Vietcong Memoir: An Inside Account of the Vietnam War and Its Aftermath* (New York: Vintage, 1986), 154.

79. Thành Tín, *Mặt thật: Hồi ký chính trị của Bùi Tín* [True Face: Political Memoir of Bùi Tín] (Irvine, CA: Saigon Press, 1993), 184–85.

80. Ibid., 184–86.

81. Ibid., 186.

82. Ibid., 184–86.

83. Lê Minh, "Huế, Xuân 68" [Hue, Spring 68], *Huế, Xuân 68* (Huế: Thành Ủy Huế, 1988), 73–76.

84. *Mậu Thân 68* (Hanoi: Ban Tuyên Huấn Trung Ương, 1988).

85. *Washington Post,* February 3, 1988, A8.

86. Interview in the summer of 2013 with Thái Thành Đức Phổ, one of the editors of the publishing house from 1969 to 1975 in Hanoi, for my research on a different project. After the war, Thái Thành Đức Phổ was transferred to Saigon/Hồ Chí Minh City in 1975 and continued to work until 2004.

87. Hoàng Phủ Ngọc Tường, *Ngôi sao trên đỉnh Phu Văn Lâu* (Hanoi: Giải Phóng Publishing House, 1971), 78.

88. Stanley Karnow, chief correspondent, "Tet 1968," *Vietnam: A Television History,* PBS, WGBH Educational Foundation, Boston, 1983.

89. Radio France Internationale broadcasts from Paris in foreign languages, including Vietnamese.

90. After the war, Burchett traveled to Cambodia, where he initially praised the Khmer Rouge, a Communist group that took over Cambodia after the end of the war and is known as responsible for carrying out genocide against the people of Cambodia. Later, Burchett condemned the Khmer Rouge. One of the sources on Burchett is Ben Kiernan's *Burchett Reporting the Other Side of the World, 1939–1983* (London: Quartet Books, 1986).

91. Thụy Khuê, correspondent, "Nói chuyện với Hoàng Phủ Ngọc Tường về biến cố Mậu Thân ở Huế" [Conversation with Hoàng Phủ Ngọc Tường about Upheaval in Hue during the Tết Offensive], RFI, July 12, 1997, http://www.nguoivietatlanta.com/index.php?option=com_content&view=article&id=769:thy-khue-noi-chuyn-vi-hoang-ph-ngc-tng-v-bin-c-mu-than-hu&catid=72:xuan-quy-t&Itemid=128 (accessed September 21, 2013). All quotes from Hoàng Phủ Ngọc Tường in the next few paragraphs are from this source.

92. Hoàng Phủ Ngọc Tường, *Ngôi sao trên đỉnh Phu Văn Lâu,* 65.

93. For the most recent ones see Nguyễn Đắc Xuân describing his road to becoming a member of the NLF in one

of the most popular current newspapers, *Tuổi Trẻ* (Youth), in a series of articles that ran in installments titled "Huế – Những tháng ngày sục sôi" (Hue: Boiling Months and Days) from January 8, 2012, to January 14, 2012, with the last installment being "Trở thành Việt Cộng" (I Have Become a Viet Cong) and a three-volume memoir, *Từ Phú Xuân đến Huế* [From Phú Xuân to Hue] (Hồ Chí Minh City: Trẻ, 2012).

94. Nguyễn Đắc Xuân, "Hậu quả của 'cái chết' của tôi" [The Consequences of "My Death"], *Nghiên Cứu Huế* [Research in Hue] 1 (1999): 255; Nguyễn Đắc Xuân, *Từ Phú Xuân đến Huế,* 3:136.

95. Nguyễn Đắc Xuân, *Từ Phú Xuân đến Huế,* 3:145.

96. Ibid., 2:259–60; 3:142–50.

97. Ibid., 3:135.

98. "Đọc Nhã Ca Hồi ký – Bình luận của một người trong cuộc" [Reading Nhã Ca's Diary: Comments of an Insider], *Tạp Chí Sông Hương* [Journal Perfume River], no. 235, September 30, 2008: 33. Nguyễn Đắc Xuân again brought the point about Nhã Ca's mistaken usage of his name in 2012 – Nguyễn Đắc Xuân, *Từ Phú Xuân đến Huế,* 3:135n1. Nhã Ca and Nguyễn Đắc Xuân met after the war and wrote two very different accounts, worthy of their own analysis in a separate work, about this meeting. Nhã Ca, *Hồi ký một người mất ngày tháng,* 477–81, and Nguyễn Đắc Xuân, *Từ Phú Xuân đến Huế,* 3:136–39, respectively.

99. Hoàng Phủ Ngọc Tường, *Ngôi sao trên đỉnh Phu Văn Lâu,* 65.

100. Nguyễn Tà Cúc, "Nhà thơ kiêm nhà văn Nhã Ca" [Poet-cum-Writer Nhã Ca], "Nhà văn như người hướng dẫn dư luận" [Writers as Leading Figures in (Formation) of Public Opinion], unpublished manuscript, cited with the permission of the author. The author arrived in the United States in 1975. In 2010 Nguyễn Tà Cúc also wrote an MA thesis, "Regarding Literary Friends and Foes: The Story of Vietnamese Exiled Writers in the United States," Pennsylvania State University, Harrisburg.

101. Markham, "Saigon Writer Finds Everyone Guilty," 60.

102. *Ngừng bắn ngày thứ 492* (Des Moines, IA: Người Việt, 1977), 75.

103. Jamieson, *Understanding Vietnam,* 243. Nhật Tiến communicated this to me in personal correspondence in September 2013.

104. Nguyễn Công Luận, *Nationalist in the Viet Nam Wars: Memoirs of a Victim Turned Soldier* (Bloomington and Indianapolis: Indiana University Press, 2012), 581–82n3.

105. Nhã Ca, *Giải khăn sô cho Huế* (USA: Việt Báo, 2008), 9.

MOURNING HEADBAND FOR HUE

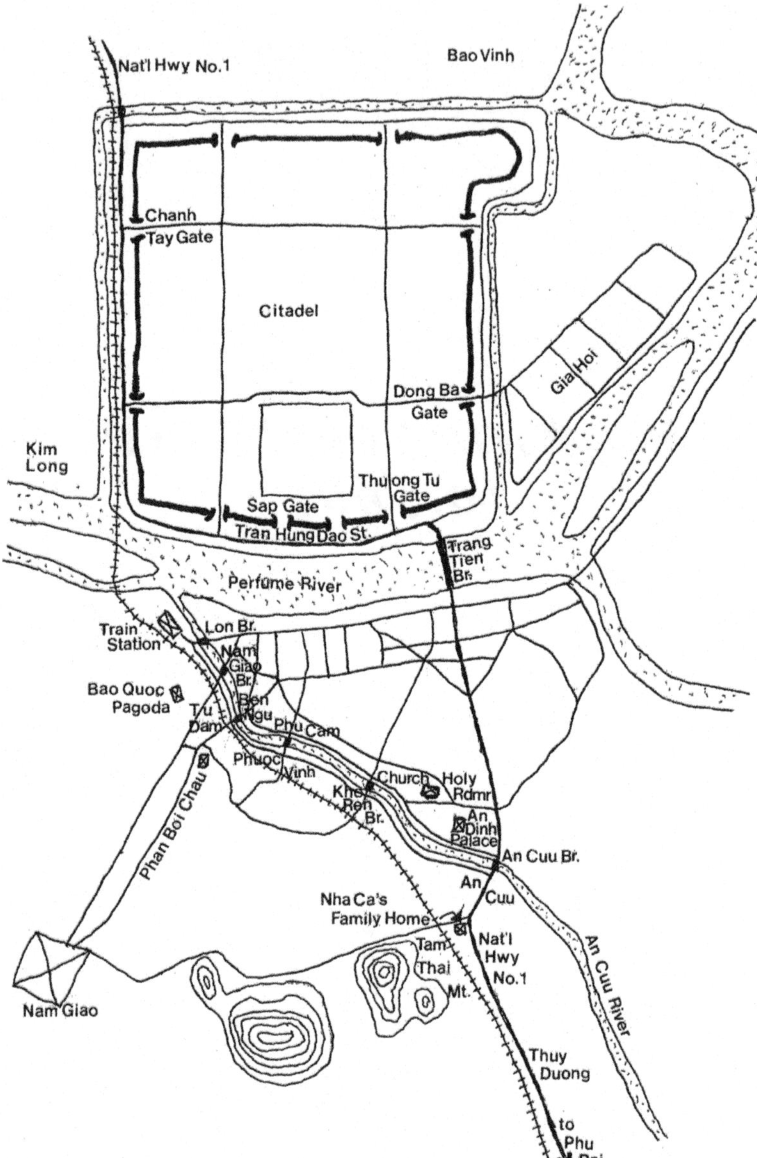

Map of Key Places Mentioned in the Book

LIST OF CHARACTERS

MAIN RECURRING CHARACTERS

Bé narrator's younger cousin; soldier in the South Vietnamese forces; twenty-seven years old

Hà narrator's younger sister; seventeen years old

Lễ narrator's elder brother; a teacher and a school principal; thirty-five years old

Thái narrator's younger cousin; member of the Rural Development Force; twenty-five years old

Vân narrator, Nhã Ca herself, using her real name, Trần Thị Thu Vân; twenty-nine years old

Vân's mother (unnamed)

Vân's uncle (unnamed)

OTHER RECURRING CHARACTERS

Ái woman living in the same hamlet where Thái's uncle Giáo lived; mother of Hiền

Bảo Lễ's cousin who joined Lễ's family in the shelter of Phan Bội Châu's ancestor-worshipping house and with whom Lễ flees

Bê wife of the narrator's elder brother Lễ

Bèo (Mr. Bèo) a noodle maker in the Citadel; during the Tết Offensive he became an informer for the Communist forces

Đắc (full name Nguyễn Đắc Xuân) Khâm's former closest friend who joined the Communist forces and returned to Hue during the Tết Offensive (see more on him in Translator's Introduction)

Điện son of the narrator's younger cousin Bé

Đoan (full name Nguyễn Thị Đoan Trinh) one of the commanders of the Communist security units during the Tết Offensive

Đội Hòa narrator's uncle, her mother's elder brother who was killed during the Tết Offensive

Giáo Thái's uncle in whose house the narrator's family finds a temporary refuge

Hảo wife of Professor Lê Văn Hảo

Hiền Ải's son, an art student

Hường younger sister of Khâm who, along with him and their mother, hid in a shelter in the Citadel

Hy younger sister of Lễ's wife; wounded during the Tết Offensive

Kê teacher who once lived in the Citadel, then regrouped to the North with the Communists and came back during the Tết Offensive

Khâm young man from the Citadel whom the narrator and Thái encounter shortly before his death

Khánh young man who brought the news of the narrator's uncle Đội Hòa's death

Lài Giáo's daughter-in-law

Lê young man who, along with his family, hid in the underground shelter of Phan Bội Châu's ancestor-worshipping house where the family of the narrator's elder brother Lễ was also hiding

Lê Văn Hảo Hue University ethnology professor who became the chairman of the Revolutionary Committee in Hue and effectively the mayor of Hue during the Tết Offensive

Mậu Tý (full name Trần Mậu Tý) former friend of Đắc (Nguyễn Đắc Xuân) from the Struggle Movement who is arrested by Đắc

Ngọc (full name Hoàng Phủ Ngọc Tường) teacher and member of the Revolutionary Committee under Professor Lê Văn Hảo (see more on him in Translator's Introduction)

Nô Răng narrator's nephew, son of the narrator's elder brother Lễ

Oanh younger sister of Lê and elder sister of Trúc; along with them hid in the underground shelter in Phan Bội Châu's ancestor-worshipping house

Phan (Venerable Phan; full name Phan Bội Chậu) prominent twentieth-century Vietnamese nationalist

Phủ (full name Hoàng Phủ Ngọc Phan) younger brother of Hoàng Phủ Ngọc Tường; at the time of the Tết Offensive he was a medical student and, along with his brother, actively participated in the events that transpired in Hue

Quế narrator's fellow passenger on the way back to Saigon

Tam boy who is perhaps either a neighbor or a relative of Khâm

Thu young North Vietnamese soldier

Thu Hồng female relative of the narrator's family

Ti Na narrator's niece, daughter of her elder brother Lễ

Tịnh neighbor's son who sought shelter with Khâm's family

Trai narrator's male cousin who came to visit her and her family upon their return to their house

Trúc narrator's younger female relative

Trúc younger sister of Lê and Oanh; along with them hid in the underground shelter in Phan Bội Châu's ancestor-worshipping house

Túc Uncle Giáo's son who is perhaps Lài's husband

U acquaintance of Bé and his wife at whose house they stopped for a night

Vạn widow, Thái's aunt, who initially stayed with Uncle Giáo's family but then joined the narrator's family

Võ Thành Minh (Mr. Minh) antiwar activist who opposed the partition of Vietnam and was the guardian of the Phan Bội Châu ancestor-worshipping house at the time

Xếp (Mrs. Xếp) woman who came along with the family of the narrator's elder brother, Lễ, when his family reunited with the rest of the family

Xuân young female Communist cadre

SMALL PREFACE: WRITING TO TAKE RESPONSIBILITY

I WAS BORN IN HUE, RAISED IN HUE, BUT WHEN I GREW UP I left my family, departed the city, and went off.[1]

Before Tết Mậu Thân, the Lunar New Year of 1968, on the twenty-third day of the twelfth month of the Year of the Goat, when I, along with my husband and children, was honoring the Kitchen God,[2] I suddenly received a telegram from Hue: "Come back at once, father is on his deathbed."

With my things hurriedly thrown together in a single piece of luggage, I – a prodigal child of the family and of the city – returned to Hue to mourn for my beloved father. And then, along with so many other people, I at once had to endure the gigantic death of the entire city when the upheaval of Tết Mậu Thân erupted.

After a whole month of struggling with great difficulties, rolling through the hell of Hue, I survived and returned to Saigon, but time and again I could not get a wink of sleep because I felt that I should tie a mourning headband for Hue, should write a diary about the death-agony days and hours of Hue. But the events of the days following the Tết Mậu Thân upheaval were deafening. And alongside Hue's storm of agonizing

1. Nhã Ca assumes the responsibility of her generation for the plight of Vietnam and of Hue for what she considers the wrongdoing of her entire generation that had fallen into a civil war that ruined the country and left a broken legacy for future generations. (All notes are by the translator.)

2. A custom in Vietnamese families: Vietnamese, as well as Chinese, pray to the Kitchen God for the health and happiness of their households. According to the tradition, several days before Tết (the Lunar New Year) the Kitchen God reports to the Jade Emperor, the highest deity, on the events that took place in every family during the year.

lamentations, people were still busy with uncovering sensational details of the fighting and of military victories achieved on ashes. Truly, at first, it was not yet the time to write about the brokenhearted self-pity and shame that, although the most mundane of sentiments, are yet at the same time the most profound for a city on its deathbed.

Exactly because of this, after I outlined a few basic sketches in the *Sống* [Life] newspaper at that time and despite requests to continue from the newspaper's editorial board and thereafter being pressed by many publishing houses, I nevertheless tried to pause. I had to pause, if not to consider more thoroughly everything that happened then at least to separate good intentions from the hectic situation, to wait for calmer, quieter moments to write about Hue.

That waiting period has lasted for almost two years. In two years, the bones of all the ten thousand people of Hue[3] who were slaughtered – buried in shallow graves in hedges and bushes, thrown down into the bottoms of rivers, the bottoms of streams – have gradually been collected. Mass graves, for the time being, have grown over with grass. Destroyed houses have been provisionally rebuilt. So, the wailings over the sufferings of Hue, the city's voices saying all kinds of things, have lost some of their clamor.

Now, in 1969, this is exactly the time when we together can wind around our heads mourning bands and light small joss sticks in the immeasurable darkness of the night of war, death, and grief, to reminisce about Hue.

A lot of salvoes of artillery, a lot of death and grief exploded and destroyed Hue. I don't know the origins of this, but regardless of the causes, it is precisely our generation, it is precisely our time that should bear responsibility for the crime of destroying such a historic city as Hue.

It is precisely here among our own generation that there was Đoan,[4] who at some point studied in the same school with me, attended a uni-

3. According to the author, this was at the time an estimate, which she believed to be correct, of the number of people who died in Hue. For the later, revised figures, see the Translator's Introduction.

4. Full name Nguyễn Thị Đoan Trinh. She studied at the University of Saigon. Being a follower of the Communists and an active member of the University of Saigon's student council, Nguyễn Thị Đoan Trinh came to Hue just before the Tết Offensive and

versity in Saigon, then suddenly returned to Hue wearing a red band on her arm and carrying a gun at her side, enthusiastic about tracking down this person and shooting that person, becoming an evil spirit on the deathbed of Hue.

It is precisely here in our generation that there was Đắc,[5] a young enthusiastic student. In times past Đắc wrote poetry, Đắc joined the struggle, and then he left the area. Later he came back to Hue to establish people's courts and to hand out death sentences to whole groups; then he forced his old classmate and friend, with whom he previously had a disagreement, to stand on the edge of a hole to carry out with his own hands the death sentence.[6] The friend of Đắc's, named Mậu Tý, raised up a red armband, the insignia of the Liberation Army, and implored Đắc:

> I beg you, elder brother. Now I am on your side, yes, I am. I am already wearing a red armband, yes I am. Long live the revolution . . . Long live Chairman Hồ!

But despite Mậu Tý's pleas and "long live" cheers, Đắc still decided to pull the trigger on his friend.[7]

It is precisely in our generation that there were crowds of people, hundreds of people, including Catholic priests, Buddhist monks, old

---

assumed command along with Nguyễn Đắc Xuân, Hoàng Phủ Ngọc Phan, and Hoàng Phủ Ngọc Tường with the security units. She is mentioned in Alje Vennema's account on the events in Hue (*The Viet Cong Massacre at Hue* [New York: Vantage Press, 1976]). See the Translator's Introduction.

5. Full name Nguyễn Đắc Xuân. See more on him in the Translator's Introduction and the List of Characters.

6. The verbatim translation of the last part of the sentence should read as follows: "then, with his own hands, he dug a hole and forced his old classmate and friend, with whom he previously had a disagreement, to stand on its edge to carry out the death sentence." However, the author explained to me that the syntax of the sentence was jumbled and her intention was to relate the idea as it appears in the translation above. This is an example of the few changes I made in consultation with, or at the request of, the author, which in some places make the translation slightly different from the original.

7. Nguyễn Đắc Xuân describes this episode differently in his memoirs. According to him, Trần Mậu Tý was a member of the Student Anti-government Movement but then switched sides and joined the Nationalist Party, which was strongly anti-Communist. Nguyễn Đắc Xuân states that he did not have anything to do with Trần Mậ Tý's demise. He heard about Trần Mậu Tý's death a year after Tết Mậu Thân. Nguyễn Đắc Xuân, *Từ Phú Xuân đến Huế* [From Phú Xuân to Hue] (Hồ Chí Minh City: Trẻ, 2012), 2:259–60; 3:142–50. This episode will be elaborated in chapter 7.

people, and children, each of them holding a white flag in their hands to signal their surrender to any side of the conflict; they stumbled around in a city full of flames and continued to run up and down, up and down, until almost all of them fell.

Also, it is precisely in our time, during the twenty-odd days of Hue's deathbed, that there was a small dog stuck between two lines of bullets, running off and barking at no one in particular on the bank of Bến Ngự River. The dog became a target for entertainment from muzzles of rifles at the ready on the opposite bank of the river. They fired until the terrified animal fell down into the river. Then, they fired again at the bank to which the small dog swam with great difficulty. These mischievously teasing gunshots were not intended to kill the small dog but only to exasperate it so that it would flounder in midstream, and thereby they would get an amusing war story. The city of Hue, and perhaps our entire suffering homeland as well: how does our fate differ from that of the small dog floundering in the water? Our generation, the generation that likes to use the most beautiful and showy words: not only must we tie a mourning headband for Hue and for our homeland, which are being destroyed, but we must also take responsibility for Hue and for our homeland.

About two years have passed, and today it is the time around the second death anniversary of the upheaval that destroyed Hue; please allow me to take this occasion to write and to send to readers this *Mourning Headband for Hue,* and please consider it as a bundle of incense and a candle that I contribute to the death anniversary.

Please allow me to invite you, friends, to all together light candles, to burn incense, and to take responsibility for the homeland, for Hue.

Saigon, Year of the Rooster [1969]
Nhã Ca

ONE

FIRST HOURS

I DON'T KNOW WHEN I FIRST HEARD THE SOUND OF GUNFIRE, but in the middle of the night I am suddenly awake with explosions shredding my dreams.

As soon as I roll out of the wooden plank bed, my ears are ringing with the sounds of guns firing from all directions. What's happening? What is this? Oh heavens! Someone's panicked scream prods me to scramble from the outer to the inner room. Someone's arms pull me hurriedly into the middle of the room. I lie there pressed against someone's body, young and cool. A faint shout drowns in the chaotic sound of guns and shells outside. When I eventually manage to collect my thoughts, a young child sits up and cuddles neatly against my heart. Is there anyone else? Oh heavens, who lights a match? Put it out! Put it out, I beg you! Voices are barely audible as if these are someone's last words on a deathbed, filled with anxiety. The matchstick dies out fast, but the glimmering light of a candle penetrates from the outer room. My younger cousin Thái crawls toward this wavering light, then sitting up bumps into my mother. That's enough. Please extinguish the candles beside the altar and also extinguish all the incense at once. I start to feel stifled and want to choke because of the human odors, the incense, and the burned candles.

The room is too cramped with people; moreover the bed takes up half of it. My elder brother Lê rolls under the bed; one person piles onto another.[1] A chamber pot beneath the bed tips over; from time to time it

1. This is the house of the narrator's family in An Cựu, a close suburb of Hue. The author's parents lived with their eldest son Lê and his family in Từ Đàm, another suburb of Hue. The author's father had built this house for worshipping ancestors, which was

is bumped and rolls around with banging echoes, adding to everyone's fright.

Lying in silence for a moment, we regain our composure; all of us begin to listen intently. I lie with my ear pressed against the brick floor. A niece has rolled down to lie next to me, holding her head with both hands, her legs entangling with mine. I ask quietly:

"Ti Na, isn't it too cramped to lie like this?"

"No, auntie. I am very frightened."

"Don't cry."

I caress her. But at this moment deafening sounds of explosions burst in. Ti Na drops her hands and squeezes me tightly; her body shivers; her teeth chatter. Oh heavens, there are gunshots even in the backyard. I hear the gunshots very clearly and with piercing pain. My younger cousin Thái whispers into my ear:

"Now these are AKs. That's it – they [the Communist forces] are now back."

I pull him down:

"Duck down."

"It doesn't matter, elder sister. Let me sit."

The window shutters suddenly burst open, and at the same time the two panels of the door open, then slam back, keeping pace with loud explosions. The sounds of bullets back in the garden become truly intense. My mother whispers:

"The Transportation Station has already been hit."

"No, it's Trường Bia military post."

"No, they are striking at the same time everywhere. I hear it from the direction of the Transportation Station, the direction of Trường Bia post, the direction of the rice fields, the direction of the railroad."

"Shhh! Be silent, please, I beg you! Oh heavens, heavens, heavens."

Appeals to Heaven and Earth suddenly fall flat on the tips of our tongues. The sky lights up with dazzlingly bright flames; the earth vio-

---

the custom in Vietnam. Because he was building the house by himself, he added some living quarters where he could stay while he worked on the house. When he became terminally ill, he and his wife moved into the ancestor-worshipping house, and he died there.

lently shakes as if there was an earthquake. Our anxiety is growing. And I cannot lie quiet to hear the sounds of shooting that reverberate and squeeze my chest. I want to sit up to hear more clearly, but the place where I lie is very tight, and it is impossible for me to move. At that moment my younger cousin Thái elbows a space for himself, his legs under the bed and his head half out the door. He strikes a match and immediately there comes scolding in a low voice: "Monkey, put out the match." The match goes out fast. But in the dark, I now begin to imagine things. We all tremble in synch: I, my mother, my elder brother, my younger sister. We all curl up together, trying to overcome our violent trembling, swelling our chests with air to keep the explosions from pressing so much upon us. My younger cousin Thái listens intently for a moment, and then he sits up and crawls into the outer room. The rest of us hold our breath and wait. In a moment, he crawls back and whispers to each person:

"They [the Communist forces] are here; our yard and garden are full of them."

"Shhh!"

Suddenly a lot of hushing sounds sift from people's mouths like the rustling of a light wind.

My elder brother Lễ's voice is a bit sharp:

"They shoot like firecrackers out there; there is no way they can hear our small noises." Then he continues:

"There is nothing strange about them coming back and hitting Trường Bia post. Last time they also struck all night long, and in the morning they completely withdrew."

I rejoice inside. By now, we have perhaps endured for a couple of hours. I try to bring my hand closer to my neck to see the face of my watch, but unfortunately my watch does not have phosphorescent hands. And, except for me, there is no one who keeps time with a watch. Anyhow, we place our hope in the upcoming morning. Suddenly, my elder brother Lễ cries out with an urgent stomachache and diarrhea. So, the chamber pot proves to be useful. We are in trouble as moment after moment our little ones demand to go pee. Over and over Lễ moans from stomachache, but the chamber pot is too small. We are all lying down, trembling and trying to keep our arms and legs under control to avoid involuntary motions. I try to think about something to suppress my bouts of fear, but no, I can't think of anything. The sound of gunfire reverberates in my brain. My limbs shudder and shiver despite all my efforts to suppress them and to overcome my worry. There are a lot of times when my limbs and my body no longer obey me.

I don't have any control over my body – only endurance. There comes a time when my shivering gradually subsides. And unexpectedly my body, little by little, becomes more spirited. It seems that we have persevered long enough and that dawn is near. I hear the morning commotion in the hen coop behind the wall, coming through the window shutters along with the chaotic sounds of shooting.

Thái has calmed down and sits leaning against the wall puffing on a cigarette. I grope for his hand and hold it tight:

"Thái, has it calmed down a bit?"

"How can I know? We all have to endure this."

I then ask Lễ, who had stretched out on the bed because he could no longer stand to jostle with others on the floor:

"Elder brother, tomorrow morning it will surely end, won't it?"

"How would I know? I'm in this, too."

I begin to despair. Flashes of fire no longer whiz past the window, but the two panels of the door still swing back and forth with the loud explosions. Large and small guns explode in salvoes from National Highway No. 1, from the pagoda area, and from behind the railway. I reckon that our house, which is also our ancestor-worshipping house, being located in a secluded spot, will survive the surrounding fighting. The National Highway and the edges of fields are directly in front of us; the railway is behind us. Two directions, two enemy sides. One side tramples on Trường Bia post, the other side tramples on An Cựu Transportation Station.

I cannot lie quietly waiting for the morning. I start a conversation:

"When it's quiet in the morning, it will be frightening to go out on the road."

Thái blows cigarette smoke right into my face:

"That's too bad; if I had a gun, it would have helped against the fear. If I had known, last evening I would have returned to my unit."

"Don't you know whether it will be quiet in the morning?"

I endlessly ask the same question like an idiot: there is no way to know. But now I must be quiet. Morning is here, and they must pull out, or else we will all be dead.

"Oh heavens. Don't talk. They are in the garden."

My younger sister Hà giggles:

"Mother, please don't be so frightened. Elder sister Vân" – she says to me – "in the morning you will go with me to watch the fighting. And you must pay close attention so that when you return to Saigon you can write a Tết war reportage vivid with details."

"Don't be so silly in a situation like this," my mother murmurs in response.

But our bouts of fear gradually abate and we start talking, and when we speak, the words also help to relieve our anxiety. The gunfire in the garden has slowly faded away, but elsewhere around there are still explosions. I am lying down but my eyes do not leave the shutters of the window above the head of my younger sister. I am waiting for when the pitch darkness of the sky out there will be sucked away to diminish the absolute blackness.

Now I need calmness; I need strength. I open my eyes wide and shake myself once; I gather up my stamina and energy. I hope for the morning sky, and now the sky is almost light. Several leaves from the trees float outside the window, first appearing vaguely and then gradually growing clear. My nephews and nieces are thirsty and cry. We wait until the sound of gunfire subsides a little, and only then does Thái go out to bring a glass of water for the two little ones. The sound of gunfire seems to be more occasional; the screen of night diminishes and with it the sense of being caught in a crossfire. My elder brother Lễ hopes more than anyone else:

"Thái, watch for when the guns are quiet and bring out the Honda motorbike; wait until all is calm, then go up to Từ Đàm. For sure, my wife and children are very scared over there."[2]

2. Lễ lived in another hamlet, Từ Đàm; his wife and children were there at that time, not having come to An Cựu.

My family is now divided into two. Lê is the most fretful. But everything must be all right. When morning comes, it will be quiet, and here is morning already. My mother's lips are less purple, and her limbs tremble less. But our joy does not last long. Exactly at the moment when I hear the sound of hens crowing in the hen coop, the sounds of gunfire again burst out. Immediately there is a loud noise of banging at the door along with sounds of numerous running feet outside in the courtyard.

"Open the door. Open the door."

That's it. We're finished. They [the Communist forces] are here. They are about to flood into the house. My mother's face turns pale; she decides to run around turning off all the lamps that she had just lit. Artillery down at Phú Bài[3] is booming. The sounds of small arms are earsplitting. The door panels are about to burst open from the banging on them. Thái crawls out into the center of the house.

"Shhh, let me go out."

Then he runs out and opens the door wide. There are a lot of familiar screaming and shrieking sounds outside. Just as soon as the door opens wide, the entire house fills with people. My uncle, who lives by the railroad close to the foot of Tai Thái Mountain, and his son Bé, Bé's wife, and the family of his daughter-in-law and other families from his village have flocked into the house. Children and adults make the spacious middle room of the house overcrowded. Several young children are startled out of their wits and collapse in the middle of the house, trembling uncontrollably and peeing in their pants. My uncle says to my mother through tears:

"Oh, elder sister, everything has completely fallen to pieces. Up there, the place is shelled by mortars; old lady Nghệ next door to us lost half of her house."

Bé, an adult son of my uncle, holding at once two children in his arms, gasps for air and at the same time talks without a pause:

"There are a lot of them. Auntie, our place up there is now full of them."

I ask inquisitively:

"How were you able to run down here?"

3. Phú Bài was an enclave with an airbase south of the center of Hue, the only airport in the area.

"All our relatives have fled down here. Up there, mortars busted all the houses. As I ran down the road I saw Việt Cộng in groups of three or five sitting in the front yards of people's houses."

Suddenly, my uncle looks around and is seized by panic:

"Where is Thu Hồng?[4] She carried little Điện[5] and ran somewhere. Oh death . . . my children, my grandchildren . . ."

My uncle attempts to tell us more but falls down with a thud because a B40 grenade[6] scores a direct hit on our tile roof. I gape and brick fragments fill my mouth.

Bé rushes out to look for Điện and Thu Hồng.

Someone kicks the chamber pot left under the bed, and it spills out over the floor. Lying pressed to the floor down here, I feel like vomiting because of the stink that penetrates right up into my head, but there is no way to move anywhere else. Children cannot endure the discomfort and join in a chorus of crying that resounds throughout the house. But the sound of crying is immediately suppressed because hands gag their mouths just in case the salvoes of gunfire might pause. Oh heavens, it's already morning; why is it not yet quiet? I turn and anxiously ask Thái:

"Did it last as long last time?"

"No, last time the shooting was less; there was not so much artillery lobbing in as now. And in the morning, they all withdrew."

My cousin Bé is back and crawls to my side:

"Oh heavens, elder sister, you cannot even imagine. I saw them [the Communist forces] covered with blood sitting near Aunt Quyệt's garden, and I ran down here as soon as I saw them."

"When they saw you running, did they let you go?"

"They ran after me shooting their guns, and I ran for my life. Up there, it is death for sure, elder sister."

While speaking, he clasps his daughter tightly to his heart. His wife frowns:

"You go look for Thu Hồng with little Điện, if not, I will run down the street by myself to be shot at."

My mother says in a temper to Bé and his wife:

4. A female relative of the narrator's family.

5. Bé's son.

6. The B40 was the first rocket-propelled grenade launcher designed in the Soviet Union.

"Death is everywhere and you don't care! Why would the two of you not run to look for them together?"

"Why would we run together? Everyone for himself; staying alive now is almost beyond belief."

The husband and wife keep silent, but just a minute later I again hear them arguing. Soon there is the sound of sporadic shooting. Bé rushes into the courtyard and gradually gropes his way to the road. Around twenty minutes later, Bé returns; in one of his arms Bé carries his son Điện, and behind his back walks Thu Hồng. Bé approaches me and lowers his voice:

"Elder sister, I went to look for Thu Hồng and little Điện. I had to cross a road behind the garden. Along the railroad, I ran into them [the Communist forces]. They asked me where I was going and arrested me. There were three of them; one was wounded. I begged them, saying that I am looking for my children who got lost. At first, they decided not to let me go. They asked me what I do for a living. I said: 'I'm a carpenter, and I have lost my children.' Then they let me go. I was thinking that if they tried to seize me, I would risk death to snatch a gun. One of them was wounded, almost dead. Another one was lightly wounded and could not hold a gun. As for the third one, he was even weaker than me . . ."

Hà, my younger sister, blusters:

"Enough. You and snatching a gun; you are just showing off."

"I tell the truth; I do serve in the army . . ."

Then he all of a sudden remembers his army camp and his fellow soldiers, and he sits down, sad. A moment later, he sighs heavily:

"Another moment and I would have been dead."

People from the upper hamlet who came into my house along with my uncle and my cousin Bé now regain their composure. One bares her breast for a child to suck. Others begin to exchange stories. Each one tells a story that roughly consists of the same elements: seeing a gang of them [the Communist forces], then running, barely escaping death, seeing their bullets, big and blazing red, as though destined to pierce people's faces but for whatever reason missing.

Suddenly, at eight o'clock in the morning, the sound of gunfire bursts from the Phú Cam area.[7] Shells from the cannons at Phú Bài stop

7. An alternate spelling is Phủ Cam.

falling. Only then do we shuffle out to the yard. The garden with its trees is tranquil, not a shadow of a person, but on the grass and on the ground there are spots of dried blood.

Some tree branches are broken, and the bamboo hedgerow at the end of the garden has fallen, opening the way to the railroad; dry branches were pushed wide apart, making an unobstructed path. Some of us siblings are extremely happy, and everyone quietly rejoices that things have calmed down. My elder brother Lễ gets ready to go back to his home up at Từ Đàm. I go out to the water tank in the front yard to scoop some water to rinse my mouth and brush my teeth. Occupants of our house, carrying children in their arms, are in a hurry to go back to their hamlet. My uncle fearlessly rushes out of the house before anyone else, not knowing whether his house is still there or has been destroyed. I try to get on my toes to see the mountains.

Thái asks:

"Elder sister, do you see anything there?"

I let out a sigh:

"It's for sure that last night, on the mountain, graves were treaded upon and disturbed. Father's grave is still fresh."

Thái hangs down his head. He goes out to the water tank to scoop water. My mother shouts, pointing at the chamber pot:

"Thái, take it out and pour it out at the back of the garden."

Lễ finishes dressing. The Honda motorbike is already waiting in the yard. I say:

"Let me go up to Từ Đàm with you."

Lễ says:

"No, it's quiet now, but no one is out on the streets."

However, my brother has not yet finished speaking when we hear the sound of many vehicles driving into town from the direction of the National Highway.

We are just standing in the yard looking out. A column of trucks carrying Americans and artillery slowly comes to a stop outside. American soldiers jump down. Thái bursts out loudly:

"Hey, auntie, it's quiet now, and the American army has just arrived. I am going outside; I will see what's going on."

My mother calls out:

"Everyone come inside; come in or they will shoot you."

My elder brother blocks the way:

"Everyone must stay where they are. Stay quiet, don't run, or they will think that you are Việt Cộng and they will kill you at once."

A unit of American soldiers jump down from the trucks and get to the gardens, crawling along the edges of the road toward the fields. In a moment, my garden is filled with American soldiers. I try to keep my cool, sitting silently and clenching my teeth.

Several American soldiers watch us carefully, then they slip to the garden, scowling, rifles pointed at the shrubs before they move to another garden. Nothing's happening here. The situation is completely calm. We are going into the house and sit quietly on a wooden trestle bed. Don't go outside now. It's dangerous. Everybody thinks this way. Perhaps American soldiers are searching here to seize Việt Cộng. We are silent, sitting and looking at each other, waiting nervously. Two American soldiers cut across the yard with their rifles ready. They enter the house. We try to keep natural expressions on our faces. My mother looks like she is trying to display joy. Two American soldiers stop; then, throwing knowing glances at each other, they enter the veranda, jerking up their chins to signal all of us to go stand next to the door. An American soldier says two words, not in the American language.

Stupefied, we look at each other. The American soldier with an angry appearance shouts out an order:

"Aitentudy sard."

My elder brother Lễ asks them a question in English, but the American still yells with distorted pronunciation:

"Aitentudy sard."

My mother is the one who understands first; she says loudly:

"Mr. American asks for our 'identity cards.'"

The American soldier nods in agreement. His companions point their guns right at us. But when I hand my card, the American soldier shakes his head. They ask identity cards only from males. Returning the card, one of them, speaking in heavily accented Vietnamese, thanks me and then slips out to the garden. We haven't had time to sit down again on our wooden trestle bed when we hear several loud explosions. Thái, acquainted with the types of weapons, cries:

"That's it – these are now the Việt Cộng's B40s."

The sound of B40s, falling like rain, comes from the mountainside and the direction of the railway. Outside, armored vehicles carrying 40-mm mortars vehemently shoot in response. Roof tiles are blasted or grazed by bullets and fall in a clutter upon our heads and necks. Everyone in the house creeps into the inner room. At the same time, strange crying sounds rise up from out by the street. What is it? Thái wants to run out there first. My mother grabs his shirt and holds him firmly. But Thái keeps begging and begging her and finally he disappears out the door, moving back and forth because of the gunfire flashing across the roof. Boom. Boom. Several big trees in the garden are knocked down. We all lie pressed to the ground, passively awaiting our fate. This time it's the end of us. Pray! The screams and crying beside the yard, just in front of us, become increasingly heartrending.

Several Americans hiding in the yard rush out toward the road from where moaning and crying are heard. At this moment bullets are raining down, while the sound of B40s gradually slackens and then entirely stops. The sounds of screaming and crying are heard very distinctly. We all together, without saying a word to each other, run out into the yard. In the yard in front of us there is a house in flames, and American soldiers are trying to extinguish the fire. I now regain my composure a little. My mother is worried, not knowing whether or not the fire might spread to our house. She shouts, calling the grandchildren to take care to wrap up whatever small part of our belongings that can be carried away. In the crackling sound of the fire and the noise of submachine guns resounding from all corners of the yard, the sound of crying becomes more distressing by the minute: "Oh my aunt, my uncle, my mother are dead. I beg you . . . help me!" Screams, crying, sounds of running feet come from neighboring houses despite all the gunfire. My mother pushes us into the house. Thái goes to help put out the fire. Several Americans circle around again through the courtyard and look in at us. The American who checked our papers only a short time ago shows several fingers and bubbles a phrase in Vietnamese, the gist of which is that outside there are some dead people.

When finished, they go to their vehicle, and the column roars on its way into the city. But several minutes later, even before their vehicles perhaps get to An Cựu Bridge, we hear frightfully violent explosions of different kinds of guns. In a moment, the American column of vehicles withdraws, and on its way back the soldiers don't spare anything or anyone – bullets are raining along both sides of the road. The returning vehicles are very few and seem to be those that were at the end of the column. Perhaps these vehicles are going back to transport more ammunition and the convoy in front has been trapped in the heart of the ambush.

The sound of gunfire in the bridge area gradually subsides.

Around fifteen minutes later, when we look out at the road, we see a unit of people in yellow uniforms, bareheaded, with rifles on their shoulders. I hurry into the courtyard thinking: that's it, now they [the Communist forces] are retreating, and our [Nationalist] soldiers are coming back. I am happy like crazy and stretch out my hand to wave when I suddenly realize that they carry haversacks at their sides. Nationalist soldiers carry rucksacks. I freeze again. The unit is not big, only several tens of people.

At this moment, Thái sees them too and gets frightened:

"It's the end of me; if they learn that I am a Rural Development[8] cadre, there's no way for me to survive."

I tell him to hand me his identity papers for safekeeping. I carefully put his papers into the pocket of my coat, which I fold into an untidy bundle of clothes wrapped in a large piece of cloth. My elder brother tries to exude confidence and tells Thái:

"I am a teacher; surely it's not a problem. If they ask you, tell them that you are a student."

Thái politely agrees but his "yes" sounds weak and deflated. Bé's family hurriedly prepares to flee with several jute bags of rice, clothing, pots, and pans. My uncle is not with them; he is already back at his house by the railroad. My mother implores Heaven and Earth to persuade Bé and his family to bring my uncle back down here, but they say that he is staying up there to guard the house. There is an old underground shelter there made after the previous shelling. My mother does not put much

8. The Rural Development units were established in 1965 by the Saigon government to assist in carrying out the local self-development programs. Organized into paramilitary groups, its cadres were charged with motivating and organizing the local population to assume their own self-defense and raise the living standards of the villages.

trust in this shelter. Thus, she nevertheless makes Bé go to call my uncle back down here. Bé goes but soon returns in a hurry:

"Aunt, they [the Communist forces] have returned and are as numerous as ants. They are gathering at Xay T-junction;[9] they are hanging flags and making appeals to the people. They have already seized all of Hue. People say that near Phu Văn Lâu road they raised a really big flag of pure silk. Just when I got close, I saw them installing loudspeakers. I quickly sneaked into Bác Ai garden and then back here; fortunately, they did not see me."

I ask if there are any wounded. Bé says he saw a lot of them in the morning, but now they have all been taken to someplace else. My mother wonders whether it is possible for us to evacuate to Từ Đàm where my elder brother's house is; Bé lets us know that all the roads, each and every corner, are guarded by the Việt Cộng. I repeatedly ask if he saw it all with his own eyes, and he becomes annoyed: he says that as soon as he saw them, he, risking his life, ran to return here; the Transportation Station looks completely deserted as though no one is there, and the walls of the Citadel are all utterly destroyed . . .

It's now around eleven o'clock in the morning. We don't stand around anymore but sit again, looking outside, waiting. My mother soon sends one of the grandchildren outside to see if anyone is going anywhere, but the roads are still absolutely deserted. Several times Bé decides to sneak over in the direction of Xay T-junction but does not have enough courage to get there. He has glimpsed a Việt Cộng flag hanging there and returns with a gloomy face:

"Heavens, if all [Nationalist] soldiers are like me then Hue will surely be lost. Had I known this would occur, I would not have left camp to come back here.[10] I left, even though I was aware of the order to stay in the camp."

Bé is sad, as he must be, for, whatever good reasons there are for thinking that Hue is still ours or has already been lost, he wants to be with his fellow soldiers. But when my father died at the end of last year, Bé obtained permission to have several days at the beginning of the year

9. Nghẹo Đường Xay is an appellation of a T-junction in An Cựu.

10. Bé left his camp to mourn for his uncle, the narrator's father.

to help take care of our family business. Now the candles on my father's altar are dazzlingly bright, and each of us lights incense and prays. This is the only ancestor-worshipping house for my branch of the family; only after a life of chaos and suffering, hard and honest work, was my father able to build it. The house was not yet fully furnished, but my father had a place to sit there. The guns and shells last night and this morning have been unimaginably kind to our family's house of worship.

At this point, we still have to think about food. Lunch can be fixed quickly, but there is no food. On the last day of the year, we finished with the funeral business. On the first day of the New Year my family was on a vegetarian diet to pray for the deceased.[11] Instead of celebrating Tết in the house of my elder brother Lễ in Từ Đàm, we, including Lễ himself, my mother, my younger sister, several young nephews and nieces, and several children of my uncle, Bé's father, volunteered to stay here to say prayers. The ancestor-worshipping house is not a place to stay and lacks what is needed for daily life. To get some household goods, we break open a door to go down to the old servant quarters being rented to a teacher from An Cựu School, who with his wife went to his native place to celebrate Tết.[12] There we get some cups and bowls and look for some seasonings like fish sauce, salt, and pepper. It's too bad that we didn't plan on staying here and didn't stock up on rice. Now, sounds of gunfire are no longer heard, or, if they are, they only resound softly at a distance, from some other area. Then where do they come from? There is not a single plane, not a single vehicle.

At this moment a column of American vehicles enters the city, dispersing in all directions. The Việt Cộng, who just recently gathered at Xay T-junction, are suddenly completely scattered. My uncle in the hamlet up there, separated from us only by the railway and several gardens, why has he not come down? Now and then we see a group of people on the street going somewhere in the city from the direction of the National Highway. Our ancestor-worshipping house is in An Cựu, close to the suburbs, right where the National Highway connects Phú Bài to Hue.

11. According to Buddhist tradition.
12. The servant quarters were in a separate building.

We can't fathom at this moment what's going on in the city of Hue. The entire household gathers together to fix the old shelter under the kitchen in the servant quarters. The sound of gunfire increases while the afternoon wears on, and the street suddenly becomes completely deserted. In the kitchen and upstairs, refugees from the hamlet lie everywhere in some small rooms sheltered by several walls. My mother sends her niece-in-law, Bé's wife, to light a fire and fix a pot of porridge, though surely nobody has the heart to sit for an afternoon meal. But just when the pot of porridge is ready, Thái again sees people walking outside. Despite the sounds of gunfire exploding everywhere and despite the shells that might burst right over our heads, our entire household spills into the courtyard and then goes out to the main road. A couple of people ride bikes from the direction of An Cựu Bridge, weaving back and forth; Thái waves at them and asks:

"Is there anyone out there?"

"All the people have evacuated to the other side of the river."

My mother shouts loudly:

"Is it possible to get up to Từ Đàm and Bến Ngự?"

"For sure it is."

As soon as we hear this assurance, my whole family is brimming with hope. Nephews and nieces urge that we must evacuate across the river or go up to Từ Đàm where Lễ's house is; otherwise, to stay here is certain death. The Việt Cộng have already returned and taken over all the houses and roads. Our house sits right between the two camps, and Thánh Giá hill lies right behind us. If there is hand-to-hand fighting here, the entire An Cựu village will certainly be reduced to ashes. My mother hastily gathers up some of my father's clothing, things of his that remain that were not used to prepare his body for the burial. She carefully wraps them up. Several younger members of my family take care of carrying the poles with containers of rice, clothing, pots and pans, and other necessary implements. I carry a purse and a small bag.

My elder brother wheels the Honda to take my younger sister Hà and his own two children to Từ Đàm first. When we get closer to An Cựu Bridge, my mother tells my elder brother Lễ to go ahead with my sister and the children, then to come back to get the others, one by one, with the motorbike, to make it faster. Thái takes a bicycle to look for a way through the streets on his own. We part in front of the Transportation Station. We see several groups of people there. Each group is in a hurry, at full stride, with people carrying children and parcels in their arms, running toward the bridge. We follow them, but when they reach the bridge, nobody is allowed to go anywhere else, to Tân Lăng or to Phú Cam, and they are waved away from the bridge. When we run up there, one of the two men guarding the entrance to the bridge stretches his hand and blocks us:

"Wherever are you are going, fellow countrymen? Stay put in your house; no one is allowed to flee."

I stand there, transfixed, behind my mother's back. The two men wear yellow khaki uniforms and have sandals on their feet. If they are not Nationalist soldiers, then surely they are part of the Liberation [Communist] Army. I stand stupefied, looking at them, not saying a word, reduced to silence. My mother sounds on the verge of tears:

"Our house is in ruins; oh, sirs, please, where can we live? I am going to my son's house on the other side of the river."

I could no longer see the silhouette of my elder brother Lễ transporting my younger sister and his two children. I think that he has escaped. Two soldiers wave us across the bridge. Several puddles of stagnant blood in the middle of the bridge have not yet dried up; coal-black flies and bluebottles swarm around. Though we have only passed a short distance, I've seen a great many sandals, shoes, stockings, torn clothes, haversacks, rucksacks, all flung about topsy-turvy and mixed with blood and pieces of flesh.

My mother says that upon crossing the bridge we must continue along the riverbank to find the road leading up to my elder brother's house in Từ Đàm. But after going a short distance, we see people in front of us turn around and run rapidly back while crying out. When we ask them what's the matter, they cannot speak but continue retreating, making waving signs. I stop a small young woman:

"Why are you going back this way, younger sister?"

"Up there, at Phú Cam Bridge, the place is full of them; they are on guard and they chased us back."

"Still, is it possible to break through? I am fleeing from the fighting!"

"They've already shot several people."

My mother clutches at us. Bé is also panic-stricken and tells his family to hurry back. "They," who those people ran into, are Communist soldiers, and surely it's not safe for us to continue.

Miraculously, as we cross the An Cựu Bridge they don't ask us for any information. When my mother asks whether we can cross the bridge, the throng of us just keep running in a file. Perhaps the Communist soldiers are busy with groups of people behind us, so we escape.

Only when we have managed to cross the bridge do I dare to look at the two sides of the road. An Cựu market looks like a battlefield; blood has not yet dried up, and red imprints of blood are on walls pitted with bullet holes. A tank had gone over the curb and crashed into a house, from which a sign still dangles. Several houses no longer have any shape. There is not a single house facing the road that has remained intact. The middle of the road is filled with barricades, blood, clothing, garbage, scrap iron, and wooden planks. We go by working our way through the debris. Not a single pair of eyes looks out of the doors, and the houses look like they are completely deserted. We don't know anymore where else to run for peace and quiet. My mother speaks in a rush:

"Enough, let's take a risk to find a road up to Từ Đàm, to get the family reunited, then either in life or death we will be together."

We make our way to the end of a short road and go down along Lê Lợi Road. The road in front of us that leads to the post office and Tràng Tiền Bridge is completely deserted. Sounds of gunfire in front of the post office explode like popcorn. One group of people approaches, another group runs away; they ask each other questions, but they have no time to hear each other's replies, and so they run in circles through the areas that are still not under Communist control. In the end, we are all driven into the church of the Congregation of the Most Holy Redeemer.

There is nowhere else to run. The people in front of us have all run back. Behind us, there is no escape. My mother implores Heaven and Earth. My elder brother has disappeared without a trace. Gradually there are fewer people outside, and the sound of many guns is getting closer. Everyone rushes into the church. All gather in the nave. The sound of gunfire seems to envelop the area around the church.

My mother shouts to us to go down to the basement shelter built under the nave, but there is no room to put a foot there. We pull each other into a corner space. Bé spreads an old sleeping mat, and the entire household, more than ten people – adults and children – jostle against each other for a small seating space. Only when I finally manage to find a place to sit do I hear a buzz coming up from the basement shelter, sounds of children shrieking and crying and sounds of quarrels and of fighting among people for a corner spot. Outside, the sound of gunfire continues to explode loudly. When the gunfire stops for a moment, a number of other people run into the church. I run out to the courtyard and meet Thái as he enters. He grips my shoulder:

"Go in, elder sister, there is still a whole lot of shooting."

I ask:

"Why did you come back? Did you see Lễ?"

"No, elder sister, I went up to Kho Rèn Bridge, decided to cross it, ran into them [Communist forces], and they summoned me to come over to them and arrested me. I nagged and begged until they let me go. I thought I would be captured again."

I ask Thái whether he saw anything unusual. Thái says that near the approach to the edge of the bridge, there are still corpses all over the place. Some people were arrested and were sitting on the other side of the bridge. Several Americans were tied up and led away.

More people burst into the church. I approach them and ask whether anyone came from the Bến Ngự Bridge area and saw there a man transporting two little children and a young woman. A small boy says: "Yes, a man transporting two little children with a young woman on a large motorbike went across the bridge at high speed. Several shots were fired at them, and the motorbike almost ran headlong into the river. They were detained, and then I saw them being set free to go toward Bến Ngự Bridge." Thái hears this and is firmly persuaded that Lễ has escaped. I lead Thái to the place where my mother sits. My young nephews and nieces sit, eating square sticky rice cakes. My mother throws me an inquiring look. I recount for my mother the story I've just heard. Thái groans from thirst and twists the tap, but there is not a drop of water. Several small children urinate directly on the sleeping mat.

People constantly ask one another about the things they saw or heard. I inquire from Thái about the road to Từ Đàm. Thái says that it's possible to cross Tràng Tiền Bridge but not to get up to Nam Giao. He did his utmost but did not find a way and had to turn back and go to the church, not expecting to meet the family here. I and Thái[13] keep listening to the gunfire. When it subsides we go out into the courtyard and stand there waiting until dusk, but we don't see my elder brother coming. Leading each other we enter the church. Thái takes an overcoat left from my father and drapes it over my shoulders:

"Wear it; otherwise you will get cold, elder sister."

It drizzles; for a whole day I was not able to pay attention to the sky or to the vegetation. I look up at the heavy, lead-colored sky. Drops of rain cling to my hair and to my face without making me feel any colder. In just one day, cold, numbness, worry, fear, and uncontrollable trembling have pressed sharply into my flesh, and my body feels frozen as if in a deep freeze. When I return to the church, I step over the feet of several wounded people, lying all over the small room next to the entrance door. Some men are dressing their wounds; they seem to be very absorbed in this. Candles are lit on several daises and on the benches. As soon as I make it down several steps from a high platform around the center of the nave with the statue of the Holy Mother, I suddenly squat down. It seems like Thái also pulls my arm down. There is a dry sound of cracking and a sound of a person screaming. When I regain my senses and decide to look around, I see that one of the two ceramic basins planted with trees arranged on two stone platforms has toppled over. An older woman lies on her stomach on the brick floor beside broken porcelain fragments. She had rested her head against the basin and dozed. When the basin fell over, it pushed the woman to sprawl headlong. Many curses resound in many dark corners. I sit, bundled, next to my mother and Thái. My mother has not eaten anything yet, and neither have I. Thái asks me whether I am hungry and then runs off; in a moment he returns with some *bánh tét* [a traditional sticky rice cake filled with green bean paste and pork fat]. Holding a piece of the cake, I bring it to my mouth but cannot swallow. I am neither hungry nor thirsty. I can feel a hundred things gnawing at my heart.

13. As indicated in the Translator's Introduction, I have kept the original Vietnamese syntax that reflects people's position vis-à-vis one another. In this case, the older person, the author, is mentioned before her younger cousin.

A whole day has passed, and I have not thought about my husband and my children. How is my family's small house in Saigon now? Is it peaceful? What are my husband and children doing? I imagine the face of each child, the appearance of my husband as he leaves the house and comes back, and also all their dull and tasteless meals. Meals prepared without a woman's hands, a vacant seat, it's very pitiful and sad. My mother holds my hand tightly:

"Child, lean against me and sleep. Listen to me, child, try to sleep a little."

Thái stands up; he says he must go to try to find a better place. I put my head on my mother's shoulder. Several nephews and nieces are crying, demanding water, food, milk. I hear the sound of iron door panels banging at the main entrance. There is no one left outside on the road or in the courtyard. The spacious nave has a curved roof with stained glass inserted in many places; the walls are thick and the partitions have ironwood doors that close tightly.

Many loud sounds of bullets fly through the area of the church, followed by the banging sounds of explosions. My mother pulls me to lean against her. I sit like this with my eyes glued to the candles set in front of my face at the legs of the benches. The flames do not remind me of anything, nor do they bring me any hope whatsoever.

I hear soft sounds of crying; they are so numerous that I can't count them. A scream rises from a corner of the room. Surely someone has just died over there.

There is the sound of sandals shuffling on the floor, from a small passage connecting to the annex. Then a huge shadow appears against the front wall. Then other small shadows crowd in, and a head with half a body also appears immediately behind them. I turn around; on the high platform, under the statue of the Holy Mother, a man in a black cloak stands holding a torch high up. A father, a Catholic priest. All the weeping that sounded softly for a long time and all the secret whispering disappear as swiftly as an arrow. I hear a voice from over there:

"Put out all the candles; I will put this torch right here. Everybody remain calm and find a place to sleep. God will protect us."

The torch illuminates people's heads; their shadows sit or crawl up in utter disorder over the wall, but the shadow of the priest gradually shrinks and then disappears.

TWO

THE CONGREGATION OF THE MOST HOLY REDEEMER

THE SOUNDS OF DISTRESSED CRYING GRADUALLY SUBSIDE, AND all the candles go out. Thái arranges a place for my mother to lie rather comfortably. I and Thái think that the best place to lie down is on the benches. Everyone is afraid; they just lie shrinking among or under the empty benches. We choose two benches next to each other. We lie on them and talk to each other in a discreet whisper. But then, hearing the sound of an explosion from time to time, I start worrying and suggest:

"Let's lie down on the floor."

Thái prevents me:

"Stop it, elder sister – no need of it."

Indeed, in the moment of panic when I lost my calm, words help me regain my composure. Hearing Thái say that there is no need to do anything greatly eases my fear. Moreover, I don't dare to lie down on the floor because I just realize that down there, very close to us, under the benches, there is the sound of someone groaning in pain. Hearing an explosion, my mother springs up:

"Get down, everyone get down now."

Seeing that her appeal is in vain and not hearing any of the younger members of her family respond, my mother grumbles a bit and then falls silent. I lie with my eyes open really wide, looking at the ceiling. From time to time, throughout the church, firelight flashes. Each explosion seems to project flashes on the roof. I become aware of brightness in the sky outside from the colors in the stained glass. I soon guess that this light comes from flares. The light continues to flicker, flicker, then dies out; now and then the glass shakes and shatters from the sounds of especially big explosions.

I lie in silence trying to review the first terrifying minutes in order to gradually get used to the frightening situation that has come up during just one day in the city. Truly, in my heart, I do not believe that this battle will last long. Before, when I was sitting at the stone platform, I heard a low voice speaking from the crowd: "Several people from the Liberation Army said they will celebrate Tết with compatriots for seven days and then they will leave." They will stay for seven days – but I can barely manage to endure one day.

I am thinking in a fog how to diminish my bouts of worry and fear when suddenly someone's hand grabs my foot. I pull my foot away, not daring to scream, and sit up filled with rising panic. Thái hears a noise and also sits up on the other side of the bench.

"What's going on, elder sister? What's going on?"

Thái asks softly but his voice is full of worry. I open my mouth but words don't come out; my jawbones are locked. In front of me, Trúc, a young girl, one of my relatives, also sits up, softly moaning:

"Elder sister, look elder sister. Who's there?"

She holds fast to my shoulders. My eyes are still open and stare without a blink. The glare of flares from outside makes the shadows in the church even blacker. Thái lightly pats my shoulder with his hand:

"Don't be afraid, elder sister."

A black silhouette scampers up close beside us. There is a sound of a foot stumbling against a bench. Then Thu Hồng's feeble voice calls for me:

"Please let me sleep with you; I am so afraid, elder sister."

Even when I realize that it's Thu Hồng's voice, I still do not regain my composure; on the contrary, my lower jaw locks up. I manage to say:

"Speak in a low voice. What are you afraid of?"

"I lay next to some woman who this afternoon clasped a small bundle to her breast; she's so stinky!"

I hiss:

"Big deal! Run for a whole day, tomorrow you will also stink like this woman."

"No, not at all, lying next to this woman gives me the creeps. She cries and mumbles like a mad woman, and it's very scary."

Thái has to bend his legs and lie very close to one side of the bench to give Thu Hồng a place to squeeze in.

The first night sleeping in a completely strange place aggravates worry. Only around two o'clock in the morning do I manage to catch a wink of sleep. It seems very short, because when I hear a wail at the end of the room I sit up like a spring, my brain is heavy, and I cannot keep my eyes open. I must dig my nails into my arm and make it really hurt to wake myself up. A lot of shouting and quiet discussions resound from everywhere, then abruptly all fall silent as though everybody had disappeared into the darkness. Then, when a matchstick flashes and a torch on the dais is lit, everyone reappears, one head after another. The priest has turned up standing on the dais, asking in a worried voice:

"How are things? Anyone hurt?"

We hear his voice coming from the far corner, then the timid voice of an old woman:

"Yes, Father, there is someone in labor here."

A lot of sighs, sniffling; many people look crestfallen. In this atmosphere, no one has enough strength to worry about others. Some heads fall forward and go back to sleep. The priest asks with concern:

"Is there anyone who knows how to help with childbirth? Is there a medic here?"

Not a single person replies. The whispering also stops. The light of the torch flickers and throws a dim light on the priest's face. The priest lights a candle, then goes down among the benches. Only with great difficulty does the priest make his way through several rows of benches. In the afternoon, people scrambled with each other to shift benches and make private spaces for each family. Those who came later were spread out around the exterior of the church; every place where people could lie or sit was fought over. While he moves toward the end of the room, the priest constantly appeals to people; only a few stand up and follow him. I don't see whether they are men or women. People carry a woman who is about to give birth up to the gallery designated for the choir during mass or sermons. Up there, it's very easy to be bombarded. I hear someone whispering; this person seems to be completely indifferent to other people and is preoccupied only with getting a good spot for himself.

Above, in the small gallery, there is crying and groaning. Thu Hồng, bolder than I, lifts up her head and listens intently, then offers her criticism:

"This woman gives birth but she shrieks too fiercely, too weird. Surely she is about to give birth. Oh heavens, she cries too terribly, elder sister."

I've given birth, I know how the pain of labor ravages a woman's body, but at this moment I don't have any strength left to share the experience. I am too tired. I lie on the bench and hem and haw about explaining to Thu Hồng. Only when I hear an infant crying do I sigh with relief. This sigh of relief is not completely for this suffering woman; at least half of it is for myself because of my brain's effort to alleviate the tension built up from everything happening around us during this time of suffering. Thu Hồng's voice:

"That woman has delivered; is it a boy or a girl?"

A small, wretched child – I curse under my breath. The baby's crying suddenly resounds boldly as though competing with the sounds rising up nearby and wanting to drown out the gunfire exploding like popcorn in the distance. I think about a phrase from Holy Scripture: "Rejoice that I gave birth to a person for the world . . ."[1]

This night, how many people are born in the city of Hue amid bombs and bullets? To be born in a house on fire, to be born at the moment of moaning by those who will soon draw their last breath because of their wounds, to be born when bullets are on their way toward them . . . No, in whatever situation, even when life is intermingled with death, we also must rejoice because a person was born. I remember my own children, now in Saigon. Is anything happening there? My heart is wrung. Oh, my children, if anything happens to you, then your mother's heart will ache; if something happens to your mother, then your hearts will ache as well.

1. Luke 1:14 reads "And you will have joy and gladness, and many will rejoice at his birth." It's an approximate reference; the author does not exactly remember what phrase she was thinking of back then.

The torch on the stone dais was extinguished but in the small gallery there is still a bit of light sifting down. I imagine a woman, still sleeping, holding a sleeping baby, and after the exhaustion and panic caused by bombs and bullets, after labor pains, that pitiful mother also rejoices in her sleep at giving birth to a person.

The sound of explosions reverberates farther away, the sound of small guns is also farther away, and I collapse into a dead sleep, not aware of time. But sometime around morning I suddenly wake up. I forget that I am sleeping on a bench and sit up quickly like at home.

I decide to stretch my shoulders several times to feel comfortable, but at the same time my mind is suddenly vigilant again. I immediately realize where I am. I open my eyes to look around at each place reserved for lying down to see whether my mother has already woken up or is still asleep. I see her lying curled up with her head resting on a bag of clothes. It's still very early and the inside of the church remains dim; the sky outside still looks like it is lit with flares. Only at this moment I realize that the flares are launched somewhere very far away, outside of the city, because the light goes dim very quickly. In that case, the entire city must now be in peril. Guessing this to be true, I decide to put my feet down to go and wake up my mother. But as soon as I start to lower my feet, even before they touch the ground, my body is like a spring shooting back upward. A dead body lies stiff in the interstice between two benches. The dead body is rigid, wide-open eyes stare, and the mouth is open as though about to cry out. I don't know whether or not I am exerting myself or if it's the invisible spring that pushes me forward, but in a flash my body flies across to Thái's bench where I fall in a heap on the heads of Thái and Thu Hồng. The two of them suddenly wake up and hug me tightly:

"What's going on, elder sister? What's going on?"

They look around in confusion. All the people are still asleep. Seeing me ashen-faced with my arms and legs shaking, Thái gapes his mouth wide:

"What's going on, elder sister, what are you afraid of?"

I can't talk but only point with my hand. Thu Hồng has also taken a look and jerks back her head:

"Oh, Heaven and Earth. So scary! What to do now? What to do now, elder sister?"

Thái gives us a sign to be silent. He is a Rural Development cadre and has become very accustomed to such sights. He goes to look for the priest. Several of my relatives keep hugging each other, not daring to open their eyes. A moment later the dead body is carried down to the annex, and only then do I regain my composure. The place from where the corpse had just been carried away still has a puddle of slimy yellow water with a piece of red string in it. It is surely the blood that ran from the person's wound; Thái ties a kerchief to cover his nose and goes to clean it up. He switches places with me:

"It's already over; elder sister, lie down and have a bit of rest. It's not morning yet."

Then he listens intently:

"How silent it is! Certainly it has quieted down by now. In the morning we will return home."

I do not believe it:

"How do you know we will return? First, let's wait and see what others do."

Thu Hồng suddenly pulls on my hand:

"Look at the woman over there. It is the woman who lay next to me yesterday; do you see her?"

From down on the floor, a woman crawls on all fours and then stands up, clasping a bundle to her heart and singing softly. The bundle is covered with a cloth and looks like a baby. But why don't I hear it crying or see it moving about at all? Sure, the baby is gravely ill. Two teardrops hang motionlessly on the woman's eyelashes; she looks at us, then suddenly bends over choking with tears:

"Baby, baby, rock-a-bye; in a shallow place, push; in a deep place, row . . . Sleep child, sleep good child . . . child, oh child."

The woman bursts into tears. I don't understand why she is crying. It turns out that yesterday her house burned down, the entire family died, and she herself managed to escape carrying only this baby in her arms. Thái, lying down, turns his face toward the woman and asks:

"Is that your child?"

The woman nods in agreement. Thái continues to question:

"Are you crying because of him?"

The woman tightly holds on to the bundle; she looks very pale and says under her breath:

"No reason, no reason whatsoever."

"Are you left all alone?"

The woman burst out crying:

"Everyone is dead, everyone is dead; no one is left."

But she immediately stops her crying short, even though tears are still streaming down her face. Thái turns to go to another place. Thu Hồng softly whispers into my ear:

"This old hag is crazy. Obviously she is crazy."

I want to scold Thu Hồng but then fall silent. A lot of people have woken up. The priest enters and says that if anyone is wounded they must be carried down to the annex. Nobody listens to him; the priest has to mobilize a group of youngsters to help him worm his way from place to place. A lot of people are carried away. Thái also enthusiastically dashes off to join the youth group. My mother has been sitting up awake for some time. I leave the place where I was lying on the bench and jostle to sit between an old woman and my mother:

"Mom."

I squeeze my mother's hand. Her eyes are not calm yet. Then I ask her:

"Did you sleep, Mother?"

"Yes, I was so tired, I fell asleep, when, where, don't know anything. Did they shoot at each other a lot?"

"A little, Mother."

I don't tell my mother what I witnessed during the night. My mother gets worried:

"Is it quiet, child? How to go back home? I don't know whether your elder brother and the children have made it up to Từ Đàm; is it still possible to get up there?"

Then, overwhelmed by worry, my mother sits and cries. An old woman sitting next to us pats my mother on the shoulder:

"Everybody suffers, not just you; if you cry, you will only tire yourself. I am still missing several grandchildren. My eldest son was arrested and immediately taken away."

The old woman lovingly admonishes us that we all share the same plight, but this evokes in herself distressing feelings of her own, and tears overwhelm her also. The woman points out an old man who tightly clasps a parcel to his chest:

"Elder sister – that man is my husband. He is so old but still has to endure these difficulties. Old, but is still alive to see young people die and to weep for them; this is a real tragedy, elder sister. Oh, what a life of such terrible anguish!"

Everybody has gotten up. The noise is suddenly comparable to a disturbed beehive. Several panels of the heavy ironwood door are slightly open, and the morning light slides in. Only then I know that it is already broad daylight. A moment later, Thái comes back and says that it looks very calm outside. A lot of people go out to the main road and, in expectation, look forward and backward, then come back and conduct fruitless discussions in low voices. Each group of several people stands in front of the church's courtyard. The roads are still empty, not a single shadow of a person; Thái leads several of our relatives to the water well to wash their faces. The area around the well is jam-packed with people waiting and scrambling merely to draw a small bucket of water. The water well lies next to the kitchen-house that connects with a long row of houses; on one side there is an immense shaded garden with all kinds of fruit trees. After a day and a night, only now I see trees, grass, and earth – all finally peacefully at rest. It drizzles. I must pull on my overcoat to shield me from the wind. Last night in the church, partly from fright and partly from worry, I did not feel cold; on the contrary, I often felt red-hot. Now, standing next to the water well, seeing the spray-like drizzle, seeing the trees and grass, I suddenly look at this scene with utter absorption as though afraid that I will never be able to see it again.

A moment later, I leave the water well area and the luxuriantly green garden. Thu Hồng runs into the church first, carrying a can full of water; Thái calls for me to go to the road to see whether there is anything unusual. Some people also stand, dazed, outside the back door of the church, which opens to a small road covered with a thin layer of bitumen leading directly to the bank of the river. Thái inquires of some people who stand there on the lookout whether anything is going on, but they, like us, only look, transfixed, at the completely deserted road, intently listening to the completely deserted city.

There is not a sound; everything has been crippled or is dead. My mind wildly produces distorted images, which make me tremble with fear and cover my body with goose bumps. Thái calls for me to walk with him to a nearby small hamlet – there all the doors are closed very tightly. In some houses there are still people; several heads stick out from half-opened window shutters: "Do you see anything strange, young lady? Where are they? Have they left, young lady?"

We respond with "don't know" or shake our heads. Thái does not dare to lead me any further, and the two of us return toward the back door of the church.

A group of people from the direction of the riverbank are running and signaling for us to come back. Thái pulls me into the courtyard. A crowd has gathered. Inquiring of them, we learn only that on the other side of the bridge there are several Việt Cộng standing guard, and when they see people appear they point their guns and threaten to shoot, driving people back. Some people, having heard this, cannot bear to return to the church; they stand, in expectation, at the gate, not taking their eyes off the road leading to the riverbank. They hope that someone will come and they will be able to inquire about the situation, but the road remains completely empty as though one of the city's hands is stretched out, paralyzed, without any strength to grasp anything.

Now in the church's courtyard suddenly appear a lot of male strangers. These people perhaps came during the night. I see them, scattered among the crowd listening for news and discussion; I decide to run over by them, but Thái pulls me back:

"Don't, elder sister; we don't know who they are, and I am very suspicious of them."

We enter the church. My mother turns her face, looking up in anticipation. "Is there anything? Did you hear anything?" The old woman sitting next to my mother also moves closer. I shake my head: "There is nothing yet, Mother; the calm is as if the city is already completely dead." My mother implores Heaven and Earth: "It's absurd to die on the road in the dust – you know this, so don't go anywhere at all." I sit down on the bench in silence. Thu Hồng comes over and sits next to me.

"I know a road to go back home."

"I heard that several bridges are completely under their [the Communists'] control; it's impossible to cross over them."

"No, I know a shortcut. Go to the riverbank; there is a boat there, for sure. Now the river is not crowded; there is no one on the river, elder sister."

I object:

"Don't rush into this. Let's see if other people go, then we will follow."

At nine o'clock sharp, we still hear no sound of gunfire and see no commotion. Several people in a panic dash in:

"The way is open now; people are rushing to cross over to the other side of the river."

I run out, jostling, in a hurry. In the courtyard is assembled a group of people who had run from the fighting, including men, old women, and children. Some are gesticulating to tell their stories to the crowd, some are weeping, and children are tightly clutching to the clothing of adults. I keep pushing my way to get close to a woman:

"Where did you come here from?"

"From below the stadium. My house was completely reduced to ashes."

"How did it get burned?"

"Got burned yesterday, burned down to ashes; I am left with just my bare hands. Oh heavens . . . oh heavens."

The woman covers her face with her hands and weeps; I try to keep asking:

"What did you see on the road, elder sister? How come you have arrived here just now?"

"Yesterday the house burned down, then they [the Communist forces] flooded into the place and did not let us go. This morning we saw people fleeing and then followed them here."

"They did not detain you anymore?"

"They forced young boys and girls to carry the wounded and bury the dead. So many dead! Then they [the Communist forces] all withdrew somewhere, and I don't know anything else. I saw people from the hamlet running, and I ran too. On the road, I saw so many dead people!"

While talking, the woman suddenly realizes that an acquaintance is pushing her way inside and she follows; she hugs a middle-aged woman and bursts into tears.

"Everything is destroyed, auntie, oh auntie."

The eyes of the older woman well up with tears, but still she tries to speak with authority:

"It's useless; what's the good in crying? A lot of people had to flee and endure hardships; you are not the only one. Now where are the little ones?"

Only at that moment does the younger woman look around and call to several children watching dumbfounded as adults engage in fruitless debate; she immediately grabs the hands of two or three of them:

"Here they are, auntie. To lead a bunch of kids while fleeing is terribly difficult, oh heavens . . . Alas, what Heaven and Earth have begotten, it's such a sin; it's the Tết holiday and the ancestral altars have all collapsed, all burned up . . ."

"Where is the boy?"

"He has been arrested and taken away."

The woman continues to weep. I elbow my way outside to get some air. It is still drizzling; my hair gets drenched, and my face is absolutely wet. I see Thái talking with an older man; beside the man is a shoulder pole with two large baskets filled to the brim.

"Certainly in a day or two, uncle, things will calm down?"

"They [the Communist forces] have already taken over everything. I came here from Phú Cam. In the hamlet there, no one dares to escape; they guard everyone very closely."

"Did you hear anything, uncle?"

"Sure I did; I heard that the Liberation Army has completely taken over Hue, and in three days Venerable Hồ [Chí Minh] will come in an airplane to visit; I heard that Venerable Hồ will also distribute rice for us to eat."

"Enough, sir. Since we came here, my family, all eleven of us, have been starving."

The man who just spoke up wears a white shirt and eyeglasses. He is surrounded by several children: one is clinging to his shirt, one to his pants, and one is sitting on the bundle of their possessions. Thái asks:

"From where did you come here, uncle?"

"From the other side of the river."

"What's going on there?"

"It has been very difficult, fellow countrymen; early yesterday morning they [the Communist forces] filled the house and yard. There are wounded; there are dead. They carried them in and tossed them into my courtyard. Then, they forced young boys and girls to transport the wounded and to bury the dead. When finished, they entered the house and asked for a meal, and after they finished eating they 'borrowed' rice. They carried away all two hundred kilograms that I had; they said that someday soon, when the liberation is complete, rice will be sold for five hundred dongs[2] per hundred kilograms. Then they immediately took off, and from yesterday afternoon until this morning, the children have been hungry; I said that at home we would also die of hunger and brought my entire family running over here to ask the priest for rice."

"Uncle, on your side of the river, is anyone dead?"

"Yes, on the morning of the second day of Tết, six were dead."

A man wearing a black overcoat comes over:

"Where are you coming from, uncle?"

The man's voice is slightly accented, northern perhaps – but not really from the North, perhaps from Hà Tĩnh, but not exactly from Hà Tĩnh either.[3] The man wearing eyeglasses looks at the face of the man in the black overcoat; then, as though unable to endure the pair of sharp-witted eyes staring fixedly at him, he stoops down, stammering. Thái touches my arm and the two of us shuffle off to another corner. Thái whispers into my ear:

"Don't say much, elder sister; a lot of people look very suspicious to me."

Several other groups of people enter the courtyard; many of them are wounded and are carried in. Thái says:

"Elder sister, go inside and tell Bé's wife to fix some food. I will stand here to watch the situation."

I go in and sit on a bench. Quite a lot of people have spilled outside into the courtyard, so the inside of the church is less stuffy. My mother

2. Vietnamese money at that time and in the present.

3. Hà Tĩnh is a province that was on the southern border of North Vietnam in the 1960s.

still sits with arms clasping her knees. The old woman is making a quid of betel; several betel leaves have already started to wither and the lime has dried up.[4] My younger cousin-by-marriage, Bé's wife, brings her small child for me to hold so that she can fix the food. But noon comes and she has not yet been able to get water to cook the rice. The well went dry after only one morning, and people crowd around the well with no place to elbow in. Thái went out to the hamlet and bought several loaves of stale bread and a bit of canned food. Only when I see the cans of chicken and beef do I understand that such supplemental things are now really precious. Usually, I don't take a bite of this kind of food.

The gunfire has started to explode in the direction of the small northern bridges across the river. The facade of the church is turned toward the big road, and on the other side of the road there is a field. This field is rather large and stretches up to the road leading to the post office. The back side of the church is turned toward the river, a small river, a branch of the Perfume River flowing from Lòn Bridge to Ga, the train station, through Bến Ngự and Phú Cam, coming back to An Cựu, and then running the rest of its length to I-don't-know-where. That afternoon there is still sporadic gunfire, but Bé's wife was able to cook rice. With bowls lacking, children of our family must eat scooping with their hands. But when the pot of rice appears, ten other kids hold out their ten chipped bowls. My mother scoops rice for the kids and reserves one bowl with rice, which she gives to me. I mix in a little bit of the fish sauce and eat it voraciously. Never before had I felt that a bowl of rice had such value. Bé is handing me an extra small piece of burned rice from the bottom of the pot, but before I manage to get hold of it, a dirty hand snatches it. I manage to see only the back of a child making his way into a crowd of people lying on their backs or sitting bent forward. The dazed woman hugging the cloth-covered bundle is still sitting. She stares at a person, shifts her glance to another, then bends to look at the bundle and sings lullabies.

An old couple not eating rice bring out *bánh tét* and sugar-coated fruits and keep sharing them with others. The old woman offers me

4. The habit of chewing betel quid, containing fresh, dried, or cured areca nut, lime, and flavoring ingredients wrapped in betel leaf, is widespread in South and Southeast Asia. Tobacco is often added.

a piece of cake. While I still vacillate, Thái grabs it: "Elder sister, eat; don't get too hungry." I hold the piece of cake, intending to bring it to my mouth, when suddenly I am transfixed. It seems that someone in the crowd is listening to a radio. The volume is turned very low, but it's enough to reach my ears: "The battle for Saigon is already over." I hear someone say that they [Communist forces] flooded into the streets and are fighting. In a moment there is a soft cry: "It's finished – the entire country has completely been taken over." I realize that the person who just said this is a youngster. An old woman sitting nearby snatches the tiny radio and crams it into a bundle of old clothes, then, fearfully keeping her eyes down, she looks around. The woman softly scolds:

"Oh, you troublemaker! Here the walls have ears."

I suddenly remember that I brought along a small radio. I decide to get it out to listen but am afraid that it will worry my mother; besides, I also don't remember whether it's in the bag or in some other bundle of clothes.

The second night at the church, the atmosphere is more familiar. Some oil lamps are turned really low. Torches and candles give only dim light, and by nine o'clock they are all extinguished.

This night there is more discreet whispering everywhere. We lie and talk, spending a restless night. Thái relates that down in the basement it is more secure but very dirty. People sitting and lying there make the place so crowded that there is no place to set foot. The space directly above, in the nave, is very large, but we can't bear to stay there either. Children constantly pee, and the stench has started to rise. Also during the second night there are a few women in labor, and the only person to assist them in labor is still the priest. Lying down and hearing newborn babies cry, I madly miss my own children. Is the situation in Saigon the same as in Hue? Is the road to my house still safe? I imagine the smiles of my children to assure myself that nothing unfortunate could happen to them. Then, exhausted, I pass out. In the middle of the night, I am startled back into consciousness by a panic-stricken voice. It sounds like a yell: "Death to me." When I sit up like a spring on the bench, there is a long continuous scream followed by sounds of wailing. There is a clatter of things falling, and everyone leaps up. Sounds of men and women hoarse with fright:

"Việt Cộng are here, Việt Cộng are here. Assassinating people, assassinating people. Save us, oh father priest. Oh Lord . . ."

Then people jump down on the ground, pushing and treading on each other. A lot of shouts appealing to Heaven and sounds of moaning . . .

"Silence; everybody stand still here."

Thái is afraid that, in a panic, I will follow everyone else; he holds fast to my hand and calls for my mother to tell the rest of the family to stay put. The torch on the high dais is lit and the silhouette of the priest appears, large and imposing. Everybody falls completely silent. The priest is solemn:

"Who – who's screaming here?"

"This man here."

"Yes, he is lying here."

Everybody looks in the direction from which the voices come. No one sees anything except for undulating heads, tall and short. The priest says loudly:

"Whoever screamed, stand up so I can see you."

A shadow rises up; no one sees its face clearly, but one can guess that this is a man. His voice is hoarse:

"Yes sir, venerable Father, I was sleeping and in the dream I saw that my head was cut off, and then ghosts and devils threw it into a cauldron with boiling oil."

"Oh, Heaven and Earth, deities and demons. He was having a nightmare."

Everyone breaks out complaining to Heaven and Earth and cursing. Several people can't contain their anger:

"Damn this fella. I got kicked and stomped right on my arms; it was excruciating."

"Someone stomped on my stomach; it felt like my intestines were coming out."

"I was kicked in the face. Goddammit, if I find out who that guy is, I will break his legs."

A sound of loud moaning from an old woman:

"Venerable Father, expel this fellow outside."

"Let him go outside under the roof of the veranda, Father."

A lot of voices chime in. But the priest tells everybody to be silent, to lie down, and to go back to sleep. The torch completely dies out; a tiny candle looks like it is stuck in a black shadow, which disappears behind the back door. The priest is gone. Everyone keeps arguing for several more hours; then people lie down and fall asleep. The guy talks in his sleep, making everybody panic once again, thinking of death; then with no reason for funny thoughts, he suddenly bursts for a while into giggles. Cursing, initially stifled, then increases. The man falls silent. No doubt tomorrow night no one will remember anymore who he is.

As it gets close to daybreak, several more incidents occur. Sometime around three or four o'clock in the morning, when we are still dreaming, we hear loud shouts. This time, it's the priest's voice. At once sitting up, we see the priest pulling a young man and a young woman from the stone dais. These two young people are white-faced. The priest's voice is angry:

"With bullets on one side and not knowing if we will live or die, at such a time you go and do this shameful thing. Oh Lord!"

Everybody stands on the benches to see the faces of the young man and woman. The two are terribly ashamed and don't dare to raise their heads. When the priest finishes speaking, he leaves. The couple, holding on to each other, slip away down to the basement and disappear. Nevertheless, in the morning several other couples are caught behind stone grottoes and in the garden. This troublesome crowd drives the priest crazy.

In only a few days so much has happened at the Congregation of the Most Holy Redeemer. Day and night the priest loudly appeals for everyone to maintain hygiene and order. But with each day the crowd gets more and more out of control. Every few hours, several wounded people die, and the corpses are carried away and accumulate below the row of adjacent service buildings. Every several hours, a number of arguments erupt with people accusing each other. People fleeing the fighting have begun to run out of rice, and the priest has to take rice from the church storehouse to distribute. But the rice distribution makes the situation even more tragic with some receiving a lot while others, although elbowing their way in even to the point of having their skin scratched, do not get a grain of rice. The woman hugging a cloth bundle doesn't ask for any rice at all, but then people give her a handful of cooked rice. She eats very slowly and reluctantly as though she doesn't want to live anymore. Seeing that the church is packed, the priest orders the doors to be tightly closed. But outside no crowds of refugees are seen anymore. The city remains quiet with the kind of silence in which it seems that there is no breath of a living person.

On the third day, the situation again turns topsy-turvy. Sometime just before morning when everybody is asleep, we all at once wake up and roll down to the ground. Guns, both large and small, suddenly explode, and the sounds reverberate everywhere. Some pieces of glass at the top of the church that are directly hit by bullets break and fall down. Thái pulls on me to roll down under the row of benches. Several of us hug each other tightly. Heavy shooting continues like this until dawn. Only when the sound of gunfire pauses for a long time does everyone dare to sit up. Some daredevils venture outside to the courtyard to be on the lookout for news. I and Thái also make our way through the panels of the ironwood door to go outside. The road leading to the riverbank lies cold and deserted like the arms of a corpse waiting to rot in the wind and the rain. The sides of the road are littered, ashes float in the air, and in the distance an entire small hamlet is burned to the ground.

I and Thái boldly cross a small road and right away enter the hamlet. Tens of houses are reduced to ashes, and the houses still standing are devoid of people. We return to the church. It is filled with the evacuees from the hamlet who lost all their possessions in the fire; they lie and sit in the church now. With the nave tightly packed, people flock down to the kitchen and the storehouse. Those who fled from the hamlet had gathered and brought along with them blackened carcasses of chickens and ducks to fix for food. Near the hedge of the church, I see a pig with scratches all over its body; blood from a small wound on its back has coagulated and dried up; there are other places with scratches where blood and fluid still continue to ooze out. A number of people venture out to the hamlet and return to the church with the burned carcasses of chickens and ducks to fix for food.

Throughout the morning guns explode in series of salvoes, then they suddenly stop, then a moment later they fire again; it continues like this until midday. My cousin-by-marriage makes the effort to run back to the kitchen to fetch a pot of rice that she fixed, but no one dares to start eating. The pot of rice is too small and the number of the children surrounding it, both from our family and the starving children of other evacuees, is too large. Bé distributes a small handful of rice to everyone. The old woman sitting next to my mother trades half of a *bánh tét* to get a small handful of rice.

At midday, the gunfire stops for a moment, then bursts out again, this time even more fiercely. Several rounds of bullets from the direction of the field directly hit the side of the church, and panels of glass keep getting shattered. My mother is afraid that the broken glass will fall straight down on our heads, so she takes a blanket to protect her grandkids' heads. Thái's hand is cut by a piece of glass and is bleeding, but not very much. My mother has to apply a dressing made with the last of the tobacco[5] we brought with us to the bleeding wound on his hand. Everybody lies very close to each other on the ground. The children have already gotten used to fear; when they hear gunfire, there is not a child who dares to let out a squeak.

Around two o'clock the sound of gunfire seems to subside in the field, but on the other side of the river, it is still very violent. Now and then I ask Thái: "Do you hear the sound of an AK? . . . What kind of gun was that? . . . So, that sound is from what kind of gun?" Thái ponders: "Too many of them, elder sister, I can't tell the difference; but there is the sound of AKs, elder sister. If you strain your ears to listen, you will hear it – a vibrating sound." We lie side by side. Thái says: "Elder sister, pull a coat over your head so pieces of glass won't fall and kill you." I hear his words, but I suddenly choke up. Fortunately, at this moment the sound of gunfire goes almost completely silent and moves farther away. Thái sits up to be on the lookout.

"It looks like it's calmed down, elder sister. Let me run outside to see what's going on."

Thu Hồng bars him:

"Hey Thái, it's no good. It sounds like . . ."

There is noise from outside the church gates and a cry for help: "Save us, Father! Father, please save us!" The priest is holding a child hit by a piece of glass; he is extracting it and dressing the wound. When he hears

5. The tobacco was brought along to mix into the betel.

the call, he hurriedly hands the child to a young volunteer medic and fearlessly runs outside.

Everybody is sitting up now, anxiously waiting. A group of people, carrying children in their arms and supporting each other, burst into the nave. A number are wounded and many of their faces are absolutely drained of blood; entering the church, they collapse on the ground, panting as if they are about to choke.

Everyone crowds around to see what's going on, but the priest shoos people back to their places. The next moment, he suddenly remembers that he has not locked the gate, and he quickly opens the door and goes out. But when he comes back, the father brings with him two white people. The crowd is stirred up: "Are they Americans or French?" They are French, for sure, and the French fellow is very short.

I look intently at the two strange guests: a middle-aged man and a woman clad in Western-type trousers and tight-fitting T-shirts. The man looks more peculiar; he wears a short overcoat made of red-checked flannel, and his beard and moustache are unkempt as though he just returned from living deep in the forest. In their hands, they hold two flags of white cloth with the word "press" written on them. When the two enter, they look for a place to sit to catch their breath. The priest talks with them in French. The woman continues to look dazed; her face is very pale, and from a glance it's hard to guess her age. A lot of adults and children swarm around to take a look: "Hey guys, a Frenchman and a Frenchwoman."

I recall my childhood, and from time to time I also join the horde of children staring at the Frenchman and the Frenchwoman as though they had come down from the moon. Everybody huddles around to see the two strange guests, the people entirely forgetting about their own situation of being on the edge between life and death. But when the Frenchwoman regains her senses, she lifts a camera and presses the shutter with a clicking sound, and only then people start to react. Scolding voices rise up in a clamor. The Frenchman with the blue eyes and aquiline nose raises his hand and laughs.

"Press, press."

"What kind of a press is this? Whatever press, it's still press."

I hear the buzz of people talking among themselves.

The female correspondent, as I assume her to be, pulls a host of kids to line up and takes a picture of them. The camera is still turned toward the crowd. A wounded man lies silently like a corpse. The woman hugging the cloth bundle, with her gaunt face and eyes wide open, senselessly looks at the lens. Furthermore, infants continue to suck their mothers' breasts and then let the nipples fall out of their mouths and cry stridently because there is not a drop of milk left. The lens turns toward the place where I am sitting. Thái scowls at the female correspondent, stands up, and turns his back toward the foreigners:

"What a monkey, to take a picture in this situation . . ."

The female correspondent smiles to ingratiate herself with the crowd, but her eyes are still fastened on the flock of filthy children standing separately. The foreigners go up to the belfry to visit the women who just gave birth and then come down to take more pictures . . .

A few scattered gunshots are enough to startle everyone. Some whispering voices arise: "The Việt Cộng are coming." Hundreds of pairs of eyes look entreatingly to the priest.

People begin to whisper: "If the Việt Cộng burst in, they will think that these two people are Americans and for sure no one in the church will survive." A number of voices rise:

"Get them out of here."

"Break the camera."

"Don't let them be here with us."

It's unclear whether the priest has heard this or not, but he deduces the discontent of the crowd. He leads the two strangers out of the door, taking them to some different place, I assume to some room out in the back. Several sighs of relief: "They are gone." The whispering in the church rises again, but all of a sudden the woman with the cloth bundle unexpectedly bursts into heartrending tears:

"Oh, my child, my child, people go through life in pairs or with friends, but I am utterly alone in the middle of the night . . ."

Every phrase from her mouth leaves her breathless. I am stunned and dare not look directly into the woman's dull eyes . . .

In the afternoon, the situation seems more settled and everybody starts to hope. When the priest enters, a number of people stand up to inquire:

"Venerable Father, did you hear any news out there?"

The priest tells everybody to be quiet, and then he says in a solemn voice:

"Brothers and sisters, do not get so excited. The situation is not at all as good as I thought. There is news that the American army is coming up the National Highway. There are big battles in many places. So, you must all be careful. Starting now, you will clean up the place. I will divide the place into many sections so we can help each other and maintain order."

The priest immediately follows up his words with action. We, right in the front row of benches next to the stone dais, have to make a fence out of pews in area number one. Each area includes ten families. The priest will distribute rice tomorrow. The priest also organizes a first aid team and a fire-fighting team. The woman hugging the cloth bundle with the child is sitting next to my family; she is all by herself. For several nights now I've not seen her get even one wink of sleep; her appearance is changing, and her face becomes paler by the day. Thanks to the priest's organizational skills, by dusk this day we can go back and forth in the house of prayer and do not have to climb over benches to keep away from other people's heads. The accommodations have become neater. Several women find brooms and vigorously apply themselves to sweep the floor. Children also decrease their disorderliness. Although the stink of urine continues to grow, everyone has gotten used to it.

When I prepare a place to sleep, Thái calls me to go toward the annex to take a look through a half-opened panel of an iron door that allows one to see the road outside. But when we get there, I immediately retreat, for several corpses that have not yet been moved away are still lying there, sprawled out on the cement floor; by now this scene is not as arresting as it was during the first days, and no one pays attention to it anymore. Everyone is busy paying attention to a man squirming on the ground at the end of the last row of benches. I pull Thái to elbow in to see. Since when has this man been like this? Is he sick with something or wounded? Didn't I see him just this afternoon sitting over there on a bench chewing on a piece of bread?

I look carefully and see his eyes bulging out, distorting his face. The man rolls back and forth, laughing and laughing, then suddenly crying and crying. Oh heavens, who has made him be in such pain? Where is he wounded? I tightly hold Thái's arm; Thái bends down to see, then asks a person who stands nearby:

"What's wrong with this gentleman, uncle?"

"He is crazy."

"How come crazy? Only this afternoon I saw him eating bread here."

"Well, his son has just died over there."

The man points with his hand out to the annex and continues:

"His son is dead, and he also grieves for his possessions. He said that his mansion and his car are turned into ashes."

"It's a disaster, isn't it?"

"Heaven and Earth, it's not the lot of the dead person that troubles him; he pities his possessions. His craziness is well deserved; evidently, it is retributive karma."

The crazy man suddenly sobs his heart out, then twists his body:

"I prostrate myself before you, comrades . . . Please sirs, no, please sirs, brothers-liberators [Communist soldiers]. Please sirs, liberators . . . please sirs, don't burn the house, don't burn the house . . . Oh heavens, fire, fire . . . brothers, comrades . . . oh, comrades."

"Make this madman shut up. If he yells like this, when they [the Communist forces] come in, it will be the death of us all."

Hearing the shouts, everybody gradually disperses. I return to my place. Thái says:

"Enough, elder sister, go to sleep. This night we are not lying on the bench; we are lying on the ground. I went outside and got a mat."

He spreads out the mat; my mother says to spread it under several rows of benches and to lie down. We jostle together to each lie on a small piece of the mat. My mother doesn't move from the wall on which she leans for the support of her back. It's been three nights, and she continues to rest her back there and dozes, nodding.

After nightfall, the crazy man again makes a fuss several times, but no one has the strength to curse him anymore. People are also not as scared as they were last night when others cried out in their sleep. I catch a wink of a sleep too, being dead to the world until the wee hours of the morning when I wake up to numerous loud explosions. They seem to be from cannons. Thái shouts in amazement:

"Elder sister, they are clashing; a big fight is underway."

We sit up in the darkness, intensely trying to hear what is going on. The artillery monotonously lobs, the sound reverberating from somewhere in the direction of the wall formed by mountains. The city is completely quiet; from time to time the silence is broken by scattered salvoes of gunfire. A short while later, I hear a lot of noise from moving vehicles. "Those are armored vehicles, elder sister," Thái shouts. The ground where we lie shakes violently as a column of vehicles stretches unendingly. Then, suddenly, explosions erupt from all directions, then a moment of silence, and then more explosions. We tightly hug each other. The situation continues to be terrifying like that until morning when the sound of gunfire gradually moves off and continues crackling without letup.

The previous evening I ate only a small handful of rice, so this morning I feel hungry and am about to faint. Bé and Thái go to get rice. Bé's wife and Thu Hồng are on duty to cook it. It must be cooked early, as it looks like the soldiers are really keen to fight each other, so we must mind our business – if there's no rice, what will we eat? But cooking rice is also a hard problem to solve. We have rice and pots and pans, but there is no firewood. What firewood was stored in the church has been completely used up. People have even broken off all the dead tree branches. Also, in the garden, edible plants have been gathered as if shaven clean. Thái decides to go to find firewood, but then the sound of gunfire on the other side of the river becomes fierce. Everybody, in panic, runs back into the church. But a moment later Thái boldly goes out to the hamlet and finds firewood. Bé's wife hugs the bundle of firewood and at once runs back to the kitchen to cook rice. Bullets from the field shoot toward all sides of the church. Around noon, Bé's wife, carrying a pot of rice, runs in, panting:

"Auntie, I ran and bullets were chasing me. The Việt Cộng are close; they have already surrounded the church."

She comes next to my mother and tells her discreetly:

"Auntie, I heard that the area around An Cựu is full of them; my house and your house are completely in their hands."

My mother bursts into tears:

"Then, what to do? Oh heavens!"

I know my mother is thinking about my father's altar, about several bead wreaths, several candles with no one to light them. Seeing my mother crying, Thái urges:

"It's enough; eat, auntie. After the meal, I will look to find a way back to Bao Vinh to see how my mother is; I am worried to death about her."

My mother has her mouth distorted by the desire to cry:

"You are going to abandon me, abandon your elder sister, too; how will we bear it?"

Tears stream down from Thái's eyes:

"How do I know how bad the situation is there? I regret I don't have a gun; I would've run outside . . ."

Bé very quietly calls:

"Hey! Bamboo shrubs have ears to hear you. You speak carelessly; you don't know who can hear you."

Bé's wife scoops rice and gives a handful to everyone. There is only one bottle of fish sauce left. As soon as I bring a handful of rice to my mouth but without time yet to chew, an explosion occurs and an entire glass panel falls down. Someone thrusts me down under the benches. Sounds of gunfire are like rain. I open my eyes looking for my mother. Bé lies close to a corner of the church, tightly hugging my mother. But there is only one direct hit on the roof of the church, and then the shooting shifts to a different area. Then, again, sounds of gunfire seem to come from the hedge of the church. They [the Communist forces] have returned and are outside the church . . .

The sound of gunfire goes back and forth for a long time, around half an hour. This half an hour feels as long as a century . . . nobody dares to raise a head. I see the woman hugging the cloth bundle with the small child inside of it crouching beside me. A stinking smell makes me want to vomit. The stench of rotten pickled fish, the stench of decomposing flesh, the stench of sweat, it seems they are all mixed together. Thái also notices this stinking smell; he rubs his nose and then looks at the woman. Meeting Thái's glance, the woman tightly hugs the bundle and moves it to her side as though she wants to hide it. But she is not quick enough, and before my eyes is dangled a child's slimy, gashed foot dripping yellow liquid down on the brick floor. It's as if the stink is glued to my nose. The foot, small and tender, black and blue, and cracked open appears to flutter about in front of my eyes. I scream, then fall into silence for several seconds.

I hear the woman screaming loudly, but it seems that something else has gotten into her scream; it's not the voice of a human being but of an animal roaring at the moment of final desperation. This scream brings back my composure. The sound of gunfire outside still reverberates in my ears as though wanting to tear apart my eardrums. Thái leaps up in front of the woman's face:

"Hand it here."

"No, no sir, no, my child, my child is still alive, surely. Oh child, oh sleep, child . . ."

The woman is very tired, very hungry, and at the end of her wits. The bundle falls from her hands, but the fabric's selvage remains in her hands. The corpse of a newborn falls down on the church floor. No, there is no body of a child there anymore, but only a heap of flesh, almost decomposed and crushed, leaking liquid.

A number of wails rise up. These are the voices of Thu Hồng, of my mother, of many other people. The woman collapses on the floor, her hand clawing toward the corpse of her child:

"My child, my child, and my husband, too, where are you? Come here, come here to be with me, oh my child."

The woman's voice dies on her lips. My eyes are wide open as though my eyeballs cannot move, as though I cannot close my eyes.

"My child, where are you, where did you go? Child, oh child . . ."

The woman's withered hand grasps the foot of the child's corpse and she pulls it back closer to her, gradually closer and closer. Her eyes roll around in their sockets and look as though they've lost the pupils; there is foam bubbling in the corners of her mouth. She talks but no sound comes out; her eyes are dry and she looks at the ceiling of the church, but it seems like she doesn't see anything anymore. She laughs and cries intermittently. My lips move in synch with the lips of the woman. Thái makes me get up:

"Vân, don't look, don't look, elder sister."

Two young people crawl over and snatch away the baby's body. The woman, as though under a magic spell and with all her remaining strength, drags herself to follow them and stretches her hands forward:

"Don't, sirs, don't, he still breathes, still eats, still sucks on my breast. He still cries, still laughs, child, oh child, my husband, oh my husband."

The woman drags herself toward the door and then goes outside. Amid the sound of gunfire I hear the woman's voice shouting very loudly, but her voice gradually weakens, drowned out by gunfire, which becomes more chaotic by the minute . . .

My tears have been soaking the sleeves of my blouse for some time. Thái's eyes are also reddish, as well as my mother's. I don't dare to look into anyone's face; the scene of the newborn's corpse still flutters before my eyes. I see only a foot, a black and blue foot, oozing liquid, so I imagine the face, the nose, the feet, and the hands of the baby.

Now not only small guns but also large guns explode in successive salvoes. And it seems that cannons have joined in. There is a great clanging sound, and a lot of broken pieces of glass fall down. From the front and from the back, it seems that gunfire comes from everywhere. I recognize the sound of B40s, the sound of AKs, the sound of all kinds of guns. From many other directions there are the clattering sounds of falling glass. There are many loud shouts. People call for each other, screaming: "Hey! Hey!" Another crashing sound and glass falls down followed by a loud explosion, and a fiery red mass flies into the middle of the church. Bricks and tiles, smoke, pitch dark. Run, run and don't die.

A scream and then many screams – the sound of crying rises without end; people run back and forth, lie down on their backs in one corner, sit with their heads bent forward in another corner, but nobody has yet dared to run out of the church. Bang – a sound and a piece of wall breaks, a lot of screaming, shrieking, moaning: "Uncle is hurt! Uncle is hurt!" "Hey Mother! Hey Mother, I . . ." It feels like blood is soaking my inner and outer clothes. A cross made of persimmon tree wood falls down from the wall. Several shouts. My legs and even my face are covered with blood. I try to make my body move, or have I already died? No, I hear shouting, crying, calling. "Thái, I've been hurt." A thudding noise as though someone fell down beside my feet. Blood spurts out from a man's hip, leaving spots across my body. "Oh, child, oh child, where are you?" "Where is uncle?" "Where is Dad?" "Where is Bé?" "Run!" "Cling to Mother!" "Hold tight to uncle's hand." In single file, we follow a group of people and run out into the yard. The field is continuously being shelled.

Boom, boom, and a lot of bricks and tiles break. The people crowd into the courtyard; the back gate is locked. A lot of bullets fly noisily past our heads. Thái yells:

"Turn back."

But we cannot go back into the church; bricks and tiles have scattered everywhere. The panels of the ironwood door are wide open, and another group of people rushes out. Near my ear there are sounds of crying, voices calling to each other, howling as though someone is wounded and is in the throes of death.

I crouch, hiding, next to a corner of the wall, but in just a few minutes we are pushed inside with a lot of other people shoving behind us. Perhaps all the glass on the walls and roof has been broken and so there is nothing more to deter us from going back in. Despite the bullets, a crowd of people with no place to hide floods into the church, and some others rush toward the back of the yard in the direction of the kitchen. Thái says:

"Run, we must run; here is certain death."

We wait for the gunfire to let up and then run, cutting across the yard. I kick what must be a wounded pig lying next to the hedge. Someone opens the back gate, and we burst out. My uncle had joined us in the church and now is fleeing with us. At this moment, I suddenly realize that my body is covered with blood; even Thái's blue shirt is also bloody in the back. A sleeve of my uncle's white shirt is soaked in blood. Panic-stricken, I yell:

"Mother, I've been wounded."

And I feel as if I am about to faint. My mother stands still:

"Where, where are you hurt?"

I check my entire body: arms, legs, face, nose. Thái turns me around, from the front to the back, and lets out a long sigh of relief:

"Nowhere, elder sister; you are not hurt, but your sandals have disappeared."

I look down at my feet. They are sticky from being covered in blood. It seems that I am indeed hurt there because I see a trace of blood at the edge of the big toenail where it feels like it is burning. The gunfire from the field becomes more sporadic. There is no one left with a pair of sandals on their feet. But I still hold a leather briefcase, and Thái still carries a small bag of rice and a bottle of fish sauce. My mother trails behind, carrying a bag of clothes. Thái cries:

"What about the bundle with my clothes?"

Thái turns around to go back, but he doesn't go far, for his bundle of clothes was dropped only a few steps behind us. He picks it up, then catches up with the others on the run. Arriving at the riverbank, the crowd scatters, some going into the hamlet and some running either upstream or downstream. We stand for several minutes, hesitating, at a three-way junction. Suddenly, Thái yells: "Run." We run, following him; in front of us, several people are also going in a hurry. All the people who ran upstream come back. My mother asks:

"What's going on there?"

They shake their heads and continue to run. My mother screams to us in a panic: "Come back." But Thái still grasps my hand and runs at a stretch. My mother, my uncle, and Bé's family, crying, run behind us. Several kids – such a disaster – have no more strength left to walk on their own feet and are dragged along the ground by adults.

My uncle points to an ancient communal house and calls to my mother:

"Elder sister, come in here. There are people inside."

But Thái still pulls me and runs at a stretch:

"Run. If you go in, it's sure death."

We run, but not much farther. At a distance of several buildings from the communal house is An Định Palace,[6] the dwelling of Lady Từ Cung.[7] In front of the courtyard, there is a group of people who ran there searching for a place of shelter. We follow inside. My mother chooses a corner room, but later it becomes too crowded and we have to move out to a back room near a water tank. Thái gathers everyone, and we put our stuff down. The gunfire has moved very far away. Here is certainly much calmer. Everybody thinks so. While running, Bé's wife was still carrying

6. Originally constructed in 1917 for Emperor Khải Định (1916–25). From 1919 to 1925 the palace functioned as a residence for Crown Prince Bảo Đại and a summer palace for the emperor. Following the abdication of Emperor Bảo Đại in 1945 it became the residence of the queen mother, the queen, and Emperor Bảo Đại's five children.

7. She was the last queen mother of the Nguyễn dynasty, wife of Emperor Khải Định and mother of the last emperor, Bảo Đại.

several scoops of rice that there was no time to eat, and now she distributes the food to several kids, a handful to each one. Only now I notice the absence of an elderly couple. Earlier, they ran together with us in the same group; I don't know at which point they got lost. Thái is sure that they entered the communal house. My mother grumbles:

"Enough. Why worry about those people when all of us are running for our lives?"

But several minutes later, before we have managed to take a breath, the gunfire resumes from all directions. Thái shouts for everybody to duck down. We roll close to each other. Boom, boom, rattle, rattle. The rattling sound of AKs resounds as though it is coming right from the courtyard of An Định Palace. Then, all kinds of guns shoot into the palace like rain. The water tank breaks and overflows into the room; a large shell hits a corner of the wall. We press into each other, unable to see anything in the smoke and dust. The house behind us shakes as though about to collapse as water floods into the room.

"Run," Thái screams.

Hugging bags and clothing, we run, following Thái. But the panels of the door leading from the downstairs room to the upper part of the house are tightly fastened. Thái strikes the door; he punches and shouts at the same time. But not one panel is about to open. Thái calls Bé and together they punch and kick until the panels of the door open wide. We rush up to the upper room; as soon as we sit down, and not yet being calmed down, the room shakes as if it wants to collapse; boom, boom in front, and boom, boom behind. A part of the roof collapses. Dust everywhere. Thái moves us down to an old-fashioned wooden couch. I am absolutely unable to keep my eyes open, but it seems like my mother still holds tightly to my hand: "Child, oh child," I hear my mother calling in my ear. My mother's voice is gradually drowned out. Gunfire rages outside as though it will never stop. This time I think there is no chance to survive. It seems everything around me is filled with shrieking, crying, screaming. It seems everybody around me has died. A dead-cold hand tightly clasps my foot:

"Oh, child, where is your foot, you still have your foot, don't you?"

A hand feels my head:

"Elder sister Vân, your head is here, isn't it?"

I don't respond anymore. At first my heart leaps as though it wants to break loose from my chest, but then I cannot distinguish anything anymore. There is a flash of light and the sound of a flying bullet. It lights up the laughter of my first-born daughter and the face of my chubby son. I clearly remember the names of my children, and I clearly remember the laughter and sparkles in my husband's eyes. I fondly remember those sparkles, from which I am far away and to which I say farewell forever.

Oh my children, your mother will not see you again. Oh my loving husband, I am not able to live any longer. But surprisingly I no longer feel afraid. It is as if having been utterly terrified I am finished with fear. I clearly hear the sound of bullets flying by, the sound of walls breaking, the sound of roofs collapsing. I close my eyes and turn on the light in my head with images of my beloved husband and children, and I wait for the blink of an eye that will carry these pictures with me forever.

At this moment, I forgive everything: I forgive myself, I forgive all my faults and those of everyone else. I wait only for another blink of an eye . . . Yet gunfire rages for a moment, then slackens, then again intensifies out to and back from the field. I have no time to open my eyes before I hear a loud explosion and the sounds of things breaking to pieces in the adjacent house. I again slide downward. Thái jumps up:

"Let me go see."

I cry:

"Thái . . . Thái . . ."

My cry is like a wake-up call for everyone to learn that they are still alive. They all get up with a lurch. Then, suddenly remembering that crying can be dangerous, they sharply rebuke me:

"Be quiet. Duck down."

Yet Thái still runs across to the window. There is a shout for him to get back. His shadow shoots past us and disappears behind the door. At the same time I suddenly hear a cry:

"It's not over; carry Her Majesty on your back, carry Her Majesty on your back and run . . ."

"Assist Her Majesty and run faster."

I open my eyes; the gloom of dust is very dark. Yet I recognize shadows of people running, appearing and disappearing. An old woman wearing a brocade dress is being carried on the back of someone – I am unable to distinguish whether a man or a woman – and they are covered by another shadow.

"Carry Her Majesty. Run. Fast."

"Her Majesty's betel and areca nut . . ."

"Hold the blanket, the blanket . . ."

Someone speaks beside my ear:

"That's Lady Từ Cung. Heaven and Earth, at such a time as this and yet 'Her Majesty this' and 'Her Majesty that' when there's no time to observe etiquette."

A few silhouettes run by here and there and then disappear. The sound of guns is booming again. I press my face into the ground. My mother hugs me tightly like she wants to protect me. This time, the sound of guns returns even more furiously. I have no hope at all, and, also as before, I tightly hold my mother's hand, waiting. Inside my head flames flash following an explosion over my head, and with them the images of my husband and children also flare up. Death is too easy. Every person has endured the same fate here. Oh my children, so it's the end.

I don't fuss about Thái's jumping out of the window anymore. Neither do I have any hope of running to break away once again, like we just recently escaped from the church. On the brink of passing out, I suddenly have a sensation of coolness on my cheek. It must be blood, isn't it? This is very possible; from my chest a current of warmth is rising up. It is my hot blood. But no, I also have enough strength to recognize a dog licking my cheek, and his entire body is closely pressed against mine as an entreaty for protection.

THREE

ON A BOAT TRIP

I MANAGE TO COLLECT MANY TRIFLING BITS OF STORIES, everyone telling something different about the first several days when the Liberation Army came to Hue. I gather some of them while I am at the church and some when we just arrive at An Định Palace. The very thought of eventually getting to An Định Palace had cut in half the misery of the difficult road leading there because I knew that as soon as I set my foot there, I would hear people chattering about what was happening:

"Here, there are airplanes of our [Nationalist] army. They call on residents to try and move to the right bank of the river."

"The right bank is here."

"There are rumors that our side lets planes take off to reconnoiter; the planes have been under their [the Communist forces'] fire that shoots up in a torrent and they have to fly very high so that they can't be seen."

"But really, elder sister, did you hear all these announcements made through loudspeakers from the airplanes?"

"Of course I did. How is it, fellow countrymen, that you did not hear them? They said that everybody must run to the right bank of the Perfume River, right here. People in other areas are stranded. People from areas up there, Phú Cam, Bến Ngự, Từ Đàm, no one has come back here from those places at all."

"Is it possible to cross Tràng Tiền Bridge?"

"Not at all! They completely occupy the post office."[1]

1. The post office was at a strategic location from which access to the bridge could be controlled.

Each person has one's own story, and I learn only vaguely about the general situation in the city. I tell my mother and my uncle that we are on the right bank and I'm certain that it's safe here. But as soon as we find a place to sit and before we are able to take a handful of rice brought all the way from home, the guns explode again, and we slip into the middle of a battle. I lie down between the legs of a table, filled with the odor of people and of dogs, and I wait for death. When I am sure that I will die, that the palace will collapse, burying us in fragments of bricks, suddenly the guns fall silent for several minutes. Survived! A loud crying sound echoes in my head, and I open my eyes to look at each person around me. They sit up in a daze as sand and dust continue to fly through the gloom while broken windowpanes have yet to stop falling. I look up at the ornate bed of Her Majesty and see there a copper tray decorated with a dragon and a phoenix for betel and areca nut and a multicolored blanket. Her Majesty has already been carried away. I don't know whether or not she has escaped with her life. No one has yet had time to exchange a word with anyone when the sound of a B40 rocket swishes over the roof. Bang, and a piece of the roof collapses; dust flies, blinding everybody, and we all pull our heads back and cower down again. In the window are only a few sharp pointed fragments of glass left that look as though they have gotten a strong kick, and then the shadow of a person jumps inside, swift as an arrow. Several screams burst out, and there are several mumbling sounds but no words. They have already burst in! Several people cover their faces with their hands. I open my eyes and look, frozen; this is not a soldier of the Nationalist Army, nor is he from the Liberation Army – this is Thái. His body is covered with blood. He looks around in bewilderment, searching, then pulls my mother and shakes my uncle and the entire family to wake up:

"Run, run auntie; run elder sister."

I pull him to duck down and shout:

"Younger brother, you made people's hearts sink to their boots. Where is there to run? It's the end now."

Thái pulls me to sit up. Only then do I see that my hip is dripping wet. Blood, blood still fresh and bright, streams down my leg. I've been wounded. Wounded – but why don't I feel any pain at all? I turn quickly:

"Mother."

My mother watches me, her eyes open but listless. I burst out crying and spring to reach my mother:

"Mother, you've been wounded."

My mother shakes her head. Thái suddenly pulls me up, and I lean my head against his body:

"Stretch up, stretch up."

I press myself against the shoulder of my younger cousin Thái. Only then do I compose myself to look carefully at a big dog huddling next to my hip, badly wounded. Perhaps it has died. I don't see it move or stir at all, but the blood from its wound still oozes. Thái says in a low voice into my ear:

"Elder sister, tell aunt that we must run right now; they are squeezing the siege outside – not running now means death."

Not running now means death. The word "death," like a slingshot, shoots me to the window and then swift as a doe I plunge headlong outside, not even knowing whether the window is far from or near to the ground. I fall out fast and simultaneously the panels of the main door open, and Thái and Bé, seeing me flee, follow in a panic, running out through the big door. Several pieces of the still-remaining glass fall with a clatter. My uncle, my mother, Bé's wife, Thu Hồng, and several small children, panic-stricken, also follow. I look around. There is absolutely not a single shadow of a person. But it's clear that the two sides [the Communists and the Nationalists] are in dread of each other and are shooting at each other. While inside An Định Palace, I had heard the sounds of gunfire as though coming from the direction of the door, or even from right inside. But now I perceive no one at all. Seeing me disorientated, Thái pulls me by the arm to run. It seems that a lot of other people are following us and also running.

The riverbank blocks us in front. We have left An Định Palace far behind.

The sound of gunfire behind us intensifies again, fiercer than ever. But the gunfire gradually moves in the direction of the field at the side of the church. We slowly move away from the dangerous place. A group of people run down from the bridge area, and Thái asks them:

"Is it possible to cross the bridge?"

Several heads shake at once. I shout loudly:

"Don't run there; they are fighting each other there."

But those in the group seem not to hear; they still keep running without turning their heads. Several children trip and fall, crying like trumpets, then crawling on all fours, getting up, and continuing to run. Then at this moment Bé's wife shouts:

"We've left all our possessions up there in the palace."

Bé screams:

"So what? We left our possessions. You don't care about death, but care about a handful of stuff . . ."

Bé's wife moans:

"There are still several handfuls left of cooked rice; if we don't bring them along, we will starve to death."

At this moment, I am running in short steps behind Thái. I suddenly gasp when I see blood on his neck flowing down his shoulder. I pull his arm:

"Thái, you've been wounded."

He sighs and keeps running:

"The entire tiled roof crashed on my head. So, I had a lucky escape. Not a big deal, elder sister."

A river wharf appears and Thái shouts for joy:

"There is a boat. There is a boat. We will be able to cross the river now."

The section of the river here is so serene, fig trees next to the river wharf are still luxuriantly green, the water surface is quiet, and several boulders on the wharf are still clean, smooth, and shiny. I am stunned; it seems that I see this scenery in a dream or else my eyes have been dazzled. We've just stopped at the wharf when behind us there are several other people running up and Thái asks:

"Where are you coming from?"

"From the church area."

"From An Định Palace."

"Did you see anything?"

"The palace has completely collapsed; shelling is very fierce there."

Thu Hồng runs down to the wharf. Several small boats look abandoned; there are no people in them. We call and call, and only a middle-aged woman emerges from behind us.

"What's this?"

"Let us cross the river with you, ma'am."

The woman shakes her head:

"Impossible. They are still fighting each other over there. If we get out in the middle of the river, how will we avoid a direct hit?"

"Elder sister, there are direct hits like that here, too."

"I'd rather die alone. I am left all alone."

The voice of the woman is cold as ice. Thái entreats:

"Elder sister, do us a favor; help us to cross to the other bank of the river. On the other bank there is the house of an acquaintance; if we are not able to get there, we will all die here."

"There are too many of you to transport."

My mother humbly requests:

"You do us a favor making several trips. At the time of war there are merits to be earned through helping others, so you could bequest them to your children."[2]

"I am alone and there is no one to get any blessing from my merits. I haven't gone anywhere but am here waiting to see whether or not my man will surface in this section of the river."

We've vaguely surmised her story. For certain, her husband has just died and she's gone completely crazy. We continue our humble requests. The woman agrees to make several trips to transfer us. When we cross this narrow river, Thái offers money and forces the woman to take it. She holds the money in her hand and turns the bow of her boat to cross the river to carry other people waiting on the other side at the wharf.

The sounds of gunfire in the direction of An Định Palace and the fields seem quieter. When we get up to the main road we don't have any strength to figure out what's going on. This area is exceedingly peaceful. Not a single house has been damaged. Bé says:

"I will look for the house of our acquaintance for us to stay there, and then tomorrow we'll return home. Our area is next to the National Highway, and certainly they've completely withdrawn from there by now."

Thái argues:

2. The concept of "merits" was similar to the Buddhist idea of karma.

"Nothing of the kind! Making such wrong assumptions will bring us nothing but death."

"American vehicles are running on the National Highway up to Đồng An Cựu, but you keep arguing and arguing . . ."

"American vehicles going up there – so what? Listen to the sounds of the guns; can't you hear them or what?"

We continue to run. I ask Bé what area this is. Having left Hue a very long time ago, I have forgotten almost all the roads. Bé says it is Tân Lăng Road and in a short while there will be a pagoda.

Hearing about the pagoda, my mother is very pleased:

"We'll go inside of the pagoda and ask to stay. Surely, they don't dare to destroy a pagoda."

Thái says:

"The church, remember? And it was fired at and destroyed. They have no more regard for pagodas than they have for churches. Try to think about it."

I am tired, unable to go anymore. Only now I feel a biting pain in my feet. I've lost my sandals. My foot has been cut with a piece of glass and oozes with blood. I plop down on the ground:

"I can't go anymore, Mother."

My mother coaxes me:

"Try just a bit more; listen to me, child, try to go a bit more. We are already close."

But my mother is also extremely tired. Now looking back at her, I see that she is still carrying the bag with clothes in her hands. Fright made my mother forget how heavy the bag is. Thái still tightly holds in his arms my leather briefcase. While talking, my mother sits down next to me. Thu Hồng, following us, is also sitting down, and several small children also plop down on the ground. In some houses, doors open to see us, then hastily close again. I don't have any hope that they will help us at this moment. Thái and Bé turn around and see us sitting right on the ground, and my uncle is torn between wanting to sit down and wanting to go; they signal with their hands for us to stop.

"Stop; we will go to the pagoda to see what's going on."

But they go only a short distance and then come back. Only then do we pay attention to groups of people fleeing from the fighting, one group going ahead and another group running in the opposite direction. Asking them, we learn that whatever directions one goes, there is fighting. Bé's wife, who is sitting, suddenly gets up:

"How could I forget, in this hamlet lives my acquaintance U; we will go to her for a while and then we'll send Thu Hồng back home to evaluate the situation."

I also hope for a place to sit and rest, to drink a gulp of water. From morning till now, I've not yet had a bite of food or a drop of water. Bé enthusiastically leads the way. We enter a small hamlet; all houses have thatched roofs. Only after Bé knocks and knocks on the door for a long time does he see a person coming to open the door. It is U.

Bé shouts with joy:

"We thought for sure that you had evacuated, elder sister. You're all right, aren't you?"

"No problem. It has been several days and nothing is happening. Nobody has left the place."

"Mortars are not firing in?"

"No, the inner hamlet was hit. But here, on the outskirts, we have dug underground shelters. Nothing to be afraid of."

Then, suddenly, seeing a large group of people standing behind Bé, U asks:

"Are those your relatives?"

"Yes, please elder sister; this is my father's sister-in-law and my siblings and cousins."

Addressing my mother, Bé says:

"Auntie, this lady is the acquaintance of my wife."

"Come in, come on into the house, don't stand out here like this; they [the Communists and their sympathizers] are keeping an eye on what is going on, and a big group of people can be suspicious."

The entire group enters the house. The house is small and cramped. Thái spreads a blanket on the floor so that we can lie down. U, the mistress of the house, gives up her small bed to my mother, to Bé's wife, who just gave birth, and to several small children. They lie close to each other, turned slightly so that they can drop down to the floor if necessary. I, Thu Hồng, and Thái are to lie down on the floor. It starts drizzling; it's terribly cold. On top of fright and cold, longtime hunger crashes in, and

I shiver all over. U hands me a bowl of cold rice, which I eat with soy sauce. I eat as though I've never had such a delicious meal, so incredibly tasty. When I finish eating, by now the evening has set in. Thái asks the woman to check to see whether the Liberation Army is here. The woman laughs brightly:

"No, no, don't you worry. They come back now and then. They walk around outside, but don't worry about them. They are very decent."

"Have they been checking the houses?"

"Only for a while at the beginning. The first several days they asked children to carry ammunition and transport wounded. But now, it's over. They are people, too. What's there to be afraid of? They are very decent."

"Did you talk with them, madam?"

"We talked many times. What's the big deal?"

U lives with an old woman, the mother of her husband, who is in her seventies, and with a seventeen-year-old son. U's husband left for the previous war of resistance against the French, and there has been no news from him since. When I learn this, I am not surprised anymore by the sympathy our mistress expresses toward the liberators.

In the evening we don't dare to sleep in the house but go down to sleep in the underground shelter dug in the courtyard. My uncle, Thái, and Bé go to sleep in the ancestor-worshipping house of a large family in the hamlet. The ancestor-worshipping house is built according to the old pattern with big stones and is very sturdy. I and the other women along with the children go down to the underground shelter. The shelter is tiny but now has to hold more than ten people; we don't have enough space to lie down.

Around ten o'clock, artillery from Phú Bài starts lobbing shells into the city. Flares brightly light up the entire sky. The sound of planes is close and then moves away. A big confrontation is in the air. The entire city of Hue seems to be completely submerged in an inauspicious omen that it will soon be demolished. I tightly hug my mother, put my head on her shoulder, and sleep. My mother never stops praying, and I pray for my children to get through the calamities. Let my children live.

I know that my mother worries for me the most. My husband and children are in Saigon – certainly they are in sorrow and distress because of me. But why do I believe that my husband and children are at leisure to worry about me? The news and rumors circulate that all of Saigon and the provinces have been lost. So, my husband and children have moved somewhere.

I want to say: "Mother, I am so afraid." But I must exhibit courage to give my mother breathing space for a bit. I say:

"They fight each other in a big way; clearly they will soon calm down."

My voice is really low, but in the cramped shelter everyone hears everything. A young chubby woman sitting next to me raises her voice:

"There are a lot of them, elder sister."

The voice of U's son follows hers:

"This girl, she went to carry dead bodies, elder sister – a lot of dead bodies."

I ask:

"Where did you carry them?"

"Carried them right up to the mountains. They have lots and lots of dead. I lost count."

"Elder sister, weren't you frightened to carry them?"

"Scared to death. I trembled carrying them. On top of it, it was getting colder. My knees were about to cave in, both of them at the same time. I was scared to death. Each corpse was also sticky with blood all over it. As for the wounded, they were piled on the vehicles like piles of fish, one person heaped on top of another. I don't know how I could have survived."

"Were all of the corpses and wounded from the Liberation Army?"

"Yes, all of them were. They ban anyone else from being taken there."

"When you were done with carrying, did they let you return?"

"They still forced me to carry ammunition, but I escaped. No doubt they will return tonight and force me to go again. I escaped and asked to spend a night here. Over there, the mortars have been firing in."

I don't ask anymore, but the young woman has momentum and continues to talk:

"They buried people in a garden next to my house. It's so scary to see protruding legs."

"You must be telling fibs!"

Hearing the mocking remark of U's son, the young woman gets mad:

"This dumbbell of a boy who hides in the underground shelter all day and night, what can he know? Go outside and see for yourself. Behind the pagoda over there, they bury dead bodies with protruding arms and legs. When you see it, it's terrifying. Now, do you know the barber named Tư?"

"I do."

"Yeah. He was forced to go outside in the garden to dig a pit to bury dead bodies, right in his own garden. He was horrified but managed to escape."

"I really hate this guy [Tư]; let them catch him at once."

"You talking like this: it's disgraceful. Why do you hate him?"

We hear U's voice, annoyed and barely audible. A flare is falling really close and sluggishly comes down. Its light brightly illuminates the entire shelter through an opening. I look at the face of the young girl. My mother pulls a torn piece of mat to cover the shelter opening. We sit through that entire night. The sound of artillery fire is deafening and omnipresent, but fortunately no shell falls into our hamlet where we are sheltered from danger. The sound of artillery never ceases and reverberates all over the place. My eyes are like a dozen fires following each explosion, and the entire night my heartbeats are very fast and thick with sticky fear until morning.

There is another stroke of luck. At dawn the sound of artillery gradually quiets down, still exploding in rumbles but at a distance somewhere in the mountains. After waiting for another hour, we get out of the shelter, rinse our mouths with grains of salt, and wash our faces with rainwater. It's still a spray-like rain and very cold. I drape over my shoulders the overcoat left from my father and together with Thái slowly go out to the alley.

Becoming bolder little by little, the two of us get to the river. From different directions groups of evacuees are still trickling in. Thái meets them and makes inquiries; there are people who let him know they were from the An Cựu field, or from the An Cựu market area. There are people who let us know that they ran over here from the church area. Does An Cựu Bridge still exist? People respond that it does, while others say that it has collapsed, and we don't know whom to believe. Thái tells me that we were incredibly lucky; last night in the church the Việt Cộng burst in and arrested all the men and government employees and took them away. He says this and his face is so deathly pale that if you'd make a cut not a single drop of blood would come out.

From the direction of the railway there are still people coming. Thái points out to me groups of people moving in different directions over the railways, appearing and disappearing behind short shrubs and trees.

When we come back, Thái suddenly looks at an electric pole. On the top of the pole there is a bamboo rod with a two-colored flag – red and blue – on top of it.[3] The flag is fluttering in the wind. The day before when I went past there and looked up in the sky to see if there were any airplanes, there was nothing on that pole. When Thái tells everybody about it, no one is surprised:

"They keep hanging them. They've even hung them in the pagoda, at Xay T-junction . . ."

But by noon of this day, no one in this entire small hamlet can keep calm anymore. Artillery has been lobbing up here. The sound of planes roars and tears the dreary ash-gray sky apart. At noon, we crawl back into the shelter. Others go into the ancestor-worshipping house. The sounds of explosions are very close; sometimes it seems like they reverberate right in our heads. Still, hearing the explosions does not yet mean death. Thái presses my hand:

"Elder sister, close your ears tight and lie down to lessen the anxiety."

In some houses there are sounds of crying. Lying in the shelter, it is extremely tight, suffocating, and impossible to breathe. Thái waits until the sound of artillery abates and pulls me to swiftly run into the ancestor-worshipping house. From noon till late afternoon that day, the artillery doesn't stop, but the shooting has moved farther away.

In the afternoon, we go outside for about ten seconds and then crawl back into the shelter. At night, I don't enter the shelter again but go to sleep under a shelf in the ancestor-worshipping house. Some of my relatives, including my mother, join me in that house. After several sleepless nights in a row, I've become dead tired. Despite the guns, despite the shells, despite life, despite death, I sink into sleep. In the middle of the night I am awakened by the sound of airplanes and the thunder of shells,

3. The red and blue Việt Cộng banner with its gold star.

but then those are also on the wane and a bout of heavy sleep takes over everything. Next morning Thái wakes me up by shaking my neck:

"Elder sister, do you know what happened last night?"

"What happened?"

"They've returned here in full. They knocked at the door but did not hear a sound; everything was quiet so they've already left."

My mother is gloomy:

"This is absolutely scary. Vân, child, I slept so deeply last night, I didn't hear anything at all. Explosions are near; surely our house and all our possessions have been destroyed."

My mother starts crying. Bé's wife crawls from under the altar, then comes my uncle's turn to get up, too:

"Obviously we have to flee farther. It's dangerous here now."

My uncle's voice is perturbed. My mother tells Bé and Thu Hồng to go fix rice but then remembers that there's only a bit of rice left; she says:

"Cook porridge to have something to eat."

My uncle grumbles that at home there is still fifty kilograms of rice left but when Thu Hồng went back yesterday she did not get to the house to bring it back. Thu Hồng indeed went back to the hamlet, but seeing it completely deserted, she got scared, gave up, and came back.

But even before the porridge is ready, we hear again the sound of airplanes coming and then artillery from down by Phú Bài lobbing up shells. The entire household is in the shelter, but the next moment we realize that the gunfire is not aimed at this area, and I and Thái crawl out because it's so stuffy down there. The two of us run outside and over to U's house, then grope our way for the alley. There are muffled sounds of gunfire, shooting like rain in the Phú Cam area. "Surely they are firing at the airplanes," Thái whispers. The flag of blood and blue colors is still fluttering at the top of the bamboo rod installed on the electric pole. There are still evacuees running around outside; we hail them and make inquiries, but nobody is inclined to answer us. They run away crying. An armed unit from the direction of the bridge pulls up to Phú Cam, and Thái shouts for me to run into an abandoned store. The unit crosses the road, its soldiers' faces taciturn; they carry rifles on their shoulders. Their hands are in bandages, their clothes in disarray; Thai whispers: this is the North Vietnamese Army. I try to watch them to distinguish whether they look any different from the Việt Cộng, but Thái has already figured it out. As for me, I give up on this and don't dare to ask Thái.

In a moment when the unit comes up, we decide to run away from them to return home, but from the side of Phú Cam suddenly reverberate sounds of feet running, of screaming, and of crying. Then another group of people appears just before gunfire goes off like rain; the sounds of airplanes shred the sky, and artillery explodes as if it has no time to pause for breath. A group of people slowly gets closer. Thái is flabbergasted:

"Oh heavens, the people, people fleeing from the fighting."

The group approaching us consists of about a hundred people; the leaders of the group are several Catholic priests and a couple of Buddhist monks. In their hands they hold white flags made of tattered cloth, flags of unconditional surrender, flags of fright. They walk, then run like children in a hurry. Following the white flags, the leaders and their followers go supporting each other. People carrying loads on their shoulders go at a jog trot. Thái stands up on the edge of the road and lifts his hand in greeting:

"Venerable Father, what's going on up there?"

The priest shakes his head, his mouth frothing at the corners. A monk carries in his hands a wounded child, blood dripping in small drops onto the road; the monk stretches out his hand and waves, giving us a sign to follow them. Don't stop; it's dangerous. But the monk does not say a word. The group of people slowly runs like this in front of us, women carrying children in their arms, men carrying loads on their shoulders, children going at a jog trot. On top of it all, they also carry the wounded. A man wounded in his leg runs, limping and hobbling. From time to time he falls on the ground, then forces himself up again. There is someone with a loose arm connected to his body by only a little bit of skin. Another person has something swelling on his head; still another one has a fractured forehead with small drops of blood on it. They chase after the several pieces of white cloth of which the white flags are made and which flap, leading the way in search of security. The people in the group run, moaning, crying, and praying; a fellow recites a Christian prayer, and another one appeals to Heaven and calls on the Buddha.

More people run, zigzagging, down to the bridge, then suddenly run in the opposite direction, turning back, then run again in the opposite direction, retreating, continuing in the direction from which they had previously run. The sound of gunfire from the Phú Cam area is still pouring like rain; several people are feeble and scuttle behind at a significant distance from the rest of the group, screaming in despair as though death is around the corner:

"Oh Father, wait for us. Oh Father, save us, your children. Oh Lord, the devil is chasing us, your children . . ."

I help a woman who has just fallen face-down on the road:

"Come up over here to take rest, elder sister; there is no fighting here yet, come in here."

The woman has been wounded in her thigh; blood is streaming, but she still forces herself to get up.

"I am running after the father; my husband and child are over there with him."

The woman resumes running. Thái follows her:

"Up there, is still anything left?"

"Nothing left, nothing left. But yes, a lot of people still stranded there, still more than a hundred young people are stranded, couldn't flee."

"How did they get stranded?"

"They [the Communist forces] shoot, they shoot . . . Oh Father, wait for me, oh Father."

The woman is running, but the group has left her very far behind. I hear the extremely loud sound of an explosion. I cover my face. Thái hugs me tightly:

"Run, elder sister, run. Hold my hand, here."

Thái pulls me by my hand and we slip into the hamlet. In the distance, the group of people is in utter disarray; then, through puffs of smoke and layers of dust, I see them again, continuing to run.

When I enter the ancestor-worshipping house, my mother is lying close to the door, waiting. She browbeats me for a while and then pulls me and thrusts me down under the dais. As in days past, my mother still thinks of me as a child, still a baby. I swiftly slide in and look for a place to rest my head, but there isn't one. My mother lies outside and I hear her question:

"Lie quietly, Vân, child, where are you? Listen to me, don't lie down outside."

My mother says this, but she herself lies outside. Thu Hồng whispers into my ear:

"The pot of porridge is burned already."

At this moment I don't feel any regrets about the pot of porridge, even though before this, hunger gnawed at me. Thu Hồng says:

"Wherever you go, elder sister, auntie insists to go look for you; I have to hold her in my arms."

I am on the brink of tears. I lift my hand and hold firmly to a bamboo brace propping up the platform holding the altar. I wish I could hold my mother's hand; it's only a short distance away, but it's impossible. In the dim light I see a small dot of dazzling fire. For sure, it's Thái and he found cigarettes somewhere. He tells me:

"I asked auntie whether it's all right to smoke here."

I ask him where he found the cigarettes; he says:

"I have an entire full box. I picked it up when a group of people passed by. For sure someone dropped it."

I think about the drops of blood scattered along the road. How far do these drops of blood stretch? Unexpectedly, I shudder. Thu Hồng asks:

"Are you cold, elder sister?"

I shake my head, but Thu Hồng undoubtedly doesn't notice. Thái hands me a cigarette and tells me to give it to my mother to help lessen the cold. As soon as the cigarette gets to me, it falls from my hands. Afraid of making a sound by my movement, I don't dare grope for it. From that moment till noon, we don't dare open our eyes to look at the light outside. Artillery shells lob in as though they are right here. In my head, around me, the sounds of explosions reverberate; it seems like they split my rib cage open, that they break my head. My mother calls everybody to duck down and press into the ground. We duck down and press into the ground, and then when it proves not to be enough to be able to bear the situation, we firmly take each other into our arms so that when death comes, we will die together, in one heap. But no, I can't die here in this one heap. I must live to be able to return to my children regardless of whether Saigon still exists or has been lost, and my children also must live to wait for me to come back. Don't let death in. Let me live.

The sound of explosions seems to grab me and throw me into red fire. One sound . . . two sounds . . . another sound. Prayers to Heaven and prayers to the Buddha have not achieved their goal. One more sound and my heart will jump out of my throat. Bang, I hear the sound of a loud explosion. So, who's lamenting my death like this now? Who is crying like this outside? Another bang. The entire roof of the house seems to be about to collapse on my head. My chest breaks open and my blood bursts like flowing from a tap. I roll back and forth. No, I haven't been hit yet; I am still alive. The sound of crying bursts in:

"Vân, Vân, where are you, child? Elder sister, where are you, elder sister?"

Thái's arm, then my mother's arm, too. Sand and dust from the house roof still keep falling down. I can't make a sound. This time, it is death for sure; artillery has not yet moved away any distance at all. After the sound of the explosion, my body is not even able to shudder anymore. That's it, all my family, everyone in this familial ancestor-worshipping house, is waiting for death.

But then the moment of horror passes. The sound of gunfire stops, then scatters in different directions. As soon as the sound of gunfire stops, it is replaced with sounds of crying. I dash out; my mother pulls me back:

"Hey child, don't, don't go."

But Thái has also already gotten to the courtyard; I can't help but hesitate at the door.

Outside, trees and plants are in tatters; bricks and tiles have fallen topsy-turvy in the courtyard. In front of the ancestor-worshipping house, a fragment of a shell whirls in a huge pit in the ground. Several glass windows are shattered into pieces; a screen covering the front window is tilted. Right at that moment, Thái runs inside, white-faced:

"Very lucky, elder sister, the place in the back corner of the ancestor-worshipping house has just been hit by a bomb; it's where the papaya tree is. The papaya tree is knocked down."

Thái lifts his hand and points at the edge of the wall in the back where the wall has crumbled into big pieces and the tiles have caved in, exposing a piece of ash-gray sky. Life is really wonderful. If the bomb had slanted a bit more, we would have been finished, for sure. Thái tells us that behind us at a distance of two or three houses there is a house that is completely destroyed by the direct hit of a bomb. Several iron-sheet roofs were blown up and thrown far away, and there is a piece that flew up and cut off the top of a coconut tree. Several houses have been demolished, several people killed. From that moment till evening, we don't dare step away from the altar's platform. Bé's wife boldly goes to fix some food, and it's only in the evening that we sit down to eat. While eating, we hear that a lot of people fleeing from the Bến Ngự area are coming here. Thái swiftly runs to the courtyard. A group of people from Bến Ngự run, straight and without a stop, up to the railway; only a father and a child, starving and exhausted, don't go; they plop down on the edge of the road. The people bring them into the house, a man around forty years old and a girl about fifteen years. After each is given a bowl of rice, they are reborn to the world, and the father and the daughter return to their senses. The girl crouches in the corner of the altar's dais; her eyes open and, with her face completely distorted by fear, she gazes toward the door. A soft noise makes the child tightly hug her father. Only when the man comes completely back to his senses does my mother ask inquisitively:

"Did you come from Bến Ngự, sir?"

"Yes, madam, I'm from Bến Ngự."

"So, up at Từ Đàm, is there anyone who managed to flee?"

The man did not have time, however, to respond because my mother, burning with impatience, announces:

"My son, my daughter-in-law, and my daughter with a bunch of grandchildren are stranded up there."

The man says something, but his lips are still mumbling indistinctly:

"I live in the area under the bridge, close to the bank of the river, so I could hide. Up at Từ Đàm is rough, they [the Communists] guard really ferociously there."

"No one managed to flee?"

"No, it's for sure."

I hear my mother's heavy sigh, full of despair. The man still hems and haws, his lips tremble, and he mumbles unclearly:

"There's not a single tile left on my house."

Thái asks:

"How did you manage to get here?"

"My house was not directly hit but reverberations knocked off all the tiles just the same. The two of us, I and my child, hid in the shelter for days, and so by now we've gone without food for three days. When the sounds of gunfire abated, I crawled out of the shelter. Horrendous, frightful. All the houses around were collapsed, and we saw not a shadow of a person. So, I went down to the shelter and pulled my daughter out to flee from the house. We ran like crazy. I trod upon people's corpses and don't even know how many of them. I heard countless moans among the piles of bricks left after the destruction of the houses. Damn it, the two of us ran more dead than alive up to here and then, exhausted, we resigned ourselves to sit down on the road to let life take its course."

"So, you didn't run into the liberators on the road, did you?"

"No, that would be the last straw. They are busy digging shelters, busy transporting wounded, and because of this we could escape. My little child, she is so afraid that she becomes stiff. We had to get off the road several times and lay shaking like epileptics. I had to pull her with all my strength; her arms and legs suddenly became completely pale and bluish."

Someone asks from the dark: "There are only two of you, you and your daughter, sir, aren't there?"

"No sir, no; it is I and my wife with my children. On the first day of Tết, my wife and children went back down to Bao Vinh, her native home place. Such a tragedy, oh, my wife and children, I don't know what's going on down there; my wife and children are stranded down there."

"Oh, who has the strength to worry? One knows whether one's self is alive or not – what else is there to worry about?"

My mother asks the child:

"Are you still hungry?"

No answer is heard from the child. The man says:

"The lady asks you, so why don't you respond? Yes, venerable lady, she is very afraid, and that's why she seems maddened. Several days lying in the shelter, starving and scared, she seems deaf like this. Enough, this trip, it's the end of me; no one else is left, oh, my wife and children. I walked and I trod upon people's corpses not even knowing how many of them. Bullets were behind me and in front of me. I thought I would not make it here to wait for my wife and children."

The man seems to choke, on the brink of tears.

There is the sound of a child crying and the sound of a young woman grumbling:

"Enough, let me sleep outside the shelter; there is more space there. Inside here it's too cramped; how can a kid endure it?"

A man's voice responds:

"Damn you, death is around the corner, and you are still arguing. Father, mother, and the child must all be in the same place. If we die, we must die together, not that some must survive and some die."

The woman cries, sniffing. Outside, the light of flares illuminates the entire sky. The gunfire starts to explode again. I don't know in what area the fighting is still going on because from what I hear it seems that each area has gunfire. At night, there are endless pitter-patters of feet outside; we all hold our breath. The girl and the man, the newest evacuees who arrived this afternoon, have no place; the two of them lean against the dais. The girl shouts from time to time: "Oh, father, I am very scared." The man comforts her: "Don't be scared; it's nothing."

There are calls begging for help, then sounds of gunfire. Thái, firmly holding my hand, whispers:

"Assassination."

I remember the face of the liberation soldier who guarded the bridge we crossed. A North Vietnamese soldier, naive and innocent, he looked for anyone who belonged to the American puppets. He shouted and arbitrarily stopped people, but finally everybody ran across the bridge. I think that he most certainly saw nothing but people fleeing from the fighting – men, women, and small children – and he supposed that with only one night of shooting, the bands of American puppets were all eliminated. I remember an empty military post [of the Nationalist Army] not guarded by a single soldier. I didn't see a single corpse thrown across the fence there either. So what does it mean that the first night there was no firing or attacks at the military posts? It's impossible that so many soldiers in the city could all be dead. The man fleeing with the child, the one who arrived in the afternoon, has just let us know that the Việt Cộng have not yet taken over a single military post, but every military post is abandoned and empty.[4]

The man also lets us know that the Liberation Army soldiers are like ghosts; they hide and appear here and there. During the three nights when he was lying in the underground shelter, the man imagined that people were continually walking back and forth on the top of the shelter, but when he ventured to run out, his collapsed house looked as though it had been deserted for a very long time.

Night comes and the air is heavy to the point of suffocation. Added to this, several more refugees arrive, and the ancestor-worshipping house seems to be devoid of oxygen. The smell of bullets and shells has inundated the place. Furthermore, the omnipresent sound of gunfire returns and intensifies. In the middle of the night there are several screams sounding hoarse with fright outside in the alleys and on the riverbank. The stampings are echoes of running feet. Moreover, there are even sounds of digging in the ground. I have no more fear of dead bodies with cracked heads, of chopped-off arms and legs, but at that moment in the atmosphere of crowding together in the dark ancestor-worshipping house, I have an impression that the smell and the coldness of death is gradually encroaching upon us, and if we stay here for several more days, we will die of suffocation or illness.

The next morning, the area of this hamlet is completely suffused with the sound of gunfire. Artillery fires at the place, then large guns and small guns. Furthermore, lying down under the dais of the altar we hear even the sounds of automobiles moving out on the road. Thái presses his ear to the ground and tries to figure out what areas have fighting going on. Some trees in the courtyard are directly hit and knocked down. Thái guesses that for sure there is fighting in the market area. Perhaps they are fighting on the other side of the river now. They fire back and forth, which means that we must flee. Perhaps this night they will strike against this

4. Most Nationalist soldiers had been given leave to celebrate Tết at home during the holiday ceasefire and, as a consequence, were not at the military posts.

Tân Lăng neighborhood. My mother listens and talks at the same time, shaking and hugging me tightly:

"What to do? I have resigned myself to death, but you, child, you still have two children of your own; who will raise them, oh my child."

I firmly clench my teeth. In this city, so many people are dead – so many children and adults; so many mothers have given up, leaving their children desolate and lonely. But those young children, can they survive until the battle ends? While in the church, I saw some children whose parents were killed by bullets, and they followed groups of refugees. They ran back and forth, punch-drunk, being bullied by some, being shouted at by others. Starving, they steal and snatch from other people. What if I die, or if I don't die, yet all the same still lose my children?

The image of the woman hugging the dead body of her child, which generated the awful smell in the church where I hid for the first several days, has ripped my heart and mind to pieces.

An hour later, we wait for the sound of gunfire to fall silent for a moment so that we can flee from the ancestor-worshipping house; each person clasps his or her remaining possessions, bags with clothes, a blanket that Bé took from An Định Palace. Thái runs ahead of everybody, and we run behind him. After several continuous days, only now do we see daylight, though the daylight is stifled in the numbingly cold spray of drizzling rain. When we rush out from the house, a number of other people also rush out, following us. The pair of father and daughter run toward the riverbank; Thái waves for us to go up to the railway. But after going only a short distance from the house, we suddenly are besieged by the sound of explosions from all directions.

They are still fighting each other. Thái calls out for everyone to take cover, and we roll into the brush at the side of the road. We lie in a heap on top of each other. The father and the daughter also duck down. The artillery fire intensifies, roaring from all directions. Gunfire also seems to surround us; we are in the middle of it. A house, directly hit, goes up in flames. Children and adults rush out of the house. The fire spreads to many other houses, and more people run out. We hear sounds of screaming and crying. Ahead is pitch-dark from gun smoke; behind, as a man informs us, there is a huge battle going on. Water rushes through the roadside ditch in search of a good, more peaceful place to rest. An artillery shell noisily explodes several tens of meters from us. It seems like we are buried in fragments of the shell and in the thick screen of dust. Thanks to Heaven and the Buddha, no one is hit. When the smoke disperses, we don't see the pair of father and daughter anymore. They were running in front when the shell exploded and smoke rose in a blinding cloud. Thái calls loudly:

"Run fast to this shell-hole that the artillery just made and duck down."

My body trembles all over and I am not able to run anymore. Leave me alone. Thái pushes me, I push my mother, my mother pushes Bé, and pushing continues from the back to the front. Thái moves us down to a very deep shell-hole with dust, smoke, and gunpowder darkening the air.

"Lie here. It can't be, auntie, that two shells would hit the same spot twice. I was in a battle and I know."

Thái's statement helps me to calm down for a couple of minutes. But why does my body still keep trembling all over? It's been almost a week. I haven't changed my clothes; the coat I wear on top of everything is full of dried blood and has started to stink. Thái rolls close to me:

"Elder sister, don't tremble, you must calm down to help ease your mother's fears."

My mother opens her eyes and sluggishly looks at me with eyes of fear, of despair, of boundless worry, and of love for me. I burst into tears. At this moment, my fear of death diminishes. I have my mother next to me; if death comes, we will see each other's faces at that moment. Sounds of weeping and of moaning echo from afar. I open my eyes wide to look around. From within the puffs of smoke and fire, from within the sounds of bombshells in front of us, a woman and a child pushing an oxcart are coming over. The woman walks while crying and screaming crazily:

"Where is the Lord? Where is the Buddha? Oh heavens!"

In the cart, there is a corpse of a man covered in dried blood and stiffened, but his eyes still stare intently. The dead body does not have any piece of clothing on it. Thái jumps out from the shell-hole, takes off his felt overcoat with red stripes, and covers the man's face. The woman and small child continue to push the cart, completely absorbed in it, and go forward where the artillery booms. I tightly hold on to my mother's hand:

"Mother."

I emit but one outcry and choke with emotion. My mother continues to look at me with that dreamy expression of hers. Thái jumps down into the shell-hole and wipes his hands on his pants:

"Whatever this woman does, she will end up dead anyway. Down there they are fighting very fiercely."

Artillery is still lobbing monotonously. I hear several salvoes of gunfire seemingly shot from within the yards of adjacent buildings. Thái suggests:

"They will certainly be fighting here soon. Run, run right now, auntie."

Thái jumps rashly up out of the shell-hole. Bé holds children in his arms so that his wife can follow Thái and jump out too. We don't give a damn about leaving behind a lot of stuff; many things are thrown out into the shell-hole. Thái takes the lead to check the road. Bé goes last. Thái carries my mother's bundle with clothes in one hand and also carries Bé's three-year-old son on his back. My mother clasps a blanket to her chest as though she wants to protect her thin, weak body. I go in front of my mother behind Thái. My uncle follows behind us, walking and grumbling. He is hungry and afraid of death, and at the same time he craves wine. He leads Bé's eldest daughter by her hand. The small child is peeing all over her pants from fear and her pant-legs get stuck together; she can't walk and is being dragged in a rush. My uncle grumbles:

"Going in a huddle like this is very dangerous. Run fast to find a place to hide. They are bursting in here."

In the gardens I see people's heads, a lot of them scattered around. Clearly they are hiding in foxholes. Barrels of guns are ready to fire from the foxholes. Shrubs and trees rustle. There is the thundering sound of a collapsing wall.

"Run fast – death is around the corner."

Then I hear a voice speaking with a slight accent from a different region. I run as though chased by ghosts and leave my mother behind by several tens of steps.

But we don't go far before the battle moves with us. The gunfire pours like rain, and we are caught in crossfire.

"Run!" Thái calls out loudly.

We run.

"Duck down."

We duck down. My body does not have any self-control anymore but is controlled by Thái's shouts. My mind is almost empty, ready to follow any command, any order, whatever it may be.

"It's not over yet."

Thái urges my mother, my uncle, Bé's family, and Thu Hồng to go into a house. But people hiding inside don't dare to open the door. We run again and get lost, scrambling from one area where there is fighting to another area where there is fighting, and I can no longer remember how to recognize whether it's a place I know or some other area. The sound of gunfire is very close. It is impossible to go back and also impossible to go ahead. A group of people in front of us has a lot of wounded; they lie in the throes of death in the middle of the road near old corpses whose stomachs are grossly distended, as if blown up with water. I have to jump into a shrub to avoid the corpse of a dead woman near a couple of baskets with hangers and a shoulder pole still leaning against her shoulder. Next to puddles of dried blood mixed with dirty sand are corpses with their chests split open, their heads broken, their arms and legs chopped off and missing as though someone stole them. I think about packs of stray dogs, roaming the city during the last several days, but I don't have any capacity to be afraid anymore. Now, first of all, we must run to escape all this. A number of wounded people are lying, moaning and groaning, with their arms fluttering around in the air, stretching, clasping, and pulling at the pant legs and coats of the people running by. There are shouts, begging:

"Bring me along. Save me, oh heavens."

But I still stomp past them and keep going; many other people stomp past them, too, and keep going. Someone's hand catches the leg of my pants and pulls it down. I pull strongly and there is the sound of tearing cloth. I don't give a damn; first and foremost, I must survive, even if only for another second, another hour, or a few more hours.

"This place is very dangerous; for sure they will soon clash with each other at this place."

Thái has not yet finished speaking when we hear the sound of gunshots from the gardens pouring down in the direction of the riverbank.

From the direction of the river, salvoes of submachine guns and heavy machine guns fire up fiercely. Thái does not have time to add any further thought. He leaps to avoid a bomb crater:

"Run!"

We run following him. The sound of gunfire from the gardens shooting down toward the river is random. We can run no more; we crawl and roll on the ground.

"Let's crawl forward, roll, roll over, roll and follow me this way."

Thái calls out loudly but the sound of his voice comes and goes:

"Auntie, run to that place over there. Run behind that wall."

Thái again firmly holds my hand:

"Let auntie run in front, elder sister."

My uncle, my mother, Bé, his wife, and their children rise up and run to escape toward the wall. Thái pulls me – run fast. But the sound of gunshots seems to come from behind the wall. Duck down. Thái pulls me by the hand, and we dive down to the ground. We try to crawl forward to a house over there. Amid bombs and bullets, amid gun smoke, that brick house still stands firm and looks to be without a trace of a shell. The house juts out like a miracle. Thái bends, lifts his foot, and kicks a panel of the door. The panel breaks open very easily. I dash inside.

But what's this? I leap inside, then feel that my legs are stuck as though firmly glued, and there is no way I can lift my legs anymore. I bring my hand up to my mouth and gasp, about to shout. But I feel like I have died standing up.

In front of me, around me, everywhere is full of dead bodies. Some lie prostrate, some with their faces up. Some are twisted; some scowl, their limbs scrawny. Pieces of flesh and stagnant puddles of blood are all over the floor. My feet cannot take one step farther, but neither is there any place to step back.

I don't understand where my reflexes came from when I stepped into the house. It seems that when I stepped in, my feet didn't even touch the ground yet, but my eyes encountered the horrific scene inside the house, and some force carried my feet to avoid landing in puddles of blood. I find a spot where I can put one foot while the other foot touches only lightly to the ground with the heel.

I want to scream; I am about to fall and pass out. But no, I am still able to distinguish puddles of blood and pieces of arms and legs; I must try to remain on my feet.

Then fright squeezes me very tightly, rushing from my feet to the top of my head, from the top of my head back down to my feet, pressing me to emit a loud shout. Thái has already gotten behind me, in readiness. He lifts me on his shoulders and carries me, running, as though flying from this horrific house regardless of the bullets and shells, regardless of danger.

When I gradually come back to my senses, Thái has just put me down to the ground. Puddles of blood shimmer before my eyes. No, oh no, I rub my eyes, real blood, droplets of blood, blood stagnating in puddles around many still fresh corpses.

"Where's my mother?" I ask Thái.

He lifts his hand, wipes his eyes, and then says:

"At the corner of the wall over there."

My mother, my uncle, and Bé run up to us. Bé says:

"Oh heavens, we thought you, elder sister, and Thái had gotten lost."

My mother grabs me by the shoulder:

"Sit down, sit down, child."

My vision is dazzled. I see how branches of green leaves in front of me undulate lightly; then spin around so fast that it's impossible to see them. Amid this blindingly dizzy spinning, it seems that someone's drops of blood and pieces of arms and legs spin with them also.

There are a lot of sounds of bullets flying and of houses collapsing. I lie and roll on the ground. From a distance of about ten meters from where I am, a man is crawling toward me.

"Save me, I beg you, people, save me, please."

The man's chest and arm bleed profusely; I roll very close to Thu Hồng. Thu Hồng screams. My uncle covers her mouth. The man, dragging himself with great difficulty, slowly gets closer. His mouth doesn't stop shouting and screaming. He lifts his bloody hand to his mouth and sucks on it; his mouth is gaudy red, his eyes glare. I watch him roll around once then squirm convulsively. My vision is overwhelmed again. I dig my fingernails into my hand and press my face into the ground.

The sounds of guns gradually move a bit farther away. There are thudding sounds of running feet, sounds of someone calling out loudly. The sounds of feet reverberate in my ears; it seems like they are stepping through my head. After the clatter of explosions, my face is blazing hot; Thái makes me get up:

"Run fast, or you will burn to death."

I grip Thái's shirt and pull him back, treading indiscriminately upon the bodies of those who are dead and of those who are alive. I call: "Mother, oh Mother." I hear my own voice, and it sounds like the last call of a person who is about to die.

"Hey, child, I'm here."

I hear my mother's voice responding to me, and she is crying too. I'm not dead yet. I can still hear. I can still see. Definitely, I am still alive. I again go back to running.

The sounds of gunfire gradually subside. We still run. I aim myself at Thái's back and run following him. Many hands from down on the ground stretch up, beseeching me for help.

"Someone save me, please. I don't have any strength left anymore."

When I run into Thái's back and stop, my entire family is sitting down on the side of the road. The sounds of guns have by now subsided. Artillery has also stopped. I suddenly open wide my eyes. My vision is not dazzled anymore. So it means that only when I have an impression of imminent death in front of my eyes do I see amazing distortions. Now I am calm and alive. We sit on the side of the railway track. How did it happen that our several children are still unharmed? I am surprised and count forward and then back again. Even in the whirlwind of war, human life still seems so full! My eyes are overflowing with tears, and the eyes of my uncle, of my mother, of Bé, and of his wife are also overflowing with tears. Thu Hồng holds little Điện tightly in her arms; the little fellow is about to pass out from fear. Thái gently pats the old railway track and says:

"We will follow this railway to get back home. They're fighting everywhere. Let's go back home, auntie."

"Go back home? But if the fighting comes over there, what shall we do?"

"Now everywhere it's still the same; to make it through, auntie, we must take a chance."

"Is our house still there or is it destroyed?"

No one responds to this. But this afternoon, before dark, we grope our way toward home. Thái says that our house is close to the National Highway, and clashes easily erupt over there. In the end, we move into my uncle's house behind the railway near several small hills at the foot of Mount Tam Thái.

Earlier, to avoid shells, Bé dug a deep underground shelter in the front of the house to hide from danger. When we arrive, the shelter gets a do-over. Thái and Bé take it upon themselves to dig soil and fill bags for piling up at the entrance of the shelter.

All adjacent buildings remain silent in a strange way. The house next to my uncle's has been half-destroyed, hit by a missile on the morning of the first day of Tết; several bamboo trees in the back of the garden were knocked down, destroying the entire frame of the house. I think that for sure there is no one left in the hamlet, but in the evening Thu Hồng finds out that there are a lot of houses with people still living in them. She discovers dots of oil lamps or hears soft sounds of cautious movement. Through the entire first night of sleeping in the shelter, we hold our breath. Thái has his doubts as he sees signs suggesting that we must stay on alert. There are people in a lot of houses, but it's not certain that they are area residents. Sometimes it might be "they." We usually use the word "they" to refer to the Việt Cộng and to avoid the word "liberators." In fact, would it not be ironic and cruel to use the word "liberation" at the sight of such pain and utter destruction in the city? Even when we just entered the narrow lane leading to my uncle's house, I saw at once a flag of the liberation, tattered, hanging on a guava tree in front of a collapsed house.

The entire night, we listen to the constant sounds of hooting owls. The sound of owls hooting from all four directions seems to carry some supernatural significance. Each time the owls hoot, I have an impression that a scythe of death from the black sky is coming down to chop, ready to hit anyone, anything.

At dawn I hear sounds of people's feet outside in the yard. The sounds of feet are very soft, sometimes close by, sometimes far away. We hold fast to each other's hands. Bé prepares to put his hand over the mouth of his youngest child, who was born a little more than a month ago, in order to be ready to silence the child in case he cries.

Looking at the large hands of my younger cousin loosely covering the mouth of his child, my heart feels unbearable pain to the point of anguish. If there is just one sound of feet stopping at the entrance to the shelter, just one flashlight shining down into the shelter, Bé's child would not have time to scream when his father's hand would tightly and strongly cover his mouth. Just several convulsions, then it would be over. This night, how many deep underground shelters are there with no sound of crying children? Has there yet been any hand pressing hard over the mouth of a child? And the faces of adults, at once self-pitying and heartless in a toxic atmosphere, ready to inflict death on anyone . . .

But another night has also passed, and we are surprised to see ourselves still alive amid a deserted, silent hamlet. However, we are mistaken, for in several houses there are still people living; there are old men and old women who could not flee, following their children and grandchildren, and a number of immobilized families that were too afraid to leave.

The following morning I hear a lot of noise, and a lot of faces stick out. Waiting for the sounds of gunfire to subside, an old lady crawls in to visit us, but then she does not dare to go back. Thanks to the old lady, I learn more about the situation. During the past several days, the hamlet has been full of the Liberation Army, and at the present time the soldiers are digging underground shelters and foxholes at the foot of the mountain.

The area close to Trường Bia post is still full of Nationalist soldiers, and from the top of the mountain behind the practice range they shower shells into the Long Thọ and Kim Long areas. My mother loudly appeals to Heaven: "We have been so stupid to come back to be near where they are." Thái pulls the old lady down to the shelter:

"Don't let them know we are back."

But the old woman is utterly sure that by day they [the Communist forces] all go up to the slopes of the mountains, so they don't know anything. The old lady absolutely advises us to not light lamps.

At noon, a family from this hamlet finds its way back; their house has been destroyed, and they ask to dig an underground shelter right inside my uncle's house. The old lady waits and waits until afternoon, when her small grandchild dashes over to pick her up; the house of the old lady is only a courtyard away and across a narrow lane from my uncle's.

The fighting still surrounds us. Night falls, and we again hold our breath in the shelter. We wait, relying on chance, but our lucky chances are indeed slim; the entire household is emaciated because of starvation, but no one has enough strength to moan about this.

There is yet another period of waiting full of horror. The sound of an explosion bursts, but we no longer listen, no longer know anything at all.

FOUR

HODGE-PODGE

AFTER A NIGHT OF SHOUTS AND SCREAMS, EXASPERATION, AND flaring gunfire, the shadows of night fade gradually away. As soon as the sky lights up, sounds of gunfire also fall silent.

The sun looks like it had exploded into pieces quite some time ago. Daylight flickers with the sadness of tragedy. This morning waking up, no sound of crowing cocks or of singing birds, no sound of temple bells and church bells, not even the sound of chickens and ducks is heard.

The sky looks as if it is about to overflow with water. Gardens are suddenly desolate, abnormally gloomy; grass is soaked with dew; apricots are trampled and crushed to bits; scattered everywhere are rags, shell fragments, and traces of blood. Streaks of blood on the surface of the road connect one garden to another. Some puddles of blood still stagnate in the courtyard, beside the water tank near a golden apricot tree that looks shy because of its own very cheerful colors.

Along with the bland morning light, an innumerable number of men and women [the Việt Cộng] suddenly appear on the roads. Men wear khaki clothes, with their pants long or short; women wear black pajamas, their hair plaited, not let down loose but tied up high in a pleasingly tidy manner. Gripping their weapons, they glance at each other with solemn faces. Other, smaller groups stand guard at the entrances to the roads and in front of many houses, or they lie and sit everywhere in the gardens. There are a lot of dead bodies and wounded people at the foot of the

This chapter is an account based on stories told to the author by various people she encountered during her time in Hue during the Tết Offensive.

slopes. A few bodies lie stretched at full length; right in the middle of the road lie several prostrated dead bodies. Next to a group of guards at the beginning of the bridge are several beheaded bodies, with pieces of arms and legs scattered all over. At the side of the road, a number of wounded are lying, moaning and crying; some men and women carry them into a nearby garden. Inside the garden there is a big house, but there is no trace of people living in it anymore.

A young woman with sharp eyes carrying an AK rifle comes out into the middle of the road; she raises her arm and speaks loudly:

"Comrades, carry the wounded into the garden; as for the corpses, gather them in one place."

She repeats the order several times. Her voice is the first sound to be heard in the morning. Her loud talk seems to shake and break through a lot of doors, and it bursts inside the tightly locked houses. Her voice also makes the sounds of moaning and crying seem louder.

For a long time, groups of wounded people are being carried away. Another unit comes up from the bottom of the slope; still another group comes down the slope from the mountain. The young woman asks anxiously:

"How is it over there, comrades? Report the situation on the ground."

"It's all over now. The enemy has been silent since four o'clock in the morning."

"I'll be in charge of the wounded. A number of comrades who sacrificed their lives are entrusted into the care of Comrade X-10."

"Up there are around a hundred wounded comrades."

"Bring them up by the pagoda on the slope."

"Under the bridge, there are more than fifty wounded; there are even more of those who sacrificed their lives."

"Bring them to the garden; we will find a location to evacuate them."

"There is some other news."

"What?"

"B-3 sent an order to the comrades to divide into groups and go into houses to prevent compatriots from running away and causing trouble. We must restore order this morning, right now."

A lot of voices say: "Carry out the order." People divide into groups and disperse. At once, there is no one left from the unit, except for several small groups of guards along the roads.

A young soldier with an AK on his shoulder wipes his forehead with his hand, even though there is not a single drop of sweat there at the moment. He waits until his comrades disappear and turns and goes toward a house in front of him.

A pathway from the gate leads to the house, which is rather far. The garden is dreary and screens an ancient house with a tiled roof. The young soldier hesitates, then knocks on the door.

But after knocking for a while and hearing no response, he leaves. "Strange, it is clear that there are still people living in the house," the soldier mumbles. He crosses a wide courtyard and stops next to the water tank beside the golden apricot tree. All the houses look absolutely identical; each has a water tank, a rock garden, and a golden apricot tree. He looks carefully at the ground. There are a lot of traces of blood stretching all the way to a corner by the bamboo thicket. The soldier raises his arm and lightly shakes an apricot branch. He throws a glance at the house, then lets out a light sigh and goes away; he leans with his back against a pillar of the entrance gate and, with his gun at the ready, stands guard.

A moment later inside the house there are sounds of light steps going through a door. It's still dark there. A silhouette of a man cautiously groping his way moves one step at a time. He approaches an ornate wooden bed. The corpse of a person lies there, covered by a sleeping mat. He lifts the mat and says in a low voice:

"Grandpa, Grandpa."

A woman, the man's wife, comes over and stands behind the man. The man lifts his hand and closes the old man's still glowering eyes, then says to the woman:

"Grandpa has passed away."

The woman takes a step back, then bursts out crying. But then suddenly remembering something, she covers her mouth with her hand to stop herself; her eyes are open and scowl at the man. She looks panic-stricken and delirious. The man wipes his tears and then also tightly covers his own mouth to stop himself. Both of them enter into a small inner room. There are sounds of discreet whispering in the pitch-black darkness; a lot of people are lying and sitting, crawling and squatting:

"What, child, is it quiet outside now?"

"Sssh. Ask quietly, did you not hear he just knocked on that door!"

"Child, how's your grandpa?"

The man presses his wife to sit down:

"Sit down – don't stand anymore."

The man sits down next to his wife.

His voice chokes with tears:

"Mother, Grandfather has passed away."

The sounds of weeping about to burst out are suppressed. There are sounds of adults sobbing and of children in distress. The man stands up again:

"Enough – stop crying. If they hear, they will be here. Mother, Mother: don't cry."

But having said this, the man himself emits a small sound. He goes out of the room and peeps through a slit in the front door. A group of men and women are entering the courtyard. The man quietly comes back. The house is completely silent.

The sound of knocking on the door initially seems rather sporadic and then becomes more persistent. A male voice belonging to a person from a different area in Vietnam rises:

"Open the door. Open the door. The Liberation Army is here."

Inside the small room, the woman holds tightly the hand of the man. Mother's hand firmly covers a child's mouth, in fear that he will moan or cry. The knocking on the outer door becomes stronger:

"Open the door. Open the door or we will shoot."

A voice of a young man:

"Just now I knocked and knocked for a long time, but there was no one. Clearly they have all run away."

"Absurd, where would they run in the night? No one has left the house yet."

Then another voice, loud and dignified:

"I will count from one to three, and if you don't open the door, I will shoot. Is there anyone in the house? One . . ."

The man's wife pushes her husband toward the entrance door; she trembles so much that it produces a small noise. Outside, there are muffled laughs, followed by a loud call:

"Two."

The man has gotten to the door; he raises his hands over his head:

"Yes, please sir, sirs, I implore you, sirs, implore you, sirs, I am opening, yes, I obey, let me open . . ."

"Ah, you got it. Open the door."

The man trembles for a moment and then opens the door. A group of people pour into the house. There are approximately ten of them, some with rifles on their shoulders, others with haversacks. The eldest man among them has really big eyes and his face is very pale; he glances quickly throughout the house:

"Comrades, guard all entrances and exits."

Several people go toward the windows. The face of the master of the house turns green, his legs and arms shiver, his teeth clatter, and he is barely able to say:

"I implore you, sirs; we are honest people."

"Damn it, then why when we kept calling to open the door didn't you open it? You're creating a chance for puppets to flee, that's why, isn't it?"

"I implore you, sirs, I am too afraid."

"There are not any 'sirs' here. We are the Liberation Army."

"Yes, please sir."

"Call all the people who are in the house to come over here. Quick!"

Then turning he says:

"Comrades. Open the windows."

The light streams into the room clearly illuminating the face of an old man lying on an ornate bed of ebony wood. The sleeping mat previously wrapped around the corpse had opened, and a blanket covering the man is covered with dried blood. The senior person steps closer and looks into the face of the dead man, then he growls in a hoarse voice:

"He is already dead, isn't he?"

"Yes, please sir."

"Since when?"

"Please sir, venerable sir . . . sir-liberator, since one AM, a whole lot of blood has come out."

"Comrades, let's take the corpse outside into the garden; give me a hand here."

Several men are about to gather around. The woman trembles all over:

"I entreat you, sirs, please sir, I entreat you sirs-liberators, please sir, allow us children to bury him."

"Leave it to them."

Several men approach the ebony ornate bed and then hesitate. One of them stares angrily around the room:

"Call everybody in the house to come in here. Everybody must come in. Anyone who doesn't come in will be shot."

First, several children come in, then a middle-aged woman and several young women and girls; one of the women carries a little child in her arms. Their faces all turn pale. The middle-aged man [senior among them] with a blue scarf barks out an order:

"You all stand in the corner."

"Whoever is in there, please come out."

There is nothing but silence. But the middle-aged man gives a sign with his eyes.

A few other liberators step up. A panel of the door from the inner room suddenly bursts open. A silhouette rushes out. A sound of a gunshot, dry and cold, cuts in. There is a shout outside of the window and sounds of women screaming. The middle-aged man snickers:

"Search this house very thoroughly."

"Carry out the order!"

They all divide into groups and go to search the house; the old woman and the young woman carrying a child in her arms cover their faces, sobbing their hearts out. The faces of several young women turn pale, drained of the last drop of blood. A man tightly hugs a little lad climbing up onto him. After a while, the crowd of liberators searching the house return, and one of them says:

"There is nothing left here anymore."

The middle-aged man jerks out his chin:

"Go see whether that guy has died."

"Yes, sir: I've already looked; he's dead."

At once, many sounds of crying burst out. Several young female cadres crowd together; their bold looks that were apparent at first have now disappeared. One of them approaches the grieving young woman:

"Don't be sad, elder sister – don't be afraid. We only execute people who are guilty; as for regular citizens, it's our duty to protect them."

The young woman wipes her tears:

"He is my younger brother, he is. How's he guilty?"

"Because he ran away. In our position, we have to act in self-defense."

The middle-aged man throws a glance at the trembling pale faces. His voice is slow and monotonous:

"Mother and elder sister, don't be afraid. We came here to give protection to our compatriots."

The young woman who was crying suddenly stops short, dazed and confused. Several girls cuddle up with each other. There are sounds of feet running in from the gate. Two other liberators come in. They also have blue scarves around their necks. The middle-aged man asks:

"Is something wrong?"

One of the two says something in a very low voice directly into the senior's ear. He nods his head in agreement, then turns around and says to the female cadres and several liberators:

"Comrades, stay here. And I will go with Comrade Thu up to Chùa hamlet."

With the sound of feet moving out of the gate, a female cadre raises her hand:

"Comrades, we will stay here and prepare provisions, and then we will help with transporting the wounded and delivering supplies."

"Comrade Xuân says the truth. Supplies will be delivered here soon."

The female cadre named Xuân smiles, pats the young woman on the shoulder, and says intimately:

"Now, let me ask you, comrades, to help the master of the house to take care of the two dead bodies. Dear elder sister, this is . . ."

Xuân points at the old man's corpse. The mother hastily responds instead of her daughter-in-law:

"Yes, please dear young aunt, this is their grandfather."

Xuân waves her hand:

"Oh hell, Liberation Mother, I ask you, Liberation Mother, don't call me 'aunt.' I ask you to consider me as your child, as you consider other women and men in your family who are here."

When she finishes, Xuân turns to her friends:

"Now, Comrade Tiến and Comrade Bình, please help take care of the two corpses, the old man here and the young one, outside in the garden."

Then, with the expression on her face changed to sorrow, Xuân turns again to the master of the house:

"It is indeed such a pity; what happened is not something that was intended. Please let me share your grief with you, Mother, and with you, elder brothers and sisters."

The man of the house turns his face away, hiding tears rolling down. The bodies of the old man and of the youth are wrapped in sleeping mats and then taken out and buried in a shallow grave in a corner of the garden. A moment later, several female cadres befriend a few young women from the household, and the liberation soldiers divide up to go to the garden to guard and establish communications. Xuân talks with the old woman.

"Dear Mother, is there rice in your house?"

The old woman is very honest:

"Rice, there are two bags of it. It's Tết, young lady. We even still have *bánh tét,* young aunt."

"Mind you, Mother, please don't call me 'young lady' anymore. Please address me as your child, like you address men and women from your family here."

She laughs and continues:

"Perhaps in a few days the army will deliver provisions here. Mother, let us borrow two hundred kilograms of rice. In several days, when we completely take over the city of Hue, Uncle Hồ will come to visit us, and I will respectfully ask him to consider your case. Now, sign your name into Uncle Hồ's golden register book."

Xuân turns around and calls:

"Where is Comrade Nữ? Bring the register over here."

The female cadre named Nữ is a chubby young woman, but her complexion is nevertheless pale. She promptly pulls out of her shirt a notebook and holds it out toward the old woman:

"Dear Mother, here it is. Please sign it, Mother."

The old woman is trembling:

"Yes, I wish to, please madam, but I don't know the letters; how can I sign there?"

Xuân laughs and tells several young women from Hue standing bunched together in the corner:

"Well then, you, elder sisters, jot down her name and then sign for her. Oh, let me jot her name down, it will also work. Please madam, dear Mother, what is your name? Yes, it's done! Please, elder sister, sign here."

A small young woman swiftly scribbles on a page in a scrawling handwriting. Nữ passes the notebook to Xuân. The old woman is silent, mopping her tears. Several young women are still standing bunched together in the corner, tightly holding each other's hands; Xuân laughs:

"This afternoon we will celebrate the victory."

Pieces of sun break into loose bits and gradually assemble again, but they are fickle, hiding in a sky full of clouds, fog, and cold wind.

Dots of blood mixed with dew scattered on the grass have dried, leaving purplish black traces. In the garden there are many marks of soil freshly dug for people's graves. All the wounded are brought up to a pagoda, and female first-aiders demonstrate their abilities in dressing wounds. The joyous fresh looks that were on their faces in the morning have disappeared. Comrades from the Liberation Army dash about, guarding approaches to the roads or, divided up into groups, bursting into people's houses.

At a T-junction, in an abandoned small tavern, some slightly wounded men sit, nursing their wounds. A young soldier named Thu, carrying a rifle, is on guard at the corner of the road. Next to a patch of grass where he sits, a puddle of someone's blood has dried and several green flies buzz about randomly; now and then some of them cruise before his nose and want to stick to his face – he brushes them aside, completely absent-mindedly.

A number of houses are wide open, and people see male members of the Liberation Army along with female cadres enter them. From time to time, some children run out into a courtyard, and immediately an adult runs out to grab them and in panic rushes back into the house out of sight. The atmosphere is absolutely calm. Just last night the sound of gunfire shredded the sky and shook and destroyed houses; now all this noise has slipped away and disappeared along with the night shadows, but it has left the sun in shatters, and panic still firmly sticks to the ground covered with blood, to the broken-off tree branches, to the green leaves fallen and amassed in the gardens.

In all the houses people sit, huddling, in groups. They apprehensively look at the soldiers from the North, whom they are allowed to call the Liberation Army and who scurry around with expressions on their faces sometimes elated, sometimes grave and mysterious. People in the houses don't dare answer any questions from this crowd of strange people.

People in the hamlet are also startled when they see a few of their neighbors, with whom only yesterday they exchanged Tết greetings, and this morning these same people are holding guns in their hands with red and blue scarves wrapped around their necks, looking back at them with threatening and haughty expressions in their eyes.

These people now openly go to visit their neighbors. A blacksmith who only last night was drunk and with a sniveling drawl got into an argument with several young women carrying water from the well now carries a gun and goes from house to house. When he meets someone, he is adorned with a big smile and brags:

"Compatriots, calm down, fellow villagers, calm down. In a few days, Venerable Hồ will come here, and then we will have a merry party to everybody's hearts' content."

Or:

"For sure you didn't know, uncle, did you? I have been following the Liberation Army for a long time. I have been underground and conducting guerrilla activities in the enemy's rear."

Everyone looks at the blacksmith with pale faces. Everyone is afraid; usually in the daytime this man was just a polite blacksmith, but most late afternoons he would get drunk, talk obscenely, and pick quarrels with children and young women carrying water. How can one know that he was not harboring grudges against many people in the hamlet? Several boys, children of a woman who sells pork in the market, excitedly show up, carrying guns for the liberation.

An old man, a beggar who usually sits in front of stalls that sell drinks, today has an extremely radiant face and goes around to all the houses propagandizing boisterously:

"Listen, the Liberation Army is here! I am so happy! I tell you all seriously, none of you has done anything here that I don't know all about."

This utterance sounds like a threat, and people shift their gazes from one to another, looking worried and sorrowful, unable to conceal their feelings anymore.

Closer to noon, the Liberation Army arrives and pushes everybody, down to the last person, outside, into the courtyards. The soldiers summon young males to go carry ammunition, young females to transport wounded. Everyone over fifteen must go; only mothers, whom they call "Liberation Mothers," and women in childbirth and pregnant women, whom they call "Liberation Elder Sisters," stay at home to help the liberation soldiers prepare food. Some wounded people unable to endure their suffering inhale their last breaths. But the Liberation Army does not bring them to be buried in the gardens anymore; it transfers them, following the groups of wounded people to the upper areas where the roads lead to Tây Thiên, up the stream to Thiên An, up to the imperial tombs. At noon, the doleful and silent houses nevertheless have steam and smoke, signs of mealtime.

A lot of sounds of crying burst out, tearing hearts apart. In many houses, a lot of people are dying from their wounds due to the lack of medicines and bandages. The young soldier Thu standing guard at the T-junction listens intently, then lights a cigarette. Several liberators in a nearby tavern are inquiring back and forth:

"Who is crying and where?"

"In some houses over there."

"For sure there are dead people, right?"

"Just residents. Our army has transported all of ours."

The soldier looks at a house hidden in a garden with trees and asks:

"Do you know what's there?"

"The ancestor-worshipping house of Venerable Phan."[1]

"A hero, a revolutionary, isn't he?"

"Yes."

People in the tavern continue asking:

"We have taken over several posts, haven't we?"

"I haven't had any news about this yet."

1. Phan Bội Châu (1867–1940) was a prominent twentieth-century Vietnamese nationalist who advocated independence from French colonial domination and favored emulation of Japan in its ability to successfully transform itself from a backward agrarian feudal society in the middle of the nineteenth century into a modernized state that emerged victorious in both the Sino-Japanese War (1894–95) and the Russo-Japanese War (1904–1905).

The young soldier is silent. The sounds of crying in many houses grow louder; he lights another cigarette, then frowns. He hesitates, then boldly approaches the closest house.

This is a thatched house located directly on the road near the T-junction guarded by the soldier. He comes close to the door and then looks inside the house. On a wooden plank bed is laid a dead body with its face upturned; the entire family swarm around it, moaning and crying. An old woman, another woman holding a child in her arms, and two young children crowd around the corpse: "Child, oh, child" . . . "husband, oh husband" . . . "Father, oh Father, oh Father." Voices of the mother, of the wife, of the children of tender age tear the hearts of those who hear them. The North Vietnamese soldier, stunned and unable to act, reaches out his hand to lightly bang on the door.

The door is ajar; as soon as he stretches his hand to knock, it moves by itself and opens. He enters straight in. Two panic-stricken women look at him; several children stop crying. He comes close to see the dead body; it's not one but two dead bodies. On the farther side of the man's corpse there is also the corpse of a child, no older than three; its face is bruised and still sticky from being covered with blood. The old woman elbows her way to stand in front of the soldier as though shielding the dead bodies; her eyes look at the liberation soldier with a beseeching, pleading expression.

"Oh sir, everybody has died; there is no one for you here to arrest."

The old woman points to the woman holding a small child in her arms:

"As for her, she has under her arm three children of tender age. Sir, please spare me and her . . ."

As soon as the old woman finishes, she bursts into tears; her daughter-in-law and small children, following her, start crying. The soldier looks around the house; the furniture reveals the family's poverty: in the middle of the house is a wooden daybed, in the upper wing there is a table with chairs, behind the table and chairs is a small altar, and on the left side sits a bamboo bed. On the altar are several rice cakes, and several dishes with jam-filled cakes are left intact. On the wooden table covered with a piece of flashy-colored nylon is a vase with a branch of golden plum stuck into it. Several cups and several mugs are turned upside down on an aluminum tray. The soldier asks the old woman in a soft voice:

"Is this house yours, Mother?

"Yes, please sir, there are my children and grandchildren here, too."

The woman points alternatively to both the dead and living people. The North Vietnamese soldier unwraps his scarf from his neck and covers the face of the man with it; then he pulls out a handkerchief and wipes away the dried bloodstains on the child's face. He pulls a blanket and tightly covers the face of the little lad. Right at this moment there is a noise down in the kitchen, a sound of a bang on the door, then the face of a woman with her hair disheveled emerges from behind the door:

"Madam Bống, do you have a bit of oil for me, just a tiny bit? Do you have a bit of the red medicine for me, just a tiny bit? She will die soon, Madam Bống."

The woman hurriedly comes into the house, sees the two dead bodies stretched out on the wooden plank bed, and then backs up:

"Oh heavens, what to do? What to do, oh heavens?"

The woman shifts her eyes and looks at the faces of all the people. When her eyes come to the liberation soldier, the woman raises her hand to her mouth, her already pale face now turning gray.

The old woman pushes the newcomer on the shoulder:

"Elder sister Trùm, go back. Don't run back and forth anymore."

The woman named Trùm trembles:

"Madam Bống, do me a favor and give me please a bit of medicine for a compress for the child Bê's wounds; a lot of blood streams out and she's passed out."

"Bê? Is she wounded?"

"She was wounded in the wee hours of the morning. Oh, Heaven and Earth, devil and spirits, my poor family, what have we done that Heaven inflicts such utter destruction on us like this? Oh heavens."

Then looking at the two dead bodies, the woman finds the courage to say:

"Oh, Heaven and Earth, and what about Tanh with the little one? Why are their bodies like this, oh heavens!"

Hearing her neighbor's lamentations, Tanh's wife bursts into violent sobbing. The old woman takes the child from the arms of her daughter-in-law, her own mouth twisting, about to cry.

"That's enough, child, go and fix a small bowl of rice, put a joss stick in the bowl for our dead ones, to honor them. Why such a woe on us? Oh heavens, incense has gone to ashes, the smoke is cold . . ."

"Who shot, who killed them?"

"Who knows, elder sister Trùm. I only know that my child and grandchild are dead."

Trùm looks at the liberation soldier and suddenly realizes that the question she blurted out could be dangerous, and she says nothing more. But the soldier still absent-mindedly looks toward the altar. The incense has turned into ashes, and two candles burned almost to the end have been extinguished some time ago. A moment later, the soldier sees the woman hurrying down to the kitchen, and he says after her:

"If someone's wounded, take her to the pagoda, and there the army's first-aiders will dress the wounds."

"Yes, I've already taken her over there, and they say there is not enough medicine for the Liberation Army."

The woman disappears behind the kitchen. The sound of feet taking a roundabout route moves off toward the alley. The liberation soldier takes a look at the dead bodies one more time, then tells the old woman:

"That's it, Mother, don't cry anymore; it is unavoidable that people sacrifice their lives for our victory in the war."

The old woman does not understand a word. The wife of the late man wipes her tears:

"Heavens, oh heavens, how will I and the kids live now? Oh heavens."

The exploding sound of a gun – only a single sound – and then silence. The liberation soldier runs to the T-junction; he looks bewildered. Another liberation soldier guarding a house approximately ten meters away raises his hand and points to the shrubs on the side of the road. The young soldier sees a youth who tries to crawl into the road; he has been hit by a bullet, and his blood trails in long streaks on the ground. The young soldier runs to him. The arm of the youth is extended as though he wants to lift it, but he does not have enough strength and his arm falls on the ground with a thudding sound. His mouth gently moves, trying to articulate a couple of phrases, and then he turns over and stays motionless. The liberation soldier stands transfixed. The voice of his friend asks from a distance:

"Is he dead?"

The young soldier nods. He raises his hand to his neck as though he wants to feel his scarf, but it's not there anymore since he used it to cover the dead man's head in the house. He grips the collar of his shirt and firmly holds it. From behind his back approach two female cadres; seeing him stopped dead, they burst out laughing:

"Comrade Thu, what are you doing standing there? The place you have to guard is there, over at the T-junction. Go back to your post; perhaps this evening our army will retreat to the mountains."

One of the young female cadres sees the corpse:

"What's this? Who shot him? Was it you, comrade?"

"No."

A friend standing farther away shouts loudly:

"He wanted to escape. I saw him. He was behind the shrubs, so I opened fire."

Another female cadre, seeing the corpse, laughs with disdain:

"This thug is awfully fat; he ate American butter and milk, that's for sure."

The young soldier stretches out his hands and looks at them, and then he goes back to his post. In another house there are sounds of moaning and crying:

"Help, I beg you, oh fellow villagers, my child, my child . . ."

No doubt another person has just died. Several heads stick out:

"What's going on in that house over there?"

"People died."

"How many people?"

The young soldier shows two fingers, then suddenly remembers and hastily adds another finger. From the tavern come loud voices:

"Thu, come in here to eat special Tết *bánh chưng* [glutinous rice cakes]. These are Hue rice cakes. Comrades, someone go replace Comrade Thu."

The young soldier shakes his head and says:

"No need."

There is a sound of running feet and some people, all of them women and children, run toward the place where the corpse lies in full view:

"Child, oh child, you went out, what did you do that they shot you, my child?"

The mother's voice is heartrending. The liberation soldier comes by and asks:

"Is it your child, madam?"

"Yes, please sir, it's my child."

"Why was he not at home? What was he doing outside at this hour?"

"His younger sister was wounded and he went to seek banana sprouts and leaves to apply a compress for her."

"Is it so?"

The soldier returns to his post. Several women and children crowd together, take the body of the youth into their arms, and, carrying it, disappear out of sight into a small alley. The friend standing guard across the way steps closer toward the soldier named Thu:

"Comrade, you have to uphold your vigilance. The upper ranks issued an order not allowing us to get close to and talk at random to the Hue residents; they are all lackeys, through and through, of the Americans and of their puppets."

The two people both return to their old positions. From under the bridge a group of people come up carrying wounded. There are several girls from Hue, still very young, their faces pale; behind them are several liberation soldiers and female cadres. They walk fast, their faces taciturn. It is obvious that the young Hue girls are terrified and exhausted almost to death. People lie on stretchers, blood all over them. The young soldier goes toward the road and looks at each face of the wounded carried past him. When the last person gets close, the soldier clings to the stretcher:

"Mịch."

The young person on the stretcher made of white cloth opens his listless eyes and looks at the face of the person who called him. The soldier named Thu bends down to the stretcher:

"They've got you."

The wounded slightly parts his lips in anguish:

"I'm sure I will not survive. Thu, when you go back to the North, remember to let my parents know."

He gives a sign to his friend to undo a silver chain hanging on his neck and says in a barely audible voice:

"Remember to give it to my mom, Thu."

Thu hastily lets his friend's hand go. The female cadre in the first-aid unit has raised her voice ordering the two young Hue girls who are working hard carrying the stretcher to go faster. The wounded tries to open his eyes wide to see his friend and attempts to extend his hand to wave but doesn't have enough strength.

The soldier named Thu stands transfixed, looking at his friend being carried farther and farther away. His hand still firmly squeezes the silver chain. "Mịch," he calls out loudly. But the stretcher has been carried far away; only the silver chain is left in his hand, and he lifts his hand to wipe his eyes as though shutting his friend's eyes on his deathbed. From under the bridge another group comes up, also carrying wounded. Thu still squeezes the silver chain tightly in his hand and, as though hypnotized, looks at each stretcher carried past him. But he does not look at each wounded person's face anymore.

Several young Hue girls walk even faster, passing by the muzzle of Thu's rifle; it seems that they are afraid that some random bullet might fly and pierce their bodies. The soldier lets the muzzle tilt down toward the ground. In one of the windows from the house near the T-junction, located in a spacious area among trees and plants, Thu catches a glance from a pair of eyes looking very hesitantly. The soldier does not dare to look again; he is afraid that this pair of eyes will disappear. Those are eyes of a small young girl around fifteen or sixteen years of age. Behind her back there is a hand grabbing her by the shoulder:

"Don't look."

A woman of around thirty years old determinedly pulls the young girl back from the window and whispers:

"Don't look. They've just shot to death a person at the T-junction over there."

The young girl pulls her head back around and sticks her tongue out.

"Elder sister, there is a Việt Cộng fellow, incredibly handsome, elder sister. He guards the T-junction."

The woman resolutely drags her small younger sister away, scolding her:

"You are talking rubbish. Go back."

The small young girl retreats from the window. The woman, holding in her arms a baby girl, stands at the door of a room and speaks to someone inside:

"Grandma, since the break of day a lot of dead bodies and wounded people have been carried past here; too many, Grandma."

The old woman's voice is shaky:

"Speak softly; come on in here and then talk."

They all crowd together in the room. The older of the two young women speaks softly into the ear of the old woman:

"For sure they will soon have completely withdrawn up over there."

"I hope so too."

"In one day so many of them are dead, Grandma."

"Certainly in the morning our army will have come up here. Clearly they [the Communist forces] are now preparing to withdraw, aren't they?"

"No doubt that's how it is."

"Grandpa, has he been seen yet?"

"He's still stranded in the Việt Cộng's hands."

The small girl suddenly leaves the room. In the room, her elder sister says in a really low voice:

"Don't let Hợi go down. Grandma, in a moment you can take a handful of rice upstairs to feed him so that he doesn't pass out."

"When they come into the house, they will look up upstairs; I'm afraid to death that Hợi will be arrested."

Outside, where the small girl is looking out, the North Vietnamese soldier still stands, watching several female cadres practicing riding a motorbike, pushing a Honda. Their hair is plaited and their trousers are rolled up above their knees.

The young girl watches two young female cadres pushing another one sitting on the motorbike; even though there are two people supporting it on both sides, the handlebar still turns back and forth.

The young cadres laugh and joke around cheerfully, but the young soldier doesn't laugh. His face is gloomy and frozen; he looks down the slope where several women are running and crying for help:

"Save my child, I beg you, oh fellow villagers, I beg you. Save my husband, save my father."

Several young female cadres scamper in front of the young soldier's eyes, laughing and chattering:

"There are a whole lot of motorbikes here; after the victory we will have them to use."

One of them says loudly:

"Comrade Thu is too zealous, isn't he?"

The young woman apes the Hue dialect in a derisive way. The young soldier Thu frowns. He looks sideways at the house in front of him. The small young girl hastily pulls her head back inside. Incomprehensibly, either out of anger or sadness, Thu lifts his rifle and aims at tree trunks in front of him as though he wants to shoot. No sound of a bullet explodes. The female cadres laugh conciliatorily, and in a flash they've gone halfway down the slope.

A dog, its body sticky with dried blood, shuffles its feet out from the brush; the liberation soldier picks up a stone and hurls it sharply at the dog. Hit in one of its legs, the dog is still able to run on the other three legs but can make only a short distance, and then it crawls and eventually lies flat in one place. The soldier comes closer to it and lifts his rifle to the animal's head, intending to shoot, but no sound of explosion comes out. The dog sticks out its tongue; its mouth is full of saliva, and its eyes look up watching the person standing in front of it. The light in the animal's eyes makes the soldier quickly turn around and return to his post. Several female cadres turn around and come back up, passing in front of the young soldier. Some other cadres continue to strenuously push the female cadre sitting on the motorbike; her forehead looks like it's been sprayed with sweat, but her face is still extremely cheerful.

Never has the city of Hue had such an atmosphere filled with death and panic. Dead bodies along with wounded soldiers have been taken up into the mountains. But each hour in each hamlet, some wounded people in the absence of medicine die. From morning till afternoon, crying bursts out, resounding from one house to another. The sounds of crying spread very quickly, catching like an epidemic. Amid death, pain, and sadness, joy spreads also like an epidemic among the liberation soldiers. In the morning, they were still cautious of the local residents, but by noon, by afternoon, an internal order was very quickly transmitted by word of mouth and they have changed their behavior, turning into modest and courageous fighters, sympathetic to the people, easily and harmoniously coexisting with them.

Bags of rice together with *bánh tét, bánh chưng,* and *mứt bánh* [cakes and candied fruits] collected from people's houses during the several days after Tết are now brought to the courtyards to be piled up on trucks to transport them to the upper areas, but, according to the liberation soldiers, they borrow all this only temporarily for the Liberation Army. In several days, when everything is finally settled in the city, rice will be dirt cheap – no exorbitant prices like those of the American puppets, who sold a bag of rice for as high as a thousand dongs. They also appeal to those whose houses have a "three-stick flag" (the three-stick flag is a flag of Vietnam, yellow with three red stripes);[2] they have to bring it out and burn it and replace it with the flag of the liberation, the flag of Uncle Hồ. Anyone who still has rice or cakes must bring them out to present to the Liberation Army; they make a special notebook to register residents' property so that in several more days, when Venerable Hồ comes, he will repay appropriately for the favor.

They also call on young people not to flee; instead, they must report themselves to receive a pardon. Funeral homes must make sacrifices to help compatriots in distress take care of interring those who are dead. No one is allowed to leave one's residential area. In the garden of every house, people bury their kin. They also heighten vigilance; residents are not allowed to go outside and are not allowed to assemble unless they receive permission from the Liberation Army, and then they can go only for studying and training.

Throughout the day, the female cadres seek acquaintance with one household after another to inquire about the state of the inhabitants; they get to know men and women of all ages. Old women who were just looked upon as evil spirits now have the title of Liberation Mother

2. A derogatory term used by Communists to refer to the South Vietnamese flag because the expression "three sticks" in Vietnamese bears a strong negative connotation. According to the author, when she was writing the book this term was not yet widely known, and thus she included an explanation in parentheses.

conferred upon them; younger women are now called Liberation Elder Sisters. All adults receive them [Communist cadres] with doubt and caution in their eyes, but children seem very elated. It's been only since the morning that the Communists forces were around, but children have already gathered around the female cadres and the soldiers. They are delighted to closely follow the motorbike antics of the female cadres or to assemble around the soldiers. In each house, members of the Liberation Army come to inquire, and they cook rice or eat and drink right there in the houses. Strong and healthy young girls are "borrowed" to cook rice for the soldiers. Young males, adolescents of fourteen or fifteen years old, are "borrowed" to carry guns and ammunition and are issued guns for themselves; they are divided into groups to help soldiers who are about to organize training sessions.

On the first day, a lot of young males and adult men hid themselves in the corners of rooms or in the lofts of houses. But by the second day, many people heard that the liberators called those hiding to come out to report themselves: "Whoever is in that house, we will never dare to touch a resident; we certainly are people's friends." This is a refrain that the liberators keep repeating. Although all areas are forbidden to communicate with each other, people in a few neighboring houses have been able to inquire about some things, and a whole lot of rumors are circulating around. For instance, by noon of the second day, a lot of people hear that the most luxurious and elegant car of an American advisor in Hue was confiscated and a high-ranking Việt Cộng commander drove it all over the city. Another piece of news says that a lot of military vehicles driven by liberation soldiers are on the streets and the roads, loaded with *bánh chưng, bánh tét,* and bags of rice. The liberation soldiers are increasingly joyous; they inquire of the people and, if some woman mentions these rumors to them, they laugh with confidence.

"The Liberation Army has already occupied Hue; now we are trying to hold it to restore order. We are waiting until the fighting is finished in the provinces, and then there will be peace."

A lot of people are stunned by these revelations. They would listen to the radio but for the fact that the liberation soldiers have requisitioned every radio in every house down to the last one. They confiscate and say that at this time compatriots need to hear only what the Liberation Army has to say because the Americans and their puppets can spread false news to make the masses confused. A lot of people manage to conceal their radios, but they don't dare to turn them on to listen anymore. People in houses that have dead relatives look for cloth to wind around their heads as mourning bands; from some houses the scent and smoke of incense floats out before the completely indifferent eyes of the liberation cadres, who indulge themselves in eating and drinking. Each and every family had put aside enough provisions for the celebration of Tết. But then as the second day and the third day pass, they run out of meat, and only some houses furtively fix pork or chicken. The Liberation Army finagles its way to find out where to buy people's property dirt-cheap. Then, on the third day, they organize assemblies: in the morning for young women and in the afternoon for young men. At the same time, they pull back the army to concentrate in several places, temporarily leaving the houses of common residents, but at any time the cadres still worm their way into each house under the pretext that they come to visit.

The first study sessions are organized in a spacious pagoda or in schools. People can't help but be surprised when they see people's representatives appear in one house after another. These people only yesterday were a cyclo driver or an old drunkard vegetating in his hopeless circumstances, and now they are leaders of their hamlets. The common residents also can't help but be surprised when they hear loud laughter among some people who just several days ago looked absolutely lethargic but now have turned into extremely animated personalities; on the hamlet's roads they walk, calling upon people and propagandizing for the Liberation Army.

On the afternoon of the second day, the third day of Tết, there are several areas that have witnessed the scenes of punishment of the guilty. A number of people in the hamlet have been arrested and condemned as followers of the armies of the Americans and their puppets. They are brought into a school, and young people, both male and female, are gathered in groups there. The familiar faces are of people who had been assigned to live in areas occupied by their enemies, and they are now authorized to judge the accused people. Verdicts are reached in a hurry. Many sentenced people are led away, then immediately in the afternoon of the same day rumors spread that those people have been executed.

No one has regained composure yet from the night of the first day of Tết when guns exploded horribly and in the morning people opened their eyes to see plenty of blood and dead bodies; they thus now start to be afraid because of the Liberation Army's search-arrest-hold-a-trial operations. Even though the Communists outwardly appear to be very kind to the inhabitants, at the same time they launch arrests and trials. Schools, preschool establishments, pagodas, churches, any other places of worship – they are all turned into locations for assemblies and for the people's courts.

From time to time there are sounds of gunfire, scattered or in a salvo. All the people, like wounded birds, quickly drop to the ground and swiftly creep under tables or plank beds. Children have also gotten used to the atmosphere of tension and fright – they have seen blood and death and thus when they hear the sound of gunfire there is no need for anyone to remind and admonish them to run; they look for adults and hold on to them tightly, or they lie with their faces pressed to the ground. But the sound of gunfire is now sporadic, and in the long silences there is nothing but the sounds of the liberators laughing and talking in the streets and in taverns.

Night falls and outside the air is silent and tranquil to the point of taking one's breath away; people hear the sound of owls hooting. The sound of hooting owls fills the entire city. People are in disbelief because, amid bombs and in the atmosphere reeking of the cold stench of death, a flock of owls dares to return to stir up a disturbance in the paralyzed city. Are these the sounds of owls or of people exchanging secret signals and thus hooting in the night? People stop breathing and wait; they don't know whether or not what they are waiting for will arrive, but the premonition is that there will be nonetheless a number of unfortunate and miserable events ahead. Husbands suddenly look at their wives with more love and tenderness; mothers hug their small children as though they are afraid that they will disappear. Grass and trees, houses, people, domestic animals suddenly seem to feel a bond that is hard to describe.

People are unable to learn anything besides the news transmitted by the female cadres and the propagandist-liberators. During assembly sessions, a lot of old men report in a detailed manner on the news. Young women go to assemble, and when they come back they say that an old man who sells *cháo lòng* – pork stomach porridge – was elected to be chairman of the training sessions; he opens gatherings and usually talks about the war situation in the country. Not only illiterate but also not accustomed to speaking, he usually gets the names of radio stations wrong and incorrectly uses terms, but no one dares to set him right or to laugh. He discusses news about the fighting and always starts by saying: "According to the radio stations A, B, and C, the Liberation Army has occupied Saigon and other cities and provinces. The Liberation Army is complete master of the situation." At each gathering the man chews these phrases over and over. Young male students exchange secret signs. Young women look with bewilderment at each other. It is rare to hear a talk that would bring such a good laugh, but at this moment no one dares to laugh. The gatherings are ostensibly mandatory, yet people whisper into each other's ears wondering how it is that fewer and fewer young males and adult men show up without the cadres noticing.

By the afternoon of the second day, the atmosphere of elation among the liberation comrades is losing its ebullience. After a tailor suspected of being a liaison for the American puppets is killed and his corpse is tossed out for display at the T-junction and after two young people in a small shelter are shot on mere accusations of evading the Liberation Army, the female cadres are completely withdrawn to appointed places to stand ready and are no longer on duty to visit people's houses. From that day on, scattered sounds of gunfire begin to explode in remote areas and return to the right bank of the river.

The liberators talk among themselves about an American tank coming up to reconnoiter in the area of the National Highway; possibly there will be a violent fight. But the source of this information is not reliable at all; in several areas there are liberators who loudly announce:

"Young males and adult men take care to prepare fifteen-day stocks of rice to go and take part in a study group to learn about the policies of the Liberation Army."

The Communist forces dig underground shelters and foxholes, and they transport weapons. The tension in the air escalates. Out on the streets, in the gardens, and at the entrances to narrow lanes resound the sounds of shovels and hoes as the liberators dig underground shelters.

Young males and adult men begin to look for places to hide; faces, young and old, stick out from behind the shutters of open windows to watch liberators with determined faces digging underground shelters – no one dares to chat merrily anymore as they did just several hours ago.

The night of the third day comes, and the entire city is suddenly awakened by flares and artillery. The soldiers and female cadres are no longer seen anywhere; they, like ghosts, have slipped away into the darkness of the night. People hear only sounds of moaning and crying that have become familiar since the night of the first day of Tết. Nobody has had time to dig underground shelters to avoid the bombs; this night the areas of Từ Đàm and of the royal Citadel, Gia Hội, and Kim Long endure the heaviest artillery fire.

The following morning, people hurriedly dig underground shelters for themselves. They dig them right in their courtyards, in their gardens, or right inside their houses. Liberators stand guard only sparsely at the intersections of roads. Residents spill out into the roads, inquiring in one house after another. Some families quarrel about evacuation, but liberators stand guard at the crossroads and signal that no one at all is allowed to leave. In a rush people dig underground shelters; all the windows, the iron gates – everything is dismantled to build underground shelters. At some houses without enough materials, people go out to lumberyards or chop down bamboo.

At some lumberyards, in a flash there is not a single board left. In the absence of boards, people take even coffins and coffin lids to carry back home and prop up the earthen ceilings of underground shelters. There are houses that have already dug underground shelters, and when the entire household goes down to hide, they feel that it's too cramped so they dismantle and redo the shelter. By noon artillery fire intensifies, and some people eating their meals abandon their food and slip down to the shelters. Liberators slip down into foxholes. They are not in the people's houses anymore, but when there are sounds of gunfire, they, out of nowhere, overflow the gardens and the roads, and they camouflage the foxholes.

When the sound of gunfire temporarily stops, the digging of underground shelters resumes. Several groups quarrel with each other, cursing each other while fighting for boards in lumberyards or for soil and sand. Shelling comes suddenly, without notice, leaving a number of residents and soldiers of the Liberation Army killed or wounded. The liberators again enter each house to seize young men and women as transporters up to the mountains. People are in a pandemonium, and rumors spread that they [the Communist forces] are establishing their headquarters over there. On the left bank, the headquarters is established at Gia Hội School. In this area, the liberators' activities are more enthusiastic; even though artillery intensifies, they still organize study and training sessions. In the Citadel, where the royal palaces are located, the Liberation Army takes over completely. There are cadres who stay behind in the enemy's rear and young people who have been missing for a long time who suddenly reappear. They wear armbands and take charge to scour each house, looking for guilty ones. Several hot pursuits end in arrests. Several people are shot and fall in the middle of the road; their corpses are left there, and nobody dares to go and bury them. There are corpses that have started to smell, blood stagnates and dries up, stenches spread, and swarms of flies mass around; it looks absolutely terrifying.

The days began when Hue opened the door to hell.

FIVE

A Person from Từ Đàm Comes Back and Tells His Story

FOUR DAYS IN A ROW I LAY IN A DARK UNDERGROUND SHELTER, and out of the four days there were two days that I had to go without food. This morning a girl crawled up out of the shelter, foraged somewhere, and found a piece of *bánh tét,* thickly covered with mold. She crawled back down, peeled off banana leaves covering the cake, and began feeding people, offering one person after another a bite.

I had already been fed up with all that was going on and was in despair. Several hours earlier, I had a feeling that if I continue starving like this I would come to the point of exhaustion, drop off, and go into eternal sleep, and that it would be really fortunate for me. But it would be even more fortunate to stay in the world of the living, though we have yet to endure a lot of ordeals. However, when I notice the smell of sticky rice and of moldy banana leaves, and when a piece of the rice cake is passed close to me, suddenly my mouth opens wide, a happy sensation makes me merry, and joy overflows me when a piece of cake gets into my mouth. Saliva gushes and mixes with the fine taste and sweet fragrance of sticky rice to the point of causing me to faint dead away.

No, death is indeed heartless and does not make people happy, as I imagined. Despite loud sounds of explosions, despite sounds of digging and scraping in the earth above as if on top of my head, despite the haunting worry about young liberation soldiers standing guard in front of the house gate, constantly aiming the barrels of their rifles in one direction

This chapter is the voice of a young man named Lê who hid in the underground shelter in Phan Bội Châu's ancestor-worshipping house in Từ Đàm hamlet, on the edge of Hue, where the house of the narrator's brother Lễ was located.

and another and ready to fire at any moment, the piece of cake in my mouth feels like the absolute happiness that only the luckiest person, in the rarest of cases, could experience but once in a lifetime. The piece of the cake is getting smaller, the saliva in my mouth runs stronger, and I can't stop feeling joy; I am obsessed and chew insatiably. Then I come back to my senses for a couple of moments and say in a moaning voice:

"Is there another piece? Give me another piece."

The young girl still has a piece of cake and intends to bring it up to her mouth. Hearing my words, she immediately stops:

"Eat, elder brother."

I see that her eyes are extremely sad in the light of the candle in the corner of the shelter.

"Go ahead, eat."

I haven't been able to stretch my arm to take the piece yet but only open my mouth for another piece, and incredible delight fills me. I am really very fortunate; happiness visits me twice in the interval of only seconds or minutes.

At that moment, I come back to my senses. I stretch my shoulders and only then realize that my spine aches in a strange way. But at the same time, I suddenly hear the echoing sounds of music and singing: sounds of a monochord, of a Vietnamese sixteen-chord zither, of a Vietnamese two-chord guitar, and even sounds of reciting poems.

"Who's there?"

My younger sister Oanh whispers:

"That's Mr. Võ Thành Minh."[1]

Võ Thành Minh is a person from the old generation of Phan Bội Châu and Marquis of Foreign Territory Cường Để;[2] he is still roving

1. Võ Thành Minh (1906–68) – in some sources his name is spelled Võ Thanh Minh – was a writer and poet from Nghệ An province who spent most of the 1950s in Europe. He was opposed to the partition of Vietnam, became a resident of Hue in the 1960s, and tried to publicize his commitment to reconciling the two Vietnamese countries. During the Battle of Hue, he was killed while trying to help civilians and stop the fighting.

2. Prince Cường Để (1882–1951) was a prominent member of the royal family. He and Phan Bội Châu were early leaders against the French colonial occupation of Vietnam.

around at this present time, enduring our common fate with the city. What has he been doing? It seems that yesterday, when we were in the shelter, my younger sister in whispers told the entire family about this strange character, but I, prone with hunger, could not hear anything. The sounds of the instruments emerge clearly, despite sounds of artillery still booming everywhere and everybody tightly hugging each other in the shelter. My younger sister Oanh stiffly hangs on to my shoulder and shivers all over:

"Call Trúc to come down."

My mother shakes her head:

"Leave her alone; no one can convince her."

Sounds of singing, sounds of instruments, sounds of reciting poems stop, falling completely silent, then we hear several explosions nearby, so close that it seems they are right on the roof, on my head. Many loud voices call out:

"Come down to the shelter."

People in the shelter inch closer to each other as more people crawl down from above. My mother asks softly:

"Is Trúc there?"

The voice of my other younger sister Trúc responds:

"I am over here."

I hear Trúc's voice whispering with Oanh:

"That guy who ran over to hide in our house, obviously he was looking for you, elder sister."

Oanh keeps silent. I guess that Trúc refers obscurely to the Việt Cộng soldier on guard in front of the house. Whenever artillery lobs in this direction, he usually hides in the house and seldom jumps down into a foxhole as his comrades-in-arms do. Right in the area of this house there is a group of three guards, and it seems that he is the head of the group. Someone bursts out with angry words:

"Monkeys – stop gossiping."

We all become silent and hold our breath; the seconds and minutes go by, the same as they have during many hours in the past.

Mr. Minh does not come down to our shelter. I surmise that he is hiding in some other shelter. I hear a woman crying. Trúc whispers:

"That is the wife of Professor Lê Văn Hảo.[3] Elder brother, she told me that her husband knew there would be a battle, and before Tết he advised her to buy several hundred kilograms of rice to be prepared."

"Damn that old hag; let her howl. Her husband went clamoring to agitate for the Liberation Army and left his wife and child to die of fear in a shelter like this. Listening to her only adds to my hatred."

But I am not as cruel as Oanh; the woman's crying makes me feel pity. For several days I haven't dared to venture out from the shelter, afraid that liberation soldiers will learn that I hide in it. Damn it, if someone says I'm a coward, let it be; I am concerned about my life first.

Despite being solidly stuck in the shelter, I get all the information about whatever is happening outside from my two younger sisters, who relate everything in full. A house near Uncle Bảy has collapsed. The elementary school is abandoned. Soldiers of the Rural Development unit came back for duty during Tết but then threw away their guns and fled. On each crossroad hangs a liberation flag. An old tailor in the hamlet has been killed, and his body is buried in a shallow grave near the local elementary school.

Mrs. Hảo, the wife of the professor famous in the liberation of the ancient capital of Hue, is still weeping and moaning throughout the entire day. When she walks or stands, she is unsteady; she holds onto Mr. Võ Thành Minh's coat. She doesn't even have enough strength anymore to care for her children. So much for magnanimity, so much for bravery and courage in a woman who completely gave up on herself for the sake of her husband – isn't that right? Despite thinking this, I am not angry with her.

When the sound of guns subsides, I suddenly hear the sound of a typewriter, clop-clop, over the shelter opening. Surely, several soldiers seized a typewriter to do important things, like type their briefs and reports; isn't that the source? No, not at all – I hear the sound of an old man coughing slightly, then Mr. Minh's voice calls:

"Where's Oanh? Come up here; please give me some noodles."

3. Prof. Lê Văn Hảo was a Hue University ethnologist who had earlier edited the Struggle Movement publication against the South Vietnamese government of Nguyễn Cao Kỳ and Nguyễn Văn Thiệu. He became the chairman of the Revolutionary Committee in Hue and of the Alliance of Nationalist, Democratic, and Peace Forces in Hue, or, effectively, the mayor of Hue during the Tết Offensive.

Oanh is climbing up to the shelter opening; my mother pulls her back:

"Don't go up."

But she is hardheaded:

"The shooting has stopped now; what are you afraid of, Mother?"

Having said this, she disappears. I stick my head out to follow her. My mother holds my head fast:

"I beg of you, please slide back down."

But I still keep sticking my head out from the shelter opening. For four days I haven't seen the sun. I linger for another moment of air outside; I long to see a leaf on a tree moving so that I will be able to reassure myself that I've not yet been separated from life, life with its grass and plants and with all its smells. Despite this longing of mine, I still see nothing; the ancestor-worshipping house, under which the shelter is located, is quite dark; a small candle is hidden behind a big column. Oanh has crawled into the corner of the house where the light of the candle flutters.

I have to rub my eyes several times before they adapt to see all the objects in the worshipping house. Mr. Võ Thành Minh sits on a padded chair; in front of him there is a low chair serving as a desk for a typewriter. He does not type but sits absorbed in his thoughts. Oanh moves her face closer to read what is on the paper. I try to look in the direction of the window but don't see anything. The window's shutters are closed tight. I desperately want to climb up, but my mother's hand is still clenching the shoulder of my shirt, ready to pull me back in.

There is a scream outside and the very urgent sound of banging on the door. Now I wait no more for my mother to pull me; my body slides down into the shelter very fast and then slips into the corner intended for me. There is this small hiding place down here; even if they shine a flashlight down into the shelter, it will still be difficult to see me. My mother firmly forces me to hide me so that they won't find me.

I hear the sound of the door opening up in the house and a lot of steps entering. Oanh slides down; she shuffles her feet toward me and whispers:

"They've filled the house."

"They have their own foxholes; why do they come in?"

"The shooting is over; they came into the house to search."

Oanh is still speaking when the steps move toward the shelter opening. The ray of a flashlight shines down. Oanh reaches out and pushes me into the wall, then pulls on the edge of a mat, spreads it on the shelter's floor, and sits leaning with her back against me. The voice of someone up above resounds downward:

"All of you – come up here into the house so we can check on you."

Mr. Võ Thành Minh's voice is absolutely calm:

"Everybody come up here. All are women and children whom you need not fear. Come up quickly."

My mother crawls first, then, following her, children, adults, old women all go up. Oanh climbs up last, and the ray of the flashlight sweeps back and forth several times. My heart seems to stop beating. Voices of the people on the top of the shelter are loud and clear:

"Anyone else still here, come up."

My mother's voice trembles:

"Please sir, it's everybody."

Mr. Võ Thành Minh's voice:

"If you don't believe us, you might search down there. Or you might shoot first to be sure."

My entire body freezes; I am trying to control my legs and arms, but they are still shivering all over. What to do if they really fire in? I want to scream, but my hand by itself tightly covers my mouth:

"Mother, oh Mother."

A shout sneaks into my head and fills me with despair. But a sound of laughter above the shelter helps me calm down for a couple of moments:

"Enough. Stand in a line. Someone there open the window a little bit to get light."

I take a breath, but my chest is heavy as though pressed down by a stone slab. I've not yet escaped. I crouch, hiding in the passage of the shelter. Vapor from the ground is cold and permeates my body with biting frost. Voices of many people up in the house burst into an uproar.

"All women and children are here. Why does that woman cry so bitterly?"

"Please sir, my husband has disappeared."

"Did he go to a meeting?"

"Please sir, my husband is Professor Hảo."

Võ Thành Minh's voice:

"The husband of this woman went to establish the Front of National Union or Peace or some other harmony kind of organization[4] and doesn't care to come see his wife and child. If you meet him somewhere, tell him that he must come back to see his wife and his kid and to share with them honor and dishonor. He is obsessed with the revolution, and whether or not his wife and child are alive or dead, he doesn't know."

The voice of the head of the group sounds softer than before:

"Ah. So this family is part of the liberation. We are all comrades here. So, is there any way that you can help the Liberation Army?"

"How can we? We have been hungry for several days."

"Is there any rice left?"

"You, sirs, have searched for it and have taken it."

The voice of another person says:

"I report to you, comrade head of the group, in that corner there are two bags of rice intact."

"Write it down: 'borrowed in this house: two bags of rice.' Write it down in the register so that we can return later to commend distinguished service for the front."

Silence for several seconds, and then I hear the sound of the already familiar voice continuing:

"There are also those two young women that must go to meetings; today at two o'clock this afternoon there is a meeting at the pagoda. All the men from this hamlet must go to study and get training, and women also have to study and train according to the policy of the front."

"They are too afraid to go, so what must we do?"

"Ah, there's also this venerable gentleman. Venerable sir, please come to meet our commanders."

"To meet commanders where?"

4. A reference to the Alliance of Nationalist, Democratic, and Peace Forces, officially set up during the Tết Offensive. It was a precursor to the Provisional Revolutionary Government of the Republic of South Vietnam formed on June 8, 1969, as an underground government opposing the Saigon government of President Nguyễn Văn Thiệu.

"To meet the commanders of this area. I am only the head of a group of three people; we are guarding the area around this house."

"Is that so?"

"Venerable sir, come with us. Please carry with you fifteen measures[5] of rice."

"Why do I need to carry the rice?"

"Carry the rice to eat. You will study and train for three days and then will come back."

"What is it that I must study or be trained in?"

"Take a sack or a bag of rice. Bring along more and it will be even better."

"What is the meeting for?"

"To study and train, I've already told you – study and train. Please, sir, follow me."

"I am not going."

Mr. Minh's unexpectedly firm voice strikes me with surprise. Certainly, since the day the Liberation Army arrived in Hue until now, no one has dared to utter such a phrase. I secretly worry about his fate. Seeing that no one is paying attention to this shelter anymore, I leave the small passage and sit, leaning against the wall. I don't clearly see the face of the head of the group, but I hear his muffled laughs:

"What have you done for the enemy?"

"What enemy?"

"Americans and their puppets."

Mr. Võ Thành Minh's voice is scornful:

"Why do you speak so perversely? I have nothing to do with following Americans. When you go back, ask if that Mr. Hồ Chí Minh of yours dared to talk with me in this tone of voice. I'm not going, did you hear me or not? If you want to invite me to a meeting, you must have a message from Chairman Hồ, not from some Liberation Front of your brazen band – what good is that? Does this brazen band of yours know who I am?"

Perhaps the head of the group has real consideration for this stubborn old man; I don't hear him saying anything else. Another voice talks instead:

5. The Vietnamese term for this word denotes a measure of 11.7 ounces.

"Uncle, please follow us to meet our commanders. Our headquarters is close by, uncle."

"I am not going. If you have anything else to say, shout it to your commanders. I am here; this is a worshipping house of Venerable Phan, and I would not be surprised if this group of yours doesn't even know him. I will go on a hunger strike; I will go down to sit under the Bến Ngự Bridge to oppose the liberation line of your brazen band. I am against both Americans and Communists."

I wait for a moment and then hear Mr. Minh's voice continuing:

"As for Mrs. Hảo, if there is a way to send word to her husband, do it. Listen, you have to send word to him to come back and bring the glorious rewards we hear about so much."

I hear a woman sobbing, then the voices of several liberators saying their good-byes and the sounds of feet on their way out. Oanh and Trúc crawl down to the shelter first. They get close to my ear:

"Afraid?"

I don't answer; naturally now they have guessed whether or not I was afraid. Even though I heard all the conversation above, I nevertheless make Oanh tell me what was said. Trúc giggles and says that there is one liberator who likes elder sister Oanh; he fastened his eyes upon her. It's been several days, and he has deliberately neglected to make Oanh go to the study and training sessions – a Việt Cộng who also knows how to like girls.

Trúc laughs. My mother scolds:

"Little devil. What are you laughing at? Death is around the corner and you don't care."

As though suddenly remembering the situation, Trúc falls completely silent. Oanh tells me the story of Mr. Minh. She says:

"When I got up there, I saw him lighting the lamp and typing. He was writing a letter to Mr. Hồ Chí Minh and the American president demanding that they stop the war. He wrote: 'Venerable Teacher Phan's worshipping house, day . . . month . . . year . . . As I'm writing this letter to both of you, airplanes roar above my head, artillery booms and flashes in the sky, the earth crumbles, and the city of Hue drowns in the sound of bewailing and in very deep resentment . . . I write then tear it up, I read it out loud for others to hear, I speak, I appeal to the entire world, too . . .'"

"In normal times he did not appeal; now he does, but who hears . . ."

Oanh is confident:

"Shame on you! Don't say such nonsense. He decided to appeal to young people and student to go down to the bridge to sit on a hunger strike to oppose."

"Oppose who?"

"Oppose the war, which is inhuman and atrocious; there is no justice in war whatsoever."

The words of my younger sister are quite simple; they seem to tug at my heart. In just a few days, so many people have died in the city; so many have been wounded. Corpses distend in the houses or are exposed outside, and no one buries them. Then, people go to study and train for the first stage, but not one of them has been seen to come back. Are they alive or have they died? I think about it and feel pity for the old man, Mr. Minh, who used to play the flute on the shores of Lake Geneva every day during the Geneva Conference in 1954. He opposed the division of his native country, Vietnam. But finally he was the only one left, and the appeal became quiet. Now the sound of that appeal has risen again, but how much weaker it is.

A moment later I again hear the clop-clop sound of the typewriter. Throughout the day, despite the bombshells, despite hunger and thirst, this man still keeps sitting at the desk with the typewriter and a dim candle. In the afternoon, several young people run to him in search of shelter, and he together with them digs a shelter.

There are thumping sounds of digging up the earth and the sound of airplanes hovering in the sky. Just as the airplanes move farther away, suddenly artillery lobs in.

Each time I hear the sound of a plane flying close by, rifles, submachine guns, and heavy machine guns suddenly fire with bullets and shells streaming upward to the sky. Liberators hide in their foxholes, exchanging stories about how they have downed a lot of planes, but, in fact, I don't hear any noise near the area where I am that would allow one to imagine that a single plane has been shot down.

In the evening, despite the constant gunfire, with large and small guns aiming to shoot down airplanes, despite the sky raining with icy drops, despite bombshells, despite flares, Mr. Minh calls all the young people over to his house to sit and play musical instruments and sing songs. I, notwithstanding my mother entreating and weeping for a long time, still crawl up out from the shelter to join them. Mr. Minh is really very skillful; I don't know when he had time to cook a pot of rice. Eating sticky rice with the salty fish sauce – how delicious it is. I think that never in my life have I had a more delicious meal of rice. Mr. Minh's voice is still confident:

"We will continue to call for peace, continue to appeal to the world. Tomorrow I will write more letters to send. I am organizing a hunger strike to oppose the Americans, oppose the Việt Cộng. Do any of you dare to follow me?"

Everyone sits looking at each other, half wanting to give support because they feel the enthusiasm in his voice, half wanting to burst out laughing because of the comic irony of what he is saying.

As for me, at that moment I want only to live in peace and quiet; at that moment, neither the Nationalist nor Communist side makes any difference whatsoever to me if I don't survive.

The city of Hue is screaming and moaning in the throes of death. The entire city is covered in dust and smoke from bombshells. Meanwhile, the study and training sessions of the liberators, according to what my younger siblings tell me, are something with which no entertainment can be compared, so comic and skillful they are. Study and train to return to the party line and to return to peace at a time when courtyards and gardens are full of voices telling stories about crimes, full of shouts about killing, about being abandoned, about destruction, full of the plaintive screams of innocent residents. Is he a state official? Is he a lackey in an American office? That one disseminated leaflets for the [Nationalist] government. As for this woman, she lives as a domestic servant for a woman married to an American. Heavy crimes heap up to the clouds. They must be killed! A salvo of gunshots and corpses line up with so many sins that the dead themselves cannot understand and cannot close their eyes.[6]

6. According to the author, it is commonly believed in Vietnam that people who die as innocent victims cannot close their eyes.

Seeing us looking at each other, stunned and at a loss, Mr. Minh suddenly says:

"If you, young brats, are not going, I'm going alone. I go to type my petition again."

But then Mr. Minh realizes that he has not played music yet and gets in a hurry to do so. He sings and plays. Being afraid of approaching death is also death. He continues to play music, sing, and recite poems to alleviate fright.

Then he suggests:

"Do any of you have a flute? I will play an old piece that I played on the shore of Lake Léman[7] at the Geneva Conference."

There is no one who dares to grope his way to get a flute for Mr. Minh to play. The entire group is sitting close to the corner of the thickest wall next to the shelter opening so that if something happens, we all will be able to go down very quickly. The rain continues outside; we sit close to each other and still tremble from the cold.

Artillery continues to detonate monotonously. The voice of a young liberation soldier outside asks a question:

"Why don't you crawl down into the shelter rather than play and sing so loudly? If the enemy knows, they will drop bombs here."

Only Mr. Minh dares to respond:

"In the whole city there is no place that is not being bombed. I and these young people want to live our last several minutes joyfully; throw away your rifle, come on in here, and have fun singing."

The liberator outside falls silent. When several students tell stories, this guy sneaks in and lets us know that for several days he has been absorbed in contemplation. Certainly, he has already seen the scenes of spilled blood and scattered body parts that move hearts, hasn't he? Mr. Minh laughs:

"For what do Communists have feelings? They only have the goal to win, to kill, to advance. I've been around them for a long time by now, and I know."

He adds:

"I must admit they are excellent organizers, but when it comes to feelings, there is nothing there."

7. An alternative name for Lake Geneva.

"Then, you are a Nationalist."

"I don't support Americans. I can't stand Communists. I am against any chaos."

"You are alone in your opposition."

In the light of the candle, the face of Mr. Minh is hard and a lot of wrinkles appear on it; he looks toward the dais of Venerable Phan's altar. Gunfire outside suddenly explodes. Are they attacking? Fighting each other? Let them fiercely fight each other and leave us alone: to live or to die. It seems to me that if we continue to sit in the shelter, listening to each other, listening to my mother's stories about dead people outside, it's like we are sitting at a campfire. I also don't need to know whether hiding like this is cowardly or not.

There is a noise at the shelter opening and Mrs. Hảo crawls out; when she sees Mr. Minh, she cries:

"Sir, this night seems to be very frightful."

A voice whispers into my ear:

"Don't you know what our professor [Lê Văn Hảo] is doing right now? I'm positive that he's at a revolutionary meeting making revolution."

Another voice responds: "If this professor arrests you, he obviously doesn't remember what the relationship between a teacher and a student must be."

Mr. Minh coaxes the woman to go down to the shelter. I grope my way to the door and look out at the darkness of the night. The night is heavy and full of secrets, threats of death, the bitter coldness of death. But I also picture myself going out to a corner with a water tank, or to another corner with Chinese tea stalls, or to still another corner with a cluster of sugarcane. Leaves on the trees are dark, and they quiver as though calling me to imagine many things. If only at this moment I could blend with the night sky, could stand in front of the courtyard with my face up to the sky enjoying the pleasant, fresh, sweet raindrops of the beginning of spring. If only I could go for a walk alone in this spacious garden as in the evenings just before this Tết, to walk in the garden with my face up to the black sky imagining the face of my beloved.

There is a noise outside in the garden. I hear people's steps moving around. It's certainly the liberators communicating with each other. The ground in the garden is bare; where have all the twigs and dry leaves gone that used to cover it? Everywhere the ground has long since been dug and hoed to make shelters and foxholes or has been plowed or crushed by shells. The trunk of some tree in front of my eyes is broken: some star-apple tree,[8] or custard-apple tree, or a longan tree.[9] I surmise that there is no garden that has remained intact, and I long for a morning to go out into the garden, to go out of the gate, to see the road and the familiar houses. Mr. Minh says:

"Tomorrow I can't stay in the house anymore. A lot of people have died; I must go to transport wounded, to give first aid. You will go with me."

I don't hear a single response from the young people. There are several young males in this house, and thanks to Mr. Minh's unbending stubbornness they've not yet been apprehended. I think this area is still under Communist control and the lives of residents are very firmly in their hands, but they have yet to show their true colors. My younger sisters says that they [the Communists] bring a lot of people from another hamlet, then pass a verdict and secretly dispose of them, executing them right here. Dead bodies are hastily buried, and there is not a single mat left for wrapping them.

There has come the hour of owls hooting. I am going back to the shelter. Mr. Minh stops speaking, dismisses everybody, and switches off the lamp. Other young students have already returned to their shelters to sleep. There is only Mr. Minh, who can't stand sleeping in a shelter. I cautiously crawl into the shelter, past my mother, past my younger siblings, then past the feet of other people, and only when I get to the place in the shelter where I hide do I feel safe. I am both tired and disheartened, so when I lie down, I immediately fall asleep.

On the morning of the following day, I hear sounds of a conversation at the shelter opening. Everybody has gone outside. I decide to crawl up, but my mother shouts at me: "Hold it!" Trúc crawls in and tells me that artillery fire has not been heard since dawn. Also, the Liberation Army has withdrawn to the cemetery and only some guards from under the bridge up the slope remain.

8. A tropical evergreen tree with milky fruit.

9. An evergreen tree that produces a small juicy fruit with a yellowish-brown exterior.

Mr. Minh says in a very loud voice:

"For sure they went to a meeting or something like that."

A moment later Trúc scoops out a bowl of rice for me and advises me not to come up. On the other side where the school is, they [the Communist forces] had arrested several young males and students. I ask her about a few other young males and students who are there in a shelter; so what about them? Trúc lets me know that they have been scattered around; Mr. Minh took care of everything, preparing for them places to hide. I think about the sounds of musical instruments and of singing in the middle of the day and night. Several liberators who guard outside know that inside of the ancestor-worshipping house hide young people and students. But I don't worry any longer about this because I listen to the sounds of a pig grunting, then people's voices exchanging remarks with each other. The pig is slaughtered. No doubt that for the meal at noon there will be delicious food. Amid all that is going on, to have a big piece of pork is indeed fortunate, such good fare, a delicacy, extremely luxurious and elegant.

I am standing anxiously at the shelter opening:

"Mother, who's making pork like this?"

"Monkey – go inside."

"How can I, Mother – it's pork."

"At Mrs. Tính's house, Mr. Tôn is slaughtering that pig. In a moment, he will give us a tiny bit to cook for a meal."

I shout for joy like a child:

"Mother, listen, don't forget to take a small part with a little fat to cook in fish sauce, Mother."

"Enough, monkey, go inside. Death is around the corner, and you don't care; all you care about is eating and drinking."

Though she is speaking like this, my mother still gropes her way to the neighboring house to get a portion of pork. At noon this day, I lie in the shelter enjoying the pleasant smell of meat being cooked, the subtle aroma of which is about to suppress all other smells. I completely forget all sufferings, all fears. At this pace, certainly soon everything will calm down. Since morning, from time to time, we hear sounds of artillery fire very far away, like in Trúc Lâm, Tây Thiên, or somewhere over there, very far away indeed.

A pot with meat seems to be stewing with salt for a very long time. Waiting makes my entire soul anxious but also makes a part of me happy. Trúc pokes me:

"Elder brother, enjoying this smell of meat? Does it make you dream? I think about the moment when a piece of meat . . . very tasty, isn't it?"

I haven't had time to express my thoughts yet when Oanh sticks her head in:

"Hey, they've come back, and there are lots of them. They are digging more shelters and foxholes, and they've assigned guards to the crossroads and gardens."

Trúc is absorbed in her thoughts:

"In the morning they withdrew."

"They are carrying with them a lot of guns and shells. There are even vehicles transporting additional shells. They've anchored outside our pathway over there."

Then Oanh's trembling voice:

"So frightening, elder brother – when I was sneaking past Mr. Tôn's house to see how they would divide the pork for Mother, I saw a dog carrying in its teeth a piece of leg or arm of a child; it gnawed on raw flesh. Having seen this, I am awfully afraid of pork."

Trúc shouts:

"It's so frightful."

Then she curls up:

"So, elder sister, you managed to get to Mr. Tôn's house."

"No, not at all. I was too afraid and dashed right back. Hearing a noise, the liberation soldier guarding outside ran in with a gun at the ready. I was afraid and screamed. He saw the dog lying and gnawing on the bone, gave it a scathing look, then laughed, baring his teeth, and asked whether or not I wanted to cross to the other side; he said 'I can clean up the road for you.' I was too afraid and fell silent. He said: 'Don't be afraid, young lady, surely this dog carried that in its teeth from somewhere else over to here.' Then he took a stone and hurled it at the dog. The dog ran away with its tail between its legs, but that piece of flesh is still on the same dusty spot. It is extremely frightening!"

"Did he say anything else to you, elder sister?"

"He looked at me. I felt at once afraid and weird. Weird and sick, and so sad. Then he said: 'Are you afraid of me?' I had to say: 'Please sir, I don't know of what, but I'm afraid.' Not knowing what to do, he was silent. Then he sneaked out of the door. I rushed into the house. Just a minute ago, Mother made me slice the pork for cooking it; I almost threw up several times."

Saying this, Oanh lifts her hand to cover her mouth as if she is about to puke. The smell of the meat cooking is still floating around and entering my nose, enormously attractive. Oanh's story does not make me feel disgusted or scare me for a second. For a long time I have gone without eating my fill; there have been days when I was plain starving.

Oanh holds my hand and says:

"Elder brother, listen, they are digging underground shelters there."

I hear sounds of digging in the ground, sounds of people's feet going back and forth. An old woman, Khái, who joined us in the shelter, says: "Close all doors and gates." I think to myself, we can tightly close doors and can hide people, but what about the smell of the meat cooking? Won't the liberators come in to visit because of the strong smell of the cooking meat? I also don't hear Mr. Minh's voice anymore. My younger sisters let me know that, carrying a sack of rice, he climbed on his bicycle and left in the morning. They say he went to distribute the rice. In a moment, a voice comes in from the outside:

"Liberation Mothers, please turn off your cooking; we are afraid that the smoke will let airplanes identify where to shoot at."

My mother is also now called a Liberation Mother. Cooking is turned off immediately, but the smell of the cooking meat, where would it go? I imagine a lot of people whose mouths are watering now. I stick my head out:

"Mother, is the meat ready yet?"

"What a monkey you are. Go back in there. Let it soak a bit first. Where is Trúc? Go get the pot with cold rice and warm it so we can eat."

Just when Trúc has intended to get up, someone is shouting loudly outside:

"Everyone go down to the shelter; airplanes are coming."

Even as this shout is heard, I see that the sky is still absolutely calm, but then at once the sounds of airplanes stream in and in a moment the airplanes are over our heads making circles. Then a few moments later rockets shoot down, falling like rain. Everyone rushes into the shelter. An ink-black dog with glaringly aggressive green eyes wants to sneak into the shelter. Only when the old woman Khái takes up a knife and shouts as loud as a gong does the dog run off to some other place.

Rockets fall in torrents, and it seems that bullets are pouring over our heads. We tightly hug each other; one person squeezes against another as though in search of a bit of additional support. There are sounds of collapsing in front and behind; there are sounds of moaning and crying in the neighboring houses and shouts of liberators, all shrieking as though their throats are being slit. Just a short time before, a pig being slaughtered also shrieked pitifully like that, and I feel insensitive to this shrieking now.

Boom. A lot of tiles break into pieces, then comes the sound of debris falling with a cascading noise. Several liberators shout and call to each other outside in the garden. I am certain they have a lot of wounded. A moment later there is the sound of fierce responding gunfire from the ground. The pouring of shells down from the sky intensifies. I feel that I am fainting, my ears buzz, my chest feels like it's hard to breathe, and I continue to lie, prostrated, absolutely flat in the corner of the shelter, not being able anymore to lift my arms or legs.

About two minutes later, the sound of shooting in the sky gradually subsides and the airplanes also disappear; only sounds of gunfire from the ground pop up sporadically and monotonously for another several minutes until an order is handed down: "Stop!" The word "stop" rolls from the corners of one garden to the corners of another garden, echoing on the surface of the ground, and gradually the sounds of gunfire die out, converging into several sparse sounds before stopping completely. My mother says that no one is allowed to peek out from the shelter opening. There is the sound of a punch on the door:

"Anyone who is inside, come out to help with the work."

I am sure they will force the people to carry dead bodies and wounded. My mother gives a sign to everyone to be silent. But it doesn't work; the panels of the door are knocked wide-open with the stock of a rifle; I hear a lot of stomping feet entering the house:

"Everybody get out of the shelter."

My mother climbs up first, then go old women and women tightly hugging their children. Trúc remains with me; as for Oanh, she can't help but to slide up. An old woman hands her a little toddler who just turned a year old; his mother had died on the day when the first sounds of guns exploded. Oanh tightly bundles the child into a cotton cloth and, trembling uncontrollably, climbs up through the entrance of the shelter. I hear a male voice asking:

"Who here doesn't have small children?"

It seems that several women must go. The voice of the young liberator who is still standing guard outside in the lane:

"This young woman has just given birth; she's still weak."

So, it's release. What a close shave for Oanh. A moment later I see her carrying the little toddler down; her arms and legs are still shaking like a leaf. I take the child from Oanh and secretly rejoice that the little toddler is well behaved and doesn't cry. Unexpectedly for me, the toddler wants milk; it is hungry and exhausted but doesn't have any strength to cry anymore. Because of that, night after night, I often hear the crying of a child, soft and feeble, like the mewing of a kitten.

I ask Oanh:

"Did they arrest anyone?"

My voice is very low, but Oanh raises her hand to give me a sign to keep quiet. The sounds of feet move outside of the house. Right at this moment, I hear the sounds of a bicycle stopping in the courtyard, then Mr. Minh's voice gradually approaches:

"How are things? Is anyone hurt? I am very worried."

I hear Professor Hảo's wife sobbing. My mother's voice relates what happened in the house. Mr. Minh's voice is still animated:

"Look, everyone go down in the shelter; airplanes are coming. Everything has been completely destroyed by now. It's sure that the army on this side of the river is lining up troops in battle array to enter the city."

I strain my ears to listen. Mr. Minh's voice drops down a little:

"Horrifying. When I was going from the road down there to come up here, I ran into so many dead bodies. They are all Việt Cộng. Dead in foxholes, dead next to the walls, dead lying prone on the roads. I came in here from the lane and saw everything covered in blood. I appealed to Heaven: 'Help. Please, Heaven put an end to this. Is anything left of the house?' When I entered the house, I saw them going on the road behind the garden. So, at least no one has been wounded here."

I stick my head up and ask:

"Sir, what's happening outside?"

"I ran into a group of their commanders."

Mr. Minh laughs and pulls out a piece of paper:

"They called me to follow them: how disgusting is that? But I told them I am against any chaos. I am afraid of neither side. My goal at this time is to give first aid to the wounded, to distribute rice, to save anyone who can be saved. That commander of this area, he appeared to be very wise and kind. He issued me a pass to go through the areas they control at any time. Here . . ."

Mr. Minh stretches his hand with the paper toward me. But my mother has scolded me:

"Hey, you go down and sit there, will you? Oh Mr. Minh, enough already; nothing is so good in that devilish piece of paper to show it off like that. Having that will make more trouble."

Mr. Minh laughs good-naturedly:

"I've already said I'm an international personality. Communism does not do anything to me – do you understand that?"

I am very curious to read that paper, but my mother has been throwing hostile glances at me. Afraid to make her sad, I hastily slip down into the shelter. Oanh raises her head:

"Sir, how do you transport the wounded?"

"I put them on the bicycle and push. The hospital has already been abandoned. I brought a lot of them into the various first-aid stations to get them bandaged. Ah, look Oanh, find for me several medical students, will you? There are some who are hiding around here. Will you serve as liaison for me?"

"Even an experienced person would not dare to do that – go outside to be shot dead?"

"You, child, are very chicken-hearted; forget it, I will take care of this myself."

My mother suddenly shouts, and her voice is panic-stricken:

"It's ruined . . ."

"What now?"

"It's ruined, damn it . . ."

Panic in Oanh's voice:

"What, Mother?"

"The pot with the meat cooking . . ."

I can't hold myself back, and, fighting with Oanh, I stick my head out from the shelter opening:

"What's this, Mother?"

"It's shattered; nothing's left . . ."

I look at the oil stove – directly above it from the ceiling a piece of the tile had fallen down and broke the earthenware pot containing the meat; pieces of meat mixed with bricks and debris are scattered around in a dirty mess. Being tensed up for a while with all the whirlwind of events, I had completely forgotten about the pot of meat cooking. And now it's all ruined. Seeing our sad dismay, Mr. Minh laughs:

"Oh, why feel sorry about this tiny bit of food? I have picked up and brought back several turnips here. I climbed up to the fields in the mountains, which was not much fun."

"Sir, you climbed up there. Oh heavens, what's up there?"

"Well, everybody must stay put in the houses. Listen, they [the Communist forces] confine people to their houses. There are several abandoned houses down the slope, and there I saw rows of turnips, very delicious. I picked up a lot of them; I have finished distributing them, and you can help yourself to what is left."

Oanh bubbles:

"So beautiful. The turnips are so beautiful."

I haven't seen such beautiful turnips. The pot of meat is broken, but the aroma of the meat still wafts around. I swallow my saliva and sadly slip down. Oanh asks me:

"Elder brother, you are sad because of the pot of meat, aren't you?"

"Yes."

"As for me, now I want only peace and quiet. For several days they said that they would stay for only one week to visit with the people; then why are they here for so long?"

"Who knows anything about that? You are such a gullible little child."

Oanh continues:

"During the first few days several young female cadres practiced riding a motorbike; it was a lot of fun. But they didn't know anything, elder brother; their comrades-in-arms from their detachment were dying violently, but they still romped so joyfully as though nothing was happening. During the first few days, the young women who talked with me said that they would organize cultural activities, festivals – and what have they organized in the end?"

"They [the Nationalists and Communists] shower bullets on each other like rain; what festivals can there be?"

"And they [the Communists] execute people, and it is so disgusting, elder brother. I saw them shooting two high school or college students or some people like that in the garden of Uncle Bốn over there. Let me tell you. It's exactly the same group that is in our garden that shot them. I heard a tiny little fellow outside the gate, the one who looks at me; he said that only trials can issue verdicts and only people's courts can condemn people but that they could not secretly dispose of people. Some of the others said that their comrades lacked fighting spirit. Then they fired. Oh heavens, I closed my eyes."

Oanh talks and talks, and I still feel sorry about the pot of meat. After about a week of food deprivation – of meals insufficient to sustain life and intermittently meals that filled our stomachs – it seems that my stomach has shrunk. I am lying prostrate on a mat with foam at the corners of my mouth. A bout of hunger suddenly pulls up to torture me, putting me through a lot of suffering. Girls are really good at going hungry: Oanh and Trúc – have a meal, don't have a meal – they still perk up like black-necked starlings. As for myself, soon I will be dead to the world.

In the afternoon, when I wake up, I see that the place around me is deserted. Has everybody abandoned me to evacuate to a different place? In panic, I lift my hand to feel around; only after what must be a very long time, I see a bit of light splashing in from the shelter opening, and gradually I clearly see my hand. But I don't dare to raise my voice to call or to crawl out of the shelter opening and instead remain calm and listen intently. It seems that up in the house there are sounds of bowls and chopsticks striking against each other, but there is no sound of the people. There are no noises outside, either in the garden or in the courtyard. I try and try to focus my hearing, and only then I distinctly recognize clattering sounds of chopsticks and bowls; clearly the entire house is eating up there above the shelter. Why didn't anyone wake me up? Why did everybody leave me in this grievous state with the pangs of hunger and exhaustion? No, I must crawl up to let everybody know that I also have a right to participate in the family meal. I am tired and exhausted but try to force myself to crawl up to the shelter opening. The clattering sounds of the chopsticks and bowls and the sounds of chewing and swallowing prove that there are people up there eating and drinking in an extremely rowdy manner. Obviously everything outside has calmed down by now and everyone is happy with a meal that will result in overindulgence. I try to hang on fast to the two edges of the earth-made wall and poke my head outside.

Am I dreaming? Am I still alive or dead of hunger? No, I am not a hungry ghost. I am still alive and well. How come there are faces of strangers around the food tray? I open wide my eyes to look around, and then I fall down, hitting the bottom of the shelter. The noise I make utterly terrifies me. They have already heard – they will come down and pull me out by my neck and a round of fire will explode. My hunger pangs have completely disappeared. On the tray with food stand cups and bowls belonging to my family, but my entire family and the other people who took shelter in the ancestor-worshipping house are sitting in the corner of the house, sad-looking, worried, and scared. Five or six liberators are sitting and eating delicious food without a single word being exchanged among them; they eat in a hurry like people who are about to die of starvation and are able to snatch a meal. I lie in silence for a moment, and when I see that nothing happens, my soul returns to me. But just at that moment the sounds of airplanes stream in, then artillery fire. I hear the liberators' steps running from the house: "Thank you, Liberation Mother." A man's voice resounds inside, then drowns in the sounds of shells and rockets that begin to shoot down. Everybody rushes into the shelter. Some fall, rolling and turning; some pile up with faces, arms, and legs all in a jumble. I dive tightly into the corner of the shelter. Trúc pushes over by me:

"Where are you, elder brother?"

I respond in a weak voice. Oanh slips me a handful of rice:

"When I served rice to them, I scooped a handful and hid it in my shirt for you, elder brother, here."

I no longer have the strength to stretch out my arm to hold anything. Trúc makes small balls of rice and puts them one by one into my mouth; I hastily chew and swallow as saliva fills my mouth. Why is it that at this moment, a small handful of rice is more precious to me than all the luxurious and exquisite meals of my life? My mother mumbles:

"We were in the process of arranging the food and were about to go down to wake you up to come to eat when they entered. It was luck that you had not yet come up. So, since they were already inside, we had to invite them, and they started to eat at once."

Oanh says softly:

"When they finished eating, they thanked us profusely: Liberation Mother is 'good'; Liberation Elder Sister is 'good'; all those 'goods' over and over again – if it continues like this, we are certainly in real trouble."

But Trúc intercedes for them:

"So, everywhere there are good people and bad people. Didn't the young liberator give us ten measures of rice? But from where did he get them?"

No one contradicts Trúc. Rockets are hurled as if right at our heads. My mother assumes:

"They are shooting here, so surely shells also pour down on Bến Ngự."

"I'm certain it's down at the market."

"Down at the railroad."

"Hush, what's the use of arguing; now they are coming to Từ Đàm."

"The area under the bridge, they still keep it closed. At noon I saw several families fleeing, being chased by them; those families ran and cried. I hear that our hamlet has a lot of wounded."

"Where did Mr. Minh go?"

"He went again to distribute rice and transport wounded."

"That gentleman has really gone mad; in times like these, everyone takes care of themselves."

I lie silently and hear how blood pulses in each of my small veins. My eyes no longer deceive me; my arms and legs no longer shake. My fear of rockets lessens, but at the same time I also understand that death by artillery or death by starvation or death by thirst are all equally horrific. But the liberators have borrowed and carried away all the rice in the house. If this situation lasts several more weeks, certainly we will all die of starvation. My mother complains in a whisper to her female friend:

"Mr. Minh, even in times like these, still brings back on his shoulders several wounded young men. To have him in the house is awfully troublesome."

My mother is no doubt afraid and worried for me. I get extremely angry at my mother each time I hear her complaining like this, but now at this moment I see that she has a point. Oanh whispers:

"Mr. Minh brought several young men back to dress their wounds and provide first aid."

I grumble:

"You'll see, they [the Communist forces] will arrest and kill everybody who helps Mr. Minh."

Oanh is confident:

"Mr. Minh has a pass to travel to and from the front. So, don't worry about him."

Right at this moment there is a knock on the door. We don't know who knocks, but everyone's heart seems to stop beating. I hear rockets outside, still loud like rain. The sound of firing from the ground also resounds with a cascading noise. This side: rattle, rattle; that side: pow, pow. Guns of all calibers point at the sky. The knocking on the door becomes more and more urgent, and then, on top of it, there is the sound of screaming, but we can't recognize whose voice it is. Oanh is extremely anxious:

"Perhaps Mr. Minh's back."

"Hush. Don't speak. Whoever this is, let him be. Be silent, for heaven's sake."

The knocking on the door continues, then the noise of something pounding on the door with a bang. Trúc is resolute:

"It's Mr. Minh come back, for sure."

Not adding another word, Trúc springs out from the shelter. My mother tries to stop Oanh but in vain. My mother can only appeal to Heaven and Earth. There is the sound of the door opening, then sounds of the feet of two or three people coming in, then the sound of Trúc screaming. I, panic-stricken, grab my mother's shoulder:

"That's the end."

My mother breaks free and runs out of the shelter, having forgotten all dangers. But at the same time I hear Mr. Minh's voice:

"Quickly, bring the medicine; bring bandages here."

Trúc's voice:

"There are no bandages. Shall we ask the medical students for help?"

"Hurry up."

More people get out of the shelter. I also timidly stick my head out of the opening to see. In the dim light splashing inside from the dreary sky, I see two men covered in blood. One person's eyes are still open but listless; the other person's eyes are shut as though he has passed away. A part of his head is of a pale white color as though his brain is exposed.

I ask Trúc:

"Who's this?"

Trúc shakes her head. Her face has turned pale. But then she helps everybody to bandage the two wounded. The blood flows and stagnates in a puddle in the middle of the house. Trúc, covering her face, shreds a white sleeve of her shirt to make bandages. Outside in the garden there are a lot of loud screaming sounds. I'm certain someone is wounded again.

Mr. Minh beckons to me:

"Come up here; they are busy fighting each other. They will not come in to arrest you; don't be afraid."

I climb up and stand next to the two wounded men. The sound of rockets gradually abates, and the sound of shells being shot from the ground also becomes more sporadic – but airplanes still circle in the sky. Then a group of neighbors rush into the house; they scream and cry:

"My house has burned down – oh my wife and children."

"My child died, but I could not carry his body along with me."

"Oh, Mr. Minh, go and bring back my little child with you. He's stuck in a heap of bricks."

The crowd shouts and cries like this. My mother inquires about the news from outside. Mr. Minh entrusts to us the two wounded people and dashes out the door. I have managed only to shout one word:

"Sir . . ."

A salvo of gunshots resounds right at the gate. Enough – surely Mr. Minh has been wounded. Oanh pushes the door open: "Mr. Minh, oh sir!" She's about to run out, but my mother manages to hold her back. We hear Mr. Minh's voice haranguing someone at the end of the alley. Oanh at once turns and comes back, and there is the sound of the door being pushed open wide. The young liberation soldier who was guarding in front of the house's gate comes in. He clasps his arm. My mother quickly pushes me down into the shelter before he can see me.

"What's this, sir?"

"I'm wounded. Liberation Mother, please give me a bit of bandage to dress the wound."

Oanh is prompt:

"No more bandages. These several days, clothes have been shredded to make bandages, and still there's not enough."

"Please help look for me; perhaps there is a bit of some medicine?"

Oanh is angry and resentful:

"So, where are the comrades to provide first aid? Where are female cadres to provide first aid to the wounded? These several days we've been waiting for them to come and to ask them for medicine, and I haven't seen any of them."

I don't see the face of the liberator, but I know that he is moved or in much pain because his voice trembles:

"I am lightly wounded; there are some others who are wounded more seriously than I."

Right at this moment I hear Mr. Minh's voice. He enters and must be carrying a small child in his arms – I hear the child crying.

"Oanh, Trúc, take clothes and make bandages; hurry up."

The sound of Oanh's feet running away – Mr. Minh says:

"Wow, comrade, you've been wounded, too, eh? Why did you come here?"

"Please, Mr. Minh, give me some medicine; please give me a piece of cloth for a bandage."

"Is your wound light or serious?"

"No, it's just light."

"You'll get over it; take lime and apply it as an antiseptic. We don't have medicine, but if only a tiny bit of medicine had remained, it would have been used to save people who are in critical condition. A lime pot is in the corner, over there."

Mr. Minh's voice again:

"There is a comrade of yours in the corner. I have bandaged him up; when you don't hear shooting anymore, take him back for the headquarters to take care of him. He is in serious condition."

Then, having sent off two people, Mr. Minh immediately brings on his shoulders another person – a Việt Cộng. Mr. Minh doesn't distinguish at all who people are – he simply saves the wounded. I hear the voice of the young soldier trying to stay calm, but his voice hides a lot of emotion:

"Thank you, venerable sir. Uncle Hồ and the party will remember and thank you, venerable sir."

"Me, eh? I don't need the party. I don't need the uncle [Hồ Chí Minh]. I only know this is a person, and he's hurt, so I help. Damn it, they shoot at each other, kill each other, but only the people really suffer."

The liberation soldier is timid:

"In this area there are many different kinds of [Communist] cadres, venerable sir; don't go outside much – if they misunderstand you, it will be terrible."

Mr. Minh gives several muffled laughs:

"Me, eh? I'm an international personality, yes! Mr. Hồ [Chí Minh] must also take me into consideration, and Mr. President of America must take me into consideration too, because I'm right."

He continues to chuckle. I don't hear what else the soldier tells Mr. Minh.

Trúc crawls down next to me:

"They're done with shooting at each other, elder brother."

"Yeah."

"The dead are everywhere, even in our alley. Are you afraid, elder brother?"

"I don't see anything to be afraid of."

"It's obvious: we have to evacuate. Here, no matter what, it's death."

I don't say a word but intently listen to the noise above the shelter opening. Several wounded people are groaning. A man's voice, unfamiliar and feeble:

"Comrade, what group are you in?"

"Group 49."

"Bring me back to the headquarters, can you? I want to meet someone I know to send a message to the North."

"Comrade, give it to me; I will send it for you."

The man's voice is weaker:

"No, I am not dead yet. I can't die yet. Take me back . . . I want . . ."

His words are cut short. Outside the door there are sounds of many feet, then sounds of people bursting into an uproar: "Transport the wounded." Then Mr. Minh's voice:

"There are several wounded here; can I send them with you?"

"No, we only transport wounded from the Liberation Army."

The sound of artillery rises again. But the work of transporting the wounded still continues. Young males and females are forced to go to work. Luckily, for whatever reason, Oanh and Trúc still manage to evade it. Mr. Minh decides not to go; the pass authorized by the Liberation Army certainly empowered him. In a moment they [the soldiers of the Liberation Army transporting the wounded] completely pull out, and Mr. Minh orders all the newly arrived refugees to find a place to build shelters. If there are no more places to dig underground, they will have to build surface shelters. The panels of the doors are dismantled for reinforcing shelters.

We also decide to repair and tidy up our shelter. Despite the sounds of airplanes, despite the artillery, children and adults go to the courtyard to dig up earth and carry it to dump on top of the shelter; the thicker the better. A few wounded people die of their wounds; their bodies are taken to the courtyard to be buried. But as soon as people go out to dig graves the airplanes come, and seeing shadows on the ground, they fire rockets and everybody flees helter-skelter. Several liberators in foxholes curse loudly and immediately fire several salvoes over the heads of the crowd running in confusion. No one thinks of burying the dead anymore and no one has enough strength to be afraid to live next to the smelly corpses, though perhaps we can die from the miasma.

The young liberation soldier has gotten his arm bandaged. He still stands guard in front of the gate. He seldom enters the house, and when he does his face looks grave. I have a feeling that it is only because of him that Oanh and Trúc are exempt from transporting the wounded and carrying ammunition.

Just as Oanh predicts, for several days thereafter not a single day goes by without airplanes coming and rockets falling down like rain. Each day there is more and more artillery fire. At first, for several days in the mornings everybody still climbs up from the shelter to get something or to run out to bring water. But now no one dares to go out to the courtyard; crawling up to the shelter opening has become the most courageous thing one can do. If this situation continues for several more days, we will run out of water and food. Such a pity for my mother – usually when anything happens she is out of her wits and overwhelmed, but when there comes a moment of true despair she suddenly is more courageous than anyone else. Despite bombs, despite shells, my mother keeps climbing out of the shelter to search for rice and to fix meals. A lot of fragments of artillery shells strike the walls; a lot of fragments of bombs fall down on the roofs and slide quickly through the holes into the houses. My mother, trembling, shuffles her feet down into the shelter. But then she crawls out again. My mother is only able to live minute-by-minute in order to do her utmost for her children.

Throughout these days Mr. Minh comes and goes; from time to time he drops by with a little bit of dry food, dividing it among everybody in the shelter. Besides continuing to help everybody outside, he also does not neglect the people who settled in this house of worship for Venerable Phan.

Many nights, we discuss the topic of evacuation. My mother moves close to the family of a school principal.[10] He, on the first day, dared to rashly transport two small children and a young woman, his younger sister, from An Cựu back to Từ Đàm. His wife was stranded here. During the day he also slips into the shelter and doesn't dare go outside, afraid of being arrested. During the first several days some female cadres often entered the house, gradually making contacts and inquiries and talking with his wife. Half of this family is still stranded in An Cựu, and the younger sister dared to go with Mr. Minh to reconnoiter the road leading there but didn't manage to slip through. My mother discusses with that family whether or not there is a way to evacuate from here. But they, like us, are also in despair. The wife hugs a small child and weeps softly for a long time. The husband has stopped worrying about his own fate and instead now worries for his mother and a number of relatives who are left

10. Mr. Lễ, the elder brother of the author.

stranded in An Cựu. When Mr. Minh comes back every day, each piece of news he brings is more pessimistic than before.

Many nights I have been lying and dreaming that I am among a group of evacuees. In our search for life we walk in long files and hold tightly to each other. We are crossing a bridge. Dead bodies are bloating and stinky. On the other side of the river is the Army of the Republic of Vietnam; on this side is the Liberation Army. No one at all hampers our progress. We walk amid the artillery, amid sounds of screaming and shrieking, and then the bridge collapses and the entire file of people, one after another, falls down into the current of the river. But we still cannot escape. At the bottom of the river there are many bloody-red mouths of water monsters, wide open, ready to swallow the entire file of people into their stomachs. I, panic-stricken, scream, then wake up. Despite the weather outside being bitingly cold, my whole body is dripping with sweat as though I had bathed. Like a child, I often put my finger into my mouth and suck on it. I suck nonstop in the darkness. I feel my bland finger gradually getting tasty. I know this taste, sweat mixed with dirty soil.

A day goes by and then another. Our ears start buzzing because of the gunfire, our eyes grow weak from hunger, and our minds are paralyzed because of the sounds of explosions reverberating deafeningly all around. But strangely, none of us has died yet. We run out of rice, and Mr. Minh manages to bring back from somewhere several baskets of dried-out cooked rice, and he divides it among all of us – each family a tiny bit. We chew dried rice but also must do our best to be parsimonious. Being so very thirsty, some people recklessly go out to the courtyard to get water at the water tank. They run but don't make it to the water tank when shell fragments pin them down, but fortunately no one dies.

None of us return to the issue of evacuation any more. Getting out from the shelter opening by this time can mean death, even more so if one goes out to the courtyard or to the road.

But then there is a morning – I lost count of the days and I don't know what day it is – when a voice calls my name from outside. My mother at once pushes down hard on my head, gagging me, and doesn't let me answer. But then Oanh recognizes the voice of Bảo, my first cousin, a son of my uncle. Oanh goes out and pulls Bảo down into the shelter. Bảo says:

"Why aren't you fleeing? They've already left."

"Why are you brave like this? Artillery lobs like rain; how's it possible to flee from here?"

"I will take the risk to keep moving. Now, are you escaping with me or not?"

"How to escape?"

"Here they will arrest you. Come with me."

"To go where?"

"We will go to a garden they don't know about. Then we'll go toward the pagoda and then circumvent past Đua-Ra Mansion.[11] We will go down there. Surely it's possible to make it – how not?"

My mother trembles:

"Impossible. Don't take risks."

But suddenly an idea flashes up in my mind. To stay here means to die anyway. To take a risk like this, with some luck, there is still a chance to survive. I tell Bảo in a low voice:

"I'm going; wait for me."

Only after I comfort my mother for about half an hour can she bear to let me go. But when I get up to the shelter opening with Bảo, I hear my mother crying heartbreakingly as though in a burial procession. My entire body shivers with fear. It's light outside, but I have an impression that the shadow of death is also loitering around here, conniving with the sounds of explosions, with rounds of shells shot here, there, and everywhere. My mother's crying makes my knees about to cave in. I want to rush back inside the shelter and collapse next to her so that if death comes we will die together and if we survive we will survive together. But Bảo has pulled me out by my hand. The door is wide open, and we worm our way outside. The daylight astonishes my eyes. I stand mesmerized near the water tank; almost all the branches of the peach trees have been broken. Certainly an artillery shell has fallen somewhere here, but golden petals are still intact and lie amid the broken branches and the bricks and tiles; the golden peach flowers are like specks of hope filling my heart with a feeling of strong passion and fondness for life.

11. An ancient mansion in Hue.

"Be careful."

Bang – an explosion really close. Bảo pulls me to lie down. Then suddenly Bảo pulls me up and I am running, either following him or being dragged by him, all the same. When we turn our heads, the T-junction near the pagoda and the ancestor-worshipping house of Venerable Phan are already out of sight. Tears stream from my eyes. Several drops of the biting cold, drizzling rain stick fast to my face. Bảo, sighing, keeps dragging me:

"Hurry up."

"What direction?"

"Đua-Ra Mansion."

I don't have time but still I admire plants, houses, and roads. Artillery shelling here becomes denser and denser. The sounds of explosions roar in front, behind, on all sides. We keep running a bit further, then we both duck down, get up, and continue running. I don't know what my face looks like, but I can't recognize Bảo's face anymore. Our clothes are covered with earth and sand; thorny bushes scratch us and tear our clothes into long strips. I am running and shouting:

"To keep going means death. Certain death."

Đua-Ra Mansion has appeared. We recklessly run toward it; I stumble over many dead bodies and many times I almost plunge headlong. We still have to run several tens of meters to make it to the mansion when we are suddenly surrounded by sounds of artillery and small arms. The two sides open fire. We try time and again, and finally we manage to get into Đua-Ra Mansion. Our ankles and feet are thickly covered with blood. The house is full of corpses: fresh corpses, old corpses, corpses of the Nationalists, corpses of the Việt Cộng. Right in front of the house I see the corpses of two Americans so bloated that they look like cows. It is strange that the two American corpses are clad in black uniforms like cadres of the Rural Development. But I don't have time to think more about it before Bảo has dragged me straight inside. Just at that moment, guns start firing in our direction. Bảo falls headlong into a corner; his entire body is covered with blood – fresh blood and dried blood. I also roll once and lie behind several bloated and smelly corpses. I tightly cover my eyes with my hand; bullets are flying over my head. The two sides engage in a really atrocious fight for a while, and then sudden silence comes. There is the sound of a lot of feet entering Đua-Ra Mansion. I hear a voice saying:

"I saw two guys running in here."

"Comrade, did you see them clearly?"

"Absolutely positive. Two guys still very young. Messengers for Americans and their puppets, for sure. They entered right when the guns opened fire."

My heart seems to stop beating. I lie pressing my face into a puddle of dried blood full of flies. Let it be; I need this mass of dead bodies to give me cover. Sounds of feet stepping over several corpses, then muffled laughter:

"Damn it, just greenhorns and they have already turned into traitors to their country."

The sound of gunfire: I hear Bảo screaming.

My shoulders suddenly are also in stinging pain. I still hear a round of bullets sweeping past me before I pass out.

"Where are you going now, sir?"

"I myself don't know anything beyond that. I ran with all my strength."

As soon as the boy tells us the above story, he looks out to the railroad. I keep asking:

"Did you get any news from Từ Đàm, elder brother?"

"I was wounded at Đua-Ra Mansion and thought they would arrest me. Fortunately, I passed out and they thought I was dead. When I came back to my senses, they had arrested Bảo and taken him away. Dead bodies were lying everywhere in utter disorder, but over the door there hung a liberation flag. I had to try and try before I could move away from under the dead bodies. I looked out – silence everywhere; there was no one on the Nationalist side, but on the Communist side there was no one either. I scrabbled my way to Phú Cam. Houses are abandoned; all the residents have fled – I met only dead people. I followed the railway, and this is how I got here."

I thought that meeting this boy who came from Từ Đàm would give us news about my elder brother's family up there, but he's completely unaware of them.

I advise:

"Now you need to find a hamlet where there are still people left and stay with them. We will also flee soon."

"I will certainly go over to the church. I heard rumors there are a lot of refugees there."

"My opinion is: don't go over there; they've searched there and arrested everybody."

My mother asks Lê:

"What about Mr. Minh?"

"Please madam, I don't know anything more."

We follow the boy with our eyes as he goes back toward the railroad. That entire section of the road is completely deserted – there are no shadows, not even of any animals. He goes farther and farther and does not turn back. I am panic-stricken when I hear sounds of gunfire near that area. I shout, but the boy has already gone down a short slope and disappeared behind thick bushes.

My mother gives out a heavy sigh:

"Here is certain death. We must flee; everyone from the hamlet has already left."

My uncle elbows his way in:

"They fled toward the area down by Phù Lương; there are rumors that it's very quiet down there."

"What direction is Phù Lương?"

No one has time to respond to him when sounds of gunfire approach. We hear vehicles moving with a lot of noise on the National Highway.

Thái shouts for joy:

"Our [Nationalist] army has advanced and entered the city and now is coming into this area."

Bé provides clarification:

"By day only – at night they [the Nationalist forces] withdraw to Phú Bài.[12] By night they [the Communist forces] come back and take over again, so it doesn't mean anything."

My mother beckons with her hand:

12. The area where Hue airport is located.

"So, go into the shelter first, then if there is something to plan, we can plan there."

A moment later we see a person [Mr. Địch, the head of the neighbor family] run into the house carrying on his shoulder a pole with two baskets. Thú Hồng crawls up from the shelter and shouts to him:

"Uncle Địch, you could not get through, huh?"

Mr. Địch responds: "I tried to go to Kiểu Mẫu School,[13] but there's no way to get through on the roads. They are firing at each other with such ferocity."

"Where did you plan to go, uncle?

"To Phù Lương."

Soon we settle his family to sit in a corner of the house, and Mr. Địch also slips into the shelter to tell us what happened. He says that they [the Communists] have completely occupied the Citadel. Some people were able to escape and come back to this side by boat, but out of those who took the risk to flee the disaster, over two-thirds died; if ten people went, with luck only one or two survived. He lets us know that the two sides are still fighting each other in the area of the post office. My mother is panic-stricken:

"If they fight near the post office, then they will soon fight here. What to do now, huh? Oh heavens."

So, we wait for the sound of gunfire to subside, then our entire family crawls up through the shelter opening and, supporting each other, we flee from the fighting. We had returned to my uncle's house several days ago, and the distance from my uncle's house to our house, which is in the same An Cựu area, is only several hundred meters, but we have not dared to cross this distance to get back to our house. After several days of constantly being in the dark shelter, Thái assigns everybody to take care of some task. We take a bit of rice and a bit of fish sauce from my uncle's house; Thái organizes it all. My mother still clutches the bundle of clothes, half of which belonged to my father; when he died, these clothes were not used to prepare his body for the funeral. I keep a small bag with some things. Bé's wife carries on her shoulder a pole with two hangers

13. A secondary school founded in 1964 and associated with the Pedagogical Institute.

and baskets filled with pots and pans, bowls and dishes, and cooked and uncooked rice that we took from our uncle's house. Everybody has their arms and legs busy, and the children are told to hold fast to the adults' clothes and run.

We run down in the direction of Mù U. At first everyone runs very fast because we hear the sounds of shells behind us and of airplanes entering the city. But when we have managed to get some distance away from the noise and panic, my legs can no longer hold me up. My mother plops on the road.

A youngster from down below drives a Honda motorcycle up here quickly. Thái waves to him:

"Where are you going, elder brother?"

"There is a rumor that up here there are a lot of compatriot evacuees – I've come up to see whether there is anyone who needs help with anything."

Thái is very jovial:

"We need help. Is it quiet down there?"

"Quiet indeed. Down there they [the Communist forces] only flood in by night. By day we just take care of our own business."

Thái is pleased:

"So, friend, please give my aunt a ride. Let her off at Thủy Dương market; we are going down there now."

My mother hastily climbs up onto the back seat of the motorbike.

"Hold fast to him, auntie."

The youth starts off as though he's flying; I only catch a fleeting sight of my mother, and then she has disappeared in the distance. I reluctantly get up and continue to follow Thái. Along the road I see countless groups of evacuees.

They move supporting each other with carrying poles on their shoulders, walking and running and turning their heads to look back. The city is filled with sounds of explosions, big and small.

A woman walks and cries: "Only I have managed to escape; I could flee over here, but my husband and children, are they alive or dead, what's happened to them, oh heavens? What's happened, Heavenly Father?" The woman looks back at the city, then looks up to Heaven. Heaven is still the color of lead, ready to flow with water but without the strength for that. An oxcart lags behind a throng of about ten or so people. Two women pull and push the oxcart; in the cart two people lie covered with an old mat.

I see four legs dangling down from under the mat; all four are completely smeared with blood. The cart cannot move faster because the two women are at the point of exhaustion. A man carries a small child on his shoulder. The child has been wounded and is bleeding, having lost almost all his blood, and his face, turned deathly pale, hangs down on the man's shoulder; the light in his open eyes is torpid, and he follows with his eyes the groups of people running behind as though to keep a visual connection with life. Drops of blood fall and splatter on the surface of the road, and other feet rushing by blur them or wipe them out. I think about the group of people who with white flags in their hands walked through the city submerged in bullets and fire, a group of people from Phú Cam that came down with several Catholic priests and Buddhist monks: those who were unharmed helped those who were wounded, and those who were alive reluctantly took off their clothes to cover the dead. The image of that group is impressed into my head; have they managed to find a road to go down to Phù Lương and Phú Bài like we have?

All of a sudden, I turn back to look at the city.

I see pillars of smoke, tall and thick. The gunfire gradually moves farther away but remains utterly devastating. Artillery shells explode with a roar, and from time to time there is a shell that, due to a mistake in coordination, falls very near the groups of fleeing people. They all duck down, and I am pushed by Thái and fall down on the road:

"Run, elder sister, now!"

"OK, running!"

Run. I must run . . . to find a road of escape.

SIX

GOING BACK INTO THE HELL OF THE FIGHTING

WE RUN THROUGH SEVERAL ABANDONED FIELDS COVERED with water and through some empty plots of land overgrown with weeds, and then a road leads us to a small hamlet. There are houses scattered here and there. Thái joyfully shouts out:

"Our [Nationalist] army has just now occupied this area!"

I recognize silhouettes of some military men on the move, carrying rifles, appearing intermittently behind the crowd of evacuees; I see them appearing and disappearing as they stand guard in front of gates and fences. Finally – our deliverance from calamity; we have arrived at a peaceful area. My mother runs out from a tavern: "I'm here, I'm here." Thái pulls me into the veranda of the tavern. The tavern is deserted; in the middle of it is an enormous shelter made of sand, occupying almost the entire building. Next to the tavern is a deserted brick house; American and Vietnamese [Nationalist] soldiers stand guard in front of it. An American soldier and two soldiers of the Republic check the papers of each of us. I don't remember where I put my identity card, but then I manage to find it.

Bé's wife puts the pole down and sits hugging her small child and panting:

"That's it; now we will live."

But Thái and Bé still look very unsure. A group of people stop at the tavern. They carry with them a wounded woman; a shell has split her chest wide open, and she is breathing her dying breaths. Several soldiers run over, and an American soldier lifts the blanket with which she is tightly covered; he looks and shakes his head. Nevertheless, the American hastens to call for a vehicle to come to transport the woman. Several other American soldiers lift their hands in signs of despair. The oxcart transporting the two wounded people has now also pulled over here. One of the people has died and the other has one foot in the grave. The women writhe in weeping and moaning. One of the women hugs the dead body; the other one crawls on the ground:

"Oh my husband, the children are dead, the grandchildren are dead, only I am left. Oh husband . . . husband, you have also gone, and I am abandoned."

The other woman with the cart also cries:

"Oh husband, don't die, don't leave us. How can you die in this situation?"

The woman opens the mat and with her hand she touches the head of the dying person; she forces open his torpid eyes that had been closed tight:

"Don't die, my husband, don't abandon me."

The two crying voices burst out, one belonging to a person in despair and the other belonging to a person who still hangs on to a thread of frail hope; the latter screams as if to die, louder than the former. In the end, one of the two women runs over and grabs the hand of one of the several [Nationalist] soldiers standing and observing the scene together with several Americans; she bows and implores him:

"I beg you, elder brother, do me a favor and transport my husband down to Phú Bài."

"We don't have a vehicle. Anyway, how would a car go through the fields? Down there they shoot nonstop. You will have to bear it."

"Please help save my husband, sir."

The woman seizes the hand of an American. The American shakes his head. Thái also intervenes:

"Perhaps there's some medicine to give them to apply to the wounds, by chance . . ."

The soldier laughs as though he has been long acquainted with this situation:

"Oh, don't waste your time. We can't do anything to save him . . ."

"Then what? Just leave . . . ?"

"But what to do even if we had medicine? Even a miracle medicine would be useless now . . ."

The woman pushes the American aside and runs back to the cart. She pulls open the mat, and with scowling eyes she clenches her teeth and falls down shaking violently:

"It's all over now . . ."

The woman bangs her head against the ground, then she turns her face up toward the sky:

"Heaven is high, earth is deep – there is no help from anywhere – my husband . . . Heaven is high, earth is deep . . ."

The woman rolls back and forth, then she suddenly springs up:

"That's enough, let's go; enough, let's go . . . go, Mrs. Tứ. We will go back up to the city."

The other woman is weeping and moaning; hearing the words of the first woman, she stops and wipes her tears:

"Going up to the city, are we?"

"We are going up there to die together with our houses, our possessions, our husbands, and our children. What is there to live for anymore – Heaven?"

Everybody rushes to dissuade them . . . but no one can change the hearts of the two women who have fallen into extreme despair. They look in the direction where guns explode and fires burn; they point with their hands and yell:

"Everything is burned to the ground. Everything is burned to the ground. I am beside myself with rage. Oh heavens."

"Go, go, they have no pity for us, do they? Who would have pity for us now, oh heavens . . ."

Heaven also has been moved and has melted in tears. Drops of drizzling rain fly down; the vault of sky in azure and lead colors flows with water.

The two women, weeping and moaning, push the cart, returning to the city. They don't look back, but the sound of their crying still merges with the curtain of rain in an atmosphere tense with gloom. The oxcart has gradually moved far away – two silhouettes: strenuously, step by step, pushing the small cart on the long road, going forward toward the area of the hell of the fighting. One of the soldiers says after them:

"These two old women have gone completely crazy."

No one else says another critical word. Two men carrying a stretcher with someone wounded suddenly ask a soldier:

"Is there a first-aid post for the wounded in the hamlet?"

"Carry him in; there are people of the Self-Defense Forces over there."[1]

The two men hurriedly get up and carry the stretcher. A little child runs stumblingly along. One of the men says:

"Go quickly, child."

The little boy doesn't respond, running to the best of his abilities. A woman speaks up:

"Certainly this is a child of one of those women."

"The little guy does not yet understand anything; how terrible it is!"

Thái gathers our entire family to discuss the situation. Bé and his wife say that we must go on foot down to Phù Lương, but Thái holds back. It's afternoon – if we go now, we won't have time to make it there before dark. The group of people that stopped near the soldiers have all scattered into the hamlet. I ask Thái where we are. Thái says that a bit further is Thủy Dương Hạ hamlet. Bé's wife negotiates with the owner of the tavern, asking him to allow us to stay for a day. The owner says:

"If you want to stay here, lie outside on the veranda; it's too crowded in the shelter."

All of a sudden Bé remembers that he has an acquaintance. Thái says:

"I also have an acquaintance; let's divide into two groups to be less of a bother for both of them."

Thái has an uncle, an elder brother of his mother. So, my mother, my uncle, I, and Thái split from the others to go to the house of Thái's uncle Giáo. As soon as he sees us, Uncle Giáo rushes outside:

"Oh, Heaven and Earth, you've made it down here. Glory to Amitabha Buddha.[2] What a blessing, what a fortune. Come in, come in, first of all, you, elder sister . . ."

1. The Self-Defense Forces was one of the groups of militia, a part of the South Vietnam Popular Force that fought against the Communists.

2. Goddess of compassion in Buddhism.

My mother bursts into tears:

"I thought we'd all die, nowhere else to go, elder brother. This journey is the end of me . . ."

"Oh, we are all lucky to be alive. Elder sister, come in here, come in here, first . . ."

I ask:

"Uncle, is it quiet down here?"

"Oh, everything is quiet. Several days ago refugees came down here, a whole sea of them. They ran cutting across here, then went to Phù Lương. When they went to Phù Lương, Phú Bài became very quiet."

My mother changes her mind:

"Perhaps we must return to Phù Lương."

Thái warns:

"Impossible. We must stay here to find out news about elder brother Lễ. Why wouldn't there be people who come over here from Từ Đàm? When they come here, we will be able to inquire of them. Rely on me, auntie."

Just as we sit down to rest on a wooden plank bed, suddenly there is a deafening explosion, making the sky flash and the earth shake. No one says a word as my mother, my uncle, I, and Thái all dive down to the floor. But the others are still sitting in silence. Uncle Giáo laughs:

"Why are you like this? They are firing in the hills over there."

I suddenly understand – on the inner side of the top of the mountain on the other side of the road is the place where [American and Nationalist] artillery is placed to fire down at the city of Hue. Artillery shells firing from there have inflicted a countless number of deaths in the city over there. But I also understand that there is nothing to be done anymore. I climb up on the wooden plank bed and sit there, but I am still trembling. One, two, or three guns in the hamlet sporadically fire. Uncle Giáo says the Self-Defense Forces go on patrol when the artillery is shooting. I ask whether the Việt Cộng have returned here. Uncle Giáo's wife says:

"By night they come back all the time, but never mind them; we are inside the house and at night we don't open the door. They go through the garden – never mind them."

"Do they search?"

"In the hamlet down from here they made some arrests, but here, no. Here, it's near the hills and there are [Nationalist] soldiers on guard; nothing to be afraid of."

But Uncle Giáo is careful:

"In fact, we must also focus our minds on this: at night absolutely no talking. If you stir around, it will be the end of us. They will enter here."

Thái suggests digging another shelter. This evening everyone bustles in and out fixing the new shelter. The house can contain another surface shelter. As dusk is falling, Uncle Giáo does not allow anybody to go to the courtyard or to show a face outside the door. Outside there is not a shadow of a person; even the Vietnamese and American soldiers have pulled back to safe locations. I suddenly have a premonition that something will happen soon. Amid this peaceful scenery, I listen to my heart, waiting for something bad to happen.

But the first night that we sleep in Thủy Dương Hạ hamlet, absolutely nothing happens. Early in the morning of the following day when we wake up, I hear the sound of birds chirping. I fumble my way to the courtyard to wash my face and rinse my mouth; then, along with Uncle Giáo's daughter-in-law, named Lài, I go out to the lane to see what the situation is outside. Life still goes on normally; in front of the house, on the other side of the road, a market is crowded as usual. But the crowdedness of the place seems somehow different. Lài pulls me toward the market. There are lanes selling porridge with entrails here; people stand, people sit, and they eat and drink whatever comes to hand. Around the group of sitting and standing people, there are also towering piles of stuff, baskets and poles. It seems that they've just evacuated this morning. I go to make inquiries. But everybody only knows one's own story. A lot of people from An Cựu, a lot of people right from the slopes of Nam Giao Bridge, but they don't have anything for me to know more than the news I've already learned. One person says to me that up there still remain a lot of wounded people. Lài pulls me away, saying that we must go up to see what's happening. The young woman has not fled from danger yet; since the day of Tết until now it has been quiet and safe at Thủy Dương Hạ, so she doesn't know what to be afraid of. But I, I am different; the sound of gunfire, even a strange noise, everything makes me twitch.

My mother stands in the courtyard; when she sees us taking ourselves away, she calls to us, telling us not to go. I say several words to put my mother's mind at peace. The words that make my mother contented the most are that, if we are fortunate, up there we will find people from Từ Đàm who came here and we will be able to inquire about the fate of my elder brother and his family.

It still drizzles. If one doesn't have to flee from danger, during the first days of spring such a drizzle is marvelous. But now I'm no longer able to admire this scenery. Groups of people who fled from Hue are still the main sight that strikes my eyes. I feel sick; whomever I meet I ask whether they know anything about Từ Đàm, but their responses are completely identical.

"Where did you come here from, uncle?"

"From An Cựu."

"Bến Ngự."

"From Nam Giao Bridge."

"What's going on up there, elder sister? Grandmother? Uncle? Elder brother?"

"Completely destroyed. Completely reduced to ashes."

The words speed away following the footsteps. Groups run as though afraid that the guns will catch up with them. Lài pulls me by the hand:

"That's enough; whomever you ask, everyone says the same thing."

I follow Lài, but if I see someone, I still ask. Some people answer; others are not inclined to open their mouths. Damn it, it's like I acquired an addiction, which is very hard to get rid of, and in spite of the fact that the responses are so similar to each other, each time I hear them I am still out of my element, surprised as though I have discovered another unknown thing.

We cross a deserted plot of land; a small food stall and a military post emerge in front of us. Here the scene is of utter disorder; people sit and lie in heaps on the sides of the road, in the courtyard, in front of the food stall. Several soldiers and civilians from the Self-Defense Forces bustle in and out, checking papers of some people, inquiring of others. Several Americans stand and gaze at the group of people, then bare their teeth, laughing inappropriately, in a manner that in no way fits the situation or the scene. The wounded have a place arranged for them, and there are several doctors in the area who are there to dress their wounds. I keep inquiring but learn only that people in this group streamed here from many different localities. They let me know that Tràng Tiền Bridge has been destroyed and An Cựu Bridge has also been destroyed. There are people from the city who managed to escape because they risked taking a boat. Each person had to pay more than five thousand dongs for a boat trip across the river.

Thanks to inquiries of those who just arrived this morning, I know that in Hue there is fighting everywhere; the Nationalist side has not yet brought its troops to the area of the National Highway and only fire artillery and drop bombs. By day, airplanes hover overhead all the time. Airplanes still call upon civilians to try to relocate to the right bank to avoid falling into the Việt Cộng's hands. I learn that Đồng Khánh,[3] Quốc Học,[4] and Kiểu Mẫu Schools have turned into temporary residences for compatriots. They stay in these places, and it's like playing with death because of the unpredictability of artillery shells or because they are trapped between the two warring sides; everyday people die. I try to inquire about the news from the area where my elder brother lives, but people shake their heads or try to make random guesses, and the answers come out increasingly pessimistic:

"Up there, everything has now been reduced to ashes; everything is leveled."

There are people who speak as though they have witnessed it with their own eyes:

"Up there is only Việt Cộng; as for people, no one has remained. Only artillery fires day and night for ten-odd days and a lot of people have already died; don't tell me about guns and shells . . . don't tell me stories of being denounced by them [the Communists]. I am from Bến Ngự and I sense a stinky smell spreading down from there. Dogs carry in

3. A school for girls established in 1917.

4. A school for boys established in 1896 and the first secondary school in Vietnam in which many intellectuals and political leaders were educated, including not only southern leaders like Ngô Đình Diệm but also Hồ Chí Minh and other leaders of the Communist North.

their teeth arms and legs, pieces of leg bones still covered with flesh – it's very horrifying."

Another person adds:

"Up there, people die and nobody buries them; there is not a house that remains intact. Several days ago there were people who fled and came here and told me this."

Enough – so I keep hoping that the family of my elder brother is still alive, not to mention my younger sister, to whose face the eyes of my father, when he was on his deathbed, remained glued fast, as though he wanted to entrust her to the care of the people who remained, and also several young nephews; I just came back after several years and, busy with the funeral, haven't had time to hold them in my arms.

Tears are about to stream from my eyes, and in my heart I don't have any hope anymore. But at this moment I suddenly hear another voice answering somebody's question:

"Up at Từ Đàm, eh? There are a few people who have escaped. They went in the direction of Tây Thiên; up there it's very calm, but what a wretched situation. That place [Tây Thiên] is full of the Liberation Army. Their headquarters is there. A lot of people are stranded there, but no one has managed to escape."

"Ma'am, don't worry. I live down the slope next to the river near Bến Ngự but have managed to escape; my house is not made of brick but is still intact."

I get hopeful again:

"No doubt my elder brother's family will manage to escape."

But thinking about my sister-in-law, who's feeble, with a flock of young children to take care of, and my younger sister, I start worrying again. My elder brother is also very feeble; the big funeral at the end of the year put him between death and life several times. During the several days of the funeral ceremonies, my elder brother didn't eat even a bowl of rice, and on the day of my father's burial procession, he almost fainted in front of the grave.

Seeing me standing stunned, Lài pulls my hand:

"That's it, we are going back; here it looks too scary, oh heavens."

On the road I meet Bé and his wife. They say that they will stay here until tomorrow and then will go down to Phù Lương; it's not quiet and safe here. I don't reply. Actually, I can't guess what place is quieter and safer than another place.

My mother is waiting for me at the gate; she asks:

"Any news?"

I reply to calm my mother's heart:

"There are people who told me that at Từ Đàm a lot of people evacuated to Tây Thiên and Trúc Lâm."

"So, why would he not flee and go up to Trúc Lâm then around Ngự Bình Mountain and manage to come to An Cựu?"

"Surely he is still stuck somehow over there."

My mother is uneasy:

"Other people have fled; why didn't he go?"

Then she decides to stay here to wait for him. When I enter the house, I see that Uncle Giáo's wife bought for me a big bowl of porridge with entrails.

The bowl of steaming hot porridge has a very sweet aroma, but when I swallow a bit of it, in my throat I suddenly feel that it's very bitter.

At this moment I still want to eat delicious food; I want to be happy. In my essence I am an egotist. I miss my children and my husband. I worry about my elder brother and his wife, about my younger sister along with all my young nephews. Will I really manage to stay alive? And my husband and children . . .

Tears stream from my eyes. Lài asks:

"Why aren't you eating? Is it too hot?"

"Yes, my bowl has a lot of black pepper. It's too burning-hot to eat; it even made tears come to my eyes." Lài suddenly laughs. I turn away to hide two lines of tears streaming down my face. My mother still sits totally stupefied in front of her big bowl of porridge. I wipe my tears and say:

"Eat, Mother."

My mother says:

"You eat, child. I pity you so much, child, for ten-odd days to endure hunger and thirst."

I blink my eyes; the veil of tears gradually thins out, and I clearly see my mother's face. She looks at me fixedly. The bowl with porridge still stands in front of her; puffs of steam gradually thin out, and soon it will be cold. Several morsels of coagulated pig's blood are floating on the surface.

I suddenly shudder; the pig's blood resembles bluish-black bloodstains, of which by now I have seen enough. I push away the bowl of porridge. My mother covers her face with her hands and bursts into tears:

"I've escaped, came here, and eat happily, but my son and grandchildren, what happened to them, oh heavens?"

My mother appeals again to Heaven. Countless numbers of people have appealed to Heaven during these days of upheaval. Lài consoles my mother:

"Don't, auntie, you are so miserable as though something bad has happened to them. There is still a chance, sure there is, auntie."

Thái has finished eating his big bowl of porridge. He pushes my bowl back toward me:

"Eat, elder sister. If there is food, eat it; people die because of artillery, and those dying of hunger fill the roads."

I try to swallow several spoonfuls of porridge for the benefit of my mother and Thái, but each swallow of porridge causes excruciating pain in my throat. When I was outside, I saw a child who looked intently at a woman in a stall selling porridge; he demanded to eat but his mother held him back and kept pushing him to run down the road ahead of her. The child stomped both his feet and cried, but his voice became so hoarse that no breath was coming out anymore.

Uncle Giáo's wife retells stories overheard from groups of people fleeing from the fighting. Uncle Giáo is worried:

"I don't know whether we have taken back Hue or not. If it's lost up there, down here we won't survive either!"

His wife throws a long angry glance at him:

"Watch your mouth. Last night, they [the Communist forces] came back and arrested some people over there. There are a couple of people from Hue who came here; they fled and also were arrested. There are spies everywhere – be careful or you will end up with a miserable death."

My mother is worried:

"If it's so, then we mustn't stay here any longer."

Thái is confident:

"Auntie, put your mind at peace; they don't know who we are. Wherever we run, it will be the same; they are everywhere now."

Thái tries to reassure my mother about staying here, but reading his eyes I understand that he is now exhausted beyond measure from foolhardily going from one place to another. Uncle Giáo scolds him and tells him to change into clean clothes, those of country people. Uncle Giáo's wife brings a set of loose black clothes for me, too. My mother advises me that I must pull my hair up into a bun, Hue-type, and raise it high up; if during the night they come in to search, then I must tell them that I am a poor farmer. I look at myself in the mirror and suddenly see myself extremely distant and strange; I don't recognize any of my features anymore.

From that time to the afternoon, I don't take my eyes off the main road. Groups of people fleeing from danger become more numerous by the minute. If someone asks them anything, they only beckon with their hands and elbows backward with one hurried phrase: They are fighting each other back there; it's absolute hell. By the afternoon, I see people fleeing over here, even carrying dead bodies on their bicycles.

The family of a doctor from somewhere down the slope of Nam Giao managed to get here to Thủy Dương Hạ; they brought along a Honda motorbike to carry their stuff. Several girls with their faces drained to the last drop of blood, absolutely stunned, sit on the shoulder of the road to give their feet some rest. The doctor orders porridge with entrails for his family; each person eats four or five bowls, eating and sighing at the same time. The features of their faces gradually change from pain-stricken to radiant.

Another family has also managed to flee to Thủy Dương Hạ; they are completely exhausted and tidy up a corner of the communal house to spend a night there. The mother of the family winds up with a bout of asthma, and in the afternoon she dies. People suddenly swarm around as numerous as ants. The corpse of the woman, big and fat, sprawls in an ugly pose on a mat with scowling eyes and hands tightly entangled, unable to separate. The husband sits near the corpse of his wife, breathing in, breathing out, throwing long looks toward the city of Hue where incredibly high columns of smoke push and push into the lead-colored sky like monsters' gray tongues. In the afternoon, this family disappears somewhere; when I go in the communal house, I see only the abandoned mat in the corner. The building is packed, and another family immediately replaces them in that spot. The mat turns into a place for an entire family of ten-odd people to sit or lie down.

Lài tells me about something she has seen. She speaks, and her face is at once moving and funny:

"In the afternoon, there was this young girl wearing a cowboy outfit; she held in her hands a coat but she cried bitterly, melting into tears. She entered the hamlet, offering her coat in exchange for a small jar of rice, but no one agreed. She was crying. I asked her to tell me her story, and she said that her sweetheart had bought the outfit for her in America and had sent it back as a gift. The young woman was very hungry and wanted to trade it for a jar of rice, but no one agreed to the exchange. I decided to go in her house to take rice and exchange it for the coat, but my mother did not allow me. She said that if this coat is in the house and they [the Communist forces] come in, then they would say that I am for the Americans and they would at once shoot me. This woman went on cajoling and cajoling, crying and begging, but no one would make such an exchange."

During these times, even gold and silver, precious pearls, jade, and ivory are not valued anymore. A plot of land is still useful to bury dead bodies, but gold and silver won't fill your stomach. A grain of rice now is a pearl, more precious than anything else in life. Uncle Giáo's wife has strongly advised that when we cook rice we must add a lot of water so that when we eat we will get full fast and that we must remember to be thrifty with rice.

In the afternoon of this day, Thái goes to mobilize the women and children to buy or to ask each house for several measures of rice, and he manages to procure almost half a bag of rice; seeing Thái coming back carrying rice on his shoulder, the eyes of my mother shine:

"This lad is very talented."

Thái throws the bag of rice on the ground:

"When we finish eating this, and if it's not quiet yet, we will all soon die from starvation. No one will dare to give or to sell another grain of rice."

Thái's aunt Vạn, who stayed with Uncle Giáo's family, runs over and asks:

"Is there anyone who wants to buy gold? Outside there is a group of evacuees; they will sell a bar of gold for several hundred dongs, or they want to exchange it for rice."

Uncle Giáo's wife laughs bitterly:

"To exchange an ingot of gold for a grain of rice, even that will not work. They must be crazy."

Thái looks at the curtain of drizzling rain and sighs:

"In rain like this it's very difficult to fight. Our side has tear gas, but in rain like this it all gets washed away."

Uncle Giáo shakes his head:

"Enough, we are all in the same boat. What's the point to moan?"

Several children suddenly dash in from outside, their faces panic-stricken. Then we hear the sound of an entire column of vehicles approaching with a roar. I look out and see American vehicles coming up from the direction of Phú Bài. A lot of Americans jump down out of the vehicles and lie down close to the sides of the road and fire in the air, their shots exploding in salvoes. They are shooting even at the area of virgin land in the mountains. Uncle Giáo shouts at everybody to go into the shelter. All the doors are closed tight.

The guns explode like popcorn in salvoes, then move away. The column of vehicles departs with a lot of noise; many people are running into the houses, and those who don't make it inside lie pressing themselves into the ground in the courtyard where the water tank is, waiting until the vehicles are completely gone. When the guns gradually move farther away, we hear a loud bang on the door. My mother whispers:

"I see that here it's not at all quiet either. Oh child, that's why I am so worried."

My mother suddenly decides to flee again. This time, it's she who suggests it. But I've changed my mind. I know that wherever we go, the situation will not be any better. My mother falls mum.

Outside everything has become totally deserted. The shadows of dusk close in very fast. The drizzling rain has gradually become denser, and the air is freezing cold. My mother sits in the corner on the wooden plank bed with her arms clasping her knees, looking outside at the vault of the sky, which gradually turns black. At the evening meal I manage to eat half a bowl; as for my mother, when she finishes eating her bowl, she suddenly cries. Tears drop down into her bowl, and my mother hastily puts her chopsticks down.

Two surface shelters are filled with children and adults; there's no place to wriggle. I want to go across to the other side to Mrs. Ái, Uncle Giáo's neighbor, to ask to sleep there but don't dare step outside into the courtyard. Very fortunately, Hiền, Aunt Ái's son, knocks on the door and calls. I follow Hiền into the nearby house. Hiền is a student of fine arts, a relative of Thái's on the maternal side. Hiền's house is farther out of sight from the road, and they dug up a deep, spacious underground shelter under the house. Hiền lights a lamp just for me to see several new pictures he has drawn. But I don't show appreciation of anything, don't even recognize anything; my brain is stretched out to the extreme. I am worried and afraid that today or tomorrow or in the near future the guns will reach this place, and I know for sure that we won't have the strength to flee anymore.

Hiền says:

"There are several young people looking for you, elder sister; they asked me, but I didn't know what you would think about it."

I smile faintly:

"Enough – spare me, now when I look like this, when my clothes are torn into shreds. Let's put it off until another occasion, if we are still alive."

Thủy Dương Hạ hamlet is the place I will remember with gratitude when I think about those days of seeking safety from the fighting. I remember a fertilized duck egg that Hiền put slyly into my pocket for me to eat. I remember a few young faces watching me with both compassion and amusement. Right, I must be looking very funny after the preceding exhausting days. But what importance will it have unless I survive?

That night I don't lie in the shelter but on a wide bed with Mrs. Ái, her daughter-in-law, and a small grandchild. The cold is biting, and I tightly cover my head with a blanket. I still always carry with me my father's overcoat, not letting it leave my side even when I sleep.

The hamlet is silent and empty in an unusual way; there are not even sounds of dogs barking, not a single sound of small arms. We hear only artillery firing monotonously from the top of the small hill and roaring sounds in the distance. Those places in the distance are the city of Hue, the Citadel, An Cựu, Nam Giao . . . It feels like each strident sound screws into my heart; I know that while I get a chance to lie quiet and safe here, countless numbers of people in that city are dying from guns, dying from shells, dying from hunger, dying from thirst. How many torsos are about to be broken open; how many drops of tears will mix with each other?

After being wakeful and restless for a long time, I fall into a deep sleep. I sink into the spell of a fiercely violent dream. I see myself fleeing from the dangers of the war all over the city. Faces of the liberators take the form of giants, always ready to swallow us. Shells fall behind me and in front of me. And I keep running. It's exactly like scenes of what I have lived through. Behind my back, dead bodies burst out into tears and chase me; even pieces of their hands and legs also run and pull me back. Under my feet, blood runs like a mountain stream. And corpses of Việt Cộng, and corpses of children, and corpses of soldiers, and corpses of Americans, and corpses of old women are scattered around everywhere, blocking the roads. Never mind, I step over their corpses and run forward.

But I am stranded between two gigantic columns of smoke: a fire in front and a fire behind. Groups of people flee from the fighting in all directions, at random treading upon each other. I recognize among the groups of people one group holding white flags that crossed the river one day. Even my mother, younger cousin Thái, elder brother Lễ, and younger sister Hà run impetuously farther and farther, leaving me behind.

On this side of the bridge, a liberation soldier holds his hands like a loudspeaker: "Compatriots, stay at home; don't go outside." On the other side a Nationalist soldier shouts: "Go to the right bank. Evacuate to the right bank." I don't recognize anymore which direction is which. Where is the right bank? Where is the left bank? Streams of blood have been flowing to the banks of the river and the surface of the water, biting cold, trailing bloody threads. Columns of smoke from behind gradually become larger, and columns of smoke in front gradually become larger. The smoke envelops me, tightly covering my eyes, then large and small guns start to compete with each other with their explosions. Groups of people run, shouting and crying; people overtake each other; people fall down. I also run following them. But I can't keep up with them anymore. A big explosion, and then the entire city explodes. It feels like my body shatters into pieces among bricks and sand. I still manage to hear my own shouts rising up, flying swiftly up toward the vault of the lead-gray sky.

Someone's hands pull me and then push me down to the ground. I hear shouts: "Run into the shelter. Hurry up." I suddenly wake up. An explosion very close to us shakes the entire house – several window shutters come loose and start flapping in and out. After I drop down to the floor, I make several rolls and get to the underground shelter opening.

Perhaps I am the last person to come down into the shelter. Another explosion follows the first one. The roof made of iron sheets cries out in fury when thousands of fragments pour down upon it. When in my dream there was an explosion causing the collapse of the city, it was identical to the explosion in the middle of the night in this place in the countryside. Someone's hands at my side are trembling. We hear a round of rifle fire from the direction of the road, then sounds of rifle fire emerge everywhere. The fighting between the two sides has reached this place. I lie tightly holding Mrs. Ái's hand. Her hand also trembles. I think about my mother, my uncle, and Thái in Uncle Giáo's house. Certainly, my mother also trembles like we do here. Hiền says in a low voice:

"Obviously the fighting has now begun here."

A thud on the door; everyone is silent, holding their breath. Mrs. Ái suddenly grumbles:

"Damn that dog, it went outside."

The dog's barking gets louder and louder, gunfire becomes scattered and sparse, and then we hear sounds of feet running all over the garden. I lie very close to the floor of the shelter. They [the Communist forces] have come to arrest the villagers. What will my fate be? I remember Hiền's words when in the evening he said that there were several young people who were looking for me. No, I was too scared and improperly suspicious; no one could still have enough strength to harm others at this time. However, my heart did not dispel my suspicions.

There are the sounds of feet running through the garden very noisily. Then we hear voices of people calling each other: "Open fire!" "Quới – at the foot of the hill." "Lục – at the edge of the river." A loud call: "Fire!"

There are beeping sounds: secret signals. But we don't know whether or not they are searching houses. This is my most important concern at the moment. The sounds of feet stop in the courtyard. Then the sounds resume – they run again. Loud calls gradually move away, and complete silence moves in. At this moment we hear gunfire again. Hiền angrily mumbles to himself:

"First they [the Nationalist forces] wait until all Việt Cộng withdraw, and then they shoot.[5] Real idiots."

A moment later there are voices of people from the Self-Defense Forces screaming outside: "Chase after them." After several minutes there is full silence. Mrs. Ái makes us sit in the shelter through the night, not letting us go up to sleep in the house.

Early in the morning, before any of the houses have their doors open, I run to Uncle Giáo's house. I bang and bang on the door. People inside listen intently for a while, then the door panels open enough for only one person to jostle in, and then immediately the lock is fastened again. Everybody is still in the shelter. My mother stretches out her hand and hugs me, crying for joy.

Thái whispers:

"Last night aunt worried about you, elder sister, a lot. She cried through the entire night."

I hug my mother more heartily and can't come up with a single word to calm her down. Certainly my mother doesn't have a calm minute anymore. Thái points to the window where the shutters were blown away:

"Yesterday evening there were several explosions, and some doors were blown away."

Aunt Vạn's voice:

"So, those bombs fell here, close to our house. I heard a boom and thought the shelter would blow up. I kept holding my head in my hands, thinking my head was about to go to waste."

Uncle Giáo's wife bursts into angry words:

"Auntie, why do you say such nonsense all the time?"

5. According to the author, Nationalist soldiers cautiously restrained themselves from aimlessly firing their weapons. Very seldom did they shoot randomly because the Communists often mixed in with ordinary people, turning the latter into targets.

Túc, Uncle Giáo's son, jokes:

"Flying heads still have two legs and can run, can't they, auntie?"

"Why do you say such stupid things? To have such a loose tongue when surrounded by guns and shells."

A moment later we see nothing unusual and people are walking around outside. Uncle Giáo opens the door. A bomb fragment had landed in the courtyard. Everybody runs out to look at it for a while. Thái goes to the road and a moment later returns to inform us that yesterday evening the Việt Cộng detonated a bridge. They used two or three mines but didn't destroy it completely, only made a big hole so that vehicles can't get through, but it's still possible to pass on foot, and mopeds can go through, too.

Thái adds:

"Yesterday evening they came back to the village but now have pulled out completely. For sure they think that the bridge has collapsed."

Outside, in the lane, there is someone's voice calling. We look outside. Bé, his wife, and his eldest son, supporting each other, stand there with a carrying pole.

I run outside:

"Where are you going like this?"

"Going down to Phù Lương; it's not safe here anymore."

"Is it far?"

"Far, but people have made it, and we can make it too."

"Do you know if it's quiet down there?"

"It's a hubbub because of all the people streaming there."

Bé says:

"I want to ask auntie and you, elder sister, if you will go with us, and if so, let's go, but if not, we'll go ourselves."

Thái shakes his head:

"Everywhere is like this. We don't know anything, so why go?"

"If you go down there, you'll find a military post and can report for duty at once. Then you will get ammunition and will be able to fight the Communist forces. I am furious with them [the Communist forces]."

Thái falls silent for a moment, considering Bé's words, then he asks:

"Do you have any news?"

"I heard that the commander of your post got his throat slit."

Seeing that Thái remains silent, Bé continues:

"If you stay here, then what? They will again come to scour and will arrest you. They know that a lot of evacuees have come here."

My mother has come out. My uncle wants to follow Bé and his wife. In this way, my family again splits up. Thái stands watching Bé and his wife disappearing over the bridge and sighs:

"Let's go inside, auntie."

"Did you decide to stay here, Thái?"

Thái tightens his lips:

"Yes, to stay here."

My mother has tears welling up in her eyes:

"Whatever happens, why go anywhere again? Here, it's near An Cựu, our home. We don't know what's going on up there . . ."

I know that my mother still misses her house, the altar of my father, and his fresh grave on Tam Thái Mountain. On the day when we were evacuating down to Thủy Dương Hạ hamlet, cutting across the fields, my mother repeatedly looked up toward the mountain. But, like myself, she could not distinguish which grave was my father's. The slope of the mountain is a realm of dead people, and from a distance each grave looks exactly like the other ones.

The first several days at Thủy Dương Hạ were calm and safe. But since the day of the explosion at the bridge, artillery lobs into this village at night. Each evening we sneak into the shelter really early. Throughout the second night, explosions continue. The bridge is completely put out of commission. By day, Americans come up to fix the bridge, but by night, they all pull out, giving way to liberators. By now, several houses in the village have been hit by artillery. Each morning we hear people everywhere engaged enthusiastically in futile discussions about the artillery shells that were shot from the other bank of the river and hit residents' houses. A couple of houses have been completely destroyed. By night, liberators come back to conduct thorough searches and arrest people. By day, the area of the bridge is blocked. American soldiers guard it and don't allow people to go back to Phù Lương anymore. We are stranded in Thủy Dương Hạ and await our fate.

A number of evacuees from Hue who came here inform us that An Cựu is completely cleared [of the Communist forces]. The American army and Nationalist soldiers have occupied the place and have full control there. Several people went up there to retrieve their belongings, but they came back crying and moaning heartbreakingly – at every house that has not been destroyed, doors are opened and the insides ravaged, the furniture gone. An Cựu Bridge was detonated and collapsed right in the middle, so the crossing is extremely difficult now. My mother makes very thorough inquiries with these people, and they say that despite the fact that the place is completely cleared, Nationalist soldiers and Americans come only by day, and at night they all withdraw back to Phú Bài. In Thủy Dương Hạ hamlet, where we stay now, suddenly there is news that the enemy [the Communist forces] is coming here soon, that it is losing control of the city, so it will pull out to the countryside. People are getting ready to evacuate. My mother and Thái decide to return to An Cựu.

For several days in succession I watch convoys of vehicles coming back through the village filled with dead bodies and wounded soldiers. But people still gather and prompt each other to return to Hue.

Yet at the same time, there are also groups of people that come here one after another from Hue. People run to and fro. My mother sends Thái to check the road first. He goes around midday, then comes back:

"A lot of people are returning to An Cựu, auntie. We're going back."

So, we get ready to go up to An Cựu. My mother admonished Uncle Giáo to go up there (An Cựu) if the artillery here is too fierce. Uncle Giáo's wife gives my mother a bit more rice: "Even if all this continues, down here we still have unprocessed rice to pound and eat, but if you are stuck up there it will be death from hunger." Uncle Giáo's wife, Uncle Giáo, and their entire family see us off, accompanying us part of the way down the road before turning and going back. Seeing many groups of people carrying poles with their belongings on their shoulders going to Phù Lương, my mother suddenly hesitates. Thái has to talk and talk with my mother until she lets out a sigh: "OK, fine, let's do it." Thái says that to stay in Thủy Dương Hạ is too dangerous; he heard rumors that during the night the Việt Cộng entered the hamlet and took away young men.

I feel a bit calmer when I see a lot of people going up toward the city of Hue; they have empty baskets on shoulder poles. I inquire of them and learn that the Nationalist Army has occupied An Cựu and is in control up there; these people are going up to see if anything is left and if yes then to take it back so that thieves and burglars will not take everything.

Artillery still explodes furiously in the direction of Hue Citadel. My mother's face turns green and her lips tremble:

"What to do now? Up there they still shoot at each other."

Thái is firmly determined:

"An Cựu is now controlled by our [Nationalist] side; the artillery is firing up into the Bến Ngự and Từ Đàm areas."

Just as Thái said, when we climb up to Mù U, I see silhouettes of military men, appearing and disappearing. They carry rifles on their shoulders and march in lines or stand guard, scattered on both sides of the road. When we get up to Trường Bia military post, my heart is increasingly assured. There are many soldiers in the post. They are very alert and stand guard outside. When we go across and I encounter their glances, I want to laugh, but no laughter comes out. I am sure they feel the same way, their eyes watching us until we are far away. Some houses on the sides of the road have their doors open. Several people stick their heads out and ask:

"Coming back, are you?"

My mother nods repeatedly and asks in turn:

"Quiet already?"

"Oh, it's OK. We dug shelters and escaped the shells; only fate knows how and why we managed, aunt."

A big explosion seems to shred my eardrums. We hastily duck down.

A voice resounds in the courtyard of some house:

"It's friendly fire. They are shooting from Trường Bia military post."

I get up, awkwardly brush away the dust, and then pull my mother up too. She looks around:

"So empty, no people have come back yet."

Then she asks the person whose head has just stuck out of the door of a house:

"Have you just returned?"

"No, I've been here for several days."

"You haven't had any trouble?"

The woman sticks her head out even more, raises two fingers, and then points toward the corner of the courtyard:

"Two people are dead."

I follow her hand with my eyes. Two graves with earth carelessly heaped on them are in the corner of a courtyard, cold and grim without a single stick of burning incense. I pull the flaps of my coat tightly together, then turn to go to some other place. The woman's face is shriveled; I don't know whether sufferings have changed her face a long time ago or just recently. But she doesn't look sorrowful at all. I shudder. Ten-odd days, and people seem to have gotten used to blood, to deaths, to wounds.

Shortly before arriving home, my legs and arms tremble uncontrollably. I am at once glad and afraid. I betray my worry that the house has been completely destroyed, that it's not whole anymore. The day when we went down to Thủy Dương Hạ hamlet to avoid disaster, cutting across the main road, I tried to get a glimpse of our house, but shells behind me seemed to push me to run forward, and thin rows of trees hid the garden area. During the days in Thủy Dương Hạ, there was no way to know whether our house had collapsed. People only spread rumors or tell a few distressing or comic stories. We heard different stories: when American army units came up to An Cựu, any house they saw intact or that had something suspicious about it, they fired into it at random, regardless of whether there were people inside. Or they dashed into a house, stood at the shelter opening, and flooded the inside of the shelter with shots. They were afraid of Việt Cộng hiding down there.

The closer we get to home, the faster my feet move. Thái and my mother are the same. When we left, my family was indeed numerous; when we come back, it's only my mother, Thái, and me. Aunt Vạn and her daughter are still getting ready; they said they would come up later. Bé and his wife have already left for Phù Lương. Thu Hồng has also stopped following us.

When we are about to step into the lane, our yard is hidden behind another house, and the lane leads in to the gate, on both sides of which are hedges of hibiscus and vines. I suddenly hear a voice behind me. It turns out that my uncle, Bé's father, has hurried to catch up with us. Bé and his wife, regardless of what they initially thought and planned, ended up leaving him behind. I push open the iron gate leading to our courtyard and then shut it, but not tightly. Our house suddenly bursts into view as though greeting us. The tiles on the roof are caved in or pierced with holes from rockets or bombs. A wall on the front of the house is cracked, and window shutters are open wide from the reverberations of bombshells. Nevertheless, the two panels of the main door are still closed. First of all, Thái jumps up to the veranda. He puts down the bag of rice and turns around to look at my mother, then fishes keys out from his pocket. I see his hands shaking uncontrollably and his face turning pale. The panels of the door open and light floods into the house. Half-burned candles, parallel sentences with condolences,[6] and beaded mourning wreaths remaining from my father's funeral suddenly fill my eyes. I rush into the house and bow my head in front of my father's altar. My mother plops on the ground crying. And even Thái, though he is Catholic and was baptized a long time ago, still looks for incense to light on the upper part of my father's altar and finally takes the incense that remains unburned from the incense burners for the more distant ancestors – relatives passed away a long time ago. I look up at my father's altar, at his picture covered with red cloth along with all the aquilaria[7] burners and the altar candles; everything is covered with a thick layer of dust. Then my eyes go to holes in the roof as my mother calls Thái; in her hand she is holding a piece of a bomb, a shell fragment or something like that, with uneven shape and the ash-gray color of zinc.

In a moment, we go to inspect whether or not anything has disappeared. Very fortunately, all the stuff we left here is intact; only the things we took along with us when we fled have disappeared. Thái is confident that no one has entered our house. In fact, why would anyone want to get into this house? My father has recently died and the house has been deserted since the day of my father's funeral procession; black and white rolls of reinforced paper for writing parallel sentences of condolences, beaded mourning wreaths, votive paper, and incense fill the house, making it feel like a crypt. If anyone got lost and entered this realm of death

6. According to Vietnamese classical literary tradition, especially widespread among educated people, when one person writes a sentence, another responds not only in accordance with the content of the first sentence but also paralleling the grammatical and phonetic structure of the first one. For Tết, every household usually composed a pair of parallel sentences on red paper to be hung in a place of honor, usually on both sides of the entrance door of the ancestral altar.

7. Sweet-smelling wood.

and grief, so desolate, certainly this person would be startled out of his or her wits. But because this is our house and over there is our ancestral altar recently established for my father, only here and now do I feel harmony and calm.

My mother tells us to close the windows and to keep the entrance door locked on the outside at all times, except for when there is need to go out for whatever reason, so that there will be the illusion that the house is abandoned. I look out of the window, thoroughly examining the neighboring surroundings. Through the window, serene and pure Nam An Pagoda appears absolutely deserted; houses around there are also absolutely deserted. But soon I see an old man going out in front of the courtyard. He stops by the pole on which a Buddhist flag usually hangs during festivals. The man stands and stares at the deserted road, his two hands clasped behind his back. I want to call the old man to ask him about his story, but my mother has pulled me inside. Thái says:

"We must redo the shelter. This shelter is definitely not reliable."

The two of us, together with our uncle, Bé's father, help each other fix the shelter. In the afternoon of this day, Túc and Lài come up from Thủy Dương Hạ hamlet. Túc informs us that down there it's not safe, and so they came up here to stay for a while. A moment later, Hiền, the art student, also arrives on a Honda motorbike. Luckily, we left Thủy Dương Hạ just at the right time.

The same afternoon Bé and his wife come back here to An Cựu and join us too. When they left Thủy Dương Hạ, they were stopped in the middle of the road and told that somewhere farther down, some vehicles were shelled and attacked and a column of American vehicles got stuck, and it was not clear whether they [the Americans] made it back to Phú Bài or not.

Because it has become crowded with people in our house, we open the kitchen house, which my father rented to a teacher from An Cựu School. The teacher and his family went back to their native place to celebrate Tết and locked the door. Down in the kitchen there is a fixed surface shelter made of sandbags; we carry the sandbags up into the house to make a surface shelter behind the altar.

While Thái is working, he asks me whether I saw anything unusual. I say no. Thái says that when he was approaching the house, as soon as he passed the gate where we turn to get out of the alley to go to our house, he saw there in the front yard a grave. On the grave, there is incense and a cluster of green bananas. I remember that the neighboring house in front of ours was shelled and burst into flames on the second day and several people were wounded there; surely one of them has already died. Thái says in a low voice:

"The lady who lived in front has died and is buried there. All of her family has now left for somewhere else, and the house is empty."

"How many more people will be wounded?"

Thái shakes his head and says: "Carry on, elder sister." Thái doesn't know anything more than I do. We bustle in and out making a shelter. Out in front there is a wooden sign from which Thái carries several boards, which are quite good, and brings them in to arrange in the shelter.

The shelter looks acceptable, at least for temporary use; he divides it into two parts. The inside part is intended for my mother, my female relatives, and myself. The outer part is intended for men. Luckily, our house has just had the funeral and there are a lot of candles; even if we keep burning them for a few months, certainly even then we will not run out of them. Thái finds a cask of oil for burning. When still alive, my father had a taste for hoarding things; he was about to retire soon and had decided to use the yard and garden together with the family ancestor-worshipping house as a place of retreat in old age.

This afternoon we have a very delicious meal. We pound rice by hand and eat it with dry salted meat. This food is from Thủy Dương Hạ, and it was Uncle Giáo's wife who paid for it. We eat a lot. Because we have been working, we are very tired and, on top of it, also hungry; and, obviously, my mother gives up half of her portion for the rest of us.

When night falls, before carefully locking the doors and gates and crawling into the shelter, Aunt Vạn, who eventually arrives from Thủy Dương Hạ and joins us, lights incense on my father's altar and whispers a prayer. Then she goes to the courtyard to light incense and to bow, with her hands joined, toward all four directions. The peach tree near the water tank still has several flowers strewn about, and she brings incense and sets it up at the roots of this peach tree. When she comes back into the shelter, we all lie on the ground, crowded very close to each other, but still there's not enough room. Lài and Túc can't stand to lie in the shelter, so they spread a mat and lie out in the house. My mother worries, discusses, and plans details of the upcoming day. Aunt Vạn grumbles, saying: "Anyhow, it would have been better to go down to Phù Lương – it's still safer there than here." But my mother says that we are done with running east then running west; we've come back here now, and even if death comes, we will have no regrets anymore. Here, she says, there is still hope of hearing news from her son and grandchildren.

In the afternoon, Bé and his wife with my uncle went up to their own house by the railroad. Bé let us know that, up there, a lot of people have also returned. Many families were intact when they fled, but when they came back they had lost some of their members. They had died on the road. My mother tells us that at night if anyone calls at the door, we must not open. Thái prudently goes outside to lock the door and then climbs in through the window. He thinks that if he does so and someone calls at the door, that person will think that there is no one in the house. My mother is in full agreement with him. In the middle of the night, suddenly we hear a lot of explosions from small guns, then footsteps in the yard. The footsteps are bold, indicating that these people are not even hiding their presence. We hear the footsteps stop in front of the house's door, then a knock on the door. A man's voice asks:

"Is there anyone there? Open the door. Open the door."

Another voice angrily bursts out:

"Comrade, it's in vain; each evening we knock here. They have abandoned the house."

"In this area, a whole lot of people have already returned. Who knows but perhaps the owners of the house are back by now?"

"There is a guy from this house whose name is on the list [according to which the Communist forces conducted searches], isn't there?"

"Yeah, there is, but that's an old man who worked for the government, and he has died."

"If that's the case, then that's it. His children and grandchildren, never mind them. I guess it's a sure thing that no one has come back yet. Who would dare to stay in this house?"

The footsteps gradually move farther away. We hear a dog barking in the hamlet. Shortly after, artillery explodes nearby. Lài swiftly crawls into the shelter. We must sit up because only then do we have enough room. The sound of artillery falls monotonously, nearby and far away. Some sounds are terribly close; their reverberations squeeze our chests and shrivel our bodies. Lài holds my hand and asks me: "Vân, where are you sitting? Here you are – it's so scary!" Aunt Vạn's voice follows:

"Keep silent. Don't make any noise."

Far away in the distance, guns explode in rumbles. The fighting everywhere seems to be very serious. We spend a restless night, worrying for one, two, three hours, then exhausted we fall asleep, dead to the world.

In the morning Aunt Vạn gets up before anyone else. She waits at the door, intently listening for any movement, and only then does she open the door wide. It is quite deserted outside; you look at any house, and each seems so desolate that it makes one scared. Thái sneaks into the courtyard first, then I go, and then Lài. The morning sky still drizzles, and leaves in the garden are green in an odd way. Beyond the low masses of grayish-blue clouds, I suddenly imagine that behind them there is a bright blue sky and brilliant sunshine. My mother and Aunt Vạn also run outside: Glory to the Amitabha Buddha, goddess of compassion, for one quiet and safe night has passed. Aunt Vạn holds her hands together and bows in all four directions with her hands joined. We all look at each other, happy and upset at the same time. We've stayed close to each other through all the dangers for a long time, but we didn't see each other, did we? However, it seems to us that, after several days of hardships and danger, standing in the front yard, happy and sad at once, only now do we really meet each other, see each other, and we are still intact.

Our bouts of joy and self-pity have not passed yet when on the National Highway a column of American vehicles comes up from Phú Bài, guns fiercely firing at the fields along both sides of the road. All of us, without saying a word to each other, run into the house and tightly close the door. The American column passes in a moment, and Thái suddenly realizes:

"The soldiers of my unit have come up."

He stands near the open window and looks out. My mother says:

"We must fix the shelter. You listen to me, Thái, remember to dig more soil to put on the top to make it thicker."

Even though we try to hope, still we haven't seen any sign to prove to us that people can live in this city after what has happened.

The first night after our return to the city, despite the artillery, despite the guns firing and echoing in the distance, we still get a calm sleep of several hours in the narrow, crowded shelter.

Unfortunately for us, only three days after the shelter is fixed, the person renting the kitchen space returns, the teacher in elementary education who works at An Cựu School.

Seeing the kitchen door wide open, he doesn't look happy. He hurriedly throws all his belongings in several big baskets and makes clear his intentions, demanding several bags with sand to build a shelter so that he can bring his wife and children back to stay here temporarily; when he's done, he gets on his Honda and leaves.

The next morning we are still working on the shelter, returning bags with sand back to the kitchen, then together rebuilding a makeshift shelter – we don't have anything to make it very solid. The renter of the kitchen returns and re-fixes the shelter there, but he brings his wife back for only one day to take care of collecting their stuff to move to another place. So, the shelter down in the kitchen is abandoned. Thái again gropes his way down to take back bags of sand to pile up for thickness.

Several days later, National Highway No. 1 connecting to An Cựu looks more bustling than before; those who are evacuating leave, others come back from evacuation, and the hamlet seems denser with people. A few families stay temporarily for a day or part of a day, sitting on wooden verandas, then they again go back to Phù Lương or Phú Bài or somewhere else.

Every day Bé and his wife come down to give us tiny pieces of news. Once, during the night the Việt Cộng came back to the T-junction. Another time: "This morning our army went to remove the flag hanging in front of the Transportation Station." Or: "Oh, auntie, soon fighting will break out here. They will soon occupy An Cựu again."

I don't have any way to apprehend what else will happen. But the An Cựu area looks more peaceful and quiet. The first couple of days we didn't see anything unusual, but every night Lài and her husband hear sounds of feet in the garden. Two or three days later, Hiền, Lài, and Túc go to Phù Lương. A lot of evacuee families go down there because they hear that refugee camps have been established down at Phù Lương and Phú Bài. Bé and his wife, intrepidly calm, stay up at their place until one day several artillery shells inexplicably fall directly in the An Cựu area late at night, either because of a mistake in calculating coordinates or aimed intentionally. At that moment we are lying in the shelter, and we all get bounced up in the air by reverberations and clutch each other tightly. Two or three explosions continue very close, then complete silence follows. When morning comes, Thái goes to check on the situation. He sees that outside there are people carrying wounded; they put them down on the side of the road and look for a way to take them farther to the American hospital. Around nine o'clock in the morning a column of vehicles with soldiers comes up; not one of them stops. Then, at ten o'clock, soldiers of the Special Forces and paratroopers from down at Phú Bài come up on foot. There are no more means of transportation, and several wounded people have already died. Two houses have been completely destroyed; a roof made of iron sheets was blown off and flew away over the railroad. Then the next night there are explosions again, this time a bit farther away, and the following morning Bé and his wife, panic-stricken, supporting each other, come down to our house:

"You must not stay here anymore. Our soldiers are arriving from Saigon, and there will be a huge fight. They are taking over the post office. All people have gathered at Kiểu Mẫu School. Last night bombs fell in the tiny hamlet and several more houses collapsed."

My mother gives a heavy sigh. Thái is worried:

"Is anyone wounded?"

"No, fortunately, everybody was in the shelter. Last night I thought we all were in danger."

And without waiting for anyone's further input, Bé, his wife, and several young children lead each other to Phú Lương, carrying poles on their shoulders and supporting each other. My mother sees that the situation is extremely difficult; half of her wants to leave, but half does not. My mother is still awaiting news from Nam Giao and Từ Đàm. But any bit of news that we get only makes us more desperate.

In the previous days, Hue residents died because of artillery, because of bombs and airplanes, because of public denunciations and informers. We are in An Cựu, which is considered a suburb bordering Hue; those who flee the fighting here flee because of the fear of being caught by the Việt Cộng or of being directly hit and dying innocently. But this time the fighting has been so violent that it has spread everywhere, out to the very extremities of the city. The Nationalist Army has managed to reoccupy a few places, and there the flags of the liberation [the Communist forces] have been taken down. At Trường Bia military post, soldiers have been seen moving in and out, but the Transportation Station is still abandoned. By day, An Cựu Bridge is guarded and repaired by Americans. First they must finish rebuilding several bridges, and only then will the army dispatch troops to the city's side of the river. On the right bank there are only a few quiet and safe areas. News comes from the Citadel that they [the Communist forces] still occupy Trần Hưng Đạo Street. Their army still occupies Nam Giao, Bến Ngự, and Từ Đàm.

We have returned to the city just as the Nationalist side is trying to reclaim every inch of ground; it turns out to be quite a dangerous game. But to flee, leaving half of our family stranded at Từ Đàm? Deep in our hearts, no one really wants that either.

At the moment, we stay in An Cựu, a piece of land that is in relatively little danger while the city of Hue has fallen in bullets and flowing blood. And from a person who escapes back here from the city, we learn terrifying news from the other side of the Perfume River.

Here's how we encountered this person.

One morning, Thái sees a column of vehicles coming up approaching the bridge and turning up toward Phú Cam; then many units of paratroopers and army Special Forces march up from Phú Bài. A moment later, he sees Americans coming to repair An Cựu Bridge. Thái shouts to me to come outside:

"Many people now go back and forth, elder sister."

My mother admonishes:

"Listen, both of you, don't go outside. When our army comes up, then soon there will be a big fight."

It turns out exactly as my mother predicts. In only about half an hour after the units of soldiers passed through, sounds of big and small guns emerge up in the areas of Phú Cam and Bến Ngự. And a number of residents, supporting each other, flee from the fighting to An Cựu, then proceed down to Phù Lương. They tell us:

"They are now fighting each other big time."

My mother hollers at me to crawl back into the shelter. But at noon we remember that there is nothing to eat in the house except for a little bit of rice.

Thái says:

"I hear that down at Mù U they sell pork. Down there it's quiet; it belongs to the Nationalists."

My mother falls silent. Thái says:

"Let me and Vân go to buy some meat. The battle is up in Bến Ngự; don't worry, auntie."

I also want to go outside to check what the situation is, so I must pitch in to help Thái:

"I and he, we'll run really fast and will be back in a minute, Mother."

My mother gives a heavy sigh:

"Yes, but listen, go fast."

I crawl after Thái from the shelter. My mother advises:

"Listen, child, go but avoid shells."

My mother's words make me both feel love and feel like laughing. How is it possible to avoid shells? But I politely say, "Yes, Mother," for the peace of my mother's heart. I and Thái don't go down to Mù U but, encouraging each other, go straight to An Cựu Bridge.

In fact, together we become bold. There are no people walking outside but American and Vietnamese soldiers who scurry up and down, moving units about.

They are not inclined to pay any attention to us. We go out to An Cựu Bridge and see that the American engineers are about to finish rebuilding it. We don't dare to take the main road but take a circuitous route, following a small road behind the fields to go back home. A lot of bomb craters broke open underground shelters that are filled with rainwater, making pools. Cutting across an abandoned garden area, we hear a noise behind a clump of bamboo.

Thái pulls me:

"Go fast, elder sister."

I inquisitively turn my head back to see through the sparse sprigs of the bamboo trees and see graves with earth hastily heaped on top of them where someone attached the victims' identification cards. Next to them is a foxhole with the body of a North Vietnamese soldier lying half in the foxhole and half out; I don't know whether he's wounded or dead. Nearby is a bomb crater and dried tree branches and pieces of bamboo that fell down, broken into small pieces. Through several desolate yards and gardens, we come to a small plot of land that is abandoned and collecting water. I don't know the road, so I continue to follow Thái. We hear the sound of an approaching airplane and Thái pulls me to duck down, pressing me into the road, waiting until the plane disappears, then we get up and cast about for the road back home. When I get up, I suddenly hear someone groaning. When I pause, Thái pulls me by the hand: "Go, elder sister." Thái says in a low voice:

"They're wounded; if we're not careful here, they will shoot us. It was such a stupid mistake to take this shortcut."

Thái firmly holds my hand and drags me behind him. But moaning sounds become clearer by the minute, imploring more and more persistently: "Help me please. Help me please. Help me please." I cannot make myself ignore it. Clearly this is the voice of a person about to die. I look around and suddenly realize that this is a youth lying face-down beside a shallow hole, which looks as though people dug it, then left it half-done, or as though a delayed explosive device created it. The young man is clad in a gray coat, covered all over with blood. Thái looks at him and knows that he is not a liberator. I pull Thái to get closer:

"No doubt it's a student from high school or college."

We stand next to him. As though sensing the sound of people's feet, the youth raises his face covered all over with earth; a streak of blood trickles from the corner of his mouth. The youth hugs his chest and wants to go down headfirst. In a jiffy, Thái jumps down into the hole to help him up. The young man groans:

"I am dying."

"Where did you come from?"

Thái bends close to his ear. The youth tries to raise his hand to point forward to gardens and trees. I don't understand. Thái asks:

"Are you escaping from the city?"

The youth nods.

Right at this moment we hear airplanes approaching. This time it seems that there are several of them and that they hover right over our heads. The youth makes a sign to us that we must run away and lets us know that the Việt Cộng are still hiding in many yards and gardens here. Thái raises his hand to signal me to go ahead and then helps the youth get up. The airplanes sound as though they will soon land on our heads. Thái shouts loudly:

"Run into the house right in front."

I run straight into an open gateway and Thái follows on my heels. We take several strides across a veranda and enter the house. The house is abandoned; there is a shelter made of sand, but as soon as Thái looks inside, he cups his mouth in his hand and pulls back:

"There is a dead person."

I decide to run out, but there have been gun explosions outside. A round is fired down from an airplane. Rockets sound as though they are falling right on our heads. Thái makes up his mind and pulls me to run down to the kitchen where there is a water tank; Thái leans the youth against the water tank, then pulls me down to the ground.

"Don't lift your head. Shells are flying over there."

I lie pressing myself into the ground, holding my head in my arms. Thái is more self-possessed; he tears his shirt into pieces and cleans the youth's wounds and dresses them. The young man is less afraid and more clear-headed now. He lets us know that his name is Khâm and he is from the Citadel. He managed to escape by disguising himself as a woman; he fled following a group of people who rushed through the Citadel gate; he scraped together all his money to bring along to hire a boat to cross the river. He opens wide his coat; the inside flaps of his blue flowing tunic are completely red with blood. A headscarf covering his head had fallen off and was lost some time before.

Airplanes still soar overhead and circle, even though the sound of firing from the ground at them is like rain, and each circle the airplanes make elicits round after round of rockets, thick and furious. Our hearts beat very fast. Certainly my mother at home is now extremely worried; based on my sense of direction, I guess that in the area of my house there is no trouble; this side is too close to Phú Cam. Lying here, I feel extremely uncertain; a direct hit can come at any moment. I think about the shelter up in the house. Thái said that there is a dead person there. I ask Thái inquisitively:

"What is it that you saw in the shelter, younger brother?"

"There's a dead person there. Very scary. I looked inside and there was a person lying with his face turned upward, his legs and arms dried and twisted; his eyes seemed to still be open and looking up to the shelter opening. Next to him were puddles of coagulated blood, and I saw several mice, busybodies, running back and forth, some of them holding in their mouths fingertips and toe tips from the dead body."

I shudder and want to escape from this house at once. But now the outside abounds in danger. Gunfire from down on the ground gradually diminishes, then fades farther away. It seems that they [the Communist forces] left their foxholes to escape when they heard the sounds of the airplanes circling back. And when the airplanes do turn around and come back, we don't hear return fire anymore from the ground around the place where we hide. Khâm looks more alert and rests his back against the side of the water tank. Thái takes a small can, fills it with water from the tank, and gives it to Khâm to get a sip. He has lost a lot of blood, his face is pale green, and his eyes are deeply sunken, betraying many sleepless nights. Although there is no sound of firing from the ground anymore, the airplanes still hover and circle over our heads, and we know that we still cannot escape from this house. Khâm says, his voice feeble:

"Several days ago, my main fear was to be arrested by liberators and executed or to die from bombs. But now, suddenly I am not afraid of anything. Everything has been destroyed."

And Khâm begins to tell us about his escape. A story of the people stranded on the other side of the Perfume River.

SEVEN

STORY FROM THE CITADEL

I DON'T UNDERSTAND HOW, THANKS TO WHAT MIRACULOUS trick, our house remained intact.

We live in a narrow, crowded shelter dug deep underground; sandbags are piled up over the shelter opening and around it. We have been living like this for ten-odd days.

What's the story? Ah, the first several days. The first several days there is no panic at all. As in other areas, the night of the first day of Tết we lie down, pressing ourselves close to the ground, crawling all the way under the beds because of gunfire everywhere. In the morning the Việt Cộng fill the house and the garden. They walk outside; there are so many of them that they seem to be everywhere. Uniforms? No. They wear all kinds of clothes. There is a small group wearing khaki, as expected, but a large number of them are clad in shorts. What is special – everybody wears colored bands on their arms or scarves around their necks.

So, what has happened? Has Hue already been lost?

We look at each other questioningly; we want to run across to our neighbors to ask them about any news, but that is impossible now. People stay put in their houses. And they [the Communist forces] issue an order that each household must dig its own underground shelter and begin to learn how to withstand hardships for the sake of victory. "We have already occupied Hue. There is still fighting in other places, and we expect to take over the entire country, which will mean victory." This is what the Liberation Army said.

This chapter is in the voice of Khâm, the young man whom the narrator and Thái met under tragic circumstances as described at the end of chapter 6.

The first several days are very joyful. They fix food, eat, and drink in our house. On top of this are rumors that they will organize a celebration. Then they bring from somewhere a lot of jam and cakes, mostly *bánh tét,* and they eat their fill. They eat as if they had never been able to eat like that before.

The first day I am very afraid; moreover, my family is very afraid for me. I'm the only male child in the family; if something happens to me, my mother will certainly not be able to bear it. But the first several days are going peacefully. I am still able to hear them [members of the Communist forces] talking. They tell funny stories. My younger sister Hường asks everything about the North; they say that in the North there is plenty of everything. But a lot of northern cadres and soldiers look very surprised when they see young Hue girls and women wearing tight-fitting pants and floral blouses. I hear them chat with each other:

"Girls here are so beautiful, and the style of their clothes does not leave anything more to desire."

Several female [Communist] cadres openly hate this. That's why on the second day young girls and women of Hue living in the Citadel[1] learn not to favor their local dressing style and immediately change their outfits. It's smooth sailing during the first several days; only occasionally do we hear gunfire exploding far away, really far away, either on the right bank or on the left, but in any case close to the suburbs, so no one here pays any attention to it.

Several female cadres take out the motorbikes and bicycles of those locals who ran away. They plan to practice riding them. A lot of families at dawn of the first day fled to Gia Hội. At first we thought they were insane to leave. Their houses are abandoned, and some female cadres rummaged through them to their hearts' content. What the cadres like the most are bicycles and Honda motorbikes. Seeing female cadres roll the legs of their trousers up to their thighs in order to practice riding bikes, we are almost incapable of suppressing laughter. But, funny as it is,

1. The seat of the Nguyễn emperors was located in the section of Hue called the Citadel, which occupies a walled area on the north side of the Perfume River. Inside the Citadel was a "Forbidden City" where only the emperors and those close to them were granted access.

no one dares to smile, for we are very worried about the future. We don't know what will happen next. Some Việt Cộng soldiers look optimistic. "The victory will be won all over the country; don't worry, compatriots." That's how they report news. And inside the Citadel we are surprised to see that they pour into the city quite easily; I don't see anything at all that looks like fighting or spilled blood. Of course, I don't venture out of the house. Right from daybreak of the second day, my mother has the door closed tight, and we are able to look outside only through tiny gaps in the walls or doors.

But even though it's only a very small slit, I still can see that there are a lot of people moving around outside. All the Việt Cộng soldiers wear blue or white bands on their sleeves.

The atmosphere on the streets changes very suddenly, with a lot of people of Hue with worried faces hiding behind doors while Communists and their supporters come out with smiling faces, glowing with extreme happiness. Teacher Kê, a middle-aged man who left for the North to regroup more than fifteen years ago, has suddenly reappeared. He has a wife who every day goes to sell tea and a son around seventeen or eighteen years old. The appearance of teacher Kê makes everyone worry. Trembling, my mother says:

"That's it – it's the end. That man has come back; he knows everybody in the area, so beware, he will be arresting people at will."

Even though we are worried like this, teacher Kê's personality doesn't panic us as much as do the two houses right at the beginning of Nguyễn Hiệu Road that suddenly bustle with Việt Cộng cadres and soldiers going in and coming out in great numbers. People spread rumors that two female students living there are undercover cadres. The two of them live in the houses at the beginning of the street; some people saw them wearing Western clothes, blouses, and conical hats perched on their heads. They go back and forth in the street carrying Czech-type guns on their backs. I don't know the names of these young women, but people tell me that the two used to be students in Saigon. I try to guess a couple of names among the circle of my old friends and acquaintances, but nothing definite comes to mind.

Also at Nguyễn Hiệu Road, a joss-paper maker who previously left with the Việt Cộng has just returned as an undercover cadre. His appearance is the most troubling for people. He lived here for a long time and somehow distinguishes himself by informing on a number of ordinary people. Worried, my mother asks me whether I did anything to make this man feel enmity and hatred toward me. I think about it over and over again, but I can't remember anything of this sort; however, I still can't put my mind at peace. For the next several days, I don't dare go outside. When my mother sees my face emerge to look through the slit in the door, she drags me back into the room and tightly closes the door.

But after several days, I still don't see anything unusual happening outside with the exception of the Việt Cộng soldiers entering each house to seize people and force them to go to study. My mother again hides me up in the loft. My younger sister Hường must go to study. When she comes back, she informs us that study sessions are organized in teacher Kế's house. I ask her what they study; she says people [the Communists] require young girls and women to join a service – propaganda, first aid, or supply. I ask her what service she picked, but she only laughs and shakes her head:

"I trembled to death. Ah, I have met . . ."

When I ask whom she met, she falls silent and her face reveals fear. I keep inquiring several more times, but she does not dare to respond. But she lets me know that lots of young people and students are forced to go study.

That entire day I can't eat; I feel that my throat is dry and bitter. It seems like I am about to get the flu. My younger sister's ambiguous words make me feel disturbed. That evening I leave the loft and come down to lie on the ground, and I ask her again. This time her voice trembles as though on the brink of tears:

"I met this young woman Đoan, the Đoan who lives at the beginning of our road over there, elder brother."

"Aren't there two of them?"

"Yes, Đoan and Kim; they live in the two houses across from each other over there."

"Did she recognize you?"

"She did. She asked where you were that you didn't come to study, elder brother. I said that you returned to the countryside on the twenty-eighth before Tết. She laughed and said that she met you when you were going out of Đông Ba Gate with your friends Hạo and Toàn on the first day of Tết."

"Then what did you answer?"

"I fell silent."

"Did she say anything else?"

"She did. She advised me that I must join the Alliance Front, Peace Front, or something else like that. I kept silent. She told me to help her. She promised she would see me again later."

"Did you see teacher Đóa going to the meeting?"

"I didn't see teacher Đóa anywhere at all."

"And teacher Kê has come back, hasn't he?"

"Teacher Kê has delivered a very fiery public speech. I was awfully afraid; I didn't hear a word, but even if I had I wouldn't have understood anything. Now, elder brother, he came back, after regrouping to the North, with a long beard down to his chest; just to look at it is scary. Oh, elder brother, I also saw someone looking like Đắc."[2]

"Đắc?"

I shout in amazement: "Enough, that's the end; Đắc has returned." But I don't believe that Đắc could become a Communist. In the past, he and I were members of the Struggle Movement.[3] Đắc was always confident that he could not accept Communism. Then, sometime later, because he was placed under surveillance and caught in a roundup, he fled.

2. In 1966, while a student, Nguyễn Đắc Xuân had been a leader of the Struggle Movement and a commander of the Buddhist "Suicide Squad," which took a very active part in the Buddhist Uprising between General Nguyễn Chánh Thi and the Saigon government. When the uprising was suppressed, he fled and joined the Việt Cộng. During the Tết Offensive he returned to Hue with the Communist Forces and is mentioned in various accounts as one of the leading perpetrators of the atrocities. Nguyễn Đắc Xuân denies this. After the war, Nguyễn Đắc Xuân became a researcher of Hue history and of the last imperial dynasty of Vietnam, the Nguyễn. He has extensively published his research (see more on him in the Translator's Introduction).

3. The Struggle Movement, also known as the Military-Civilian Struggle Committee, was an offshoot of the opposition movement against the Saigon government that came into existence in 1965. Prior to and during the Buddhist Uprising of 1966, the Struggle Movement was active. It supported Buddhist general Nguyễn Chánh Thi, a commander of the area that included Hue, against the then prime minister Nguyễn Cao Kỳ. The movement mainly consisted of Buddhists and students.

Some people said that Đắc had fled with Đoan and Ngọc.[4] If Đắc has returned, surely Ngọc and his brother Phủ[5] have also returned. I am secretly worried and afraid. In the past Phủ had a sweetheart who lived here in the Citadel; soon after Phủ left, she had a sudden change of heart and followed another person. In addition to being miserably unhappy because he had to flee, Phủ at the same time also lost the one he loved. Now, if he has returned, Phủ definitely will feel utterly wretched and extremely resentful. Just think what will happen.

I keep questioning my younger sister very closely: "Did you see Phủ or not?" "Did anyone see Phủ?" She is certain that she did not, and even her friends who went to the meetings also said that they did not see him. I feel a tiny bit more at peace and secretly glad for his ex-girlfriend. If Phủ has returned, add in another feeling of hatred here – his beloved who changed her heart certainly won't escape tragic consequences. But my younger sister forces a laugh:

"Elder brother, you think that Phủ only now learned about this [his former girlfriend]? I believe that Phủ bears no resentment. But neither Phủ nor Ngọc is here in the Citadel."

I can't get rid of sadness and feel on the verge of tears when I remember my old friends. Though Đắc, Ngọc, and Phủ left, though they followed some other ideals, though they were hostile toward me, I have still kept good memories about them. I am confident in myself; I am confident in my friends. Earlier, Đắc was driven to the end of his rope; he had to escape and follow the other side. Đắc's presence doesn't make me worry or afraid anymore, but it makes me think of him. I suddenly feel a little bit calmer and safer. In my gut, I decide that I must meet Đắc. I don't believe anything can harm our friendship. Today or tomorrow,

4. Hoàng Phủ Ngọc Tường was a teacher at Quốc Học School, an elite secondary school established in 1898, and subsequently during the Tết Offensive he became a member of the Revolutionary Committee under Professor Lê Văn Hảo. He is a prolific and renowned author and poet and currently resides in Hue.

5. Full name Hoàng Phủ Ngọc Phan. He is a younger brother of Hoàng Phủ Ngọc Tường and like his brother is also a writer. At the time of the Tết Offensive he was a medical student. Together with Nguyễn Đắc Xuân, he is also mentioned in Alje Venne-ma's account (see Translator's Introduction).

whatever happens, I will still have an opportunity to meet Đắc again. I must meet him. I ask my younger sister:

"Did you talk with Đắc?"

"I saw a person who looked like Đắc, that's it, but I didn't dare to take another look at him. That guy was wearing a blue armband and also had a gun."

"But how did he look to you?"

"He had a contemplative look, not lofty like some other undercover cadres. You know, elder brother, our hamlet is full of undercover cadres, but you don't know anything about it."

I keep asking:

"So, what kind of study do they organize?"

"Elder brother, you could hear the entire conversation while lying here in the loft in the morning. They came to the house and invited us to go to a meeting. I decided to dodge, but Đoan, she stood at the head of the lane and immediately called me by name, so I had to go. They said to go to the meeting, but they additionally forced us to study. Then they delivered a public speech with their propaganda about the victory."

"What did they propagandize about? I feel sick."

"They said that the victory, taking over Hue, is possible thanks to the contributions of the people. So, children are to go back home to find pieces of bamboo and short pieces of sticks covered with black lacquer, and whenever they hear sounds of American and their puppets' airplanes coming, they are to bring them out and aim them up to the sky so that the Americans and their puppets will think that those are guns, and they will be frightened to death by the spirit of the people of Hue against imperialists and their lackeys. They also said: 'Compatriots, don't let even a single American or a puppet or a Vietnamese malefactor hide in your house. If you encounter any such case, you must immediately report it to the Liberators.'"

I am terrified:

"Is it really true that they excite children to make fake guns out of lacquered bamboo pieces?"

"I clearly heard this. They still propagandize a lot. Listen, elder brother, before the meeting, the Liberators continually recite slogans, then the seven tasks of a party member, then the words of Uncle Hồ;

I remember it like this: 'Be loyal to the party, be dutiful to the people, complete any task, overcome all hardships, gain victory over every enemy . . .' They shouted loudly many times, and I've memorized everything by heart."

I burst into angry words:

"Damn them! Why must I learn and listen to slogans of loyalty to the uncle and the party?"

These are soldiers from North Vietnam who came to the South; they learned these slogans by rote, but no doubt there are also people among them who don't understand why they must be loyal to Uncle Hồ and the party and why they must die.

But this propaganda talk had harmful consequences. Later on, when battles broke out, it was not possible to understand whether they happened because of guns firing from foxholes or because of the sticks of small children who were forced to bring them out and aim them up at the sky, and airplanes would fire down at them thick and fast.

I cannot sleep that night. The next morning I have to climb up to the loft and lie there. My younger sister still runs across to the neighbors to check on the news, but I don't dare show my face down in the house, not to mention go outside. I'm afraid they will recognize me, especially the joss-paper maker, who has been with the Việt Cộng for a long time and now has returned to be an undercover cadre. He doesn't favor students like myself. Then there is still teacher Kê's family, including the lad of seventeen or eighteen years old or something like that, who seldom openly talked with me. My younger sister lied that I am stranded out in the countryside, and I am afraid that she will bring misfortune on herself because of my presence.

That morning, in front of my house and back in the garden I hear sounds of someone digging in the ground. Then, a moment later someone bursts into an uproar. I hold my breath, lie quietly, and listen intently. I hear the voice of an old man with a northern accent from Quảng Bình province,[6] and it seems that he is talking with my mother:

6. A province of North Vietnam on the coast, located on the border with South Vietnam.

"Liberation Mother, you must allow us to dig an underground shelter. We still face a lot of hardships. The armies of Americans and their puppets can bring airplanes over here to drop bombs to kill people. But it doesn't matter, for they will suffer a heavy defeat."

Sounds of footsteps accelerate around the house. My mother's voice implores:

"Yes, please kind sir, my family is small, their father passed away a long time ago, we are a widow mother and orphan children . . . Yes, sir, help yourself to *bánh tét* . . . Yes, please sir, here are some more rice cakes left after worshipping rituals . . ."

"In the North our people celebrate Tết very joyfully."

"Yes, sir."

"This year, Uncle Hồ comes to celebrate Tết here with us. We are very happy to meet with mothers and sisters here in the South."

"Yes, kind sir."

"Oh, I forgot, for how much per bag do American puppets sell rice?"

"Yes, please sir. Two hundred kilograms is several thousand dongs, some for three thousand dongs, and some for two thousand dongs."

"American puppets sell at outrageous prices; they drink the people's blood. Wait until the liberation is complete, and then rice will be sold for only five hundred per two hundred kilograms."

"Yes, sir."

"Do you have anyone in your family, Mother, to help you dig shelters?"

"Yes sir, myself and my child can dig it. Besides me and my young child, there are other helpers, like this ten-year-old boy, and several nephews. My aunt and grandmother also help. Please sir, I would not dare to bother you."

I hear feet moving toward the altar. I guess that these are my mother's quick steps as though she wants to prevent something:

"Please sir, the altar has been set up now for several days."

I hear a man's ringing laughter:

"Nothing, Mother; sure, continue to worship."

"Please sir, to worship . . . but during the last several days who has a heart for worship? On the first day of Tết, I thought we were dead, but thanks to our ancestors we survived . . . Please, sir, in there is nothing at all. Please, sir, here are cakes, *bánh tét*. Yes, please sirs, help yourselves to them, sirs . . . oh, please, help yourselves to them . . . comrades."

"Thank you, Mother. People of the South are very good to the liberation. We will record our gratitude to you to the best of our ability, Liberation Mother . . ."

I hear footsteps going out of the house and then gradually moving away. Having waited for a moment, I stick my head down. Pieces of cardboard covering the entrance to the loft have just been lifted; I see my mother's face looking up, her hands clasped together in front of her chest:

"I beg you, God, God on high, help me. They've just grabbed all the cakes."

I am afraid that my mother will worry, and I quickly pull my head back up and put back the pieces of cardboard. Throughout that day, I lie prostrate in the loft. I wait for whenever my younger sister, very quietly, will bring up food for me or pour me a cup of cold water.

Several days later a few of them [Communist soldiers] come into the house; perhaps they don't have suspicions about our family anymore. My younger sister still has to go to the meetings, to go study. She comes back and brings me an update:

"It is indeed Đắc himself."

"Did he recognize you?"

"He did. He laughed and said: 'Hường, is Khâm here?' And then he gave a neighing loud laugh. I remember how in the past Đắc often patted my head."

"So, were you afraid?"

"No, Đắc is very kind, elder brother. He asked about you; then he asked about our mother. He said that when he has free time he would come to visit Mother."

"Oh heavens, did you reveal that I'm hiding in the house?"

Hường laughs:

"I am not a fool. Nor was Đắc very hard on me while inquiring. He only asked: 'Did something happen to Khâm?' I said: 'Please sir, nothing.' Then I remembered and said immediately: 'Because he got stranded somewhere out in the countryside.' Đắc asked whether it's in Bao Vinh. I nodded my head and he got a bit angry. He also looked worried and afraid for you, elder brother."

I feel moved and secretly ashamed. So, it turns out that Đắc is still my friend. Đắc has never changed toward me. So, why did Đắc return? With what task did he return? My heart languishes more and more in my desire to see Đắc. I open up to Hường about my desire to participate in a meeting. Hường says:

"It's impossible. Đắc is kind, but some other people are very cruel. They say brutal things, and it's very easy to get scared."

Then Hường whispers in my ear:

"Now, elder brother. When cutting across a T-junction I saw someone looking like Mậu Tý, who was also in the Struggle Movement. He carried clothes in his arms as though he wanted to flee down to Mai Thúc Loan Road."

"Wow, that Mậu Tý guy. He dares to flee, does he?"

"I don't know, elder brother. But I also saw that he wore a white band on his arm. Perhaps he is also with the Việt Cộng now."

"This man is very daring. He's the one who can do anything."

I feel vexed. But at the same time I am also afraid. If he is with the liberation, he will have the guts to find and arrest me or will report me. I tell Hường:

"Little sister, don't let him see you or he will start asking you in a roundabout way and will figure it out."

I am afraid he will see my younger sister and then will remember about me. Perhaps because of how busy he must be, he has forgotten about me, but meeting someone related to me can remind him of me. Ordinarily I am not fond of him or of our time together in the Struggle Movement; many times I talked with friends:

"That Mậu Tý guy is not trustworthy. But he dares to be in the volunteer suicide team – how many people has he deceived?"

Seeing my contemplative look, Hường quickly says:

"If I see Mậu Tý, I will escape at once; I am afraid to death."

"Why would a girl like you be afraid of him?"

"I'm afraid he will arrest me. I saw that guy snatch some of my friends with whom I go to the meetings."

I laugh, trying to calm the girl down.

"Never mind him; we don't have anything to be afraid of."

"Elder brother, you don't know this, but Mr. Ích Khiêm from down the road, they have already arrested him. Government officials, army people – all of them have been arrested. Especially those who worked in American offices."

"We don't work in American offices, do we? So, there's nothing to be afraid of. We are not government officials, either."

"Down there a lot of people have been arrested. Many didn't do anything either but still were arrested."

Exactly like my younger sister predicted, throughout the next day, all young males, government officials, and military men are arrested in my neighborhood. A few people who try to escape are caught on the spot. Our family finishes building a rather solid shelter from sandbags and pieces of board from the precious wooden plank bed that has been in the family for several generations.

So during the day I continue to hide in the loft of the house, and only at night do I dare to come down to sleep in the shelter. I begin to feel dispirited and exhausted. At that time, everybody is dismayed because artillery shells are being lobbed into our area. Lying prone, I press my ear to the ground and hear constant murmurs as though tanks are moving somewhere outside of the Citadel. A couple of times I vaguely hear the sound of airplanes.

A few houses are directly hit by artillery fire. People say that direct artillery hits fall mostly on the city walls. People also say that the flag at Phu Văn Lâu has been lowered and instead a liberation flag is hanging there now. But when artillery fire hits the Citadel, everybody panics. Add to this the harsh arrests by the Việt Cộng, which make the atmosphere even more terrifying.

One day, I'm lying in the shelter chewing on some pieces of dry bread and hear at the beginning of the alley sounds of feet in hot pursuit. A voice shouts:

"Stop. Stop."

I hear sounds of feet running in circles back in our garden, the sounds of stomping feet chasing someone; there seems to be a lot of people in a hurry. An explosion and a scream – I tightly cover my ears. My mother holds Hường fast in her arms, and several small siblings of mine lie flattening themselves against the shelter floor; a child hugs my mother's legs and another one hugs Hường's legs with his mouth distorted by the desire to cry.

A moment later, the sounds of feet from the garden enter the courtyard. I hear the sound of an uproar:

"Because he attempted to flee. He's certainly a military lackey of the Americans and their puppets."

"Is he completely dead or not quite yet?"

"Not yet, but he will die later. But is it true that he worked for Americans?"

"He worked for Americans, indeed. I often saw him with tons of dollars."

"That's correct then."

"If not for me, he would have escaped. In this hamlet, when anyone flees, even if into the sky, I will still know. Their [those who work for the South Vietnamese government] gangs must pay the debt by blood, mustn't they, dear comrade group commander?"

"You're very active, comrade."

I hear the familiar voice of the informer. It seems that this person is everywhere in the hamlet. Hường also decides to raise her voice, and my mother gets a bit vexed:

"Be silent; if he hears you, he will come in."

We keep silent. But then we hear that someone is pushing the door, and then feet enter the house:

"Is there anyone at home? Please come up here for a short chat."

My mother hastens to creep out. Then Hường also creeps out.

"Please sir."

"Back in the garden, there's a person who has just been shot. We'll have people come here to carry him away and bury him. We want to again advise you not to shelter anyone from the gangs of Americans and their puppets. Please, auntie, help us – that is, help the party; help the country to get independence."

My mother immediately responds with polite "Yes, sirs." Some other voice speaks:

"In this house there are only a few people: the woman and children, that's it."

"That's why we have just advised them because if they [the Americans and their "puppets"] enter, they will kill the entire family, and we will not be able to save them."

Hường innocently asks:

"Please sirs, dear elder brothers, whom did you just shoot over there?"

The familiar voice of the official informer responds:

"That guy Minh.[7] Before the liberation, he was the one who showed off his power the most in this hamlet, isn't that right? Please, young lady, identify him here for our brother comrades."

I hear Hường's very soft and subordinately polite "Yes, sir." Then, the voice of the informer asking:

"This lad Khâm, where is he? Not at home?"

My heart beats fast. That's it, it's the end; he has remembered me. My guess is not mistaken – this is indeed the person who makes noodles in the hamlet. Usually, he only stays in his house grinding flour to make noodles and then his wife takes them to sell to fellow traders, wholesale and retail. He also talks very little with anybody. Hường attempts to keep her voice calm:

"Please sir, my elder brother is stranded down at Bao Vinh. That day they went there to congratulate our uncle, then didn't have time to come up back here when everything happened . . ."

"If he's down there, stop worrying; that place now completely belongs to the Liberation Army and to the people."

Hường smartly adds for form's sake:

"Yes, sir, and here also now belongs to the liberation."

"Yet in just this short period of time, our division has still not finished liquidating the enemy. But now they will all die of starvation. Soon we will get more reinforcements from Quảng Trị[8] to complete the takeover, and from the North will also come more reinforcements, so nothing to worry about."

He continues to stand there blabbing and singing verbose praises, and then he leaves together with his comrades.

I sigh, relieved, thinking that I have luckily just escaped death. My younger sister sneaks down to the shelter and tells me in a low voice:

7. Not to be confused with Võ Thành Minh, who appears in several other chapters.

8. A province in North Central Vietnam, the northernmost province of the Republic of Vietnam, located north of Hue.

"That's the noodle-seller guy from the hamlet, elder brother. He was as slippery as an eel; who would suspect him?"

"So, did he shoot anybody?"

"Mr. Minh. He's now dead."

"Who did he come with?"

"With several Việt Cộng, who else? When he was talking, I saw Đoan and Kim walking outside."

"Did they see you?"

"They did, and they waved 'Hi' to me."

"Have you stopped being afraid?"

"Not at all. At yesterday's meeting I met them and both were as slick as shit; they greeted me and didn't ask anything. Here, elder brother, today it seems they are scouring and conducting arrests very fiercely. Be a bit more careful, elder brother."

"People have their own fates, younger sister."

"To meet Đắc is certainly out of the question now, elder brother, isn't it?"

I exhale without any confidence:

"I don't even know for sure."

My mother has come back:

"Mr. Bèo, the one who sells noodles, he's a Việt Cộng."

"When I heard him, I also guessed it."

"Fortunately, there's no bad blood between him and our family."

Hường says:

"No bad blood, but he owes us, doesn't he, Mother? The day his hag of a wife gave birth, he came to borrow money from you, Mother, several hundreds. The day before Tết, you, Mother, sent me to go request that it be returned, and luckily I forgot, so it didn't make us enemies."

Just at this moment we hear a woman in a nearby house shouting and crying. My mother signals for us to be quiet, then strains her ears to listen:

"Mr. Bình's house."

"It's Mrs. Bình screaming there, and certainly someone else has entered her house."

Hường tightly holds my hand:

"It seems they [the Communists] are arresting people."

Sounds of screaming and crying from the nearby house become louder by the minute:

"Pray you, sirs, my husband is innocent, and my child goes to study."

A man's voice is unruffled:

"It doesn't have anything to do with that, Mother. Please, you and your son, come with us to a meeting, and then you'll come back. Go to the meeting, then come back, Mother, put your mind at peace. We came here to liberate Hue; we ask for the help of the people of Hue."

The shouting and crying gradually weaken. A moment later there is the sound of someone banging on the door. Hường opens the door and Tịnh, Mrs. Bình's son, comes in, his face deathly pale:

"They have just now arrested my elder brother Định. My father has also been arrested."

My mother asks:

"What do you think to do now?"

"My mother said I must run over here to ask you, auntie, to shelter me. There, they will come back anyway to arrest me."

My mother gives a long and heavy sigh:

"Enough! Go down to the shelter."

Tịnh brings me a lot of very strange news. Now, outside the city gates there are many dead Việt Cộng because of the direct hits by artillery and bombs. And one can hear outside of Gia Hội School public denunciations; it gives me the creeps. And some people suspected of working for Americans are executed; their bodies are buried in the garden area down the road. I ask why they took away Mr. Bình, Tinh's father, from the house nearby, even though he's quite old. Tịnh tells me that when they entered the house, Mr. Bèo, the noodle maker from the hamlet, accompanied them. He said something in a low voice, and then several liberators immediately invited her to leave with them. At that moment Tịnh escaped down to the kitchen; surely Mr. Bèo forgot about Tịnh and didn't inform on him.

My mother says:

"Fortunately, there's no bad blood between us."

"It seems that there's enmity between him and my family. Before Tết, the guy came to borrow some money, but my mother did not give him anything. He had borrowed several times before but didn't pay back.

On top of that, when the guy is drunk he curses profusely; my elder brother Định used to speak his mind about this, and clearly this noodle maker hates him so now he harms him."

Tịnh intently listens to the sad crying still heard from the outside and grimaces with an apprehensive expression:

"My mother begged him, but I was just burning with anger. I wish I had a rifle; I would shoot a round then and there and let it be, whatever comes, even if death."

I comfort him:

"Surely there is no guilt of anything; your mom is already very old. They force her to go and then they will let her return home, and there is nothing to worry about."

"Yes, please sir, may you be correct."

"There is a rumor that down in the hamlet there's a house directly hit by a bomb; is that right?"

"It seems like that. Just now in my house Mr. Bèo threatened that any house conniving with Americans and their puppets will be the easiest target for bombs because they will suspect that the Việt Cộng have occupied those houses."

"They are just talking bullshit."

My mother moans. At night artillery shells do not reach the area I live in, but from time to time there are shells that go astray, hitting some gardens, making roofs fly off, making houses shake. Outside, the number of Việt Cộng soldiers going back and forth has decreased. They pull into solid shelters to hide from danger. Guards on the street also dig individual foxholes for themselves.

From that day on, my younger sister continues to be invited to go to meetings and study sessions, and then she manages to be set free to come back. Each time I inquire about Đắc. One day she says that she saw him. Another day she says she didn't. But suddenly one day I hear Đắc's voice.

That day, when the entire family is eating down in the shelter, someone knocks on the door. My mother quickly tells us to squeeze into the end of the sand shelter and then she climbs up to open the door. It seems that there is only one person there, and my mother greets him; her voice is slightly happy:

"Wow, it's you, young man, isn't it? When did you come back?"

In a flutter of excitement I wait to hear the answering voice.

"Please madam, I've come back with my comrades into the Citadel."

I don't hear my mother asking anything else. A moment of silence, then the young voice asks:

"Auntie, surely you've dug a shelter, haven't you? You must get ready for a long resistance, auntie. The situation seems to be wearisome."

"Yes, sir."

"God, auntie, the way you talk to me, you make me feel very weird. I am still the same guy, Đắc, who I was in the past, auntie. Oh, where's Khâm?"

My mother pretends to sob softly:

"Oh, it's a disaster, elder brother. He has been gone since the first day of Tết; he went back to the countryside at Bao Vinh and then there has been no news from him anymore. I am so very worried, afraid that he, as hot-tempered as he is, was coming back up here but was arrested somewhere along the road. He's my only son; you know this, elder brother: if his fate led to his death, I will not be able to bear it . . ."

It's Đắc, for sure. I want to climb up from the shelter to meet my friend. But Hường has tightly clasped her hands on me:

"Don't, elder brother, are you out of your mind?"

Đắc's voice:

"Don't worry, auntie. Those who are guilty must pay for their sins. Khâm and I are still friends . . ."

"I know that you are fond of him, but there, on the roads, he will not encounter you but someone else . . ."

Đắc seems to think about this for a moment and then says in a less confident voice:

"Death indeed is a fate, auntie. If I had been destined to die, I would have been dead a long time ago. Auntie, don't call me 'elder brother'; it makes me very sad because I'm still a child for you. Oh auntie, I hear Tịnh has come here, hasn't he, auntie?"

I get angry; Tịnh is lying next to me and shivers from head to toe. Fortunately, my mother answers on his behalf:

"He has been here and has already left. He went to a meeting and then was going to go back somewhere."

"Huh, so who could it be that detained him? All right – let me ask around and then I will let him out to go back. I've just met Định, Tịnh's elder brother. Định must go to study; otherwise no doubt he will be taken to Gia Hội or down to the mulberry field."

"Why so far?"

Đắc doesn't respond to my mother but asks instead:

"Where's Hường, auntie?"

My mother doesn't dare to hide the truth:

"She's been so afraid the entire day, she has crawled into the shelter or under the bed; this child, she's afraid of sudden gunfire."

"Auntie, call Hường up here. I am none other than Đắc; so there's nothing to be afraid of."

"Hey, Hường. Đắc has come to visit."

Afraid that Đắc would come down to the shelter, Hường quickly crawls up from the shelter opening. I hear Đắc's voice laughing loudly:

"Hường, it looks like you think that when I went up to the mountains I turned into a tiger eating human flesh, isn't that right? And that's why you got so awfully scared when you heard my voice?"

Hường forces a reluctant smile:

"I'm not afraid of you at all, elder brother, but these several days I am very afraid of death."

Đắc sits down and talks with my mother and younger sister for a very long time. He tells them about the hardships he went through before he went up to the mountains. Đắc talks half-jokingly, half-ironically:

"Back then I only struggled against the South Vietnamese government; I was arrested and unimaginably beaten up. Do you know, auntie, they crushed both my hands? My body is still full of scars; I was dead and then came to life again. Gratitude and hatred must be paid back, auntie. I went up into the mountains to study and practice with the Việt Cộng; now I return to pay back my persecutors in kind. I don't want to harm anyone, but the debt of blood must be paid, auntie."

I don't know what my mother's face looks like right now, but Đắc suddenly laughs:

"I tell you my story, and your face, auntie, turns dead white. I'm just joking for fun, but I was indeed forced to go up to the mountains. Wherever I went, I couldn't forget about Hue. I still bear a lot of grudges, auntie."

Right at this moment I hear many people entering the house. I hear a lot of stories, and it's Đắc who talks about recent arrests in nearby houses. Someone's drawling voice:

"That guy is real good at hiding: if not for comrade Đắc, who knows whether we would have found him."

Another voice, laughing:

"I knew that he hid under the mattress. That guy here in the hamlet, who doesn't know him?"

Perhaps this is a group of undercover cadres. They loudly tell stories and merrily joke around. Tịnh pushes my hand and is about to speak, but I cover his mouth. I am afraid that up there at the shelter opening they will hear him. Hường asks about Ngọc and Phủ. Đắc replies:

"They've come back. Phủ along with Ngọc are at Gia Hội School."

Hường's voice:

"I haven't heard anyone mention meeting those two at all."

"Hường, you don't go out, so you don't hear or see anything. Oh heavens, this girl is really timid."

Then Đắc talks with my mother:

"It's a pity that Khâm is stranded out in the countryside; if he were here I would make him go to work with me."

Then suddenly Đắc ponders.

"But certainly I wouldn't force him. When you see him, auntie, tell him that I am always and everywhere his friend."

Đắc stays and talks for a long time. He asks my mother whether there's still enough rice in the house. Then Đắc promises that he will bring rice to supply the entire family. Seeing Đắc being happy, my mother and Hường seem less scared. My mother inquires about the situation. At first Đắc's voice is quite positive, but then the confidence in his voice seems to decrease. Đắc advises that the shelter must be made very carefully; a lot of houses inside and outside of the hamlet have been directly hit by artillery fire. Đắc also says that the American army has advanced to National Highway No. 1, and in daytime it advances to An Cựu. But Phú Cam, Từ Đàm, and Bến Ngự hamlets are still under the authority of the Liberation Army. My mother can't suppress moaning out her grief. Certainly, a lot of civilians have died. I don't hear Đắc's response, and the merry laughter also stops for a long time.

Before leaving, Đắc promises to come back to visit. Đắc advises Hường about some things that I don't hear clearly, only occasionally

Hường's responses: "Yes, elder brother." Just as Đắc and several liberators and cadres leave the house, artillery fire resumes. My mother and Hường again crawl down into the shelter. Hường tells the story about her meeting with Đắc despite my having heard almost everything. Hường says that among those who came into the house there was a person, still young, wearing thick glasses, surely also an undercover cadre. My mother advises me to be careful because Đắc promised to come back. She reminds me that Đắc promised to supply us with rice and told Hường that if she needed anything to go find Đắc himself. I listen and feel moved. In fact, no ideology, no ideals can divide human feelings and friendship. I also think that perhaps I am too shallow. But after several days pass by, Đắc doesn't find time to come visit with us anymore, even though I know that he has passed by our house many times.

Once, when the artillery had calmed down and the large and small guns outside the walls of the Citadel were also taking a break, I suddenly hear deafeningly loud shouts outside. My younger sister, by now very much accustomed to the situation, dares to crawl up, open the door, and look outside. I hear a familiar voice and recognize Đắc's voice. Hường sticks her head down to the shelter and says in a low voice:

"Damn it. Đắc has just now arrested Mậu Tý."

I don't have time to ask more when Hường goes back up and continues to peer out at the street. Đắc's voice resounds from outside:

"Comrades, let me try this one. Give me the right of priority. In the past, he afflicted our lives with misery on so many occasions! He must pay for his terrible crimes."

Mậu Tý, Đắc's former friend, pleads:

"I beg you, elder brother, to spare me. Now I also follow the liberation. Here, I am wearing a band, elder brother; here, I am wearing a band. For several days I've been very active with the liberation; I've already publicly denounced and arrested a lot of American puppets. Please let me work to redeem my crimes."

Đắc gives a few muffled laughs; his voice is biting:

"So you also know repentance. No, I must try you. You go down and stand in the foxhole, and I will ask about your crimes."

A sound of jostling, then Mậu Tý's screaming:

"Oh, pray you, elder brother, please spare me!"

"Spare you? In the past, I put our friendship on trial with you, but did you spare me? I was arrested, imprisoned, and beaten."

Đắc gives a few muffled laughs and keeps joking:

"Damn it. I went up to the mountains to study and practice with the Việt Cộng and then I came back here; this time you don't have any hope."

Mậu Tý's voice sounds as though he's crying:

"I beg you, elder brother, spare me. I beg you, elder brother – I now know my mistakes. That's why I followed the liberation right from the start of the offensive."

"You have a knack to follow very fast. That's exactly why I was beaten and imprisoned. You stand there in the hole and bend down your back and listen to my questions."

"I will, I beg you, elder brother, don't shoot me dead. I, I . . . by the will of Heaven, elder brother . . . elder brother . . ."

Đắc erupts into a boisterous outburst of laughter.

"Shoot you? No, you cannot die such a fast and easy death. You must die gradually, die in weariness . . . die in pain and in misery. In my life, I was a victim of glaring injustice; now I don't want to judge anyone unfairly."

I shudder. Đắc's voice is very angry and resolute. I hear someone's voice saying:

"Enough, comrade. He has already shown repentance for his crimes and mistakes; he has come back to the liberation with the people . . . Comrade, you have to – "

" – have to restrain my personal hatred? No, my personal hatred is also the hatred common to all my friends. You, comrades, don't meddle in this case; please, comrades. I only ask for this case; that's all I ask, comrades."

Đắc's voice storms blusteringly upon Mậu Tý:

"Stand quiet there. I haven't shot yet, but don't have any expectations."

"I beg you, elder brother, stop . . . spare me from being shot to death – release me from this misery."

"No."

Mậu Tý screams loudly as though someone is breaking his neck:

"I beg you, elder brother . . . I beg you, elder brother . . ."

Đắc's laughter resounds loudly. The laughter full of deep resentment pierces my head, making me giddy, and then the sounds of a gun firing. A loud scream – it's all over. But no, there is another gunshot and another scream. And it goes on like this. Several times my heart sinks, then I breathe a small sigh for the accused person. Death is the end. But strangely, it's not over yet, and each gunshot brings another scream, adding another round of Đắc's mad laughter.

The gunshots end after a terrible scream from Mậu Tý. By this time my mind is at peace about Mậu Tý.

Now the guns are somewhere outside the walls of the Citadel, farther away; it seems like in the market area near Tràng Tiền Bridge or somewhere over there are explosions, and then I hear artillery. My mother calls Hường to hasten into the shelter. But Hường looks terrified by the scene she has witnessed and stands transfixed near the open door. My mother has to run out and drag her into the shelter. I ask her what she saw. She stammers and stammers, trembles and trembles, and only then she tells me about what she witnessed from the beginning.

Đắc managed to find Mậu Tý. He forced Mậu Tý to stand down in the foxhole and then started to ask him about his crimes and to abuse him. Đắc asked the comrade-liberators who were there to let him settle his old score of personal hatred, and none of the comrade-liberators intervened. Mậu Tý stood down in the hole, and each time Đắc raised his gun and aimed it at Mậu Tý's forehead and placed his finger on the trigger, Mậu Tý would close his eyes, his face frozen . . . waiting. But the awaited gunshot did not come. And when the gun did fire, Mậu Tý still was not dead. Each bullet passed close by his ears, by his head, or by his shoulders, and each time Mậu Tý thought that he had given to the world his last scream. After that, Đắc pulled Mậu Tý up and then led him away.

Several days later in that vacant foxhole, according to what Hường told me, a liberation soldier died with his head at the opening of the hole and his face turned toward my house. I suppose that before he died, he surely had a chance to see the golden peach flowers in the courtyard and a part of a roof that had collapsed from a shell or from shots by B40s during the first night when the battle began.

I don't remember anymore what the days after this were – whether the dates were in single digits or in ten-odds. The battlefront had spread into the Citadel. By night, the sounds of exploding artillery are nonstop. The Citadel walls collapse in many places. There are rumors that Đông Ba, Thượng Tứ, and Sập Gates of the Citadel have all been hit and destroyed, and the ways out are all blocked. The first few days we can still get out from the shelter to cook food. But several days later, artillery fire falls nonstop and guns from outside shoot into the Citadel like rain. My mother and Hường have to pull several bags of rice down to the shelter, and we eat raw rice to alleviate hunger. We eat raw rice and drink cold water, and on top of this the weather is cold, as though cutting through our guts, and the vapors from the earth penetrate into our bodies; everyone in the family has indigestion. We have to pay close attention to the sound of artillery when we climb up from the shelter to urinate right inside of the house. A couple of times, our business still unfinished, we hear the roaring sound of an airstrike and without running we automatically fall directly down into the shelter as though someone has punched us with a fist down the hole.

We live like this for several days, and our bodies turn sickeningly green. Hường can't bear to go up anymore; she weeps softly throughout the days. So, how would it be possible to be calm? Despite artillery shells, despite airplanes, liberation soldiers still find a way to come to the door of each house, calling for compatriots to contribute to the struggle at the front. The slogan is: "Don't hide American enemies, do not give shelter to Vietnamese malefactors, do not lose heart at the onset of artillery fire. If necessary, all compatriots, adults and children, must flood outside to fight against the Americans and their puppets."

Each time we hear this, we shiver. People around us die, each day more and more. Right in the back of the garden of our house there are three or four abandoned dead bodies, we don't know whether ordinary people or liberators. By night we occasionally hear the sounds from back in the garden of screaming and shrieking. Or they arrest people and lead them past the house with sounds of entreating and imploring and screaming and crying assaulting our minds and bodies.

As another day passes away, we are still alive. But the house next to ours is hit and destroyed by an artillery shell. The iron-sheet roof of the house next to it breaks into pieces that fall pell-mell everywhere; a shelter inside that house turns into an open-air shelter. Daylight shines into the shelter, making everybody in there scared. So they, oblivious to death, run outside and into my house asking for refuge.

Even though it's more crowded and foul-smelling now, still the presence of many people makes us calmer. People who just arrived let us know that there are a lot of groups of refugees fleeing along the riverbank toward Gia Hội. But Hường is firmly determined that Đắc talked about Gia Hội School as exactly the place where the Việt Cộng headquarters are and where the people's tribunals are conducted. I warn my mother. Any refugees who go there are thrusting their heads into the jaws of a tiger.

Only two hundred kilograms of rice are left, but there are so many additional mouths. We must ration our rice and eat sparingly. Fortunately, the refugee family that has come over doesn't have children [who would inevitably cry without food and water and would be heard], so it is bearable to stay hungry and thirsty. Each morning we chew on a handful of rice and have a handful for lunch and a handful for dinner.

Even so, the bag of rice goes down terrifyingly fast. Perhaps when the bag is empty and we are not yet dead from artillery we will still die from hunger and thirst. Each day everybody looks at each other and gives a long sigh or has tears overflowing from one's eyes. No one has any strength for long discussions.

One noon, when everybody is sitting in the shelter, chewing raw rice, there is the sound of the door being pushed open and then someone calling:

"Hey aunt . . . hey aunt."

My mother hears and recognizes the voice of a child from Mai Thúc Loan Road. She shouts for joy:

"Here, here, here down in the shelter; hey child, come down quickly."

A head sticks in. It's Tam. He shivers all over; his face is pale green. My mother pulls him close to her body:

"Where are your mother and father? Why do you go about alone?"

Tam bursts out crying:

"Mother died when we ran outside. Mother told me to keep running; Mother waved her hand, opened her eyes wide. I couldn't bear to leave. I left only when my mother died."

My mother bursts out crying:

"Oh, Heaven and Earth. Where is your father, child? Where is your father? Let me know."

"Father has been arrested. He was led, tied up, along with many other people. People say they were led to a gate of the Citadel so that artillery would shoot down at them. Oh aunt . . . oh auntie . . ."

Tam cries bitterly. My mother does so too. I appear to be covered with goose bumps all over my body. Why do they lead people up to the city gate for the airplanes to shoot down at them? What are these people's crimes? It's several damned local cadres who satisfy their personal hatred, that's all. We are a small hamlet, we are neighbors, and we kill each other like this? I am angry, full of deep resentment; I want to scream wildly to diffuse my anger. Tam continues to sob:

"They are so ruthless, auntie; they arrested several suspects and took them up to the city wall, tied up, for the American airplanes, so they would think they are Việt Cộng and shoot them. Yesterday, ten-odd people . . . today, several tens of people. No doubt my father too."

My mother taps her hands and her feet in anger. Hường's feeble voice:

"What to cry for, Mother? Sooner or later we'll all be dead anyway. To be set free by death sooner is even happier. Now I want to run outside so that airplanes will shoot me to death. To live like this, how's it different from being condemned to death, being threatened by death?"

The sounds of gunfire from small arms resound widely on the road. My mother and Tam completely stop crying. It seems that the Liberation Army leads a group of convicts past the house. There are loud sounds of screaming, crying, and shrieking. My mother wraps her arms around her chest. Hường opens her mouth wide and then falls on the ground, shaking violently. I touch her with my hand and feel that she is deathly cold. Fortunately, the neighbors who came over have a bottle of oil and rub it all over Hường's body. A moment later she comes slightly back to her senses and groans:

"Oh Mother . . . so terrible. Oh elder brother . . . so terrible . . ."

Then she cries. It seems that she is crying in a fit of delirium. I hold fast my younger sister's hand. I feel such pity for her. She ate raw rice for many days and could not bring herself to go up; her stomach has swollen up hard like she has a gastroenterological condition. Foam brims over from the corners of her mouth. Soon she completely regains her senses and heartily hugs my mother:

"I can't bear it anymore. Surely I will die."

Amid bouts of raining artillery outside, my mother, crying, crawls up out of the shelter. She rummages for something for a long time. I am concerned, so I stick my head up and call:

"Mother, come down to the shelter at once."

My mother comes down only after an eternity. In her hands she holds a piece of *bánh tét* with mold all over it. She peels off layers of banana leaves covering the cake and gives the cake to Hường, who at that moment is lying close against the ground and breathing as if about to expire.

Since then, horrifying nights turn into horrifying days.

I am unable to sleep. No one dares to climb up from out of the shelter anymore. The food is gradually used up.

The bag of rice is almost finished and, on top of this, there has been added another mouth to feed – Tam is stuck here with us. He doesn't dare go back home alone.

Hường is seriously ill; she lies completely motionless. My mother continues to listen intently to the sound of feet on the surface of the ground, hoping for Đắc to come back. If Đắc returns, we still can depend on him for help. One afternoon we hear the sound of light steps entering the house, then the sound of a person falling down with a thud. A moment later we hear a lot of other feet chasing in after him. A gun fires. A shriek. An uproar of talking and laughing bursts out: "He has fled to heaven." Another voice seems to be surprised: "Definitely no one is in the house. There's a shelter; they are certainly down there . . . Search thoroughly, oftentimes puppets hide in places like this . . . Oh, thick shit, certainly there's no one there. Such a stink comes out of there." The sounds of feet gradually move away; my mother is happy to the point of tears. Stinky piles of excrement and litter lying topsy-turvy in the middle of the house have saved us. My mother takes a deep breath and nods her head: "Only now have we seen the value of the piles of excrement." I feel the same way; there is no disgust or fear in me anymore about the foul stink penetrating down here. I think to myself: "Obviously, when they departed, they left a dead body right in the middle of our house." I am confused, not knowing whose body it is. I think about Mậu Tý. But it can't be Mậu Tý either. Đắc[9] has already arrested him, and he would not let Mậu Tý pay his debt so easily. But I feel confused only for a minute; my biggest scare is that in several days the corpse will swell and stink, and certainly the stench of the dead body mixed with excrement will not be as easy to breathe in as the smell we breathe in now.

Then the bag of rice is used up down to the bottom. That morning, my mother alerts us that no food remains. Those in the family who came for temporary refuge look troubled because they think that they are responsible for the imminent onset of hunger and thirst. But even if they had not been here, the rice would have come to an end and we would die of starvation anyway. A quick end or a struggle for two or three more days, it's the same at the end. My mother cries:

"Real suffering has not yet started here; not to die from artillery but to die of hunger is real suffering."

Then she hugs Hường and buries her in tears.

After that we chew the last grains of rice very carefully as though we are afraid that a few grains will fall down and scatter and there will be no way for us to find them.

The refugee family has decided to abstain, but my mother still divides the last grains fairly for everyone: "Oh, if death comes, we'll die together. Go ahead, eat, and then die." Everybody is weeping and moaning for a long time, but no one dares to cry loudly, afraid that someone up there on the surface will hear.

It seems that a lot of houses around us have collapsed. Many loud explosions reverberate and squeeze our chests. Occasionally we imagine how the explosions will plow and upturn the earth under the house we live in, and we close our eyes, waiting for death to come, and a moment later the sounds become less sharp – only then we know that we are all right.

The sound of small guns firing comes closer; it seems that they are right here in the street. Suddenly a decision pops up in my mind:

"Mother, we are going to escape; here it's death in any case."

9. In the original the name is mistakenly written "Xuân." See a discussion on this issue in the Translator's Introduction.

"I don't know anything anymore. Let's do whatever you decide."

We go without food for two more days. Hường is exhausted. Our two families discuss and plan the escape. Tam tries to crawl up from the shelter, despite the gunfire, and he fumbles his way out the door to see what's going on outside. A moment later he crawls back down into the shelter; his voice is very pleased:

"There're a lot of people walking outside. From time to time, there's a group of people running toward the city gate."

My mother springs up:

"We're going to follow them."

But Tam rejects her idea outright:

"No, only women and old people. I didn't see men. Men, they don't go anywhere anymore."

My mother discusses a possibility of disguise. The women, carrying Hường, would flee first; as for me, I will disguise myself in women's clothes, cover my head with a scarf, and follow them. I ask:

"And what will Tam do? It's absurd to disguise him too, because it will be too evident if two people are disguised."

Tam looks very sad:

"Life or death, it is fate. Elder brother, you go ahead and take care of your own fate."

Right before noon of that day we climb up from the shelter, supporting and encouraging each other. What jumps into my eyes is the dead body of a man, huge and bloated, lying in a prone position, blood already dried up. His two arms are stretched as though he embraces the earth. We don't clearly see his face. Tam is absorbed in applying makeup on me. I am wearing Hường's clothes, my head very tightly covered with a scarf. My mother gathers bits of trifles, wraps them into a bundle, and then drives everybody outside.

The door suddenly opens. My eyes are dazzled; I stagger, about to fall. Only after I get used to the light do I realize that the entire scenery has changed. Nothing of the old shapes has remained. Strangely, our house has not yet gotten a direct hit from the artillery and still stands desolate amid destitute gardens, among houses reduced to piles of loose bits of brick. Everywhere are dead people: in the courtyards, at the ends of alleys, out in the street. Some puddles of blood have dried, and some are still fresh. Artillery still lobs monotonously from the inside of the Citadel, and groups of people continue to flee. They run, screaming and crying, lamenting to Heaven. No one asks anyone about anything; no one looks at anyone.

Right in the middle of the road and on both sides of the road are big holes dug by people and also dug by bombs and shells. Just as we get to Mai Thúc Loan Road, we hear salvoes of small guns pouring like rain outside the city walls. In the group of people running in front of us, several individuals fall down. At once others turn their heads and run back, like a scattered swarm of bees. I quickly pull everybody to run and hide in a destroyed house just at the edge of the road. The house has collapsed and only some desolate walls still remain. We crawl to the back of a wall and climb up on a large pile of bricks. This house has a sand shelter, but it has been reduced to smithereens by a direct artillery hit; sandbags are completely torn up and a lot of broken pieces of wood are thrown all over the place. Amid the sandbags that have been dug up and amid large slats of wood lies the corpse of an American in a prone position with his face looking out. His hand is tightly clenched in front of his face. I look at him carefully from curiosity; from his fist sticks out a small photograph of a Western woman pressing her cheek against a small plump girl. The two, the mother and the daughter, are laughing together, fresh and beautiful, in a lushly green garden of fruit trees. The American is still very young, not yet thirty years old; his fair hair is smeared with stagnant blood. Around his dead body lies an open leather wallet with papers and letters that had fallen out, scattered around, along with a lighter and strings of unused cartridges broken into pieces. Tam is more curious; he looks closely into the hand of the American and manages to read lines of small letters on the backside of the picture. Tam translates under his breath: "My husband, I implore God to send you our words of prayer and best wishes for the New Year in Vietnam. The war will be over and our family will be reunited." In the pile of letters scattered around, Tam manages to pick up another picture, also of the same woman, almost without any clothing covering her body, lying exposed in a prone position on a wide bed with a line inscribed on the back of the picture expressing a tragic and heartrending yearning for her husband.

I don't know what day of the month it was, ten-odd or twenty-odd, when Americans came here. Perhaps they came and were pushed back. Fortunately, we have found our way here. When we got outside from the shelter it seems that on the road where we live there is not a single family left anymore. They've all died or left a long time ago. Hường, dejected, sits leaning with her back against a pile of bricks; she raises her hand and covers her eyes, not daring to look at the dead body.

The oldest woman in the family of the neighbors who came for refuge in our house crawls out to look around and then waves to us:

"People are now continuing on the road. Let's go."

Again we go, coaching and supporting each other. But wherever we pass at a run, we instinctively look for places to avoid bullets and duck down, pressing ourselves against the ground whenever we hear the rattle of gunfire over our heads. Each time there is a rattling sound over our heads there is also an explosion of artillery. In front of us a bullet hits someone, and behind us a bullet hits someone. A group of people fleeing the fighting suddenly gathers near the city gate. My body shivers. I think: "Surely, it's a checkpoint." We approach the gate. There is a unit of the Liberation Army there. They don't stop anyone, but the group of people automatically stops in front of the dreadful barrels of the guns that look like they are about to cough out bullets. I pull the scarf to cover my hair and the lower part of my face.

My mother quickly slips into the pocket of my undershirt a small packet with money, and then she picks up Hường to carry her.

"Women can pass. Young males and adult men go back."

Soldiers from a unit of the Liberation Army sit with their backs leaning against the gate; a firm voice from the unit issues the order. Tam's face turns pale; he tries to mix with the crowd of young women and children. I hold my breath to pass through. Several pairs of eyes glower directly at my face. Suddenly a voice says:

"You, elder brother over there, stop."

I am startled but don't dare to look back. Are they talking to me or to someone else? But someone's hand has pushed my back to go straight ahead. Hường groans like she is in a huge pain. I know that a part of her is really in pain and another part, screaming and shrieking, simulates it. Suddenly Tam shakes himself loose and runs forward in a rush. A round of gunfire chases him, but it seems that the guns are fired only into the air. A very large group of people rushes out of the city gate. Thanks to this, Tam keeps running, elbowing his way forward. Hearing the gunfire, guns from the outside fire back in response. The two sides fire at each other at random. We are separated, running more dead than alive. A round of bullets lashes out past my ear. I hastily duck down to the ground, and when I manage to get up, my mother, my younger sister, Tam, and the neighbors are now out of sight, having run away somewhere and disappeared. I am stunned – my mother and younger sister, are they among the people of that group that dispersed in all directions, or do they lie in the pile of corpses that have just fallen behind my back and are still warm, overflowing into the next life? I want to turn back, but it's impossible. The gunfire pushes me to run forward nonstop. I'm now on Phan Bội Châu Street.

Just a while ago, I clearly heard a lot of guns shooting at Đông Ba Gate, and the Việt Cộng army from the inside of the Citadel responded. But why, while getting up to here, haven't I seen even a shadow of a single living person? There are only dead bodies – Việt Cộng corpses dead for a long time or still fresh and corpses of civilians seeking refuge. I see a lot of very pitiful scenes. Dead women firmly holding their children in their arms, dead pregnant women whose newborns have spilled out. Seeing how dangerous it is to run outside, I push a door into a nearby house.

The house is deserted. I am surprised when I see a big gaping hole carved in the wall, connecting this house with other ones. I wonder whether the Việt Cộng used this passage to move about. But I don't dare to venture climbing over into other houses. This house has not been completely destroyed, but after a long search I can't find any food whatsoever. Reluctantly, I have to move to another house to find something, absolutely anything edible to alleviate my hunger. Just as I pick up a bag with dry bread next to the body of a long-dead girl already bloated and smelly, I am directly hit in my arm by a bullet. I dress the wound by myself with the shirt of the dead girl. The bullet is still firmly stuck in my flesh, and perhaps what hurts me the most is this wound.

I don't understand how I manage to survive when I run to the bank of the river. I don't know, I don't clearly remember what part of the river it was. When I see the water, my throat burns from thirst; my body is shriveled up with not a drop of sweat left. Behind my back and over my head I hear guns firing. I suddenly feel a sharp pain all over my body, and it seems that blood runs out of my body like a spring. Regardless, the current of the blue river in front of me is very calm; at first the blue color dazzles my eyes, and then the current catches me and takes me down to drown. I flounder toward the shore. My face dips into the water and my entire body goes down; the water is fresh and cold as though it wants to turn me into a block of ice. Then a distressed shout is heard: "Someone, save, please save." I am lifted up into a boat, and I pass out.

When I regain my consciousness, the boat has crossed the river. I have been wounded rather seriously in several places. I empty my pockets of whatever money was there to pay the boatman who saved my life. I say good-bye to the boatman and try to crawl, dragging my feet up the road.

It seems that I am crawling past a lot of dead bodies. I come to Kiểu Mẫu School. Here it's already very crowded with people fleeing from the fighting, so crowded that there is no place for me to lie down. I get a simple dressing for my wounds and get something to eat and drink. People advise me to go to An Cựu hamlet. According to them, over there it is quiet now, and if I am fortunate and run into the [Nationalist] Army, it will transfer me to Phú Bài, where there is medicine and bandages. I go down many small roads and also cut past the post office; if there is gunfire in one place, I move to another place. Near the post office, I see several Việt Cộng corpses with their legs chained to machine guns. Dead. In another place I see something similar. When I come to An Cựu Bridge, I see our [Nationalist] soldiers and Americans there. I don't have time to approach them before gunfire breaks out, and I hastily shuffle my feet onto a small road to avoid bullets.

Just as I went across this part of the road, you, elder brother, you saved me. I was shot and immediately fell down to the ground. I kept trying to crawl to a bomb crater to avoid a random bullet. When I was at Kiểu Mẫu School, I saw a lot of new graves there. People said that each day several people die – those who were wounded earlier or those hit directly by bombs. I thought that if I could make it here, perhaps I could make it down to Phú Bài. But now I've lost all hope. I don't understand why now I still feel alert enough to be able to tell you, elder sister and elder brother, my story. Perhaps the airplanes are now far away.

Enough, elder sister and elder brother, don't mind me; run from here before they [the Communists] flood in. Please set me up near the door – no, near that column, it will also work. I will still be able to see rain, grass, and trees. The shrubs in front of my face don't have any traces of shells that come to destroy us, and the rain will wash everything up squeaky clean for me to see . . .

Thái puts the youth's body up against a column so he can see a corner of the garden. There's a pot containing a shrub. Several flowerpots with dahlias are still blooming in white and purple. Farther away there is a large shrub bent over as if listening to the rain patting it. Perhaps airplanes will indeed return. Thái wants to take the youth along. But the youth smiles and shakes his head. His hands start shaking; his lips have turned black and blue; his eyes blink fast as though they want to take in the sky and the scenery before him. His eyes gradually turn empty as though a curtain has been pulled over them. Thái tightly holds the youth's hand. From the corners of the youth's eyes, which are about to dry up, there suddenly slip out two tears, and his mouth gently moves. He tries to open his eyes wide as though he wants to collect all the images, and then his eyes stop moving. Thái shakes his head. I pull back and stand behind Thái's back. Thái lightly closes the eyes of the young man and then puts his corpse to lie in the open near the water tank.

The drops of rain are becoming heavier. Dazed and confused, I follow Thái out into a lane. At the entrance of the lane are several corpses of Việt Cộng who have just died. Some lie prone with their faces down, others on their backs with their faces upward. Thái closes the eyes of each of them and then pulls my hand to go. I am suddenly panic-stricken and want to spurt out to run forward. Thái asks:

"What's this, elder sister?"

I am saying something but only my breath comes out; I stretch out my arm, but it drops down dead. The eyes of a Việt Cộng that Thái has just closed by mistake suddenly open and glower as though following us. Thái pushes me forward:

"Enough of this, damn it . . . go . . . go elder sister . . . go . . . go fast."

Thái's own legs are also out of control. The two of us, going hand in hand, run, escaping by a small road. The next moment we get to An Cựu post and see somebody's basket of duck eggs turned upside down with the eggs scattered all over the road. Thái picks up a few of them, which are still intact, and puts them into his pocket.

The image of the youth named Khâm who has just died in a strange house will haunt me forever. He was telling his story with such full possession of his senses; why on earth did he die so fast? Death occurs easily, and sometimes no explanation comes for it. He had been living in a place that was shelled by artillery for so many days, and he had been wounded so many times. He hid and fled, hid and fled, and he almost got to a quiet and safe place, but he suddenly died because of some bullet shot from behind a bamboo grove. Death really seems to be a joker.

So my fate, the fate of my family . . . there's no guarantee for us. I have fled all over the place – I left for the countryside and then turned and went back to Hue. In the countryside there are also dead people because of stray artillery shells. When I came back to the city, looking for the safest place, there also were stray, absolutely senseless bullets. I am suddenly completely stunned thinking about the days in the church, in An Định Palace, about the days of flight from Tân Lăng back to the railroad. Each place is full of death but we don't know yet that although we are not yet dead, it certainly does not mean that we cannot die.

At first I hear that Việt Cộng soldiers have been carousing at the An Cựu post for three days; then I hear that it has been for seven days. And then there is news that Venerable Hồ [Chí Minh] is coming to visit with the people. Venerable Hồ has not yet arrived but half of the city is already dead, almost completely destroyed, reduced to ashes. On the day of his arrival, surely nobody who is still alive will come to cheer for him. Looking at the dead compatriots, my heart can't help but feel stinging grief; but looking at the corpses of the Việt Cộng, neither can I feel hatred. They also died en masse so that Uncle Hồ can enter Hue. Thái says:

"Why, elder sister, are you crying for no reason?"

I can only respond that I am awfully afraid. Certainly, Thái also thinks about the same things that I saw, and his eyes are full of grief. As we return home, my mother looms at the door. She dashes to pull us into the house, crying and scolding us at the same time:

"You're really insolent. Insolent you are; I lost my soul, my senses worrying about you."

Then she pulls us into the house. From my father's altar I smell the aroma of incense. Aunt Vạn is fixing rice on a kerosene stove in a corner of the house. She says:

"Listen, you insolents, for lunch we had a cooked papaya. It was brought up here from Thủy Dương, sent over here by Uncle Giáo's wife."

Thái is stunned:

"Who came up here? How's it possible to come up here? They've just been fighting with each other, haven't they?"

"So, he came up and then got stuck in Mù U. He drove here very fast as though flying, and when the gunfire subsided he immediately went back."

I then understand who this "he" is that Aunt Vạn is talking about. It must be the son of Uncle Giáo.

My mother says:

"Listen – don't open the door. By now people have returned to a lot of houses. If you open the door, I'm afraid the Việt Cộng will know that we're here."

That noon while eating our meal we hear an explosion like a thunderbolt over our heads. The entire family drops everything, and covering our heads we scurry into the shelter. Are they fighting each other again? But there's only one loud sound and then it's over. The shutters of the window, which were closed, burst open and some more tiles shatter, exposing pieces of sky the color of lead. Only several hours later do we learn that a unit of American soldiers was passing by An Cựu post. They had sat down for a break on the side of the road, and when they checked they found that a gun was missing. So, they went into the most beautiful deserted mansion, laid a mine, and detonated it to vent their anger.

EIGHT

RETURNING TO THE OLD HOUSE

SOMEONE HAS RETURNED TO THE HOUSE IN FRONT OF US. Before Tết, I saw that this house was very crowded; children filled its courtyard. When my father died, the head of that household came by to express his condolences. But now only two boys have come back. They wear clothes of profound mourning and have white hats on their heads.

I learn that they are back because I hear the sound of crying. One day, right before noon, when we have just crawled out of the shelter to help Aunt Vạn by bringing water to wash the rice, I suddenly hear sorrowful crying in the house across the lane. Aunt Vạn waves her hand:

"Be silent, someone's crying so scarily. Someone's crying as though at a funeral."

I say:

"It seems to me like it's a male voice."

Thái inches outside:

"The crying is from the house in front of ours; it seems to be Uncle Năm's house, don't you think so, elder sister?"

"It sure is."

"Let me go to the courtyard; perhaps I will hear or see something."

Thái rushes off into the courtyard. I hastily run behind him. Indeed, the crying comes from the house in front of us in the lane. On a grave in front of the courtyard someone has lit incense; very fragile wisps of smoke hang low, close to the ground, then, thinned, they melt away very quickly. Thái stands in front of a coconut tree, looking in. A head, then two heads stick out – the two elder sons of this family. Their faces are reddish and their eyes have not yet dried from tears. Thái inquires:

"Have you all now come back?"

"No, just us, and we are leaving at once. We've come back to see what's happened to the house."

Thái points at the grave:

"This is the grave of your mother, isn't it? She was lucky to be buried given the current situation."

"My mother died right here at the house. My younger sister was not yet dead, but her life was in danger."

"Your sister was seriously wounded?"

"She is now also dead."

The elder brother raises his arms to the sky and points back toward the city with rising smoke:

"I swear that I will not walk under the same sky with them.[1] Look, elder brother, my younger sister was wounded on the first morning when the house was in flames. My father took my sister to a hospital. When they were somewhere over there, they learned that the Việt Cộng had completely occupied the city. It was clear that Americans and Việt Cộng were firing at each other, and then our house was burning. My mother inside was directly hit by a bullet – not by B40s but by an American bullet fired from outside. My mother died because of an American bullet, not a Việt Cộng's. Then my father took my younger sister – my elder sister also went along – and in the middle of the road they were directly hit by artillery or something like that and died at once. They are buried outside of Kiểu Mẫu School. Oh heavens, I went there but saw only several ID cards and a thermos with boiled water that had already grown cold. All these things were placed next to several shallow graves."

"Have you found your father's grave?"

The two brothers melt in tears. They wipe their tears:

"Several days ago I heard that they [the Communist forces] are coming here, so we had to run for our lives and I thought we would die. Then we came back here to hide from the shelling when it started. There was

1. The author indicated that her use of the pronoun "them" here was not supposed to condemn either side of the conflict but reflected the grief and frustration of the son who lost beloved members of his family. Implicitly, however, again according to the author, the son was accusing Communists who seized Hue and provoked American and South Vietnamese forces to counterattack.

no one in the hamlet. It was so terrible – a bomb or something like that, I don't know what it was, fell down and the roof of the house collapsed, and we quickly crawled into the shelter; the warhead was stuck upside-down, pointed upward like an arrow, but it didn't explode. We closed our eyes waiting for it to explode; it didn't explode. Then we ran out of the shelter. Now we've come back, and it's still here and has not exploded yet. When we fled, I kept worrying that when it explodes, it will destroy everything."

I am so afraid that I turn pale. It turns out that for the several days since we have returned, we've been living next to a house containing a large warhead. If it explodes next to our house, we will not escape calamity.

Thái asks:

"Where are you going now?"

"Now we are going back to Phù Lương. It's very scary here."

The two put together several necessary things, go out to light more incense on the grave of their mother, then bid farewell to us and leave. Thái runs behind them to ask:

"Are you walking?"

"No, when we got down from Mù U, there was a Lambretta motor scooter[2] there. The scooter took us up this way."

I'm happy as though I found a gold mine:

"Really? Please, elder brother, may I ask if the motor scooter can pass by Thanh Lam?"

I suddenly remember a place where I can rely on support. In Thanh Lam there is a small office, a branch of the place where I work. If there is a motor scooter, I will get off there to ask the workers to help me return to Saigon. One of the two responds to me while he still keeps going:

"Sure, sure."

I rush into the house. My mother asks who cried there. I don't respond to my mother's question but instead chatter nonstop and boast:

"I will soon be able to get to Saigon."

"Hee-hee. You go to Saigon."

"Now it's possible to get to and from Thanh Lam. I will go there and ask for transportation to get to Saigon."

2. Referred to as *xe lam* from the trademark "Lambretta."

My mother is doubtful:

"Is this so? I can't believe it."

I tell her the story of the two brothers from the house in front of us in the lane. My mother understands and rejoices. If I manage to escape, I will join my husband and children. I suddenly feel absolutely dumbfounded. My husband and children in Saigon – are they still safe and sound? There is fighting in Saigon too; people flee too, and die too, like in Hue. My children. Do they wait for their mother to come back? My tears suddenly stream down. My mother scolds me:

"You think rubbish. Surely nothing has happened there."

My mother's words don't comfort me a tiny bit. If something has happened to my family in Saigon, I'd rather die here with Hue. But being afraid that my mother will be even sadder, I quickly wipe my tears.

That afternoon, Thái takes me back to Mù U to wait for the motor scooter. But there is no motor scooter.

I hear that Bực Bridge was detonated and heavy traffic can't go through. But when the day draws to a close, a lot of American vehicles drive up here. Then a lot of American vehicles drive back. Each column of vehicles coming up here brings a few families returning from evacuation; columns of vehicles going back down take some families who are evacuating. Even in this situation with people leaving and people coming back, still no one knows what place is safer than any other place. People continue to flee; if you are still able to flee it means you are not dead yet.

When that day draws to a close, Túc comes up to visit. Túc tells us that National Highway No. 1 is very quiet by day because Americans guard it. By night Americans withdraw, and Việt Cộng flood down from the mountains and conduct searches in every house, forcing young people to follow them up to the mountains.

That evening, I and Thái discuss our plan: tomorrow the two of us will walk back to Thủy Dương, then will borrow Túc's motorbike to go to Thanh Lam. That night I am not able to get a wink of sleep.

My heart pines in a way that is hard to describe. Only now do I sense how infinitely self-centered and narrow-minded I am. Amid death swarming around, I alone feel happy because of a fleeting hope that comes from nowhere and leaves for nowhere. Oh Mother, Mother. Oftentimes when the artillery lobs and roars in the night, I, in a flash, vaguely hear something like the voice of a child, either bursting out of my memory or echoing my grief and love.

The battle that went on for so long is now coming to an end. And how many more dead bodies has the city gotten today? Lying in silence in the dark, in the deep shelter, I can't imagine the scale of the destruction of the city, the misery of the city. So many guns, so many cannons, so many bombs have torn to pieces this entire small city, the beloved native place of mine. I am surprised when I think why all the artillery from America, from Russia, from Czechoslovakia suddenly lands in the hands of North Vietnamese and South Vietnamese to pour down on a small city that is as good-natured as is the city of Hue. Ammunition from all the faraway countries, sent here in the name of helping the South, assisting the North, suddenly focused on a small city, tearing into pieces its innocent flesh, chopping off the arms, legs, and faces of so many people. Images of pieces of arms and legs seen along the roads; scenes of furtive love expressed amid gunfire in a corner of a solemn Catholic church inundated with screaming and crying. An image of the corpse of a newborn baby bundled in its mother's blouse . . . oh life . . . why must life still go on? It seems that I can still breathe during this terrible night here. No, it seems that not only in Hue but in so many other provinces, including Saigon where my children and my husband live, there too, there are such images. Also bombs and bullets, burned houses, destruction, and death. But I suddenly feel certain that there is no other place that has endured such utter suffering as Hue, the place where we are enduring.

Outside it looks like the rain has become heavier. But the sound of rain tries to weave a melodious and refreshing curtain that is being torn into shreds by flares, gunfire, blood, and tears. I think about fresh graves hastily filled up with earth – tonight the rain will penetrate down there; the rain will open the eyes of the dead, will suck out even more of the tiny bit of vitality of life that has not had time to melt from the body because death was so sudden. The rain will also wash the ears of the dead so they can hear better – the sounds of the earth sighing, the sounds of bombs and bullets making everything shake violently. This night, how many more dead bodies yet will there be with no time for burial and no one to close their eyes, whether they lie with faces downward or upward. So many eyes will be open and staring with one image or another still glued onto the ground or up in the high, ponderous sky. How many roads or how many streets and alleys are like arms and legs? Those arms have already died, are torn to bits and scattered everywhere, and there is no longer any strength left to comfort persons searching for their way.

And this night, the group of people that includes Catholic priests, Buddhist monks, and ordinary people supporting each other and carrying white flags, running back and forth, where has it gone? How many people remain along the roads; how many legs and arms continue to move in desperation? And I still lie here. Praying to Buddha. Praying to God. Asking Buddha, asking God to protect me. I suddenly feel awfully ashamed. Because now for so many years, I haven't been thinking of Buddha, I haven't been thinking at all of God. But it's useless . . . futile hopes. Why would Buddha or God save only me, take pity only on me, but not take pity on so many other people?

In the morning when I awake I suddenly feel a tranquillity that makes my body shiver. I stare for a long time into the darkness. The oil lamp in the corner of the shelter with its wick turned down low has run out of oil and has been extinguished for some time. I touch my arms, my feet – they are so cold. Why is it so? Why is nobody breathing? No, as soon as I touch someone's chest I feel it's steaming hot.

"It's morning – get up."

I wake up everyone. My mother is exhausted:

"Yesterday evening I couldn't sleep; in the morning I fell asleep and don't have any idea what time it is now."

So, it turns out that last night everybody remained awake the whole night. Thái gets up with a start, crawls out of the shelter, and opens a window. A bit of light shines in and makes the darkness fade, but we still aren't able to see each other. When outside of the shelter, I still feel wrapped in thick silence. Have they stopped fighting already or what? No sounds of small guns; there are not even sounds of large guns anymore. Thái gives me a sign to stop at the door and then he runs outside. In a moment he runs back in:

"Elder sister, people are evacuating. Isn't it strange?"

"Where are they going?"

"They're going back down, surely to Mai market in Phù Lương."

I shout for joy:

"Let's go down to Hương Thủy."

"Elder sister, will you be looking for your office?"

"Yes."

I express my intention to my mother. At first she stops me, but then she sees many people going to Phù Lương and agrees to let us go. Coming out to the lane, my mother still admonishes:

"Listen child, if you see that it's not possible to get through on the road, turn back."

I have to promise time and again for the sake of my mother's concern. We follow a group of people who are evacuating on foot and head to Thủy Dương. When we get to the market, we stop at Uncle Giáo's house to borrow a moped. But the moped is out of gas, and there's no way anymore to find where to buy gas. We resign ourselves to continuing on foot. When we cover some distance, we meet up with a group of people in front of us. They are carrying loads of goods from down in the market, loads of fresh green lettuce leaves. It turns out that here the market is still going as usual. The Việt Cộng flood into these areas only by night and conduct arrests, but by day the market is absolutely secure. Even so, looking at the group of houses, I still sense that there is something terrible ready to break out.

In another section of the road, passing by wide fields, we have to go close by the edge of the road to yield the way to a column of vehicles hurrying up in the opposite direction. The vehicles are full of American soldiers. Thái pulls my hand to crouch down close to the edge of the desolate field, soaking wet. This column clearly goes up to Hue as reinforcement. When the middle of the column is passing us, there is a big explosion, like a mortar opening fire, then a barrage of guns, large and small, pouring like rain from inside of a green grove beyond the field. The front part of the column keeps moving forward and fires at the same time. The back part of the column stops and all the American soldiers get off the vehicles and rush into the edge of the field. We quickly roll down into the field with half of our bodies soaking under awfully cold water and our heads sticking out over a wet grassy edge. Thái immediately commands:

"Bow down your head really low, elder sister. Lie quiet and don't run."

Fire and returning fire from both sides fall like rain and glide over our heads. We are caught in crossfire. I am at once awfully afraid and repentant. When we were leaving, my mother dissuaded us from doing this, but I didn't listen to her. Now if we die here, it's really meaningless. But luckily, guns inside the grove gradually move farther away and then fall completely silent. They've withdrawn. No one has been wounded, the column of American vehicles is only slightly damaged, and five minutes later they continue on their way.

We wait for the column of American vehicles to completely disappear, far away, and only then do we climb up to the main road. On the edge of the field, on the other side, there are a lot of people who also strenuously crawl out and then get up. They are also evacuees. When we cover some distance, we run into a woman with a load of lettuce; she is seriously wounded and her load of vegetables is scattered all around. We stop to check her wounds and don't know what to do yet when, fortunately, a motor scooter comes up from Phù Lương. The driver sees a big crowd, jumps off, and asks:

"Has there just been a clash here?"

"Yes, right now, right here. American vehicles were passing by and they [the Communist forces] fired at them."

"The vehicles have managed to now get through, haven't they? This woman, is she wounded?"

"Very seriously. Please, sir, be so kind as to take her down to Phú Bài where the American hospital is located; if she gets into the American hospital, perhaps she will survive."

"I thought the same thing; I was hiding down there and as soon as I heard the guns calm down over here I drove up to check whether women, children, or anyone was hurt. Oh heavens, in this situation, if we don't pity each other, who will?"

The driver, together with several other people, carries the wounded woman and puts her on the scooter. He says:

"I will give a ride to anyone who needs to go. I don't take money. But you have to sit tightly together."

Thái says:

"Take us over there to Thanh Lam."

"Get on."

The scooter takes off at once. I look back at the place where just now there was fighting, and there is no trace of it there except for the load of vegetables that fell and got scattered around. Fields are still glossy with water and groves in the distance are still silent, keeping their secrets. The driver tells his story in a loud and powerful voice that mixes with the noise of the scooter's engine; sometimes he can be heard and sometimes not. In general, he informs us that since the start of the fighting he has transported a lot of wounded. Also, on the road are a lot of wounded people who cannot bear the pain and die, and our driver has been taking them back to his village and immediately burying them.

We have to shout really loudly until our voices become hoarse, and only then the driver hears us and stops the scooter so that we can get off in Thanh Lam. I enter the office alone. Only when I stand in a spacious room do I feel that my body is wet and cold; the water not only runs from my clothes but also seems to ooze from my skin and flesh. My body is as stiff as a block of ice.

The person in charge of this small branch of the office runs out:

"Oh heavens. These several days have been frantic; we didn't know what to do, how to find you, elder sister. How come you are here? Sit here, sit down here . . ."

I don't have enough strength anymore to sit down. My arms and legs have completely disappeared. Only my brain remains, not yet hardened, and it issues orders to me to produce words . . .

"Elder brother V– –, do you have any news from Saigon?"

"Ah, you're worrying about your husband and kids, aren't you, elder sister? Nothing happened, nothing happened to them. Just yesterday evening they called to ask whether there's news about you. A couple of days ago your husband went to the main office to ask for news about you. Put your mind at rest, elder sister."

"Have you heard anything more specific about my family, my children?"

"The children are fine. Over there, there was also a big fight, but everything is calm by now. Your place over there is safe and secure – no problem. I guarantee it. Don't worry."

A wisp of warm air suddenly bursts out from my chest, and now it seems that my heart at once beats and exudes fire, exudes hot air. This wave of warm air very quickly runs through my veins; I suddenly sense my arms and legs. I softly move my lips:

"Are you telling the truth, elder brother?"

"I guarantee you that your family over there is completely safe. The other day the main office called to make us go look for you, elder sister. But we did nothing. Still, you've managed to get down here."

"I walked on foot."

"Now, elder sister, stay right down here so that I can find a way for you to get to Saigon."

I think about Thái, who's standing outside waiting for me, and also about my mother, my younger sister, my elder brother and his wife, and my nephews. No, I must stay, I can't allow myself to walk away alone at this time. But there's no certainty that if I stay here, I will later find a way to leave safely. By night, military posts and offices are still their [the Communist forces'] targets, their delicious morsels of prey; here it's also very dangerous. I say:

"I will come back tomorrow. Now I must go up to An Cựu."

Having lingered for a moment to hear what's going on in Saigon, I turn and go out, carrying with me a liter of gasoline so that when we get to Thủy Dương and borrow the moped, we can return to Hue early. Thái is waiting for me at a small tavern. The two of us walk on foot to Thủy Dương.

Fortunately, nothing happens along the road. When we get to Thủy Dương, we go to Uncle Giao's. His wife has put aside for us a little bit of sweet potato leaves, sweet potatoes, and a bit of pork. Having poured the gasoline into the moped, we take the provisions back to An Cựu.

I tell the story about Thanh Lam for the entire family to hear. When my mother learns from me that nothing has happened to her grandchildren, she is happy to the point of tears. But being this happy for her daughter's grandchildren, she feels miserable and worried and starts crying about the brood of her son's grandchildren still stranded in Từ Đàm.

As that day draws to a close, suddenly in the abandoned house on the other side of the road there are two men, strangers, who come and stay there. They look very pale and very frail. Cautiously, they come over to our house and ask for temporary refuge. As soon as my mother saw them entering the lane, she gave Thái signs and pulled him into the corner of the shelter. The two men converse with my mother while at the same time they look around the house with disrespectful eyes. They try to modify their voices; I can't guess what their regular voices are like, but the manner of their speech doesn't seem very familiar:

"Dear aunt, we have fled back here from the dangers of the fighting; please, aunt, let us stay here for a short while."

My mother quickly responds, drowning their voices:

"Please, sir, in my family there are only I and children. Yes, sirs, by day down here Nationalist soldiers take control; by night gentlemen-liberators come back and take control. The house is really in plain sight; please look for another quieter place."

"Why haven't you fled, aunt, but have come back – to do what?"

My mother pretending to wipe tears, points at my father's altar:

"Please sir, three grandchildren have just disappeared without a trace . . . I and my children don't want to go anywhere anymore; enough, we completely entrust ourselves to fate."

"This woman is your child, aunt?"

"Yes, sir."

"Surely she does a government job."

"No, sir. She and her husband are tailors. She came back for the funeral, and her husband is stranded in Quảng."

One of them asks me while sneering.

"Elder sister, do you make European or Vietnamese clothes?"

I respond at random:

"Please sirs, neither European nor Vietnamese. I make several items of peasant clothes for relatives and neighbors over there."

One of them points at the house on the other side of the road:

"We are over there, aunt. If something happens, just call us, aunt, and we will come and help you."

"Yes, elder brothers, thank you."

The two men enter the house, look around, and gradually move toward the shelter opening. My mother quickly runs after them:

"Please, elder brothers, please sit down: be my guests, and drink some water. Please, elder brothers, it's very smelly in that shelter. For several days we didn't go outside, several small children pooped and pissed, so there is a stench. Please, elder brothers, sit down and be my guests."

But the two strangers bid us a farewell and then go directly out to the lane. They enter the house across the road. Dusk falls and we don't see them anymore.

When night comes, the sounds of guns resound in the areas of Phú Cam and Bến Ngự. Artillery continuously falls in that direction. We lie in the shelter, listening to the reverberating sounds of artillery buzzing in our ears. Then, two or three explosions bang and it seems that some part of the house is blown off. Bricks and tiles rain down on the roof of the shelter. We lie close to each other, reaching out in search of each other with a constant feeling as though another beloved person is getting ready to depart into the darkness of the night.

Only in the morning do we learn that the shutters of the window that Thái closed tightly with a steel cable were blown away and fell behind the veranda. More tiles fell from the house, breaking down the walls a bit more. We go outside into the garden to see the place of the explosions. Two or three houses away beyond the veranda were directly hit by artillery fire. We have to make a circle out to the road and enter an alley, and only then can we approach a house that was shelled. The house has completely collapsed, and there is a large pit right at the base of the house. A coconut tree in the front yard was uprooted, and several pieces of sheet iron were propelled up on the roof of a nearby house, damaging a third of the roof. Because the owner of the house had dug a shelter in the courtyard, no one died; only several people are lightly injured.

Another nearby house has an old man who still remains there; his children and grandchildren have all fled from the dangers of fighting. The man is very old, definitely over eighty, and cannot go anymore. He didn't dig any shelter or hole and keeps sleeping on a wooden plank bed, but he has not yet been hurt. I and Thái enter the house of the elderly man and see that the fragment of a shell flew through and destroyed the front wall of the house. The old man looks at us with his eyes half-closed:

"You're back? Why haven't you fled? If this place gets a direct hit, you'll die."

I ask:

"Dear sir, where did your entire family go?"

"When hell is here, there's nowhere to go. Damn it, I told them don't run away; my entire family has fled, and I hear they have all died somewhere near Kiểu Mẫu School. I've remained alone, old but not dead, but children and grandchildren have all died."

The man raises his eyes up to the altar; a vase with withered marigold flowers, several desolate incense bowls, and cups of tea from the evening of the first day of Tết that have almost dried out – all these are covered with a thick layer of dust that turns their gold color into red. The old man sits on the wooden plank bed, raising his hands and repeatedly rubbing his eyes. I don't know whether it's dust in his eyes or he's crying. The man sits with his back to us, mumbling something nonstop. The crumbling, deserted house gives us shivers. The old man is like the shadow of a long-dead person. On the altar, there's a picture of an elderly person, absolutely toothless and smiling; the eyes have completely lost the photograph's tin-like color, turning white like the eyes of a ghost . . . I and Thái don't say a word to each other . . . together we hastily slip back out the door.

A big crowd is still assembled outside the house directly hit by artillery. It turns out that in this hamlet quite a lot of people have come back, but no one dares to show their faces outside; they dig shelters and live inside, in hiding. Thái says that there are families who evacuated from other places and came over here, then stayed put right here and didn't move anywhere else.

Those in the crowd discuss many things but without any sense of resolution and then suddenly rush out to the road. Another big crowd assembles at the end of the alley. Thái pulls me to run over to it. This crowd surrounds a small young girl who is seriously wounded. The girl is set down to lie on an old piece of canvas spread on the edge of the wet grass.

According to the people discussing matters back and forth, the house of this young girl is up near the railway tracks. At dawn, an artillery shell hit directly in the back garden of her house and its fragments pierced the girl's body. One of the fragments entered her stomach and pierced the intestines, which now dangle outside. The entire body of the girl is tightly wrapped in an old blanket, but blood has completely soaked it; if you could squeeze her body, there would barely be a drop of blood left. The face of the girl is pale green; her eyes are open and listless. Her father sits on his heels next to his daughter, crying and imploring obsequiously:

"I beg all of you, fellow villagers, please find a vehicle to help me transport my child down to Phú Bài to the American hospital to save her."

But there are no vehicles on the roads; there is nothing but groups of evacuees, from what areas we don't know, who go through here and then continue right on to National Highway No. 1. Thái bends down to examine the wound of the young girl, then shakes his head. A person says:

"If we give her help at once, with some luck she will make it."

But the young girl continues to lie waiting on the side of the road until noon; she tries to open her eyes wide but has lost her spirit and looks up at her father, making a hiccoughing sound and scowling.

Her father wails loudly for a long time; he takes his child in his arms and holds her, and then he runs with her along the National Highway, running and crying absolutely heartbreakingly. Several soldiers standing guard at Trường Bia post run after him to hold him back, but no one is able to hold him back anymore. After going for a stretch, the man sits down on the edge of the road and waits as with each minute his daughter's breath becomes weaker and weaker. Thái says:

"Enough, elder sister, go back to the house."

We go back along the road. Thái asks a group of people running by:

"Where're you coming from?"

"Từ Đàm."

"Where're you from?"

"Bến Ngự."

Thái shouts for joy and, holding my hand tight, pulls on me to run. When we come into the house, Thái yells loudly:

"Evacuees from Từ Đàm are coming over here. There are people coming from there."

But when my mother runs outside, the group of people is already long gone. Other groups of people continue to come by. They are from other areas: from the city center, from Bến Ngự, from over by the station, from Phú Cam. A person from Bến Ngự informs us that up at Từ Đàm people are still very much confined; the Việt Cộng headquarters is still set up there and the American army has lined up on the other side of Bến Ngự Bridge.

My mother is desperate again. At our midday meal, even though there is delicious food sent up from Thủy Dương Hạ, no one appreciates it. The image of the young girl with a dangling pile of intestines awaiting her death by seconds and minutes on the side of the road makes me anxious.

When we finish eating, we see several units of [Nationalist] soldiers outside, entering the city through An Cựu from the direction of the National Highway. They carry rucksacks and guns, keep a distance of around half a meter from each other, and are completely silent. They don't look at the houses on either side of the road. Thái recognizes special task force troops, then another group – paratroopers – and then marines. Regardless of how much my mother dissuades him, Thái still runs outside, raises his hand, and waves. I also run after Thái. In a number of courtyards of other houses there are a lot of people who stand and, raising their hands, wave and ask questions. These soldiers seem to come from afar; they are covered with dust and look very weary. They smile and respond to waving hands and to inquiries. Thái gets out close to the road:

"Elder brother, where are you coming from?"

"This group has just got out from Saigon."

The soldier responds to Thái while still moving on. The next soldier who follows right behind slips his hand into his rucksack, gets two small cans of food, and tosses them at Thái's feet:

"Gift, friend. Glad you're still alive, friend."

The next soldier pulls out a pack of cigarettes; the next one after him tosses some more canned food. I run after them to return them:

"Elder brothers, hold on to them to eat; there is still a lot of fighting ahead."

"Stop it, young lady; keep them. We don't even know whether we'll survive, so food doesn't mean much to us. We are on a suicidal mission."

Some smiles, some shrugs. I stand motionless, following them with my eyes. These several days there is a lot of news disseminated about [Nationalist] soldiers[3] coming to pacified areas and putting their grip on everything, taking the stuff of the people who fled. People hasten to come back to protect their property, and because of this hurriedness a lot of people die as victims of injustice. But this army unit is certainly

3. According to the author, the Communists spread these rumors to agitate people.

completely different from these stories. In addition, a candy bar lands at my feet. I don't have strength anymore to bend down and pick it up.

"Glad you're still alive, friends."

Several soldiers at the rear keep shouting. Hands of people along the road wave, stretching to return the goodies, and we continue to greet each other with smiles. Gradually, as the unit passes by, I am able to bend down and get a firm hold on the chocolate bar, and unintentionally at some point I crush it into bits. Never before have I seen such amiable soldiers. They are soldiers who've come here from faraway places to die in Hue. They are men from Saigon, men who migrated from the North, men from provinces in the South, in the Center, in the North. They've come to die with Hue. Oh heavens, I think about the Regional Forces soldiers,[4] some of whom deserted their posts on the first day, some of whom are waiting for a bit of quiet to rush outside and carry off some rice on their shoulders, to enter deserted houses to loot them. The good food had been carried away by the Việt Cộng during the first several days of the upheaval; what remains goes to the outcasts who fish in the murky water[5] of the lawless situation. I once saw two soldiers taking away a Honda motorbike and several other people carrying a chest, chairs, or bundles with useful things taken from destroyed houses still reeking of dead bodies. Thái has picked up several boxes with stuff and prods me to return back inside. When my mother hears what we have seen, she gets very emotional, on the brink of tears.

"Shame on you; why take from them? You should've left it for them so they could eat and get strength to fight."

Aunt Vạn expresses her concern over and again:

"They indeed deserve pity. Who would think that they're so friendly, unlike those bastards who cast their fishing lines in the murky water, stealing and looting in the hamlet? And those bastards are still alive, while these soldiers have to endure suffering and enter rough battles."

We hear the sound of gunfire resounding in the distance. Surely, men are fighting each other again. I think about the soldiers who just

4. Another group of local militia along with the Self-Defense Forces.

5. A common Vietnamese metaphor for those who use war as an opportunity to loot.

tossed me tins with meat and candy bars. They laughed there on the road, but by now, among them, there are those who have fallen down. What will Hue do for them in the days to come? Nothing... Hue is also emaciated, only bones and skin, already completely destroyed. But certainly Hue will still survive, even if it will be made of dying flames, cold ashes, and human bones. Among those soldiers will be men who survive, who even will return to their homes, and who will remain to protect Hue.

Thái has lit a cigarette. He puffs out the smoke that turns into rings; a dot of fire on the end of the cigarette flickers, now small, then big, like a hope that gradually gives me wings and then extinguishes again in my soul.

Precisely at that moment I am suddenly stunned by a noise in the courtyard. Then a voice calls:

"Oh Mother."

A girl's voice. My mother sits up, on alert. The entire family flocks out of the shelter. "Oh, Mother, oh Mother, oh Mother, oh Mother . . ." The voice calling "oh, Mother" doesn't stop. The panels of the door are wide open. A bicycle flops with a thudding noise on the ground and Hà jumps and rushes to throw her entire self on my mother's chest: "Mother, Mother, Mother . . ."

"Child, child . . . Oh, good God, Hà, three souls and seven vital spirits,[6] Hà . . . you've managed to come back, you've managed to come back."

I suddenly look out to the courtyard and see an old man wearing a long black traditional tunic holding the handlebars of a bicycle; he smiles, looking into the house.

My mother shouts:

"Mr. Minh. How did you come back?"

Then my mother cries, cries with happy tears, cries noisily:

"Oh, sir, sir come in here. Sir, please come in here, sir."

6. This expression reflects the Vietnamese belief that a person has several souls and vital spirits, which can disappear in the moments of danger. According to the author, the mother here appeals to Hà's souls and vital spirits to return into her since the mother thought they had deserted Hà on her way full of dangers.

The old man, unruffled, sets his bicycle upright, strokes the flaps of his long black tunic, and then, ascending the doorsteps, enters the house. My mother still holds Hà firmly in her arms. The old man whom my mother calls Mr. Minh points to Hà:

"I've brought this little devil down here for you, aunt. She has been demanding to go for several days now, and she has been tormenting me, indeed without any fault of my own."

Hà wipes her tears:

"Mr. Minh has brought me down here, Mother."

Mr. Minh, while sitting down on a chair, looks around the house:

"What luck, the house hasn't been seriously damaged at all."

My mother, prodding me to bring some water, at the same time asks Mr. Minh:

"Sir, how are Lễ and his family up there?"

"Not bad. They indeed are still up there. Your son teacher Lễ burns with impatience; he was so determined to go down here to look for you, aunt. I had to prevent him. The two of us, I and your child, every day were looking for a way to come down here, but it was impossible to do it."

"Have any of my grandchildren been hurt?"

My mother stops; her eyes turn pale in expectation. Mr. Minh drinks a mouthful of water:

"Not bad. Oh, only Hy, the younger sister of Lễ's wife, was directly hit by a piece of shell, which entered her leg. But not bad, there are several medics over there, and they have bandaged her."

Thanks to the old man wearing a black silk tunic and Hà, who give us their accounts, I learn much more about the situation up at Từ Đàm. My elder brother Lễ's family had to abandon their house and move to hide at the ancestor-worshipping house of Venerable Phan. Around it, everything has been almost completely reduced to rubble. During the first several days, the Việt Cộng occupied a pagoda for a barracks and a makeshift hospital, but later they gradually withdrew up to the mountains and assigned only a few of their people to stand guard and dig underground shelters for combat. Mr. Minh tells us that now in the pagoda there are hundreds of refugees, and around the pagoda a lot of houses have completely collapsed. On both sides of the road from the ancestor-worshipping house of Venerable Phan going down to Bến Ngự Bridge, not a single house has remained intact. My elder brother's family fled to the house of Venerable Phan along with a lot of other families and refugees. Hà points at the old man:

"Do you know who this is, elder sister? This is Mr. Võ Thành Minh."

Seeing me stupefied, she adds:

"Mr. Minh is the person who played a flute on the shores of the lake in Geneva where he opposed the division of our country in 1954, elder sister."

I look at the old man, who is still busy recounting stories for my mother. Hà continues:

"You don't know Mr. Minh, elder sister? He is also called Võ Song Thiết."

I surely know about him but never before met him in person. I ask in a low voice:

"What does he do now?"

"He is in charge of the ancestor-worshipping house of Venerable Phan; he was Venerable Phan's comrade, elder sister. Listen: during the several days of fighting, thanks to Mr. Minh, a lot of people have escaped death. It's very joyful."

I frown:

"You're calling it 'joyful'? Oh heavens, death is everywhere, and you say 'joyful'?"

"Mr. Minh says that in any circumstances we still must try to enjoy life. Mr. Minh isn't afraid of death at all. He is on the go throughout each day, elder sister. He goes to distribute rice, to transport wounded, to visit places . . ."

I look very attentively at the old man. He wears a black silk traditional tunic, pants made of white fabric, and on his head a black beret.

I don't know where my mother found betel, but she brings it out and offers it to Mr. Minh to chew at his leisure. His face is intelligent and kind. Looking at him, it is easy for people to quickly feel at ease and to be sympathetic with him rather than to be suspicious or to want to cross-examine him. Two bicycles are still in the courtyard. The drizzle has not yet stopped, and the sounds of guns still resound in the distance. My mother suddenly asks:

"What road did you take to get here, sir?"

"We took all kinds of roads. We've been trying for several days. One day we went down past Đua-Ra Mansion and saw fighting there with heavy gunfire, so we had to turn back. Hà was boiling over with impatience."

My mother raises her eyes full of reproach and looks at my younger sister. Hà bows her head and gives a light smile.

Mr. Minh continues his denunciations:

"When I would tell her to stay in the house, she wouldn't listen to me. When I went somewhere, she would go with me. Several days ago the two of us climbed up Ngự Bình Mountain to watch the fighting, with an intention to again look for a road to come down here. While they were fighting, artillery lobbed in – bang, bang – we climbed up the mountain to find cover and the two of us rolled down from halfway up the mountain and then lay buried in a bomb crater. A real horror. But somehow Hà liked it very much. This child, her guts are indeed the guts of a courageous revolutionary."

My mother attentively listens to Mr. Minh, and her face is at times pale, at times joyful. She sighs when she looks at Hà, who looks at her, and she laughs:

"Ah, you're really something!"

"Yes, the two of us went up to Đua-Ra Mansion and Hà took along a still brand-new pair of shoes."

"It was so scary, sir. The entire Đua-Ra Mansion is covered in blood, isn't it?"

"Monkey, it is so, and you still went. You're really . . ."

Perhaps afraid to worry my mother, Hà turns a deaf ear to her words and switches to another story:

"Mr. Minh, here, my elder sister is here, sir."

I have to nod my head to greet Mr. Minh. Having just met him, I immediately feel sympathetic toward him. Thanks to the words of the youth Lê[7] who escaped disasters, came here, and told us his story some days before, I don't feel a stranger, even for a moment, with Mr. Minh.

"Hà has been always talking about you, elder sister."

I laugh:

7. Lê is the youth who related his story in chapter 5.

"Oh, sir, please don't address me as 'elder sister' anymore. I'm just a child for you. Consider me to be like Hà."

Mr. Minh nods:

"All right. It will be easy to address you the same way. What a pity. You, child, have come here and gotten trapped, right?"

"Yes, sir."

"How many children do you have?"

"Yes sir, two."

"What a pity."

Hà pitches in:

"Listen, elder sister, Mr. Minh is very artsy. Up in Từ Đàm they are fighting and the shooting is roaring, but Mr. Minh keeps getting together with young people who escaped in the ancestor-worshipping house of Venerable Phan, and, moreover, he plays musical instruments and sings songs all day long."

I ask:

"The Liberation Army left you in peace, sir, when you were making such a noise, correct?"

"The first several days it was the case. Then, we started to worry about getting young people out of there. I told several young people to go down to Bến Ngự Bridge and to go on a hunger strike opposing the war."

I find this hilarious:

"Sir, surely you're joking."

Hà winks at me, giving me a sign not to talk anymore. Then she turns to Mr. Minh:

"Sir, show my elder sister the paper the Liberation Front gave you to be able to travel."

Mr. Minh laughs, gently and good-naturedly:

"Hà, you're saying nonsense. This paper is nothing. I can go anywhere because I'm nobody's slave. I am absolutely against war – the war itself is what I am against."

Hà keeps talking:

"Mr. Minh still writes letters to Hồ Chí Minh and even to the American president expressing his opposition, and he also appeals to the world."

"I act alone, so what goal can I achieve? But even so, I still keep doing this; right, child?"

He raises his eyes to me and smiles. I nod. He continues:

"Will you dare to go out with me to sit on the bridge to oppose the war?"

"You're kidding, sir."

My mother pitches in:

"Sir, could you help to bring Lễ with his wife and children down here, sir?"

"I and Hà scrabbled our way to come down here. It's so difficult to escape. Today we had to circle around Đua-Ra Mansion, then circle down to the railroad crossing, but it didn't work. We then circled around to Tây Thiên intersection. Up there, artillery was shooting like rain, and only when we went up to Tây Thiên did the explosions abate."

Seeing tears running in long streaks from my mother's eyes, Mr. Minh comforts her:

"We are in the same boat with others. Listen – if I were you, I wouldn't worry about anything."

Hà adds:

"Elder sister, look outside, see? Mr. Minh's bicycle is over there. It has a bag for rice. He has carried and distributed a lot of good rice, and what remains are only broken pieces. All day long, Mr. Minh distributes rice and transports the wounded. He has only that bicycle."

Mr. Minh's bicycle is set against the pillar of a flower arbor, and from the handlebars dangles a rice bag made of fabric stretched to its utmost. I look at Mr. Minh; he had taken his hat off, and now suddenly he hastily puts it on:

"That's it; I must go. I must go back up to Từ Đàm."

My mother begs him insistently:

"Sir, stay to have a meal; then you'll leave. Now, sir, listen, they are fighting."

"Fighting each other, never mind them. I am leaving. See, this afternoon, I still have to go to transport wounded and to find provisions. Up there they are now out of food."

Hà asks:

"When will you come down here, sir?"

"Tomorrow."

"Tomorrow when you, sir, come down, I will go up again with you, OK?"

My mother scolds:

"You are just inventing funny stories, aren't you; why would you demand to go?"

Mr. Minh sides with Hà:

"It doesn't matter – the matter of life and death is all in the hands of fate, aunt. Listen, this child is very brave. If I'm still able to make a revolution, I shall immediately let her follow me."

My mother, careful not to hurt Mr. Minh's feelings, keeps silent. Hà reminds Mr. Minh time and again to remember to come back tomorrow. I and Hà take Mr. Minh outside and up the lane; he says:

"That's it – now go back inside. It's very dangerous to stand outside."

I say:

"Oh sir, when you get back there please tell my elder brother about us, in case he's worried. Say that mother and I and the entire family are down here and are completely safe."

"Yes."

Hà asks:

"Sir, will you remember tomorrow to come down here, sir?"

"Yes."

Mr. Minh gets on his bicycle and pedals away, his black robe gradually disappearing behind a turn. I say:

"That's it. Let's go inside."

"Down here is very quiet, right, elder sister?"

"Yes, quiet."

I don't have the heart to tell my younger sister about artillery lobbing at random at dawn. I also keep quiet about the clashes occurring each day on the National Highway. If there are a few shots of AKs or some B40 grenades behind the fields and our hamlet, then the entire road can be destroyed by the returning fire. Right on the first day of gunfire, the American army also managed to get up here to An Cựu to check the situation, then later went back to lie low at some place, letting the Việt Cộng rampage here. While they were cutting across to avoid an intersection, a gunshot from somewhere in the direction of Đại Càng Shrine was fired. A unit of the American army stopped, and several Americans went inside the closest house and dragged out a young man. This guy could speak English; he was a student in a pedagogical school in Qui Nhơn who had come back to visit his family. He handed them his papers and conversed with the Americans. But what did they need to know? One gunshot exploded and the unfortunate young man fell down to the ground, his body twisted in death. The Americans climbed on their vehicle and drove back to Phú Bài. From the nearby house everybody poured outside, hugging the corpse of the young man and wailing. Several liberators garrisoned in the houses behind that one came out:

"Down with the American army ruthlessly killing people."

"Please accept our condolences. This is a valiant death, a person who died for the people, for the country."

A flag of the blood-red color was placed to cover the face of the dead. A moment later everybody went away. Only the relatives of the dead person remained, their crying and wailing not yet abated, but then their crying was gradually drowned in the sounds of gunfire and explosions resounding far and wide. There are still a lot of other things, but why would I tell them to my younger sister? Only several days ago, the American army lost a rifle and so the soldiers blew up a multistory house. Only several days before that, a family had just returned to one of the houses on the other side of the road. That night, the Liberation Army came in and arrested the head of the household, and he disappeared. That person was a custodian, or bike keeper, or did some kind of a similar job for a branch of the police. He was old and definitely by now has passed into eternity.

Hà is still at my side as we return into the house. She asks:

"Has our family already dug a shelter?"

"If we hadn't, we would have been dead by now. Each day there are stray bullets, and artillery shells fall close by. It has been quiet here only for the last few days."

"Over there is very scary. Elder sister, do you know artillery shells fall nonstop, then bombs from the airplanes? The other day several people died, and people are too afraid to go out to the garden to bury them. Airplanes fire down shells like rain, awfully scary."

My mother has met us at the door. As soon as we slip through the door, she closes it tight once again.

Thái also crawls out of the shelter:

"Hi, elder sister Hà."

"Wow, when I came, where were you?"

"Hiding in the shelter."

"Why didn't you come out?"

"It's really scary to get out. If I had known it was you, I would've come out. But if you turned out to be someone from the liberation, then what?"

"What a monkey you are. I came back and you are not glad."

"I'm just joking. When I heard your voice, I was as happy as I could be. When I heard a male voice, I thought there were a lot of people, so I got scared. Listen, elder sister, these several days they come back and arrest people; they are very cruel. If you hear the hooting of owls, it means they're back."

"Wow, is it so similar to what's going on up there? Up there each night the hooting of owls is heard everywhere. Awfully scary."

"This is their secret signal."

My mother has not completely clarified some things for herself:

"But how is it that they let you go, child?"

"The first several days they forbade it, then artillery fired up so much that they let those who wanted to leave go. But if adult men or young men wanted to leave, they would be arrested."

That evening, fortunately, I and my younger sister lie next to each other, with Hà telling me stories from Từ Đàm. She lets me know that all the pagodas have collapsed. The Liberation Army hung a flag and established its headquarters right at Linh Quang Pagoda, and it organized classes and training there. The first several days no one got out of the houses. In the houses, shelters were made. Outside, the Liberation Army dug foxholes. The atmosphere seemed to be very tense. But the first several days were quiet; no one was very worried or scared . . . but then when artillery started lobbing up there, people began to panic and evacuate. But to go outside meant death. I ask Hà whether they had hung a red flag with a yellow star. Hà says they had only blood-red flags. During the first day they were ordered to take down the "three-stick-flag" and to find fabric to sew blood-red flags.

Thái inquires about a group of Rural Development cadres who were stationed at the high school several days before Tết. Hà turns melancholy – they ran away somewhere and completely disappeared from the time the gunfire started; their belongings were scattered all over. When

Hà went up there, there was nothing left of them. Hà describes for me young female Việt Cộng cadres. They would go to visit with people, entering each house to inquire about those inside, but when they would enter any house they would scare the hell out of the children and old women. Hà tells me a story of a stout Mrs. Xếp. She says:

"Listen, elder sister, it's very funny: liberators elected Mrs. Xếp to be Liberation Mother. In no time, they [the Communist female cadres] also started to call her Liberation Mother. She was very scared of them. So, each time she saw them coming into her house, she blubbered nonstop: 'Liberation Mother, Liberation Mother. Here, children, take the bottles with oil from the mother.' No matter how many bottles of the 'Double Heaven' oil were for sale in her shop, she gave them all away to the cadres. When Mrs. Xếp saw them, she would fall down and bob her head up and down on the floor kowtowing – bruising her face and brow."

I ask Hà whether she was afraid; she says that yes, she was, but the first several days, thanks to having Mr. Minh, it was very merry. Mr. Minh gathered young people to sing songs at the ancestor-worshipping house of Venerable Phan. He requested them to write letters opposing the war. The first several days there was no gunfire and Mr. Minh was sitting and typing, clop-clop, and then he would organize singing. He said that singing like that decreases the amount of spare time to be scared. Hà tells us that when she was walking in the ancestor-worshipping house of Venerable Phan, she encountered the wife of Professor Lê Văn Hảo, the person whom the Liberation Army made mayor of Hue. I am curious and inquire further. Hà says that the wife said that before Tết, Mr. Hảo told her to buy rice to keep in reserve but didn't inform her about anything else. Contrary to the words of the young man Lê who also gave us an account of her, Hà says that Mrs. Hảo is very easy to like and also has a child named Nai. Mr. Minh has been helping the woman with all his heart. Mrs. Hảo, like other women, is afraid of artillery fire and is, in general, easily frightened. She is not at all clear about what exactly her husband does.

My mother says that whatever it takes, we must bring my elder brother Lễ and his family down here. It seems that Americans have advanced to Nam Giao Bridge. The two sides are spoiling for a fight and hold defensive positions. If they start fighting, how many people who so far have survived will die?

Hà says:

"Tomorrow Mr. Minh will come back and I will go up to Từ Đàm."

My mother falls silent. Hà asks:

"Elder sister, will you go up there with me tomorrow?"

I don't promise Hà; I am still in an infinitely dangerous position. If they know about me, they will find me, and I will certainly be arrested as so many other government officials have been. Thái asks:

"What way can be taken?"

"Go toward Ngự Bình Mountain. There's no one there; they [the Communist forces] have already completely pulled out from there. The other day, I went with Mr. Minh up Ngự Bình Mountain to observe the two sides firing at each other. Artillery lobbed up to there, and it was very scary . . . we rolled down the mountain and there are still plenty of scratches on my arms, elder sister. I also went with Mr. Minh to Đua-Ra Mansion. Everywhere is covered with blood and stinking dead bodies . . ."

"When you were going there, did you see corpses of Americans?"

"Behind Đua-Ra Mansion I saw a few of those. They are bloated and very scary to look at."

Hà raises her hand and, touching the wall of the shelter, says:

"A shelter like this is very scary. Let's redo the shelter. It's quiet here now, but I'm afraid if artillery lobs up here and there's a stray direct hit, it will be the end."

My mother remembers several artillery shells that at dawn made a house collapse, killing people, and she gives a heavy sigh:

"What will you use to make a shelter?"

Hà says:

"Tomorrow I will go up there and will buy sandbags and will bring them back. Over there, there's no shortage of anything to buy."

Thái also pitches in:

"Up by uncle's, Bé's father's, place, there are still a few sandbags. Tomorrow I will go up to ask elder brother Bé."

We keep discussing the issue of digging the shelter. Hà says we must not make a shelter in the house, that it's very dangerous. If the house collapses and the shelter does not collapse, we still can't exit and might end up dead because everything will be clogged up. In the end, we discuss making a shelter tomorrow outside in the courtyard. My mother says: "That's it; go to sleep now." Hà hugs me, and I also circle my arms around her. It's really fortunate that while so many people have died and so many families have been destroyed, I and my younger sister can still lie next to each other. Talking and talking, we forget even the sound of gunfire, which is still roaring, now close by, then far away. A moment later Thái says:

"Shooting is very fierce, elder sister."

Hà gives her opinion:

"It's not really fierce here. Up there, explosions roar everywhere; it always seems like they are about to explode on top of your head."

"So are the Việt Cộng dying?"

"Sure, they are. We stayed in the house; in the shelter it was good but still not completely quiet, much less for them when they are in those tiny foxholes. In front of our house, there was still a guard-liberator."

"Did he talk with you?"

Hà falls silent. My mother bursts into angry words in a low voice:

"Sleep now; you are talking nonstop. Go to sleep; tomorrow morning we will need strength to dig a new shelter."

I think about my elder brother; now he is with his wife and children in a dark shelter, not knowing whether or not American and Vietnamese armies will attack Từ Đàm tonight. In just an hour or a minute everything can change completely. Who knows whether tomorrow my younger sister will be able to come back from up there? The same for myself – who knows whether or not we are now in a safe area and whether or not it will still be possible for me to go to Saigon to see my husband and children again?

But then I don't have strength to keep thinking. I close my eyes and sleep peacefully amid the sounds of artillery exploding fast and thick, plowing and crushing a dreamy, romantic, and beautiful city.

NINE

A DOG IN MIDSTREAM

WE SLEEP THROUGH THE NIGHT; WHEN WE WAKE UP, IT'S already light and the roads are suddenly bustling. A lot of [Nationalist] soldiers from Phú Bài are coming up National Highway No. 1. They go on foot along the road one by one, carrying their rucksacks. They walk and look around, looking at both sides of the road, and smile, greeting people who stand by the road following the soldiers with their eyes. I don't know for how long she had kept it, but an old woman displays a basket full of cigarettes to sell at Xay T-junction. Several soldiers stop:

"Mother, sell me a box of Ruby, Mother."

"If you want a box, go ahead and take it. How would I know which one is Ruby?"

Someone's voice asks:

"So, where are these cigarettes you sell from, Mother?"

"Ah? Where are the cigarettes from? Yeah, I evacuated and came here; I saw an abandoned house, and there was this basket with cigarettes under the bed there. When I saw you passing by, I thought to sell them to buy food."

"How much do you want, Mother?"

"How would I know? Anything will do."

The soldier pulls out his wallet and takes out a banknote of two hundred dongs and hands it to the old woman. The woman is astonished:

"So much? A few tens are enough."

"Mother, take all this and spend it."

"No, no. You are going to fight the enemy; take it and buy food for yourselves. I give you the cigarettes as a gift, not this . . ."

Several other soldiers stop; they draw out banknotes – a hundred, two hundred – and take cigarettes. In a moment all the cigarettes are completely gone. The old woman holds a fistful of money, banknotes of hundreds. She runs after the soldiers:

"Oh, elder brothers, I don't take money. Why did you give me so much?"

Several heads turn, laughing:

"Mother, keep it and buy food. As for us, we don't know if we die or live."

"We are going to face the bullets, Mother."

"Wish you luck, Mother."

The unit goes ahead and leaves the old woman far behind. Another unit is coming up; seeing the old woman, running and shouting, they don't understand what's going on. They pull from their rucksacks small cans and toss them down at the woman's feet:

"Are you hungry, ma'am? Here, take something to eat."

"Ma'am, are your children still alive?"

A lot of inquiring voices. A lot of small cans fall next to the woman's feet. She has not yet managed to pick them up when several children appear out of nowhere and pick everything up. Several soldiers chide them in good spirit:

"Shame on you. Leave all this to the old person, you brats."

The children break into a run. Some cans are handed to the old woman. Several soldiers are solicitous:

"It's enough, ma'am; please go back home. Don't run after us; it's very dangerous."

The soldiers continue to walk. I and Thái stand, expectantly looking to see whether any groups of refugees are coming back. But when people see many American soldiers coming up, they do not risk being out there anymore. My mother rushes into action to make the shelter; she forgets that we do not yet have any sandbags. Units of soldiers keep going by until around noon and then stop. With our minds at peace, we set the table to eat. For a long time we haven't had such a complete and sumptuous meal. Uncle Giáo's wife continues to regularly send up food to us. Today we have meat cooked in a fish sauce and fresh papaya. Aunt Vạn is thrifty with food; the cooked meat is really salty, but we eat it and it still tastes as delicious as ever to us. When my mother inquires about what the situation with food and drinks is at Từ Đàm, Hà says that, thanks to Mr. Minh, food and drinks were very much in abundance. Whenever Mr. Minh came back, he brought meat and vegetables. But during several days when the fighting was really intense and he was busy with transporting wounded, the house ran out of food and several children started crying.

Having finished eating, Thái walks down toward Mù U hamlet, hearing that a market gathers down there. But at Trường Bia post, soldiers chase him back up.

Mr. Minh keeps his promise and indeed returns. When we have just finished eating and are preparing for our noon nap, he wheels his bicycle into our courtyard. The entire household rushes out to invite him into our house:

"Sir, how are they up over there?"

"It's completely quiet and nothing's going on. Your son, teacher Lễ, heard that I found you, aunt, with the entire family, and he was very happy."

Hà bustles in and out:

"I'm going up there with Mr. Minh. What road shall we take, sir?"

"We still go by way of the mountain. A lot of shooting's going on. I had to tie up the flaps of my tunic, carry the bicycle on my shoulders, and run."

Hà looks enthusiastic:

"I'm going with you. Mother, I am going to get ready to go with Mr. Minh."

My mother is worried:

"Is it possible to get through, child?"

"Possible, indeed possible."

"If so, why hasn't Lễ come back yet?"

"It's possible to get through for people who are just by themselves, but he's tied up with wife and children, and on top of it, Hy, Lễ's wife's younger sister, is wounded, so how would they go?"

Then Mr. Minh speaks:

"Hà, go get ready. Vân" – addressing me – "pour me a bit of water."

Aunt Vạn asks:

"Sir, have you brought rice to distribute?"

"Certainly I have. There's a bag of rice over there."

Hà has finished her preparations; she wheels her bicycle out and is ready to go with Mr. Minh up to Từ Đàm. My mother takes a little bit of food and forces Hà to take it up over there. Hà says she'll be back in the evening, and we'll have sandbags. After they go, I and Thái look for a place to dig a shelter. We decide to dig right in the front yard. Thái starts working. We disassemble the old shelter to make another new shelter.

This afternoon, Hà comes back without Mr. Minh; she also doesn't have her bicycle. Two students are with her; their faces are pale green as though they have long been deprived of sunlight. Their hair is disheveled and tangled. Hà says:

"Here are a couple of students – Chữ and Hát."

My mother asks:

"How come these young guys were able to leave and Lễ couldn't?"

Hà recounts:

"Mother, it's impossible for him to escape from there. They watch very thoroughly up there. If elder brother Lễ goes, they would know immediately. I had to pretend to go in and out tens of times and only then managed to sneak these guys out."

Thái asks:

"So, they didn't see?"

"They did. There was a guy there on guard in front of the door and he saw. I was scared to death and was afraid he would shoot. But when he saw us, he didn't say anything at all. He just followed us with his eyes."

Thái jokes:

"Did you wink at him, elder sister Hà?"

"Monkey, I was afraid to death, and you're annoying me. But that guy, he's still young, and he's very kind."

"Has he ever talked with you, elder sister?"

"No, very little."

"Has he looked at you, elder sister?"

"Monkey."

"Looks like he likes you, elder sister."

The two students smile reluctantly. My mother invites them inside:

"Please, come into the house – don't stand outside there, or else they [the Communist forces] will be spying on us."

Hà leads the way:

"Come in, come into the house and take a rest."

The two students trudge in, each carrying huge bundles of sandbags. "It's now enough to build a shelter," says Hà. My mother asks why Mr. Minh hasn't come down. Hà says he's busy transporting the wounded. Americans have already gotten to Bến Ngự Bridge; thanks to them getting up to the bridge, the Liberation Army had to withdraw to the mountains, and then all at once a lot of people were able to flee. Hà tells us that up at Từ Đàm, artillery lobs down like rain, each day more and more fiercely.

As soon as evening comes on that day, the entire household joins efforts to dig the new shelter. Not until the following day do we finish building it. We still keep the old shelter inside the house because there are too many of us. We have been able to buy some food, and each time Mr. Minh comes down we send up there with him a little food for the family of my elder brother.

The next day, an audacious family escapes from Từ Đàm by way of Tây Thiên and is able to come to An Cựu. They carry on their shoulder poles a lot of their stuff because the husband and wife are owners of a provision store. Passing by our house, they rush in and ask to stay with us temporarily. My mother agrees immediately. They at once occupy the kitchen quarters and hurriedly take off the door to make a shelter. The head of this household was also able to bring along a moped and even kerosene. He has a daughter named Nga of the same age as Hà. Thus, the two young girls discuss with each other how to go up to Từ Đàm and get in touch with the people who are still stranded there to help them escape to An Cựu.

They make several attempts to get through, but only once are they able to sneak up there. My elder brother Lễ sends word back that they will escape down here to An Cựu, but for fear of being detected they are waiting for the Liberation Army to withdraw first. My mother is the most anxious, and throughout the day, whether sitting or standing, she cannot stay calm. She goes out and comes in; she makes inquiries of evacuees who come by from the Bến Ngự or Từ Đàm areas. Communication with Mr. Minh is cut off for several days. Artillery strikes the road in the mountains, and Hà and the other young girl Nga don't dare to venture out anymore. But several days later, Mr. Minh comes again; he drops his bicycle with a broken handlebar in the middle of the courtyard and then, sighing, comes into the house. My mother asks immediately:

"What? What's going on up there, sir?"

"Very dangerous. They are lining up troops and are about to fight each other. Artillery pours down like rain; in a few more days everything will be utterly destroyed."

"Oh heavens, so what will happen to Lễ's wife and children?"

Mr. Minh gives a heavy sigh:

"I'm also worried. Whatever it takes, we have to save his family."

"So, what road did you take here, sir?"

"I went along the side of the river; bullets were falling like rain. Plenty of people running from the dangers of the fighting were wounded. I've just taken a wounded person to a hospital in Hue, and then I came here. Over there is now quiet and one can go back and forth. At the post office and the treasury building, several Việt Cộng corpses still lie sprawled with their feet tied to machine guns; it was so sickening to see . . ."

The two students run out, and Mr. Minh says:

"And you brats, you haven't gone to the hospital yet? You must go to the hospital and help people there. Out there it is quiet, so nothing bad will happen."

Mr. Minh turns back to Hà:

"Child, go check if there's a place that can fix the handlebar for me, child."

Hà carries the bike away on her shoulders and then brings it back:

"There's no one to fix it. Sir, take my bicycle."

"Yes, fine. Auntie, give me a piece of betel. I have to leave now."

My mother again sends a bit of food up to Từ Đàm. These several days near Trường Bia post there was a market and people slaughtered a whole pig to sell for meat, and there were vegetables brought up from Mai market to sell. I hold Hà's hand and we see Mr. Minh out to the road. Hà looks hesitant and keeps reminding Mr. Minh:

"Sir, listen sir, remember whenever you have some spare time, come down here. Sir, don't stay over there anymore."

Mr. Minh turns back to Hà and scolds her:

"Silly child, don't be sad. I'm still taking care of many people over there. Let me bring your elder brother with his family here. Put your mind at peace – don't worry."

When Mr. Minh finishes speaking, he climbs up on the bicycle and immediately pedals away toward An Cựu Bridge. Thái runs out, and the three of us also walk toward the bridge. Americans stand guard there, and the Transportation Station also has soldiers guarding it. Our area is now completely safe; we worry only about our elder brother and his wife who are still in the most dangerous area. Young people who fled the fighting and came back here have pedaled bicycles out to Kiểu Mẫu School to check on the situation in the streets. The battles on that side seem very ferocious. Certainly, up at Từ Đàm it's also like this. When we are walking, we meet a group of people coming from the direction of the bridge, some by motorized transportation, some on foot. We hear a moped stopping next to us. I look up and shout for joy:

"Elder brother Trai."

Here's my cousin sitting on a moped, happy and asking excitedly:

"Has Lễ already come back here? Is all your family fine?"

I reply sadly:

"The family is fine, but Lễ and his wife are still stranded at Từ Đàm."

Trai laughs. His attitude toward us continues to be very cheerful:

"I have already returned back to my home. Listen, when things calm down, come to visit. Don't worry about Lễ; nothing has happened to his family. Is there any news for him?"

Trai intends to leave, then puts down the brace of his moped:

"Shame on stupid me . . . I have this."

He slips his hand into the pocket of his coat. There's something big bulging in it. Trai fishes for something in his pocket and pulls out a fertilized duck egg, still warm. He keeps pulling out several more eggs:

"To each person a fertilized duck egg."

Before he leaves, Trai recommends:

"Don't go out to the bridge. Americans are guarding there and they shoot incessantly. People who flee the fighting are crying out there."

"From where are they coming?"

"I ran away from there as fast as I could, so I didn't ask."

There are several sounds of scattered gunfire, and Thái pulls me to go back.

That day, Bé comes down to help us pile more earth on top of the shelter, and he says that he will go to report for duty. He says that tomorrow he will bring his family down to Phù Lương to a refugee camp because they have run out of rice for food. Thái is also burning with impatience and asks to go to report for duty, too. Several Regional Forces [Nationalist] soldiers pedaling their bicycles past us let us know the news: the [Nationalist] army has closed up on the right bank and has successfully completed suppressing the Việt Cộng, so people are just now returning, and all those who are members of the military or government employees must report for duty immediately. One can go up to the Provincial Seat or to Kiểu Mẫu School, where there is also an office. Thái goes at once to change his clothes, even though my mother and I attempt in vain to hinder him.

Two hours later, Thái comes back. He says that it's now possible to use the road on the right bank; American and South Vietnamese armies have completely occupied it. In the streets, bullets fall like rain and smoke rises, darkening the sky. At Từ Đàm, Americans and Vietnamese have not yet completely suppressed the Việt Cộng, and they dare not rush across Bến Ngự Bridge or Nam Giao Bridge. Civilians who are fleeing the fighting shout and cry on the other side of the bridges. Thái also tells us that the buildings of the Provincial Seat and the Bureau of Representatives are still full of Việt Cộng corpses, which no one has buried yet. The two students who came with my younger sister Hà say good-bye to our family to go to Hue hospital to care for those who are hurt from the fighting. Seeing that it makes sense, we don't hold them back. I ask Thái whether he has already reported for duty. Thái says that he has and will go tomorrow to receive his weapons and assignment. Thái lets us know that his commanding officer was killed, and furthermore a woman, who was a low-level cadre at the Ministry of Rural Development, was beheaded and her arms and legs completely chopped off. The Provincial Seat is vacant, and it seems that the head of the province has also been killed. A lot of rumors – random and awfully disgusting.

Also on this afternoon Thái leaves for a while; when he comes back, he brings our family half a bag of rice, which he procured thanks to his talent in conducting a lively conversation. My mother looks at the bag of rice and is happy to the point of tears.

Since the day when I was able to get in touch with my office, I have been without any means of communication. I borrow a moped belonging to the family temporarily lodging in our kitchen quarters and call for

Thái to go down to Thanh Lam with me again. This time we are more fortunate, and I manage to get in touch directly with Saigon and am assured that my family is still safe and sound. I only need to wait for an airplane, and then I will be able to escape. Another day passes. Từ Đàm is still mired in smoke and fire, amid bombs and bullets, and we have absolutely no news about my elder brother. Then people from Bảo Quốc Pagoda[1] flee here, and people from Bến Ngự are able to get here. Mr. Minh disappears without a trace. Everyone is absorbed in his or her own business. I try to do my best to discover any information about his whereabouts but have no luck. Two days later, a young man named Khánh passes by and drops in for a visit; he gives us the news that Uncle Đội Hòa, my mother's brother, has passed away. Uncle was in charge of music at the royal palace. He was old but still in very good health. His house is next to the steps of Bảo Quốc Pagoda. It was a simple thatched hut, and in the courtyard were flowerpots and pots with ornamental trees. In his house there was an abundance of different kinds of musical instruments, from really ancient ones to the most modern. When I was little, I always dreamed that uncle would give me a zither, and he would say:

"If you study well, child, I will give you an instrument from the old times, which belonged to His Majesty; His Majesty played so skillfully that ghosts would stand outside to hear him."

But I didn't learn anything about national music, and I didn't dare ask for that precious instrument, either. Now Uncle Đội Hòa has died? Where did he die? When he was fleeing the fighting or at home? What about the fate of the instruments, of the thatched hut? My voice trembles when I ask the young man. Khánh says that Uncle Đội Hòa fled to the place in front of Khánh's house near the post office. Over there it was still quiet, but suddenly a stray artillery shell fell down. Uncle was directly hit by a small shell fragment that went into his temple, and so he fell down and lay there, his body spread out; he was in full possession of his heart and mind, waiting until all his blood would run out, his body would dry up, and he would die. Tears overflow from my eyes. I have cried too much. Before the upheaval of this Tết, I cried because of the death of my father. When the city was crumbling into pieces, I cried together with

1. The largest Buddhist temple in South Vietnam.

so many people, and now I'm crying for a kind uncle-artist who always tried to maintain an old-fashioned, dignified appearance in front of the children. And I also cry for the instruments; so many of my uncle's treasures were also the last treasures of our national music, and they, like my uncle, are no more either, buried in the smoke and fire of war.

My mother also sits stunned for a moment. I'm certain that my mother calls to mind times when she, together with uncle, lived in the resplendent Royal Citadel – the sounds of musical instruments and the sounds of castanets, mornings with elegant music resounding far and wide, dresses and hats and the sound of music on the days when the king held court. My mother also used to study music with my uncle when she was small. When Grandfather became angry over her lack of talent, my uncle would protect her from his wrath.

"But are you certain that it's Mr. Đội Hòa himself indeed, or did you only hear someone talking about it?"

"No, I saw with my own eyes. He died in my house."

I firmly hold my mother's hands. Her hands are shaking. A moment passes and then my mother asks, choking with emotion:

"And what about his wife?"

"Please madam, nothing with her, she has survived."

My mother turns to me:

"There's nothing we can do but to go fetch her and bring her here, child."

But Khánh shakes his head. There or here it can be safe and quiet, but it can also be that stray artillery shells will fall at any moment. Besides, there's no certainty that my uncle's wife has not yet left. Khánh tells us that my uncle's family left their house when it was burning. My uncle turned back, appealing to Heaven and Earth, wanting to rush back into the house to die together with his instruments. People had to drag him away. Since then, uncle did not say a word to anyone until he was directly hit by a shell fragment and died.

So, this is the end, from the eldest person, the most ancient one like my uncle, to little crossbred Vietnamese Americans – they all have been killed in the whirlwind of war. How many tons of ammunition are pouring down on the heads of people in the city of Hue? These several days the airplanes flying over the city are countless. Standing by the National

Highway, we can see jets flying swiftly like lightning and dropping load after load of bombs, followed by the sounds of explosions, which even though reverberating from far away are still endlessly terrifying. We go out farther and stand on this side of the river looking across: Đông Ba market has become flat ground; houses in the downtown area seem to be tightly wrapped in smoke and dust. With each explosion, dust and bricks and tiles fly up in bits and pieces, as if a gigantic firecracker explodes, throwing corpses up into the air.

My mother hears the news about Uncle Đội Hòa's passing, but when no news comes about Mr. Võ Thành Minh, she becomes dismayed. Sometimes when she's sitting and eating, she sets aside her bowl and chopsticks, takes her face into her arms, and cries. I am afraid that my mother is going crazy. In this situation, anyone can go crazy – like an old acquaintance of my family fleeing the fighting and passing by whom my mother takes in. The woman cries nonstop; she tells stories that don't make any sense. Then suddenly she bursts out laughing:

"I've never seen such a huge blaze. Dead people burn like pigs on a spit."

After finishing laughing, the woman suddenly again takes her face into her hands and cries. Any moment she can lose her mind.

At noon the next day, Thái manages to get in touch with his unit. When he comes back, Thái reports the news:

"A lot of people from Từ Đàm and Bến Ngự have come here. Our side used airplanes to appeal to people, advising them to flee from there so that the army could stream up there, unobstructed, to fight the enemy."

My mother jumps up and down like a child:

"Really? Who will go to pick up Lễ and his family? Go at once."

I, Thái, and Hà immediately volunteer to go. We go out toward An Cựu Bridge. I suppose that my elder brother and his wife, if they go, would be able to go only by the riverbank. The Liberation Army will withdraw up into the mountains, and surely up there gunfire is shaking the sky. We walk out to the bridge. Many people are fleeing the fighting. They run, carrying poles on their shoulders with two baskets containing their belongings, putting even children into the baskets. Thái wanders about, inquiring, but no one wants to reply or, if there is a reply, the response doesn't help us in any way. Several American soldiers stand guard at the two ends of the bridge watching groups of disheveled and bedraggled people fleeing the fighting; the soldiers laugh among themselves, narrow their eyes, and make jokes, and sometimes they raise their guns up and fire warning shots into the air. When the groups of people hear the gunshots, they take to their heels and rounds of amused laughter explode behind their backs.

People run with dogs; dogs run with people. Dogs from somewhere run following the groups of people, and there are so many of them. A black dog is trampled upon by jostling feet rushing from the end of the bridge down to the river shore. Suddenly a gunshot rings out and the dog emits a pitiful sound, rolls, and falls down into the water; noisy laughter bursts out. Several black and white Americans stand on the bridge and keep shooting to prevent the dog from swimming to the shore. The dog gradually gets farther and farther away from the shore, howling plaintively; it's absolutely heartrending. The bullets are still fired nonstop, but it seems they don't intend to kill the dog, only to prevent it from getting to shore. Some bullets are off target and hit the road on the riverbank; other bullets ripple under the water. A group of evacuees runs up in confusion; their shouts and cries echo in the sky. The louder grow the shouts and cries, the louder the laughter of the Americans. The people fall and then get up, get up and then fall headlong. Why is my nation in this position? Why is the dog over there still trying, with great difficulty, to get to the shore to regain its life? I feel such a pity for my people, for my country, that human life is worth less than a joke, less than a dog. I bend down and pick up a stone and hold it firmly in my hand. I tightly squeeze the stone as though I squeeze my own heart. Throw it – sling it into their faces: barbaric inhuman thugs. At some point I see a group of people running with difficulty, shrieking and crying, frightened. I suddenly feel deep resentment inundating me. A small yellow-skinned nation – what profit can be gotten from it? The dog has roamed nonstop during so many days that its saliva has dried out, and it is covered with sores all over its body; its heart fails. I raise the stone up. Go ahead – throw it. Throw it into their faces, then whatever comes, let it be. But no, what will the stone achieve? The dog is very far from the shore. It tries to make several more sounds, then its front paws can't swim anymore and it strikes the water right and left at random. I release the stone, and it falls down on the ground. The screaming group of people has passed over a section of the road where a number of parcels fell down and did not get picked up. Another group of people continues to go forward. The dog now has completely sunk under the water, letting the cold stream take it along while the red blood turns to pink on the surface of the blue water. I swallow my saliva, my throat is dry and bitter, and tears are about to well up in my eyes. Thái stands at my side, silent. Both his and Hà's faces are pale in an agony and a humiliation that will never be possible to wipe out.

A black hand raises and waves to us. A tin with meat is tossed and rolls to my feet. Not knowing what to think, Thái strongly kicks the tin with meat. It rolls, falls down into the river, and sinks into the deep. Several peals of vile laughter resound. I raise a kerchief to wipe tears and, choking with emotion, tell my younger siblings:

"Let's go back."

Before leaving, I again pick up a stone and hold it in my hand but eventually do nothing with it. Just a single stone, but the consequences of throwing it at the soldiers could trigger three shots – and three lives. At this moment, any yellow-skinned person could be an enemy with just a glance from the foreigners with blue eyes.

Cry . . . cry . . . scream without restraint, cry with the beloved native land that is squirming as its spine is being broken. A group of people passes by, and then another one follows. Faded, soulless eyes, hands firmly clasped to bundles with clothes and possessions that remain – they continue to go by. Burned grass, fallen trees, and collapsed houses. The turquoise stream of the river, poetic in springtime, has been swollen with the blood of people and of dogs. Piles of bricks grow higher day by day. The stone I firmly hold in my hand – what is it for? I hurl it at a destroyed house. The stone disappears at once without a trace.

By the end of that morning I hear more very sad news. In the city of Hue, it looks like the fighting is almost finished. Tràng Tiền Bridge is destroyed, and American army engineers try to install a temporary bridge to transfer troops across the river; heavy machine guns, automatic rifle fire, and airplanes shoot down like rain on houses already destroyed. In the city, people do not dare to run outside to escape, so they dig holes in walls from one house to another and in this manner escape toward Gia Hội or run in the opposite direction up to Kim Long. People tell about the death of Mr. Tinh Hoa, the owner of a bookstore, who, being extremely hungry and thirsty, rushed outside. Before going outside, he had researched a way to flee by zigzagging, crossing back and forth to avoid bullets. But bullets were still shot at him, and he fell face down and died on the spot. Some people guess that it was the Việt Cộng who shot him, and other people are absolutely sure that it was the Americans who shot him; but whoever fired the shot, Mr. Tinh Hoa nevertheless got killed.

I think about the people still trapped in Từ Đàm and in the Citadel. The entire Citadel is enveloped by high walls: Chánh Tây Gate is the evacuation route for Việt Cộng troops, and in the directions of Thượng Tứ, Đông Ba, and Sập Gates, bullets from airplanes, American bullets, fall like rain. How many people are nervously struggling with this? The sturdiest underground shelters can withstand guns only of small caliber; how can they withstand the penetration of missiles and tons of bombs dropped down each day? And furthermore, what about the venerable old Citadel, the last vestiges of a historical era with golden branches in jade palaces, ancient porcelain vases painted with flowers from hundreds of royal generations, and an abandoned, empty golden throne? Now it's all finished; Soviet Russian and Czech guns along with American guns have razed to the ground and crushed into bits a venerable old city, a city of history. Never can it be rebuilt again. I have no more hope. Usually I pay little attention to such things as preserving our inheritance from the past, but now, watching tons of bombs being dropped on the Citadel, my heart is squeezed with pain. My mother used to tell me stories about the imperial palace in times past – about the golden mansions and jade palaces and about His Majesty's residence, and about music in early mornings, and about bells ringing in the evenings, and also about the days of the funeral rituals for Emperor Khải Định, when white tigers were brought to court. So many of these legends, so many of these fantastic episodes were woven into the stories I heard during my childhood; they were even more beautiful and interesting than ancient tales.

That afternoon, something else happens unexpectedly, to the point that our entire family is stunned and flabbergasted; we pinch ourselves to be sure what we see is happening in reality. Having finished our lunch, the entire family sits around, retelling stories for everyone to hear, when there's a voice calling from the outside:

"Mother, oh Mother."

My mother forgets everything, slips into her shoes, and rushes into the courtyard. A child named Mai, a maid for my elder brother Lễ and his wife, is carrying one end of a hammock; at the other end is a strange man still very young; and in the hammock is Hy, a younger sister of my sister-in-law. Lying in the hammock, Hy is trying to lift her head to see what's going on. Mai is shouting, "Mother, oh Mother," and energetically waving her hand. Hy is carried into the house as Mai points to the road both crying and saying:

"Oh Mother, Master Lễ is running behind, and he is still out on the street."

I rush outside before anyone else and my mother follows me, then Hà comes, then Thái. Just as we reach the lane, my elder brother comes into view. He pushes a metal children's stroller in front of him and goes barefoot with his hair hanging down to his ears. In the stroller are two small boys, their faces covered with Mercurochrome,[2] and they are about to cry.

I hold my nephews in my arms. The elder niece Ti Na, who runs behind in short steps, also falls onto my chest. My eyes overflow with tears. My nephews also sob. My elder brother points back, behind him:

"My wife is behind over there."

I leave the children and run up to the bridge. But just as I turn onto Xay T-junction I see her sitting plopped on the ground, her ragged hat on one side. She holds in her arms the tiny one, the newborn, and her face is soaked with tears. I hug the baby and show the way. My sister-in-law doesn't wear sandals; exhausted, she follows me. Entering the house, my elder brother and his wife stand in front of my father's altar. My sister-in-law bows her head and cries. Following her lead, the young children cry too. From the eyes of my mother, myself, and Hà, tears stream down, tears of joy and self-pity.

A bit later, only when my elder brother and his wife fully regain their composure, they tell us the story of how they managed to flee the fighting. I inquire what road they took, and my elder brother recounts:

2. Mercurochrome is the trademark for merbromin, a green crystalline organic compound that forms a red aqueous solution used as a germicide and an antiseptic.

"Shells over there are shot awfully fiercely. The Việt Cộng could not control the area anymore. The American troops came to Nam Giao and Bến Ngự Bridges. Yesterday at nightfall an underground shelter collapsed and crushed to death a little child, a great-grandchild of Venerable Prince Cường Để,[3] and another child was wounded. I carried in my arms two little children completely covered in blood. Mrs. Xếp carried another child in her arms. The little ones were set to go first, holding white flags in their hands, and we went down to Bến Ngự Bridge to bring the children to the hospital. Several people also ran following us, and when we got to Bến Ngự Bridge I asked for permission to cross, but I saw that it was very crowded with Americans who were very suspicious and who waved their hands to drive us back away. But our entire group didn't have time to turn back before the Americans fired at people's feet with bullets that also grazed next to people's ears and swished over their heads. The children were crying awfully, and our entire group had to withdraw. The little wounded child could not bear the pain and died."

My sister-in-law adds:

"Lễ was very brave, Mother. He carried in his hands two small children and was himself all covered in blood. Lift your shirt, Lễ, so that Mother can see."

My elder brother lifts his shirt; bloody traces have turned bluish-black. He's thin as a lath, his eyes are dirty yellow, and there's no blood in his face at all. The children demand food. Hà rummages for food for our nephews. My mother assails Lễ with questions:

"When you got out from there, what happened then, son?"

"Oh, there is nothing left to tell, Mother. Our house is destroyed. There was nothing to take with us. My children had only the sets of clothes they wore. When the guns quieted down, our maid Mai went back to bring some of our stuff stored at the ancestor-worshipping house of Venerable Phan. I don't know whether in a couple of days the altar there will still be intact. Last night, guns still rained down bullets; when it was dark, they [the Communist forces] came back, raised their flags,

3. Prince Cường Để (1882–1951) was a prominent member of the royal family. He and Phan Bội Châu were early leaders against the French colonial occupation of Vietnam.

and trapped our troops. The two sides fired at each other. I was sure that the next day our side would manage to get up over there. I knew that to stay meant death because of the ferocious fighting. Mr. Minh advised us to leave immediately."

My mother has not yet calmed down after her excitement:

"What road did you take, son? Where was it possible to come down?"

"We followed the railway, Mother. All thanks to Mr. Minh."

My elder brother points at the young man who had helped to carry the hammock with Hy:

"Mr. Minh had to go up to Tây Thiên and asked this young man to go down with us to help carry Hy. Alone, I would have had to deal with several little children, with Bê who has just given birth, and also with our stuff. Mr. Minh took care of everything; I feel so sorry for him."

Bê is the name of Lễ's wife, my sister-in-law. Hà is confused and she asks:

"Why didn't you ask Mr. Minh to come with you?"

"Mr. Minh was still helping wounded, transporting them. He said that he still couldn't leave; if he left, he would leave so many people stranded in the circle of artillery, and Mr. Minh could not put his mind at peace about this."

I pour some water into a cup and invite the young man to drink it. He is around thirty years old, and the features of his face are firm. My elder brother doesn't hold back his words of gratitude. Hà looks immensely sorrowful and worried about Mr. Minh. My mother inquires about the neighbors. Bê, Lễ's wife, lets us know that the stout Mrs. Xếp, of whom Hà told us earlier, is coming along behind; her maid is lightly wounded, and she limps while helping her mistress. My mother keeps hugging one grandkid after another. I feel sorry for them; they, like a flock of small wounded birds, tremble and shiver whenever they hear the sound of artillery from behind Trường Bia post and raise their hands to cover their heads.

When he finishes his cup of water, the young man who helped to carry Hy is determined to request to take his leave to go back to Tây Thiên. My mother invites him to stay, but he doesn't want to listen to it as he's made his decision. He says he must go see Mr. Minh. My elder brother is afraid that something unfortunate may happen on the road.

The young man borrows a bicycle and says he's going by way of Ngự Bình Mountain; surely there won't be any problem there. My mother solicitously advises time and again that the young man in any case should convey to Mr. Minh her invitation to come over here.

A moment later the stout Mrs. Xếp arrives. Her maid limps, holding her mistress's hand. When she enters the courtyard, Mrs. Xếp starts to sob:

"Has teacher Lễ arrived yet? Has he arrived yet?"

My elder brother comes out to greet her and invite her into the house. The woman leans her cane against the leg of a chair and looks around and around, and when she sees my mother she starts crying again:

"Oh auntie, I thought that we wouldn't see each other again . . . Heaven and Earth, it seems that everything has turned upside-down. Our family is all safe, isn't it, auntie?"

"Please, ma'am, sit down and rest. Our family is safe. Thanks to Heaven, thanks to Buddha."

"Glory to the Amitabha Buddha, goddess of compassion; I was so afraid that they would arrest teacher Lễ."

"I was down here and in a torment of worry about you all the time, ma'am."

My mother also bursts out crying. Seeing this, Hà jokes with Mrs. Xếp to distract my mother:

"When the Liberation Mother departed, why didn't the Liberation Children [the Communist soldiers] detain her?"

"Yes, yes . . . they [the Communist soldiers] have all fled now. They even abandoned their own fathers and mothers."

The words of Mrs. Xếp make everybody sad, then they also make us burst out laughing, but Mrs. Xếp herself wipes tears:

"Well, aunt, to see each other is precious by itself. The family is still here, and the property is still here . . ."

Hà asks my elder brother:

"Up there, have they [the Communist forces] completely withdrawn yet?"

My elder brother makes a wry face:

"In fact, they are extremely smart. They have almost withdrawn; only several Việt Cộng guys have remained; they run to a corner and fire back several rounds of bullets, then they get to another corner and fire back several rounds of bullets. The American troops down by the bridge thought there were a lot of them, so they didn't dare to come up and waited until the Việt Cộng had almost completely withdrawn, leaving only several tens of people with orders to hold their position like that. I have to say, it's really funny that several of those Việt Cộng guys who stayed behind to tease with their shooting were able to stop the American troops. As for the roads to the mountains, they [the Communist forces] lined up their troops to withdraw there and departed while singing. It seemed that they went as reinforcement to somewhere in the area of Chánh Tây Gate."

I inquire about an old friend of mine, also a grandchild on the paternal side of Prince Cường Để.

"Has Thạch Hà been able to evacuate?"

"She was hiding together with us at the ancestor-worshipping house of Venerable Phan. When the shelter collapsed, Thạch Hà lost a child. So, I carried that small child in my arms down to Bến Ngự Bridge, and the children, Ti Na and Nô Răng, carried white flags. Mrs. Xếp with several other people followed us. But they [American soldiers] were shooting at our feet to scare us off. Thạch Hà evacuated up to the Tây Thiên area. Thanks only to Mr. Minh, who checked the roads, were we able to come down here."

My little niece boasts:

"Auntie, auntie, our family's milk fruit tree has broken down; I picked up two pieces of fruit and they are ripe and smell good."

I feel both pity and joy. A good healthy tree that for years had been supplying so much fruit – it is nothing to celebrate that, broken and withered, it now yields only two pieces of fruit, which nevertheless the children will enjoy.

After returning to An Cựu, my elder brother becomes calmer and more peaceful. We take care of reorganizing our life. There certainly won't be enough rice to eat if this situation continues, but our family cannot go back into the evacuated areas to obtain rice or money. Thái has to both report himself and take care of buying rice. I again go to get in touch with my office to see about an airplane to Saigon. But before going to Saigon, I must take care of Hy because her wounds have been left unattended for a long time and now are getting infected. I no sooner request assistance at the office than the roads are again becoming difficult to get through. I reconcile myself with trying to wait.

The next afternoon, more families come down from Từ Đàm, and among them is the family of an old teacher of mine with his children, who are also teachers, and their little children. My elder brother Lễ greets them and brings them into the house; everyone is barefoot and looks exhausted. We get to know more about the situation in Từ Đàm. We learn that after my elder brother had escaped, the Việt Cộng returned again and took away with them some young people. Only those very clever at hiding were able to escape. Mr. Minh, it seems, has also been detained. Hà, frightened, shouts out:

"How can it be that Mr. Minh was also arrested?"

Teacher Liên, the old teacher of mine, has aged; he shakes his head in despair:

"Last evening they still shot several young people near the school."

My mother asks:

"Up there, have the guns subsided yet, teacher?"

"Oh, they explode like rain with a cascading noise, each day fiercer and fiercer. We took the risk of dying when we decided to leave. Thanks to Heaven and thanks to Buddha, only when we got here did we know that we will live."

Our house is filled with utter joy. Next morning, everybody is making underground shelters. Each family occupies a corner of the courtyard; anything still remaining in the house that can be pulled out for making shelters is used. But we don't worry about anything; even if we disassemble the entire house to make one more shelter, everyone works with all his or her strength and is happy to do it.

Families from other nearby houses are coming back, making a lot of noise; they also make underground shelters to protect from artillery. A small market assembles in front of the road leading to Trường Bia post. A few taverns have opened. Vitality rises really fast; only several days ago houses and neighborhoods were desolate, as though they would never breathe again. And just two or three days later, people have returned. Everywhere there are people, there is breath, and it means that there are taverns, there is smoke from cooking, and there are meals to eat. But it's also absolutely heartbreaking that next to this scene, about a kilometer away, perhaps two kilometers, blood still continues to flow. In the morning, units of [Nationalist] Special Forces troops, paratroopers, and marines cross the National Highway, their faces still ruddy. In the afternoon, their corpses are brought back to the same road.

Although our area is calm and quiet now, by night the Việt Cộng continue to come back and arrest people. By day American soldiers come up to guard roads and garden areas and to watch people's activities with suspicious eyes, without a trace of sympathy. If they hear so much as a single suspicious noise, a magazine of bullets is shot into a shelter full of people. A single gunshot fires and an entire small hamlet behind the field bursts into flames. American soldiers standing guard wave their hands, prompting people to run out of the houses, but they can't take anything with them. The sounds of screaming echo into the sky and resound over the earth. People run out of their houses to stand and watch the flames. The area becomes increasingly populous as new evacuees arrive. When the Americans' gun barrels point at them, they resign themselves and weep as they once again run from danger. Each time my elder brother sees an American soldier entering our courtyard, he calls up the entire house and urges people from all the shelters to get out of the shelters and into the house. Seeing how many people there are in our household, with a lot of women and children, they [the Americans] do not suspect anything. It is clear that residents returned earliest and in the largest numbers to the hamlet where we live. No one has yet dared to return to neighboring areas, even though it has now become calm and safe.

[Nationalist] Regional Forces soldiers seize the moment when the owners of houses leave; they break in and carry all the stuff out of the houses. A lot of people become rich. I even see men carrying past my house Honda motorbikes that are still locked. I also see scenes of [Nationalist] paratroopers coming from afar to chase after Regional Forces soldiers caught looting. A marine from Saigon comes out and shows Thái a mechanical pen with two engraved names overlapping with each other. He says that he picked it up from the corpse of a young woman. Every young woman of Huế even in death would still have her long hair, making him go from one deep regret to the next.

A few other families who have just been able to escape from Từ Đàm and come here confirm that Americans have crossed Bến Ngự Bridge but have not yet gone up the hill and are still lying in wait. I think about the artillery shells that will lead the way for the military units. Everything has been reduced to bits; surely there will be more that will be squashed into the ground even deeper. People talk about corpses along the roads. The young people don't have time to bury them, so they are thrown topsy-turvy into the bushes or buried among piles of brick. Packs of dogs, hungry for a long time, suddenly have an opportunity to get full. Some people are in agony, some die abandoned, and there is nothing but packs of overindulging dogs. I notice that around my area there appear a lot of dogs. In addition to worrying about protection from artillery and from the Việt Cộng who come back to arrest people, we also have to save some bricks to throw at the dogs. Each time when we arrange for a meal, a pack of dogs flies into a rage outside. Although the dogs are many, so is the number of people in my household, so the dogs can't flood into the house. Thái regrets:

"Several days of starving, almost to the point of death, I didn't see a single dog – otherwise I would have caught one to fill up my stomach."

Day after day we go outside and stand watching airplanes dropping bombs near the Citadel. The airplanes roar as though shredding the sorrowful firmament to pieces. Columns of smoke continue to rise up, as high as the mountains. There are a few people who have managed to escape from Gia Hội; when asked, they cry and say:

"Death – it's all death . . . death . . . nothing but death. They established a headquarters at Gia Hội School, set up trial courts, and killed people there day after day: so abhorrent."

"What about the Citadel?"

"People evacuated to Gia Hội."

"Elder brother, is there anyone else in your family?"

"I'm the only one who survived. To cross the river by boat I had to pay three thousand dongs. Well, good-bye everybody."

"Come in here; rest two or three days and then leave."

A lot of people invite him in, but the lonely man declines. Surely he wants to go farther from the puffs of smoke, from blood and death, and the sooner the better. He walks so fast that it seems like he runs down the National Highway.

Another person recounts:

"They [the Communist forces] have started to kill people very ruthlessly. When they see a man, they shoot. If an informer accuses someone, they shoot. I was hiding for twenty-odd days on top of a water gutter; some days I was so hungry that I had to pull out moss and chew it. I had to catch the water in the gutter to drink. Look, people, my stomach got swollen like a woman afflicted with ascites.[4] I must go to Phú Bài and ask to be put in the hospital."

People also tell a story about how an entire family died because of a television set at Gia Hội.

The family was asked by a Communist soldier who came to search the house:

"Is this device to communicate with the enemy?"

"Please sir, but no, sir, the TV machine is to watch songs and dances."

"Turn it on – let's try to listen to it."

When the TV was turned on, there were no programs with songs or dances on the screen. One magazine of bullets – a woman and her little children fall dead on the ground. The verdict was announced: it was done to give compatriots a lesson. Small children died not having time to close their eyes. And again, two crossbred children of a Vietnamese mother by an American father: their mother had gone to Vũng Tàu and left them with a woman who would breastfeed them. "These are children of an American imperialist who are left here to harm the future of the nation" – such was the Việt Cộng verdict. No need to waste bullets. The heads of the two little children were smashed against the wall. Brains and blood splattered and spilled all over.

There are still wounded to transport. They are either the ones who flee the fighting and get wounded, or they are those who long for their property and return exactly at the moment when the two sides clash and are then hit with a bullet. So many deserted houses, so much abandoned property. The Liberation Elder Brothers liberate only bones and blood, and they grab "by mistake" inconsequential things like watches, mechanical pens, and tiny, pretty, funny, or curious objects. As for what was

4. An accumulation of fluid in the peritoneal cavity.

left after them, it's saved for those who take advantage of murky water to cast their lines, and however much they take it's still never enough.

People also say that a hunchback youth, still very young, the son of a jewelry store owner, fled, taking with him ten-odd *liangs*[5] of gold. He was shot to death right in the street: one gunshot – which side's bullet it was is not known – and the gold flowed out together with his blood, leaving only the corpse of the unfortunate person lying on the ground.

But there is more. There's still much more destruction and death. Youth and men are lured with the sweet words of the Việt Cộng and go to study for fifteen days – no one has ever seen any of them again, and more people are still being taken away. What will be the fate of these people? They [the Communist forces] have intentionally detained people to bring them along to make targets for warding off shells and bullets when they make a last stand. But as for the people: some died, some escaped – certainly, not many have survived. The screams in the middle of the night, the verdicts, the sounds of guns killing people with no reason – how do people dare to stay, dare to believe?

Day after day I go out to stand on the road, hoping that in the crowds of refugees there will be Mr. Võ Thành Minh. I met him only several days ago, but I appreciated and loved him with all my heart. Some people are vile while others are courageous in this period of turmoil; everyone shows their real face. Today, hearing news that Americans have advanced to Từ Đàm and that the two sides are fighting each other, disputing every inch of ground, I think that undoubtedly Mr. Minh cannot remain safe over there, but in his spirit of setting an example, he continues to transport the wounded. No one still with the strength to survive until today should die from a bullet. I hope that Mr. Minh will return. Why would they arrest him? Surely, he will manage to escape and I will see him before I leave Hue. I have been able to get in touch with my office and am preparing for the day when I set off for Đà Nẵng. But why is it that I still don't want to go? I am waiting for that gigantic pillar of smoke rising up from inside the Citadel to gradually stop. Certainly it must abate little by little. A woman leading a little child goes to the National Highway and with tears recounts:

5. A *liang* is approximately thirty-seven grams or 1.3 ounces.

"Oh fellow villagers. My house has burned down, my husband has been arrested, and also my child has gotten lost."

People inquisitively ask her:

"Who is that little fellow whom you are leading behind you? Isn't it your child, or whose is it?"

"My child has gotten lost, neighbors. I was holding him by his hand and pulling him along and running. Then when I looked back he was not there, and I met this child."

The woman keeps crying, keeps talking, and keeps dragging along the little fellow. She calls out for her own child, and the child whom she is pulling along calls out for his own parents. The scene looks really funny, but tears also well up in people's eyes. In my native place, how many children and how many mothers have suffered like this? There is no way to tell everything. Another day goes by and then still another day. An Cựu area looks more calm and peaceful than before. In the morning, I have been able to eat a bowl of porridge with pig intestines and also some pork sausage that peddlers sell. We don't have to huddle down in the dark shelter throughout the day anymore. But the air outside seems extremely venomous. Everybody's eyes are always stingingly hot. The tear gas of the allied armies spreads everywhere to force out the liberation troops that still remain. Right behind our garden, a few houses from mine, there's an abandoned house and an abandoned shelter; people [American and Nationalist soldiers] spray tear gas to force out a wounded liberation trooper who was abandoned by his comrades-in-arms. And when he comes up and sees the light, he breathes his last and dies. In the shelter, even though being in pain, the man also was writing a diary, writing letters to his mother and his girlfriend. What was special is that he also had a letter, written in unsteady hand, opposing the war:

> When I die, I want to put my head on the land of the North, even though my legs are in the South. I've caused bloodshed in this city and I must leave my blood here too, so that it dissolves together with the streams of blood from the people of Hue and of my nation that is being unjustly spilled.

The Special Forces soldier, when he finishes reading the above lines, hastily crams the letter into his pocket, then silently takes the enemy corpse, the corpse of a Vietnamese, and goes out into the garden. He digs a small hole to bury the corpse of the northerner who died together with the people of South. He looks around, calculating back and forth to figure out where North is to make the place for the head of this fellow in an unhappy grave.

I want to ask the soldier for the letter, but I see that his face is taciturn and that he carries a very heavy rifle on his shoulder, and I stop short. Only a moment later, when I get out on the road, I see this same soldier firing a salvo of gunshots into a shrub. There are no people, only a sick dog there. The dog runs out, its eyes blazing with fire; it holds in its jaws a piece of human bone. Enough, I don't want to tell anything anymore.

People continue to spread rumors that in the Citadel the dead bodies of the residents and of the Việt Cộng have piled up high. People fleeing the fighting who are hit by bullets lie in heaps on top of each other. Corpses of Việt Cộng fill holes; corpses are down in the ditches and on the sides of the roads, scattered like dead fish caught on dry ground.

Also starting from this day, no one comes here from the areas of Nam Giao and Từ Đàm. It seems that no people remain there to flee. Nearly all have already left, and those who remain are now trapped in crossfire, between two long lines of bullets and shells. I continue to lack news about Mr. Minh. My elder brother gives a long sigh each time he hears me mention Mr. Minh. My mother is able to buy a bit of areca and betel to keep for him. I don't understand the basis for it, but my mother believes that Mr. Minh will be safe and sound.

I myself do not believe this. Perhaps he was arrested and led away, as the rumor has it. According to the rumor, Mr. Minh was taken away along with Master Đôn Hậu.[6] So, perhaps he has not been killed. Isn't it possible? But I still doubt it very much. Two crossbred Vietnamese American children – what was their fault? A Buddhist monk like Master Đôn Hậu, a scout, and a fighter like Mr. Võ Thành Minh. Heavens, why amid sounds of gunshots, amid the bloody scenery, amid the innocent deaths of so many people, why am I still uneasy about things like that? The necessary things that I must do are to get out of Hue, to survive, to return to see my children, to meet my husband. I will get out, leaving behind a devastated, destroyed, and shattered Hue. I will leave my mother, my elder brother, my younger sister, nephews, relatives, and

6. Full name Thích Đôn Hậu, who was a leading figure in the Hue Buddhist community.

neighbors. Perhaps if I stay for another night, my turn to be arrested will come. Sounds of hooting owls, foreshadowing death, still persist each night – sometimes in the distance, sometimes nearby. I bring up all these thoughts of mine with my elder brother. My elder brother advises:

"When you manage to find a way to get to Saigon, you must leave here at once; don't wait around. When you get back there, I will feel that our family is more at peace."

What has he seen that my elder brother dares to be so firm? I look up at the altar of my father. My sister-in-law has lit two candles and a big joss stick. The smell of the incense is like subtle perfume. In this city, how many graves are cold and desolate, are lacking the smoke of incense? Oh Father, despite dying, you are still lucky. Does not the fact that we were able to properly perform all the burial ceremonies give my elder brother hope, Father? Father, if you with enormous effort had lived a few more days, what would have happened to you? I don't dare to keep thinking about this. Oh Hue, on the day that I returned to mourn for my father, I also had to mourn for the city.

In this upheaval, how many of my old school friends are left? To what extent has the destruction taken the building of beloved Đồng Khánh School, a nurturing place of my childhood and of my growing-up years? Flame trees,[7] hollows of tree trunks full of memories – why do I still have an impression that the hollows of tree trunks full of my memories in the courtyard of the school are also full of blood that oozes from them?

I want to see again the Congregation of the Most Holy Redeemer, the place where I escaped calamity during the first several days, and I want to again drop by An Định Palace to see how huge the piles of bricks and debris are there. I want to go to Tân Lăng to check on elder sister U's house and to check on the family ancestor-worshipping house – whether it is still intact or full of what is left from bombs and bullets. I want to go to the places where I took refuge and where I entrust a bit of memory, those places where I saw blood, saw death, and also saw birth. Oh, the gallery in the church where so many babies were born – amid abhorrent scenes of agony, the sound of a newborn infant crying was both a huge struggle and a stretching up to the utmost of pride in the vitality of life. It

7. *Phượng vỹ* or "phoenix's tail" is a popular urban tree in much of Vietnam. Also called "students' tree" because it usually blossoms at the end of the school year.

happened not only in the gallery but also in the bell tower of that church. It has been almost a month that all over the city of Hue, in dark shelters, on roads, on edges of ponds, in puddles of blood already grown cold, next to severed arms and legs, so many other children have also been born. The earth muffles doleful shouts, and life also opens for the sound of crying newborns.

No, Hue will never be reduced to ashes and destroyed as if it were the end of the world. In a ring of fire and a scene of bombs and bullets, people again gather in markets, and those who survived have returned to their daily routines, determined to wait it out. And down in the ditches on the sides of the roads, in the dark soil, how many dead people with open, frowning eyes are waiting? I also meet more people who fled from various places and came here – from Gia Hội, from Bến Ngự, from Kim Long. So Hue has been emptied. A survivor recounts that in order to save more than several tens of people who were stranded in a small hamlet, [Nationalist] soldiers had to sacrifice their lives in rather significant numbers. Another person says that just as he was almost able to escape from hell, he was arrested by the Communist forces:

"A group of us were arrested and a long rope bound one person to another. The group was led up toward the mountains. When it came to an empty plot of land, a liberator issued an order to release the rope and forced people to dig trenches. Those brand-new trenches were next to trees and plants that were still fresh and green. A group of people was lined up. A round of bullets does a favor: liberation. Some of us were spared: 'Push them down into the trenches and cover them with earth,' ordered the Communist soldiers to the survivors. Afraid to cry, we swallowed our tears, so no teardrops flowed out of our eyes, but hot as fire they ran burning down through our chests and guts. And was not the fate of the remaining to be the same? But I, why am I so fortunate that I escaped death? My ancestors have saved me. Heaven and the Buddha or demons and spirits have saved me. Farewell everybody, farewell! I must run and hide from them [the Communist forces]. I must go and find my wife and children. I'm going to run away from here – all you people go and hide. Hide right now."

The man finishes his story; he's very anxious and has clearly gone mad. I wish him to go mad so that he can forget. To be able to go mad – what a blessing it will be for him.

Another person holds a different point of view, and he tells his story with tears. He is not crazy; on the contrary, he remains lucid and full to the brim with emotion.

"They [the Communist forces] stayed in my house for ten-odd days. They brought in a lot of wounded. Many who suffered could not make it through and died. Do you know, my fellow villagers? They also know how to be compassionate. They saved my son when he was wounded by a fragment from an artillery shell. A young North Vietnamese soldier lamented and sighed with me – think again, my fellow villagers, don't hate their young ones. They only know how to carry out orders from above. Their families are also far away and poverty-stricken. Seeing how compatriots die is painful for them, too. Out in the North, they hear propaganda to go to the South to fight the Americans – how would these youths know what reality is like here? They also deserve pity... they also hate the war very much."

"Why have you fled here, uncle?"

"They're all gone now. In my house, there were only dead bodies. There was also one young guy, wounded, who remained; he advised that I must go, because to stay would mean death. Now I'm going; I'll go to the safest place. Here it's still not safe yet."

They [the Communists] are also people, aren't they? Oh Hue . . . do you, Hue, do you hate and resent them? Eyes that remain open deep down in the black soil, glowering there in that lightless world, do you hate and resent them? Surely you do, right? But you must not hate and resent them; rather you must hate and resent the bullets brought into this country to transform us into people who are killed or arrested, forced to kill people, kill siblings, fathers and mothers, those of our own flesh and blood. I have seen so much of torn human flesh and entrails during the past month. How much more will be enough so that we will never forget? My younger male relatives, Thái and Bé, have gone to report for duty. Thái was able to get back to Phù Lương, and Bé returned to his unit. On the right bank of the river they have started to check the population. People who returned gather in groups to go and get control cards. My elder brother has already received a card.

Around the area where I live, it seems that nearly all the people have now returned. One family has lost its mother; another has lost its father; some have lost children. Sounds of heartrending cries burst out, connecting one house with another. People tell us about the days when they fled the fighting, about tragic deaths, and they cry inconsolably. Mourning headbands have started to appear.

My office has sent word that there will be a helicopter to take me from Hue to Đà Nẵng, and that from Đà Nẵng I will get a plane to Saigon. I am very happy. But I don't dare to show this happiness of mine to my mother or my elder brother. As days have gone by, my mother and my elder brother increasingly express their sadness and are overcome by bouts of emotion; our initial panic has gradually settled in and turned to stone in everyone's heart. At night we still must sleep in the shelter, and by day we choke on our tears from the tear gas. But we still have confidence that the disaster will soon be over. I dare to break the news from the office about the airplane to my mother and elder brother only during the evening meal of that day. My mother advises:

"Child, you must find a way to go early. Look, Hue is not yet safe; I gather there are still a lot of unfortunate things happening."

I know that my mother wants to tell me about stray bullets, stray artillery shells, the sound of owls hooting by night, footsteps groping for a way in the dark. I tell the entire household:

"I can't put my mind at peace yet and just leave like this. If I go, I alone escape, and then what if something happens here at home . . ."

"If anything else happens, we will brace ourselves to endure. Such is fate, younger sister."

Those are the words of my elder brother Lễ. His eyes look up at my father's altar. The candles still glimmer and the columbine still emits a subtle aroma.

My mother says:

"Perhaps, child, you will go on the morning the day after tomorrow. Tomorrow afternoon you must go to Phù Lương and stay there, child. I'm afraid that something unexpected will leave you stranded on the way, child. To take care in advance is better."

My nephews get into a ruckus:

"Auntie, you're leaving because you are afraid of guns, aren't you?"

"So, are you children afraid of guns?"

"We were afraid only the first days, when we came down here, but we're not afraid anymore at all."

That night I can't sleep. There's only one more night left to sleep in this house, the house where I returned to mourn for my dad, and then later I shared mourning for the entire city. I have an impression that in the darkness of the night, our garden is still filled with feet walking around. From time to time, hooting sounds and screams still reverberate in my subconscious. My mother doesn't sleep either; she lies close to me, and in the darkness with her hand she gropes for my wrist:

"Sleep, child; you must be in good health, child. Why are you still awake?"

I turn over, sigh, and talk with my mother:

"Guns fire quite a lot, mother."

"Sure, it's in the Citadel."

"I don't know whether at Từ Đàm the fighting is over yet or not."

"Child, put your mind at rest; when it's quiet up there, we'll go and get our stuff. Surely, not much has gotten scattered around."

"Mother, you don't believe that the house of elder brother Lễ has collapsed?"

My mother is confident:

"No, even if it collapsed, it's still not razed to the ground."

"When it's safe, Mother, will you consider leaving Hue? Or will you let me come and arrange to move our entire family to Saigon right away?"

"No."

My mother responds "no" very quickly, without thinking. Why leave, right, Mother? Right, Hue? I imagine my father's grave on a slope of the hill, surrounded by the graves of my grandfather, my grandmother, my uncle, and other close relatives. Then there is my garden and the ancestor-worshipping house that are still here. Only after being defeated so many times during his entire life was my father able to create this garden and to build this house. Trees and plants are still striving to live, even if they are withered and broken. My father's hands nurtured everything in that garden. Now my father is dead. During this calamity in the city, so many people have also died. But trees and plants will continue to grow, will continue to be green, as though the deaths of the people who are in the graves under them continue to give more strength for life to the abundant vegetation above the ground. My mother's voice is still flat:

"I think we will still be alive; we will still be able to reestablish everything."

Then she changes the topic:

"Child, when you get to Saigon, remember to find a way to let me know how the family is there."

I assure my mother that Saigon has become quiet and safe again, and there's information that my family is also safe and sound. But my mother remains uneasy:

"When you get there, child, remember to make a shelter. During these times, one must make a shelter to be on the safe side."

For my mother's peace of mind, I politely agree with her over and again. That night I keep crying silently for a long time. Lying there, I hear gunshots exploding in salvoes from within the Citadel; the monotonous lobbing of artillery shells is like the voice of someone seeing off the souls of innocent victims. Tomorrow I alone will leave Hue to find security for myself. But is there still any secure place? In my native land, everywhere is blood and everywhere is fire. What do I wish for Hue in this?

Next morning, Hà, along with several young girls who stay with us, goes for a bike ride, trying to find a way to Từ Đàm. But in the afternoon Hà comes back, her face covered with dust. She says that it's impossible to get through on any road. Up there, there's still fierce fighting. All the roads going up and down are completely blocked.

I am busy preparing to go down to Thanh Lam. I say just for the sake of words that I'm preparing, for in reality there's nothing to prepare, apart from the fact that I loathe to part with my relatives in the house.

Before I leave, I and Hà go around the area where I live. We go up to my uncle's house; the entire family has gone down to Phù Lương for safety. Around there, there are only a few neighbors who have come back. The houses have been directly hit by shells, and every day they get damaged more and more; it is utterly desolate. Walking around on this small road leads us toward the mountains. Over there is my father's grave, but I don't dare go any farther.

The two of us go down to An Cựu Bridge. There are still plenty of American soldiers standing guard there; we want to go farther, but someone says that it's very dangerous. The area of Kiểu Mẫu School is eaten away by shells fired from the opposite side of the river. When we return to the house, we see that there's a stranger in the house. An old gentleman is sitting and drinking water and talking with the whole family. This old gentleman is about eighty years old. My mother explains that he lives in one of the houses behind our garden. All his children and grandchildren evacuated, but he remained alone in that house from the first days when gunfire started up until now. I am curious to inquire more, to ask something so that he would tell us another story. But just a moment later I realize that he is both weak-sighted and deaf. I say loudly:

"Great-grandfather, living alone do you have anything to eat?"

"I sure do. A whole lot. My kids and grandchildren left for me dried bread, special Tết cakes, rice, now . . ."

"Great-grandfather, you're not afraid of guns, are you?"

I have to repeat this question of mine two or three times, and gesticulate too, and only then does the old man understand me:

"What guns? What for? I am deaf – if I hear anything, I hear sounds as though popcorn explodes – that's all."

"During those first days, Great-grandfather, did you meet them?"

"What?"

"Did you meet them?"

"Who are they?"

"Việt Cộng, Great-grandfather."

I shout up to the point that even my throat gets dry. The old man nods his head and looks like he understands:

"Yes, yes. Việt Cộng. I did, I did. They entered the house, saw that I'm old, what to do with an old man, to eat his shit . . ."

I'm sad but also can't hold back laughter. The old man tells us more:

"The bunch of my children and grandchildren, I told them, but they didn't listen. I told them not to go, but they still went. People say a bomb hit their group and they died. All dead and left me all alone. Is it not painful?"

"Now, Great-grandfather, what are you planning to do?"

"I heard a lot of people have come back here, and I wanted to go to ask for the way to find their corpses. Such a disaster, aunties and children. I told them not to go, but they didn't listen. Look at me, I eat my fill, then

I fall asleep. Though I don't care about guns or bullets, I am still alive to die somewhere like this, oh heavens. And them, they didn't know that devils and ghosts led the way, and they all went."

My mother advises:

"Sir, go back home and don't go to look for them. Whoever died, people have already buried them, and who knows where to search?"

The old man lifts his hand and rubs his eyes:

"Are buried already, eh? Buried where?"

"Wherever they died, people have buried them there."

I look at the two sparse streams of tears that run down the old man's shriveled cheekbones. He doesn't say good-bye, doesn't ask anyone anything, but just goes out the door. I follow him to help him; I give him my hand, and he lets me lead him back home.

Indeed it's extremely strange. Half of his house has completely collapsed, and it is still full of debris from bombs and shells. But the old man is unscathed. I point at the traces of shells on the wall. He says:

"They shot here."

He searches near the collapsed wall:

"The house is about to fall down. I heard something and there was only one bang and my body bounced a little bit, and when I opened my eyes the wall had already collapsed."

I see at the corner of the house several liberation flags covered in blood; a few flies still swarm over them. The flags emit an unbearable stench. Seeing me looking at them, the old man explains:

"They belong to some mister-liberators who left them here. They were here only during the first several days and then they died, and then there were a lot of wounded. They brought them over here and over there, put them to lie in that corner of the house, and then carried them away – I don't know where they went."

"Who do you live with now, Great-grandfather?"

"Alone."

"Do you have anything to eat?"

"In another few days it will be quiet and I will ask the government. My children and grandchildren are all dead now. I will ask the government for help."

I say good-bye to the old man and go back. When I get home, I see the office car, ready and waiting. My mother is standing and talking with several people inside the house; when she sees me, she runs out:

"There, they've already come to pick you up, child."

I clasp my mother with sudden haste. I want to cry but can't. However, my mother bursts out crying easily:

"Enough, child, go in; get ready and go."

"Mother."

"Go get ready child; go."

In the atmosphere of disarray on a chilly day, my mother seems to dry her tears, and she looks at the tops of high hills. Up there is my father's grave.

Before I leave, I light a joss stick on the altar. It seems like I want to pray for something, but my memory is completely fogged.

I carry a small bag. I hug . . . cry . . . and wave good-bye to everybody. I go out on the edge of the road. The car's engine starts, waiting, ready to go. Right over my head, airplanes roar without cease, hovering in circles. And in the distance, over there, at the Citadel, pillars of smoke rise high, squirming amid the sound of explosions that blast debris into the air.

How can it be that I am now about to really leave Hue?

TEN

LITTLE CHILD OF HUE, LITTLE CHILD OF VIETNAM, I WISH YOU LUCK

ON THE TRIP FROM THANH LAM TO PHÚ BÀI, OUR CAR RUNS AT full speed. We could be attacked at any moment. But nothing happens. OK, I can't die yet. The Phù Lương market appears, and the car stops. A bowl of noodles with beef and hot pepper tearing my mouth apart is my light breakfast before we set off again. I eat greedily. This dish makes tears flow from my eyes. In the desolate house in An Cựu amid the denuded garden, my mother's heart is now certainly on fire. "Oh, child, listen child, have a safe trip," my mother advised me from the courtyard when I was leaving. Several nephews, some of them holding my hands and others grasping my shirt: "Auntie, you are going to Saigon; you're afraid of guns, right, auntie?" Those children's voices made me want to stay in Hue until I can see Hue quiet and safe again or until I die together with Hue. But my children loudly call for me. My insides ache as though someone cuts through them. The sound of artillery has become muffled and distant, but it still seems to pound a cadence in my heart, never subsiding: boom, boom.

A grassy plot, which makes a helicopter pad, can now be clearly seen. I jump from the car. There's also a fellow passenger, Quế, who goes with me to Đà Nẵng. The grassy plot is empty; there is nothing waiting for us on the pad, but a lot of people are sitting, stranded outside a barbed wire fence. We present our papers to several guards and then enter the gate to the grassy pad. Pandemonium breaks out among the people sitting along the barbed wire fence; they get up, intending to flood in after us, but the guards block them.

Poor Thái and Bé, whose posts were near our house, before seeing me off went and bought some boxes with American cookies and several chocolate bars: "Elder sister, you are setting off – eat while on your trip."

I put my small piece of luggage on the grass and sit on top of it. My fellow passenger with whom I am going to Đà Nẵng brought along his old mother and two small children. The two little ones run, romping out on the grass, picking up pale-violet flowers. They lightheartedly frolic around, reminding me of my own sweet children. At the same time, the image of small children who hold their bowls of rice in their hands and listen to the reverberating sounds of artillery and whose faces have turned pale green, who drop their bowls and run to press their faces against the wall, stretching their small hands and hugging their heads, this image rends my heart. My mother, elder brother, younger sister, and a flock of nephews are lying on the bank of the river of war. The flaming ring of war, will it shrink in size or will it expand and spin further? I am the only one who has left it behind and has heartlessly escaped, fleeing by myself. My heart is suffused with a harassing and painful misery.

The people in the group gathered outside of the encircling barbed wired ring are more and more numerous by the moment. They inquire about flights. These people have escaped from Hue, have come to Phù Lương, and are still anxious; they want to escape even farther from Hue. Bundles and suitcases are heaped on each other topsy-turvy. Few of them are able to get the soldiers to allow them into the grassy pad.

Arguments erupt, very insistent, imploring, and begging. Then those who are left outside watch the people sitting inside with angry and envious looks.

Quế, my fellow passenger, informs me that every day now for more than a week these people come up to the barbed wire fence and wait and wait in hopes that perhaps they will be lucky enough to get a helicopter ride to Đà Nẵng. A person says:

"There's a ship near Gia Hội transporting a lot of refugees to Đà Nẵng."

"It's very dangerous. People say the Việt Cộng have shot and sunk several ships, and all the refugees are drowned in the sea."

No further discussions. Then suddenly the weather dries up for good. The drizzle that had started early stopped some time ago. Soft light comes from the sky. The grassy expanse is covered with fresh green color. Never before have I seen such an utterly clean, brilliant, and vibrant shade of green. Blades of grass soaked in rain now stretch up with all their strength. Here trees and plants remain absolutely calm and quiet. The mountain ranges and rows of hills spread far and wide, calm as a picture painted of a landscape in a time of peace and prosperity. But into this scene jostles the groups of absolutely pitiful and desolate people outside and inside the barbed wire fence. These people still seem to be full of smoke, to be scorched by fire, and to be punctured with bullet holes. But grass still grows here, right?

I plop down right on the wet grass and lean my head on my luggage. The wind from the mountains permeates my body with cold. I have to take my father's coat and drape it over my shoulders. During the days of fleeing from the fighting, I wore this coat like a talisman, and now it has become a keepsake of my dad. My eyes attentively observe the grassy surface. The grass is so long that it looks like it wants to reach my face. A few small clumps of grass growing along the barbed wire fence, fertilized by the iron, grow taller than clumps elsewhere; a few violet flowers with small fragile petals are in bloom. Suddenly, I am stunned. The violet flowers that come back in springtime to the courtyard of Đồng Khánh School – have they now managed to bloom under the feet trampling upon them? When still at school, we called these flowers "dazed with longing." Before leaving for Phù Lương, I heard that the roof of my beloved former school had collapsed and a lot of people died; many people who fled the fighting were staying there.

We wait until noon and still there's no aircraft. Some waiting people bring out bread and other provisions to eat. I eat only a small piece of cookie and feel half full. The bowl of noodles with beef that I had in the morning still feels like daggers drawn in my stomach, and its stinging hot taste from time to time engulfs my throat. Perhaps because of the long days of food shortage, I have forgotten the dainty taste of delicious food.

The two little children put their heads on Quế's feet and fall asleep. Quế hugs his children; he sits next to his old mother, who is moaning out her grief to a fellow passenger also waiting for a ride.

"My entire family is no more."

"Nothing is left of my family. I lost two children. They were taken away [by the Communist forces]; I don't know whether they are alive or dead, or what happened to them, or where they are."

I'm fed up with hearing stories about the people who fled the fighting, about deaths, and about arrests. I close my eyes, trying to sleep for a moment, to forget the burning impatience of anticipation.

But in a rather short time, up in the sky there seems to be the sound of something moving in the distance, then the sound of approaching helicopters gradually grows clearer and clearer. From behind the mountains appears a group of helicopters, five or six of them. Everyone gets up in excitement. The group of people outside of the barbed wire fence starts to scream, weeping and moaning. They carry their stuff to the place where the guards stand on both sides of the barbed wire. But out of five helicopters, only two are landing, while three continue flying forward. The people outside of the barbed wire fence have still not despaired; they elbow, call out to each other, and beg boisterously. The helicopters come in low, and I can't hear anything anymore. The sound of the engines is too loud and two sets of propeller blades are whirring, making a lot of people bend down, about to fall over. The grass that was just stretching up boldly suddenly bends all the way down to the ground. A moment later, the engines come to a complete halt as the propeller blades stop spinning. People and vegetation draw themselves up again. Two Americans and two Vietnamese officers step down from the helicopters. My fellow traveler, Quế, calls to me and then leads his mother and two little children to go to present their papers. We are allowed a place to stand for boarding. The group of people on the grassy patch is evenly divided up for transport in the two helicopters. But the sound of noisy protests, weeping, and moaning from the group outside of the barbed wire fence becomes more and more ferocious with every minute. The guards are not able to restrain them and a lot of people flood in. Several gunshots are fired into the air. Hearing gunfire, the people being left behind recoil. They stand stupefied, looking at each other. Gunfire here is somehow quite gentle – the bullets fly and disappear without hitting anyone; however, several people here and there think that they are bleeding.

The two divided groups of people are led to board the two helicopters. I am surprised when I turn back and see a small lad tightly clasping a flap of my coat and following each of my steps. When I get up into the helicopter, the little guy steps up too, following me, but someone's hand keeps him back. An officer blusters:

"Hey, who's this little guy with?"

The boy is pulled down. He stands hunched over, his eyes moist with tears, looking at all the people climbing onto the helicopter. I get a seat next to the door, so the boy's eyes seem to be firmly glued to my face. I move a little so that I can give the boy a tiny spot to sit. The officer, after he pulled the boy down, rushes up and sits next to the pilot. The small guy's eyes suddenly brighten, and he looks at me making signs, begging for help. I hold tight to the seat with one hand and stretch the other one down and pull the child up. He climbs up with alacrity and sits down so swiftly that he tumbles inside behind the luggage. But all this doesn't escape the eyes of the officer. He jumps over and browbeats the boy:

"The helicopter is cramped; you can't go. Get off."

The boy is white-faced; his arms and legs tremble. The little fellow is alone; clearly he got separated from his family or his family is dead. I tell the officer:

"This little boy was sent with me. I didn't put his name into the papers because he's just a child."

The officer looks at me with suspicion. But then he leaves. I look at the little guy, trying to give him a friendly smile. But he's not through with his fit of trembling yet; his arms and legs shake convulsively as he tries to shrink his body to fit amid the baggage and the careless feet of adults wanting to step on his body.

The helicopter starts to take off. The propeller blades start to rotate. So, I have escaped. I bid farewell to Hue, to underground shelters that continue to be smashed and broken, to unburied corpses. I also bid farewell to Phù Lương with its church entirely filled with refugees, hungry and suffering.

The engine of the helicopter grows louder. The propeller blades spin faster. We are able to take off. The helicopter gradually rises higher. The people outside the fence and those who are still on the grassy pad follow us with their eyes in despair. We make another turn, really fast, and fly high so that I no longer see those eyes following us.

I put my hands into my coat. The higher we get, the more a cold wind numbs my skin and flesh. How far has the helicopter been able to get by now? No doubt, soon we will be out of the town. Looking down, now I will certainly see a green mountainous area. I greedily want to lock this green color into my eyes, but when I do look down I am abruptly spellbound. It seems that the helicopter is returning to the city of Hue. I raise my eyes to Quế. Quế and his small children are sitting on the front bench, next to the pilot. I make a questioning sign. Quế says something really loud, but his voice drowns in the noise of the wind and the engine. I vaguely guess: Making a circle or something like that . . . but it is certain that the helicopter has now returned to Hue. When it gets to the beginning of the National Highway, near the entrance to the city, the helicopter suddenly spurts up higher and picks up at a frightfully fast speed. With my hand, I clasp the seatbelt more firmly and tighten it, then turn my body around to look down at the city.

What is that over there so tattered like a colored parasol, shattered, smashed, torn into shreds by the wind? Oh, is it the city of Hue, or what? Destroyed houses and desolate gardens look like the fur of a poor dog exposing a hundred gaping wounds.

Who has just squeezed my heart, and who has just squeezed tears from my eyes? A gigantic dead body is lying with arms and legs outstretched – fallen, torn, with skin and flesh coming apart. The enormous corpse of Hue has lost its face, its arms, and its legs, and whatever remains is but a heap of slime turning to mud. The spine of the city is broken. And my spine has also been broken.

The propeller blades of the helicopter still whir, pressing down on my heart that has become like a hard callus. My heart has died and has gone rigid. How is it that I still breathe? How marvelous is the strength of life.

I blink my eyes so that I can see. The helicopter flies past a hilltop and dips slightly. Does my father's grave lie down there? Why does the grave still shine brightly in my memory, with fresh buds breathing dying breaths under a new layer of earth while waiting for a chance to stretch up toward sunlight? Is it my garden over there? Broken-off coconut trees, a collapsed roof, and an empty gateway join with other houses and gardens, bridges and roads, turning into the slimy skin of a corpse. The eyes of Hue are still open and frowning at the fire and the bullets. Another blink of my eyes so I can see and another spin of the propeller blades to let something else appear, and then the engine, trying to ascend, bursts out crying as if to break. I've already heard it – the sound of crying, isn't it? It is the terrifying screaming in the middle of the morning, at noon, in the pitch-dark night – isn't it? The woman giving birth and falling down in the church; the corpse of the baby wrapped in a bundle being sung its mother's lullabies during so many days of fleeing from war . . .

Let the eyes blink one more time, shall I not? A group of people from Phú Cam is fleeing, staggering with panic, carrying food, children, and dead bodies, following priests and bonzes with tattered white flags. Where's An Định Palace, the place ruled by the obsolete empress, where she could still hear soft sounds: "I will carry thee, Your Majesty, on my back, and run"? Where has Her Majesty fled . . . how many steps has she been able to take in the circle of fire? A corner of the roof of the ancient palace collapsed; now where are the traces of its bricks on the corpse of the city? That group of people fleeing the fighting – have all of them managed to cross the bridge yet? The dog drifting in midstream is dead and drowned, thanks to a bullet's favor; otherwise it would still be trying with great difficulty to swim to shore. Enough – now go.

The sounds of screaming, shouting, crying, and the sounds of American soldiers laughing as they shoot at the dog floundering farther away in midstream while it struggles to the shore – why are these sounds still stuck tight to my eardrums?

Now we approach something closer – is this streak of blood the span of a broken bridge connecting the two parts of the city? Where's the post office with corpses of the liberation soldiers? What else is there to wait for when one's feet are tied to machine guns? Who tied their feet? I blink many times and open my eyes many times; tears stream from my eyes many times. I watch gigantic pillars of smoke licking up the lead-colored sky like the tongue of a demon. If I try to bend a little bit lower, I can see waves of shells and bullets whizzing like rain, destroyed houses, and deserted roads.

How truly surprising when under the bloody-red tongue of the demon, amid bombs and shells that plow up the earth in such a way, there are still groups of people fleeing in all directions, seeking a way to survive. I'm even more surprised when I see myself sitting in a helicopter flying back for another look at the destroyed city.

The helicopter has not yet reached the Citadel walls when it abruptly turns around and goes back. There seem to be streams of fire shooting down at those walls – so many innocent civilians have died over there: groups of people tied up by the Việt Cộng so that the airplanes would shoot them from above.

Those people have reconciled themselves to connect their fate with Hue; they have contributed to Hue's slimy piles of skin and flesh.

The helicopter returns to Phù Lương, one more time hovering above the hilltop where my father's fresh grave is. The area of my father's garden has been diligently tended. During so many days on the patch of earth trampled by war over there, I hardly ever thought about the close bond between the land and myself. But now sitting high up and looking down, I clearly see why suddenly I think about the land with such sadness and longing. Down there, isn't that the land where my father is buried? Not only that, but also exactly on this big expanse of land I also buried a small and innocent child.

I am up high but there is no separation; I am indissolubly connected with the land. Down there lives my family. The land is very close and dear to me. Right down there, now being broken into bits, is Hue's body with my footprints, not only from each and every day of running away from the fighting but also from so many years of childhood and of growing up to adulthood.

The land beloved by so many people and with which so many people are bonded . . . The expanse of land down there is for me not only the keeper of my customs and habits, of my ties, of my kin, but even more, something to which I have entrusted a part of my own bones and blood.

The helicopter gradually moves farther away and approaches slopes of green mountains. A blink of an eye, and the entire destroyed city has disappeared. My body convulses. It seems that there are a lot of small drops of water like dust sticking to and covering my face. The sky starts drizzling again. The rain is light and gentle; how can it overcome the red tongues licking the blackness of the entire expanse of the sky? Over there now the Citadel is still dark in the shellfire. How much longer will it take to cease fighting? Let me keep blinking.

It seems that in the helicopter there are still long discussions about Hue: about a woman whose head, arms, and legs were chopped off; about two crossbred Vietnamese children fathered by an American who were detained and their heads smashed against the wall – guilty of being American imperialist thugs; about another familiar personality, Mr. Tinh Hoa, a bookstore owner who hid in his house for the entire month but because of hunger and thirst had to venture out to look for water – one gunshot and the man was dead and his story has become the talk of the town. It's not over yet; the war very much continues wantonly without restraint. Everyone has a right to suspect others. Over there, they suspect that these little Vietnamese born from an American father will grow up to be a danger to society, so – kill them. The American soldiers, as soon as they hear a noise, a small sound, they immediately burn an entire hamlet, they destroy a house, or they fire salvoes of bullets into underground shelters swarming with women and children. There are shelters that still have the breath of living people, and there are shelters full of the flesh and blood of dead people. And then, for example, there is the small story about a pharmacist who no sooner made it out of his shelter with his two hands still raised up over his head than he was hit by a full magazine of bullets.

There are so many of these stories: why do I remember them all, why bother to carry all these bloody images in my small head? It's such punishment for me now. My memories are really chaotic – an image of my elder brother hugging with both arms two wounded neighbor children gasping their final breaths, a flock of my young nephews going in front of the group and carrying white flags to cross Bến Ngự Bridge. Bullets from the bridge fall like rain, scratching people's heads, landing under people's feet. Americans are very good shooters, like in the movies, and a small flock of people fall; they roll on the ground in somersaults, screaming and crying. My elder brother makes up his mind to carry two small kids in his arms, children of a neighbor woman at death's door who turns back to go up to the area occupied by the Liberation Army. It's no fault of Americans here, right?

I hear soft sobs. Are those sobs my own or someone else's? I raise my hand and rub my eyes to gradually melt away those haunting memories. But as the helicopter gets farther and farther away from the city, those images cling; they stick fast to me more and more. I think about the group of people still sitting on the grassy pad – will they be as lucky as I am to get a seat so that they can go and search for a more peaceful place? But it's not only on that grassy pad. My Hue compatriots are also inundating Phú Bài Airport. Only when I come there do I see hundreds of people standing and sitting outside of the fence, screaming frantically, begging Americans to let them get on a helicopter to seek refuge. They scream, weep, and cry as American military men sit, doleful and exhausted, next to the corpses of their comrades wrapped in nylon bags, arranged in a long line and left waiting for an aircraft to come and take them away.

The helicopter passes over rows of green trees and mountain slopes to get out to the sea. The wind is biting cold and the raindrops are thicker. Raindrops fanned in by the helicopter's propeller blades splash into my face, painful as pricks from needles. All the people sit bunched up together. One person rummages through his luggage; another opens a cloth bag to get a raincoat and puts it on. A woman holds a bamboo hat in her hands, not very firmly, and it gets blown away from the helicopter by the wind and slowly falls down to the sea, turning into a small round dot on the blue surface of the water rippling with waves. I don't know whether or not these people are like me and have left their souls back in Hue and so now are crying, but is everyone's face now soaking wet from rain or from tears? A few soft sounds of sobbing – I have to look very carefully and listen very attentively and only then do I get it: several small children lie snugly against their mothers' hearts covered by two or three layers of blankets. These small children also fled from the war by many routes and through many places in the city during the past days.

The rain is beating down terribly. The little lad who followed me while I boarded the helicopter now simply sits shriveled up into a ball among the bags and parcels. The boy appears to be stuck there and unable to move and seems to not dare to take a deep breath. He has no space to move or to even turn his back to the outside. Only now do I notice that the little lad is clad only in a very light shirt and underwear. His face has turned pale green and is about to turn the color of lead; it seems that he's filled with frost and cold to the point of absolute misery. As if without the strength to endure it, his lips cannot stay calm but tremble, and his teeth are clattering. Noticing that I'm watching him, the boy opens wide his round reddish eyes and looks back at me. In these eyes I read: "Oh, what have I seen making goose bumps cover my whole body – a city, a stream of blood, pieces of arms and legs. Stray dogs running in the streets, uncontrollable, with pieces of human leg and arm bones in their mouths, running to hide in the shrubs, rushing across the roads and behind verandas of the houses. What else have I seen – a city whose wings were clipped, whose future is wiped out, youths with sad and pitiful deaths." "Enough, little brother . . . blink your eyes, don't open them wider: the glimmers from your glance are enough to chill all your future days." It seems that the little lad's lips stammer indistinctly. "Do you want to say something, little brother? It's only a short distance between the two of us, but even if you, little brother, scream out, I will still not be able to hear you." The sky is covered in thick fog, the rain is covered in thick fog, the sea is covered in thick fog; the helicopter flies high and the noise of the machine wipes out all our small noises. "But you are very cold, little brother, aren't you? I must share something with you." I take my bag in my hand and only with great difficulty I manage to drag out the only overcoat that remains from the days of fleeing from the fighting. I throw it straight to the boy.

His two arms spring out with unexpected strength. And hastily, with great difficulty, he unfolds the coat and puts it on. The boy's arms and legs still tremble, but regardless of this, the coat helps him to get a bit warmer. He doesn't say anything but opens his eyes wider and looks straight into my face. I turn to look outside so that raindrops splash into my face.

Getting out from the dangerous area, the helicopter leaves the sea and flies over the land. Houses and vegetation appear below. The helicopter flies lower, and sometimes it seems like we are too close to the tops of the trees; the roofs of houses are clearly seen and gradually become bigger and bigger. I look down and see a few thatch huts in square plots of land. And in their courtyards, several children raise their hands to the sky and wave vigorously.

A moment later, the helicopter descends gradually. I can see a big river, then dirt roads looking as though they were just recently constructed, rows of houses covered with sheet iron, and smokestacks of factories. "Have we already arrived in Đà Nẵng?" I ask myself. The helicopter suddenly stops and hovers, the engine works more lively and strenuously, and then we go gradually down and slowly land.

Seatbelts are unfastened very quickly. People compete with each other to jump out, carrying their stuff. I wait until everybody else gets down and only then do I jump down too. There are people's voices calling each other: "Hey, hurry up, don't be late for the ferry; staying on this side of the river will not do any good."

Where is "this side"? Is it Đà Nẵng yet or not? I ask Quế:

"We haven't got to Đà Nẵng yet, have we?"

"This place is Sơn Trà; to get to Đà Nẵng we have to cross the river. We have to take a ferry."

I make a little sigh; the sound of my sigh vanishes, swallowed by the sound of the engine. The second helicopter also comes down. The place where the two helicopters perch is a grassy expanse on the side of a road that is carefully covered with earth. The wind from the propeller blades makes the vegetation bow low to the ground. The words of people calling out to each other scatter and fly away without leaving a trace. People hold tightly to their clothes and their scarves, and they bend down low to avoid the wind as they go up to the edge of the road.

The sky dries out completely, but as the day draws to a close, clouds are very low and gloomy. Surely it drizzles in Đà Nẵng just like in Hue. I stand on the main road and wait for Quế, who leads two small kids and his old mother to come up. Now I can clearly hear the voices of the people calling to each other. People hastily get into a group and go quickly forward.

It seems that someone pulls down on a flap of my coat. I turn back. It's the little lad. His eyes are big – he blinks and then opens them, letting me see many images of destroyed Hue reflected there. I softly ask:

"What's this, little brother?"

The boy silently hands me back the overcoat that he has carefully folded. His eyes are still wide open; he watches me and his mouth very softly says, "Thank you." I keep asking:

"Where are you going now, little brother?"

He shakes his head. His eyes look down at his small feet. Then suddenly he says, "Thank you," one more time and leaves, walking really fast. The boy's disappearing figure is lonely, pitiful, mixing with the crowd that hastily gets on the ferry to cross the river and enter another city.

Little beloved child, little beloved child of Hue, little beloved child of Vietnam – I wish good luck to you.

Nhã Ca